Protecting Mama

Protecting Mama

Surviving the Legal Guardianship Swamp

Léonie Rosenstiel

2021

Minneapolis

Protecting Mama: Surviving the Legal Guardianship Swamp
Copyright © 2021 by Léonie Rosenstiel.

All rights reserved.

No part of this book may be used or reproduced by any means, graphic, electronic, or mechanical including photocopying, recording, taping or by any information storage retrieval system, without the written permission of the publisher except in the case of brief quotations embodied in critical articles and reviews.

10 9 8 7 6 5 4 3 2

SECOND EDITION 2022

ISBN 978-1-959770-29-9

Design by Sue Stein
Photos used with permission
Cover photos: motortion / Dreamstime
GulArt / Pixabay
Author photo: C&H Productions

To the memory of David A. Garcia, a surprising and extraordinary combination of Perry Mason and Matlock.

DISCLAIMER: This book is based on my recollections, on family documents and on the more than 40,000 pages of documents that became part of the three guardianship-related cases in which my mother was involved and that were ultimately released from sequestration by the court. My family's reality is typical of the struggles of thousands of other families who have been placed in similar situations. For that reason, I have only used names when they are essential to the story.

My family's story is a common one in the guardianship universe. Many relatives of people under guardianship and conservatorship live the rest of their lives under gag orders or non-disparagement agreements. Furthermore, they might also be denied any documentation or refused the right to publish it, due to court-ordered secrecy, and so might be unable to prove that what they say is true.

Contents

Prologue	ix
Chapter I: The Failed Great Escape (Darkness Closes In)	1
Chapter II: Lies and More Lies	63
Chapter III: Money Takes Wing and Truth Flies out the Window	133
Chapter IV: As One Nightmare Ends, Another Begins	225
Chapter V: Waking Up	317
Acknowledgments	389
Index	393

Prologue

This volume will expose the accumulated, horrifying result of generations of secret-keeping and misinformation. "Misinformation" is the kindest word I can find. As I was to discover so painfully, my branch of the family and its openness about financial matters did not entirely compensate for other secrets it was keeping. Nor did my mother's lack of candor on certain subjects with my father, her sisters, my cousins and me help matters.

I sincerely hope that you never need to attempt to survive events like those I describe in this book. And may you find a way to protect both your loved ones and yourself against ever being sucked into the slavering jaws of our cannibalistic adult guardianship system!

Under current conditions, there can be no guarantees that you and your loved ones are going to be spared, even if you do everything the authorities say you should. Failing the rethinking and radical restructuring of the entire process, no one can promise you that—as the result of the current laws and rules and customs in your state—all existing legal documents will not be arbitrarily shredded in a court of law. No one can promise that you will not be capriciously excluded from your loved one's presence or allowed only a limited list of topics to discuss or emotions your loved one is allowed to experience. Or that court personnel and contract players in the guardianship process will not place egregious lies about you and others into the court record, without suffering any consequences.

Even if you do not have a lot of money, you may find yourself emotionally devastated by this system. I know a mother who received no notice of the hearing held when her adult son's guardian (who was on his way to prison for embezzling money from her son) was going to be changed; the court did not even consider her as a potential guardian. An elderly man in New Jersey ran out of money. His two adult children were not wealthy either. When they could not care for him anymore, they allowed the State of New Jersey to name a guardian. They visited him frequently, until COVID-19 hit his facility. The state then closed all eldercare establishments to visitors. The guardian no longer returned calls. Citing HIPAA restrictions on releasing health information, except to the state-appointed guardian, the facility refused to tell the man's adult children anything about their father's condition. Not until weeks after their father was buried did they receive notice of his death.

You deserve the right to prepare for battle. The events in this book can warn you about what might happen once the process starts. In addition, you will also see where the holes in the system might be plugged up so it does not mangle more of us than it already has. Right now, adults under guardianship are helpless; their families and loved ones are simply considered collateral damage. As Patricia Wooten, a Las Cruces, New Mexico attorney who represented people in adult guardianship cases for many years opined, after she gave up this area of the law, "I have found it so dysfunctional in so many ways...I have generally given up on that mechanism...[The guardianship system] is just not working."

My own trip through the Salvador Dali world of guardianship has led me to question the legal process and the assumptions of individuals within the legislative, legal, medical and guardianship systems. Most of these folks seem to believe that, at best, all families consist of bumbling, meddling fools who present inconveniences to beneficent, efficient bureaucrats and, at worst, consist only of sadists, murderers and thieves from whom elders need protection.

On December 2, 2020, a radio show called "Speak Up, Las Cruces" presented a panel of invited guests who discussed eldercare and adult guardianship. One panelist, attorney Patricia Galindo, represented "the Administrative Office of the Courts," which oversees the organization and funding of the entire New Mexico court system. After emphasizing that everyone acknowledges what a fine job the commercial guardians and conservators do, and estimating (without actually producing any firm statistics) that only about 10 percent of cases result in complaints, she went on to assert that almost no one ever complains about any aspect of the adult commercial guardianship system. She said, early in her presentation, that families get first preference to become guardians. If a family member did not, the reasons were "either the family is unable to, unwilling to, or not physically in New Mexico." It sounded as if she was denigrating anyone who might complain, relegating their problems to some sort of personality issue or hurt feelings. "If you feel as if it's [the court case] not going in your favor it's very easy to feel that you were slighted," Galindo asserted. She went on to attribute what sounded like the rest of the complaints to simple ignorance of the law.

I always call people who earn a good part of their living from being guardians or trustees or conservators, *commercial* guardians, *commercial* trustees and *commercial* conservators. They are not volunteers. Normally they are not family members either. They are independent. Up until recently there were few *enforceable* requirements for them to satisfy; any standard they met, regardless of their status as "nationally-certified" guardians, seemed to be entirely voluntary. Even today, states like New Mexico have not yet passed any statewide standards or board requirements. At best, the requirements would be created to jibe with those of the current national association of guardians. Even so, given my experiences, I have come to believe that potential guardians ought to be screened for psychological fitness to undertake the job, the way police officers are. They have almost unlimited power, once in place. What these workers do to care for wards earns them their livelihood in the eldercare industry that provides various services for people who are aging. In other words, whether they work at a non-profit or a for-profit firm, this is how they put food on the table.

They prefer to call themselves "professional" guardians and conservators. This always sounds (to me, at least), as if they are saying that family members who are appointed as guardians or conservators, or who are appointed trustee of a family trust, are simply dabbling in this field. That is because we automatically think that "an amateur" is the opposite of "a professional." By that way of figuring, family members are mere amateurs.

Ms. Galindo's statement about any complaints coming only from a few fringe people conflicted directly with my personal experience. Just about everyone I meet or correspond with who has had experience with the adult guardianship system, whether in New Mexico or in any other state, has horror stories to tell. This contradiction practically forced me to run a Google search on the term *guardianship abuse*.

What did I find? About 8.5 million websites discussing guardianship abuse by commercial guardians perpetrated on older adults. A number of individual sites contained thirty or more horror stories on a single page. A few cited hundreds of cases. These results seemed to rebut this New Mexico bureaucrat's statement quite neatly. However, that is not the end of this story.

There are only about one thousand certified guardians in the United States; they belong to the National Guardianship Association (the NGA). A few states have adopted individual standards, but they usually base them on NGA standards. It may take a week or less of online courses and a test to acquire initial certification.

Let us say that you arbitrarily discredit half of those complaint websites, to account for the likelihood that at least some complaints have no merit, or that some guardians complained about are not commercial guardians (those caring for three or more unrelated adults). That would mean about 4.25 million sites likely have valid complaints. Is the spokesperson for the courts trying to say that she is the only person who is sane and several million other people are all crazy? And even if every single one of the thousand members of the NGA think everything is fine, when you compare the number of "certified guardians" to the number of people who feel aggrieved, you find hundreds of times more people are unhappy than happy—especially with the state of adult guardianship and the care being given to the aging who suffer from varying degrees of mental incapacity.

As of 2018, the AARP estimated that there were 1.8 million individuals under guardianship in the United States, and that 85 percent of them were over the age of 65. That would mean that 1.53 million elders were then under a guardianship. Why would there be a couple of hundred times more complaints than there are wards?

My guess would be that there are far more people now living under guardianship than the AARP realizes, because so many guardianship cases are kept secret by the courts. According to Rick Black of the Center for Estate Administration Reform, in 2021, 48 of the 50 states and six United States territories still kept adult guardianship records secret. New York is supposed to hold open hearings unless a judge sequesters them for cause. Recently it was discovered that more than 200 cases were kept secret in a single county over a limited period of time. Was all that secrecy warranted?

If my estimate of the number of sites that are offering valid complaints against commercial guardians is correct, it might also mean that there seem to be more than 4,000 complaints per certified guardian. It is highly unlikely that most family members will be taking to the internet to excoriate their brother or their cousin. I have seen this happen occasionally, but from what I have seen complaints against for-hire guardians are in the majority. And even if Uncle Harry or Sister Sue started a complaint for incapacity against an elder, frequently a commercial guardian eventually took over anyway. For this reason, the high number of complaint websites is definitely not a good sign. To make the situation even worse, given the number of commercial guardians and conservators, the people complaining are overwhelmingly in the majority. That is exactly the opposite of what Ms. Galindo was trying to tell the public in December 2020.

Multiple federally funded-studies have estimated that there are 1.5 million wards. However, that is just an invented number. The federal and congressional agencies are up-front about the fact that no one truly has reliable statistics. They have not been able to get them from the states, despite repeated requests over a period of several decades, starting during the 1980s. Is that any way to get reliable information? You bet it is not.

These reports generally go on to state that 80 percent of guardians for adults come from the same family as the ward and are not professionals. Where did this 80 percent figure come from if there are no reliable statistics? From the guardianship industry and their lobbyists, I am guessing. Or perhaps from their friends in the state bureaucracy, like Ms. Galindo. And just because family members are initially named guardian does not mean that they stay as guardian. Many are later ousted by commercial guardians and conservators. I had heard about this happening before I saw it in those relatively few court records that are now open to public view.

When I checked Ms. Galindo's background, I discovered that—like many state bureaucrats in this field—she herself had been a guardianship attorney in private practice before taking on her state job. This makes it easy to imagine where the sympathies of this particular bureaucrat (and many others like her in other states) might lie.

Ms. Galindo claimed that overwhelmingly, egregious abuse of helpless wards stemmed from evil family members. (It helps to remember that "family guardians" are only in place for as long as the judge pleases. Often, after six months or a year, the judge names a commercial guardian instead.) As far as I can tell, this claim that "family members are the primary guilty ones" is just a belief of hers because she did not (and in my opinion likely cannot) provide any verifiable statistics to back it up. There is no valid census of people currently under guardianship.

Thus far, the two largest New Mexico cases of the abuse of wards—adding up to more than $15 million stolen from 1500 helpless individuals—were prosecuted in New Mexico District Court and Federal District Court in 2017 to 2018. Ayudando Guardians and Desert States Trust saw their firms shut down and their principals sent to do hard time. Even though the court dockets referred to the firms as "guardians" and "conservators" when Rick Black brought these events up to Ms. Galindo, she saw fit to quibble over the words "guardian" and "conservator." Instead, she called them "trustees" and "designated payees." She claimed that most were neither guardians nor conservators. However, when these wards were reassigned after their original commercial "keepers" folded, a number were given to the same firm that cared for my mother and the firm was still called "guardian" or "conservator" (or both) on the court docket. As of this writing, not one of those hundreds of victims has gotten back one cent of their portion of that stolen $15 million dollars. It had all been spent on cars, jewelry, real estate and other luxuries in the names of the embezzlers.

If you look at the Congressional reports on guardianship abuse, 50 percent, and sometimes as many as 75 percent, of those are cases in which someone is actually found guilty of guardianship abuse are prosecuted against commercial guardians, not family guardians. Because commercial guardians often handle multiple unrelated people, sometimes one single court case can complain about the fleecing and mistreatment of between twenty and two hundred wards (and sometimes even more) who have all been abused by the same commercial guardianship, conservatorship or trust firm. If 80 percent of guardians are relatives, that leads to the conclusion that 20 percent of the guardians are generating 50 to 75 percent of the cases of abuse so bad that they have not been able to defend themselves against suits in court. And this does not include all the other commercial guardians who might have lost in court but instead made settlements to prevent that judgement.

One major complaint that I have heard judges make is that the public has no right to require them to assess blame or innocence. Judges do this every day in criminal cases. However, guardianship cases take place in a civil court. Strangely, the same civil court judge who sits on an insurance case on Tuesday and assesses 20 percent of the fault to one litigant and 60 percent of the fault to another, refuses to do the same in an adult guardianship case on Thursday.

Does this mean that some enterprising pollster or psychologist cannot devise a way around this, so that there are clear benchmarks? No. Likely, they can. But no one will bother unless either the law or the court's rules are changed to require them to do so. They do not because no one is requiring them to do it. The insurance company has a powerful lobby. Individual families do not. A coalition of numerous aggrieved families might.

I have heard judges say, repeatedly, that they feel overworked. A new way of approaching adult guardianship would mean they would actually have to try the guardianship cases themselves, instead of punting when they make their decisions and giving their friends years' worth of fees as guardians and conservators. They think the old way is easier for them. I predict that they will continue to do things this way until change is absolutely required. What a shame! The judges (as a group—with a few notable exceptions) will likely experience far less hostility from the public if they allow people to have their say in court instead of working as hard as they have, so far, to prevent them all from speaking.

If all the interested parties—including an elder whose thinking faculties might be seriously compromised to the extent that s/he has no real understanding of having already lost the capacity to function independently—do not come into court in complete agreement, judges generally appoint outside experts (guardians or conservators or trust officers) to take over. The most deplorable aspect of "family disagreement" may be that often the entire situation is manufactured or augmented by unscrupulous court-affiliated individuals or through manipulation by court-appointed doctors and psychologists of vulnerable elders. And there is a specific stage of dementia during which individuals are far more easily manipulated, in part because they deny anything is wrong.[1]

Another complaint I have heard judges make is that the families would not be in court if they were "good families." Furthermore, any deviation from this imaginary standard of perfection means the members are worthy of punishment. If they were not dysfunctional in some way, everyone would be in agreement, goes that argument. And if they did not have disagreements, they would be compliant with each other and make things easy for the judge; s/he could then simply ratify the family's own already-made agreements. In other words, these judges demand human perfection. Is not "human perfection" an oxymoron anyway? As if there are any perfect families out there. Are the judges' families perfect? Do judges ever argue with their significant others?

---

1 *https://www.dementiacarecentral.com/aboutdementia/facts/stages/*

My family was not perfect. We were (and those of us who survive still are) all too human. What I tell you in this book is the collective experience of my family, some of whose secrets and lies go back for generations. The earliest lies (perhaps some of them might charitably be called "tall tales") led to later cover-up lies. Over the generations, these compounded exponentially. They created various levels of what might be called "dysfunction" that affected each individual, according to his/her own background and circumstances. What sorts of lies? Lies about religion. Lies about preferences. Lies about relatives. Lies about money. Lies about the past.

Am I guilty of creating the lie someone told in my great-grandparents' generation and the cover-up some long-deceased relative invented to hide its falsity? I do not think so. Is my mother? I do not think so. I did not even know about these specific lies and attendant cover-ups until long after Mama passed on. And she did not know about most of them either. In fact, it took me years (detailed fully in the prequel to this volume) to trace as many of them as I could. Mama wanted the truth to be told, and I promised Mama to tell it. That meant I needed to separate the lies from what might be called "objective fact."

Mama's life started out skewed because of lies and cover-ups perpetuated by her parents, grandparents and great-grandparents. And then she added her own, in what seems to have been an attempt to balance things out a bit. The new lies and cover-ups only made an already-terrible situation far worse. So how can a judge, looking at us today, say that either of us is guilty because the lies and cover-ups of past generations have survived until the present? Up until recently, I had no idea they even were lies!

Mama's lies and cover-ups gave her a strange and frequently painful relationship with her own parents and sisters. Not to mention her other relatives. They also prevented me from knowing one of my aunts well and most of Mama's other relatives at all. Later in her life, Mama's hidden experiences hurt her (and me) in so many ways.

Mama's family engaged in an ever-escalating demand that every relative be perfect. Anyone who was not, was considered unwor-

Mama always said that a Russian émigré nobleman took this photo of her in 1933, after they met at one of Gertrude Stein's famous Paris salons. It was almost certainly taken in Paris during 1933, but by someone else.

thy to be a relative. I think this contributed to Mama's misplaced and incredibly destructive rivalry with Dad, as I was growing up.

Maybe this pretense of perfection would have made the judges in family court happy, but it certainly did not make us happy. When Mama was young, she looked so much like Greer Garson that she was often mistaken for the actress. That put stress on her too. Several careers later, she thought she was buying security through her work as a college professor. To her chagrin, she later discovered that she could not.

One of the things that most upset me about what happened to Mama was the one-size-fits-all attitude of her all-powerful, court-appointed guardian. Mama's legal guardian took away (and made to disappear forever) the Egyptian bark paintings that Mama loved (and that reminded her of her long and successful career teaching anthropology to college students). Mama had chosen to hang these on the wall nearest her bed. The commercial guardian substituted large photos of people who had abused Mama, simply because they were members of Mama's "birth family." Mama had photos of these people carefully hidden away at the bottoms of old cartons and trunks; her guardian simply did not know this. They had been hidden all my life, because that was where Mama wanted to keep them. The guardian apparently thought the thing to do was to get copies from a relative and post them near Mama's bed.

Their constant inhibiting presence during Mama's last years prevented her from finishing working through and coming out on the other side of her early traumas when I was not there to protect her. They also inhibited her from telling anyone the truth about her early life (even her always-welcomed Presbyterian chaplain from hospice) because everyone involved was always searching for Mama's happy memories from childhood for her to remember.

Mama essentially spent the last four years of her life in bed, the vast majority of that time inside her own bedroom, often staring at that wall, with her disapproving relatives staring right back. In my opinion, the stress triggered by having her abusers "watching" her at all times likely hastened Mama's dementia process. Additionally, all that time spent inside did not help; Mama did not get sunshine and likely developed a Vitamin D deficiency. Long-standing, quasi-religious precepts of dementia treatment instruct us to keep the patients in touch with their early life memories, to emphasize early memories so they remember them for as long as possible. It is supposed to be comforting. Mama's guardian (and all their hirelings) believed that dogma absolutely.

It is here that the observation of Pedram Shojai ("The Urban Monk"), who co-founded Whole.TV, might serve as guidance. "Experiencing post-traumatic growth," he said, "requires us to look back and sometimes confront the past traumatic events that we carry with us…If left unrecognized, our trauma can dictate everything we do, whether we know it or not…"

By the time we pick up Mama's story and mine in this volume, Dad has just died at the age of eighty-four, while in the midst of an otherwise-placid conversation with Mama. Mama, at the age of eighty-two already long retired from teaching anthropology at the college level, is in the midst of a new career speaking in library programs and for groups throughout Long Island, New York, and occasionally writing. She has just had a visit from her next-younger sister and a niece. They had managed to arrive at Mama's home sooner after Dad died than I could. None of us was prepared for the journey ahead.

CHAPTER I

The Failed Great Escape (Darkness Closes In)

By the time I had reached Manhasset, my aunt and younger cousin had managed to arrange the basics of a Reform Jewish funeral for Dad, but they had already left town. Mama had not contacted a rabbi, nor had she even given anyone the name of a rabbi, because she and Dad had not had contact with any for about thirty years.[2] She did not seem to want to engage any of the local rabbis.

Mama asked me to help her find one she could tolerate. From my years of study and then teaching at The New Seminary, I knew Rabbi Joseph Gelberman, a former military chaplain who specialized in ceremonies that included interfaith elements.[3] I wanted to avoid the sort of guilt provoking accusations I had heard at my maternal grandfather's funeral, where the officiant had blamed those present for having done something wrong that had angered

---

2 Judging from what I had heard them say, over the years, they had never found a Jewish congregation, either in New York City or on Long Island, in which they had felt welcome and, despite one Kabbalah class they had taken in Great Neck some years before, they definitely did not feel at home there, either. Nor did they feel comfortable in churches.

3 The New Seminary, from which I had graduated, was the first ministerial training organization of the Modern Interfaith Movement. Clergy from various religions served on the faculty. Rabbi Joseph Gelberman, the former military chaplain who had founded it, and then headed it, had had to provide services to soldiers of various religious persuasions while he was serving in uniform during World War II. This was one of the inspirations convincing him to co-found this movement. I had been teaching at the seminary, in addition to my other work, since 1990.

Annette and Raymond Rosenstiel on New Year's Day 1994.
Dad died on the morning of March 17, 1994.
Photo: Léonie Rosenstiel

the Creator, thereby bringing about my grandfather's death. Rabbi Gelberman was the quintessential optimist. I asked him if he would officiate.

Dad had died on a Thursday. The funeral would not take place until Monday, March 21, 1994, and fortunately Rabbi Gelberman—a short, slender man who had a goatee like Dad—was free. Held five days after Dad's demise, the ceremony might have been nominally Jewish, but it was certainly nothing even vaguely approaching Orthodox, up to and including the baby blue velvet lining of Dad's open casket, that Mama had picked herself, after I got there.

Almost all of the hundred or so people at the ceremony were Christian.[4] Rabbi Gelberman used the fact that Dad had died on the anniversary of my parents' engagement as a sign of Dad's ongoing commitment to Mama, which I saw gave her some solace. He welcomed all Dad's acquaintances from the community and declared this proof of Dad's active engagement in life, up until the moment of his death.

---

4 When I called Naomi and Phil, Arthur's sister and brother-in-law, to let them know that my father had died, Naomi begged off from the funeral, saying that she had a board meeting that morning and it was "too far" to go to visit Mama's home later. She said Phil simply did not feel like going. He was busy.

Mama was very happy to hear Rabbi Gelberman recite the 23rd Psalm, to send Dad on his final journey; it was her favorite psalm. Mama was much calmer, after the ceremony. I even saw her smile, then, for the first time since Dad's death.

My fiancé, Arthur Orrmont, sat next to me. Louise (Mama's next-younger sister), Betty (the younger of Mama's nieces), Sondie (Mama's elder niece) and Serge (Sondie's husband), sat with us, but none of Mama's other family members attended. Dad's younger brother, Uncle Adrian could not come; I do not recall his name being mentioned at all. My cousin Betty had volunteered to bring food for those who came back to the house after the ceremony. "What would you like?" she asked us a day or so before Dad's funeral.

"Something simple and not spicy," we answered.

When we got back, after the ceremony, we discovered that only pastrami and corned beef, and a couple of other similarly spicy dishes were to be seen. "Did you bring anything that's not spicy?" Mama asked her.

"No. I only brought what I want to take home with me later."

Fortunately, a friend of mine from the seminary, Ife Majkia, and her fiancé, Herbert Gaston, came to the house after Dad's funeral and brought a huge dish of homemade macaroni and cheese. That way, Mama and the rest of us who had not eaten much or slept in a few days could have something comforting to eat.

Arthur and I returned to New York that night, somewhat anxious about how Mama would adjust because she and Dad had not been apart in years. After all the commotion of the past few days, and the seemingly endless procession of people from Manhasset and nearby towns with whom she had been interacting, she would now be totally alone, for the first time.

I went out to Manhasset the following weekend, to see how Mama was doing. "I've been talking to people who didn't know, telling them about your dad," she said. "One of them told me he simply didn't believe it, because the day before, Ray had been out, driving the car. He had not been sick at all. That's the way I want to go, too."

There followed, of course, the myriad practical details that always ensue. Dad and Mama had kept all their documents in order; they had made sure to take care of this, years before. However, Judge Alfred J. Loew, who had been their attorney for many years, had died in 1980. Mama needed a new lawyer. She found an attorney in Manhattan—Mortimer ("Mort") Lipsky was both an accountant and an attorney, so she would not have to search, separately, for someone to do her taxes.[5] He had a cavernous office on Fifth Avenue, in the 40's, with a dozen or more accountants, each with a private cubicle, working under him and his son. A tall, affable man with a rosy complexion, Mort said that he had been Eddy Murphy's accountant in the 1980s, and also that he was one of the models for the salty Jewish old man character that Murphy played on *Saturday Night Live*. Arthur was Mort's literary agent, too, for a book Mort had written about the Nobel Prize,[6] so we all already knew each other.

Dad had named Mama the executrix of his will, of course assuming that I would help her as necessary. Mama was very pleased when I discovered that, although Dad had never received income from the seat on the New York Mercantile Exchange that he had bought back in 1959, its value had soared to more than $600,000 ($1,059,036.44 in 2021), up from the $10,000 he had paid for it. Because it had split, two-for-one, in June 1981, she now had two seats, each of which was worth that amount. Her gain would, in 2021 dollars, have been more than $2 million. "Even so, we've never seen any income from it so far," Mama said.

Dad had mentioned, a few years earlier, that he was buying two other seats on a new enterprise called "The Twin Cities Board of Trade" (TCBOT), in Minneapolis, but he never discussed them afterward. After he died, we quickly discovered that these other "seats" had not done as well as the one he had bought on the Merc. On December 6, 1989, Dad's ledger shows that he had purchased two TCBOT seats, for $2,500 each. The TCBOT had just been created

---

5 At the time of his death, Dad was doing his own taxes, something so complex that Mama would never have attempted to do it herself.

6 *Quest for Peace: The Story of the Nobel Award*. South Brunswick, NJ: A.S. Barnes, 1966. Mort wanted to publish a revised edition of this 1966 book, but that never happened.

as a legal entity the previous year. Money woes kept delaying its opening, however.

The TCBOT promise, when Dad bought in, was that commodity and currency contracts would start trading any day. In March 1991, the ebullient, ever-optimistic thirty-year-old Sean O'Toole, the president of TCBOT, told *The Chicago Tribune* that there would be trading on the exchange within 90 days. However, in June, TCBOT informed *Business Times* that it was still negotiating funding.[7] As of September 20, 1991, only one contract had been authorized for trading, but no trading had ever taken place. Mr. O'Toole left the exchange when it folded, in 1992, never having hosted any trading at all.[8] By the time of Dad's passing, this exchange had gone bankrupt, rendering both of Dad's seats there worthless. I had to remind Mama about this investment. She found the documentation for it while looking through Dad's papers. Mort was the one who got confirmation, for her, that TCBOT was a defunct company.

The process of finding and re-titling assets kept Mama and me occupied for months, because Mama really had not interested herself in Dad's business affairs, even after they were both retired. By then the internet existed and I was able to use it to help Mama by doing research. Although she had learned how to operate several computer programs, Mama was never comfortable working online.

Mama seems not to have known about a vault Dad had leased from a private company. When we were collecting and evaluating Dad's assets, she never mentioned it. I found the key to this vault only after Mama passed away, by which time the vault company was long defunct. Considering that Mama had not been paying any bills from them in the years after Dad died, they might easily have sold off the contents of the vault, whatever those might have been, many years earlier.

Although Mama had gone back to driving after Dad passed away, she clearly did not enjoy that activity as much as Dad had.

---

7 In the article "TCBOT Still Negotiating Funding," on p. 14 of its June 8, 1991 issue.
8 Mr. O'Toole is now a politician. His official biography lists his experience as "President/Chief Executive Officer, Twin Cities Board of Trade, 1988-1992" which, I suppose, is technically accurate. *https://votesmart.org/candidate/biography/123743/sean-otoole*

Arthur and I did not have a car; finding a permanent parking spot in Manhattan could run $300 or more per month ($529.52 in 2021), and we were convinced that we had better uses for the money. Therefore, when Mama came to visit Manhattan, she traveled by train, and later on, in a car with a driver. Mama continued to drive her Acura Legend locally, on various errands and to her classes. All events seemed now to be scheduled during the day, and it was a long-familiar as well as short route to the library—only about three-quarters of a mile. Mama did not seem to have had any plans to give more night courses or classes in other towns.

For many years, both before and after Dad's death, Mama continued to work on a book she had tentatively titled *Letters from the Iron House*. She had intended it as a sort of sequel to *Red & White*. It had, if possible, a darker and more painful subject than that of *Red & White*. Mama had been gathering first-hand accounts of either Native Americans who had been incarcerated or, alternatively, the accounts of Native American children whose parents had been incarcerated. In one instance, a child had ended up in prison as what seemed like at least an indirect effect of watching his father murder his mother, then commit suicide. Mama collected boxes of material, continuing to work at it even after she moved away from Manhasset, but she never seems to have submitted a proposal to a publisher for it. Eventually she projected a work, darker still, on Native American suicide.

One of the nasty storms, during the winter of 1993-94, had taken down an old pine tree. The tree fell right through my parents' roof, requiring major restoration work. At the time of Dad's passing, my parents had been having extensive home repairs made. I had never met the contractor, because he generally worked during weekdays, and of course he worked during daylight hours. I was normally there over weekends or in the evening.

In the spring, after the repairs had been completed and the contractor paid, Mama complained to me that she still was getting calls from him. He kept saying that he wanted to see Mama socially, but she clearly did not want to see him. Judging by her agitated demeanor when she discussed him, it seemed that Mama might have been a bit afraid of him, although she never said this.

One day, I was the passenger in her car. We were driving south on Community Drive, the wide road that separates Manhasset from Great Neck, when I saw her frown.

"What's the matter, Mama?"

"It's that deuced contractor!"

"What about him?"

"He's following us! He's already done this to me three times so far this week."

"Are you sure?"

"I know that truck. He's following us."

"There's a big police station coming up on the right.[9] Why don't you pull into their parking lot and let's just sit there for a bit?"

I figured at least we would be close to help, if we needed it.

The truck did not follow us into the police station's parking lot. After that, Mama said she did not hear from the contractor again. Since that was the only time that I saw this particular vehicle, I do not know whether it was the contractor's truck, and I certainly do not know whether it was the same truck Mama had just told me that she remembered seeing, following her car, several times before, earlier in the week.

Without Dad as a steadying influence, Mama suddenly began to ascribe to supernatural forces any breakage or losses of household items. She started telling me that some "evil entity" had broken things in the house. Since I never experienced any such activity, I was forced to assume that Mama herself broke or lost these items. The breakage was likely an accident, but Mama simply did not want to take responsibility. Reading psalms and performing cleansing rituals in the house did not stop Mama's claims.

This went on for months. Finally, I was determined to find a way to confront Mama without having to do so myself directly. Through friends, I arranged for Mama and me to see a Candomblé priest who lived in Brooklyn. He was a tall, distinguished-looking man, in his mid-50s, I would guess, wearing white, flowing robes that contrasted with his dark skin. I had not told him about the details of Mama's case, so when she recited her story for him, I have every reason to believe that he had never heard it before. He

---

9 That station is still there, at 100 Community Drive.

sat across the table from us, in his ritual garb, listening respectfully and carefully to everything Mama said.

An air of additional dignity and authority descended on him. "I have every reason to believe that you should look to a human entity, in human form, as the source of your problem," he intoned, the lilt of the Caribbean Islands infusing every word. He nodded his head for emphasis. "However, if you would like to be initiated, we can make the appropriate arrangements for you to come back. If you do this, then you must bring two live chickens to be sacrificed as part of the ritual. Only remember: once you have received a command, as part of a ritual, you must obey it, no matter what it is. You must obey, without question."

We thanked him and said our goodbyes. I had no further contact with him. Mama never told me that she did either. Poring over Mama's papers, after she died, I found no evidence that she had ever seen or spoken to him, or even written to him, again.

Although Mama never directly admitted that she had made up those stories of supernatural destruction, she did confess to me, on the way back to Manhattan in a taxi, that she really did not want to live in her Manhasset house anymore. "It upsets me to live where I saw your Dad die," she said.

A little further discussion revealed that Aunt Louise and Betty had been pressing her to move to New Jersey. Apparently, they had started to ask right after Dad passed on.

"Is that where you want to live, Mama?"

"Never! I don't want to go back to New Jersey. The privacy factor is just about right, where it is. That's where it's been for years."

Arthur and I had been considering moving out of Manhattan as well, so the three of us got together to discuss the whole idea of relocating. Arthur and I had taken a few trips to upstate New York, already, just to see how we liked various areas. However, our explorations did not end up making us want to live there. We discussed our experiences with Mama. She, herself, had absolutely no desire to go back to New Jersey. Arthur and I had never considered any New Jersey community a serious option either.

The past few winters had been particularly rough in the New York area, which led the three of us to narrow our search for possible new homes to three areas, all of them warmer than New York—North Carolina, Florida and New Mexico.

Toward the end of the summer of 1994, I wanted to attend a two-day meeting in Orlando, Florida. Perhaps, if we all went, Arthur and Mama could see how they liked the area. We flew down to Florida together.

Arthur and Mama planned to explore the vicinity while I was at the meeting. However, it was so steamy outside that Arthur and Mama told me later that they did not even want to open the door to the street. They said that they had tried to go out, but it was like attempting to walk through a hot, wet towel. The extreme humidity also seemed to make Mama's arthritis much worse—and very quickly, too. Before this, Arthur and I had visited points in Florida as far south as Key West, so we knew that, even in winter it was hot and humid there. Orlando was further north, but we now saw that it had similar problems with heat and humidity. The Jacksonville area had never attracted any of us. Florida came off our list.

North Carolina was the next place, in order. Even though Aunt Vicki was living in Charlotte, we never considered living there. We did not because of a letter Aunt Vicki sent me, in answer to one I had sent her, describing our experience in Florida. She said that between 10 AM and 4 PM, there were about five months of the year—but never less than three—when you would not want to open a door to the street in Charlotte, either. Indeed, Charlotte has what most people refer to as a "humid, subtropical climate." Why did we assume that cities further inland in North Carolina would be much less humid?

For Mama, the possibility of moving to North Carolina had nothing to do with wanting to see more of Aunt Vicki. Other than contributing this information from her letter to our discussion, her name never came up. We decided that, given the results in Florida, Arthur and I should go first, to scout out the place, and that we would only involve Mama if we found some compelling reason for her to go there.

Arthur and I prepared to spend Christmas that year in North Carolina. The first area we looked at was Raleigh-Durham, where the climate was far milder than what we had faced in New York over the past few winters. Raleigh and Durham seemed similar, on the surface anyway. Arthur and I were sitting in the hotel in Raleigh, eating dinner, when we heard two men talking in the next booth. One had raised his voice. The phrase that caught our mutual attention was, "He's one of those G_D_ white N__s!" Arthur called for the check and we left, only to discover, in glancing over to see who had been speaking, that the two men we had heard conversing were both police officers, in uniform. Scratch Raleigh.

Our next stop was Asheville, for which we were leaving the next morning. After boarding, we could not imagine how Mama would be comfortable in this cramped, regional plane. Getting to it required passengers to walk long distances in the airport, and then climb a steep flight of stairs, just to get in and out. When we arrived in Asheville, one of the passengers was taken off the plane before anyone else, directly to the hospital. Because of the close quarters and lack of proper air filtration on that trip, I suspect that most of the other passengers were as sick within days of arriving in Asheville, as Arthur and I were. It took us a couple of days more to feel well enough just to get out of bed. The temperature in Asheville might have been a little higher than New York in late December, but the humidity made the cold penetrating. Although Asheville was seductive to Arthur as the nurturing-ground of Thomas Wolfe and he loved the Biltmore Estate, even he had to admit that the area seemed awfully inhospitable in winter.

Durham, a cosmopolitan university town, remained a possibility. Neither Arthur nor I wanted to take our book publishing or agency business with us. Florida, North Carolina and New Mexico all had acupuncture-friendly laws at that time. The final decision-maker on moving to North Carolina came when I called the North Carolina Board of Acupuncture to ask about licensure, since by then I was about a year from getting my diploma. "We won't license anyone who doesn't agree to live in the mountains. There are already too many acupuncturists in Charlotte and Raleigh-Durham. If you want to live in Asheville, we'll consider licensing you."

That left New Mexico, the last place on the list. This was a trip Mama wanted badly to make with us, if for no other reason, then in memory of Dad. We all made that trip in August 1995, arriving on the redeye, about 3:30 AM, on the first flight of the new day. Or was it the last flight of the old day?

We took our time collecting our luggage and going outside. The terminal was deserted. At that hour, no cabs waited at the exit, so the three of us got about 90 minutes to watch from the airport, in the comfortable, cool morning air, as the sun started to rise.

The Manhasset house was surrounded by hills. They seemed like some sort of insulation. You could not have a clear line-of-sight to the horizon on any side. Albuquerque had a clear line-of-sight, to the west and north and south. Then, of course, looking back a few miles to the east, we could see the Sandia Mountains. Mama loved her ability to see for miles in all directions. In a time when Manhattan was becoming a city of huge buildings with shaded, dark gullies in between and the skies were often choked with smog, it was a great relief to Arthur and me to be able to see clouds with Tintorettto colors and wide-open vistas.

I suspect that, before we left the airport, all three of us had already decided on New Mexico, although we were too tired to talk. We still wanted to believe that we were planning to make logical decisions, so probably none of us would have said this yet. By the time we reached our Albuquerque hotel, the only question that remained to be answered was exactly where, in New Mexico, we were going to move. Which city, which neighborhood? We hailed the first cab of the morning, got to our hotel rooms and crawled into bed.

Arthur told me, that first morning, that he really, really wanted us to marry before we flew back to New York. That way, he said, Mama could be there but the rest of our negative relatives on both sides of the family could not. Ife Majkia and Herbert Gaston, now married, had already moved to Albuquerque. Both were ordained ministers. It seemed to me that Arthur had already spoken with Herb, asking him to officiate. Mama would certainly be the first witness. Ife could easily be the second witness.

Mama was delighted. We used a good part of the time we would have spent house-hunting preparing for our marriage instead. Mama needed a dress, and so did I. Herb and Arthur were running around, doing their preparations also. We were frantically busy.

The wedding party on August 14, 1995. Left to right: Rev. Ife Majkia-Gaston, Annette Rosenstiel, Arthur Orrmont, Léonie Rosenstiel, Rev. Herbert Gaston. Photo credit: Ife Majkia-Gaston.

In 1992, Dad had bought, at $5.4375 per share, 1,000 shares of SBS Engineering, a company then located in Albuquerque.[10] For reasons only Mama knew, she contacted the company before we arrived in 1995, letting them know that we were interested in looking at houses. The wife of one of the officers wrote Mama back. She was a real estate agent. In the spare time we had, she started taking us around town—always, it seemed, to places she described as "an area a New Yorker would like," where any visible names looked Jewish, or she simply drove us, without comment, around areas where it was clear that all the names on the mailboxes looked Jewish. The architecture there made them look like New York suburban subdivisions, too, which was exactly what we wanted to avoid. We had already tried to explain that to her. Mama did not want to move to New Mexico so that she could buy a Levittown house or a New England colonial, and neither did Arthur and I.

Just for completeness, we explored a bit in Santa Fe before we left in August, but Arthur said it reminded him too much of

---

10 It had split two-for-one before it was bought out by what was then GE FANUC at $16.50 per share in 2006, so Mama received $33,000 for Dad's original $5,440 investment. Dad was 82 years old when he bought shares in this company, thereby proving that there are at least some people whose financial acumen does not necessarily diminish with age.

Greenwich Village; Albuquerque seemed more real to him. Mama did not much like the ways in which Santa Fe had changed from the sleepy village she and Dad and I saw there in the 1960s. Albuquerque it was.

I complained about this issue of real estate "steering" to Ife, who referred us to the real estate agent she and Herb had used, but we did not have the time left to explore much more on that trip. Arthur decided to deputize me, because he could not leave work much more to house-hunt. Mama and I decided to come back to Albuquerque again, just to search for homes. We had already decided that we wanted to live much closer than the twenty miles or so that separated Manhattan and Manhasset, but Mama wanted to have her own home.

It took about as long for Mama to get final approval to inherit Dad's seat on the New York Mercantile Exchange, and have it retitled in her name, as it had for Dad to be approved to become a member in the first place. There had been no increase in the efficiency of that process between 1959 and 1994. I helped Mama get the paperwork together and submit it. It was the end of 1995 before Mama finally was the official owner of her own seat on the Merc.

There was a provision in probate law that a spouse could disclaim part of an inheritance and give it to someone else. Mama said that she wanted to give me the other seat, but I did not have any need for a non-producing asset, so she sold it and gave me the money instead. I then invested some of the money and kept the rest to pay for the house in Albuquerque that Arthur and I were going to buy.

Mama had to sell her home so that she could leave Manhasset. In fact, she was just getting ready to list it, late in 1996. Moving, although an effort for Arthur and me, did not involve selling anything because we had been renting both his office and our apartment. It only remained for us to give a month's notice and move out.

Mama wanted help deciding which objects, from among the thousands she had collected over decades, needed to be weeded out before she could sell her home. I went to Manhasset for a few days, to help her to sort out clothes. That is when I discovered the 200 boxes of never-worn shoes, dozens of new dresses and coats and other never-used wearables in the attic. And many more in the basement. Sorting these turned out to be a job requiring sustained effort, and multiple trips. When he had time, Arthur came out, too. In preparation for showing the house, Mama put most of the furniture in storage or sold it.

Mama determined to rent an apartment in Manhattan while the remaining preparations were being made. She loved the idea of living in New York City, temporarily; she said it would make her feel young again.

Most non-furniture items, Mama donated to local churches. What they did not want went to a second-hand shop. Among the donated items was Dad's Rolls Royce. The then-inoperable Rolls became one of those donations in which a person gives the Archdiocese a car, as a donation, and the Church sells it to a pre-chosen buyer who also donates the money for that payment to the church. When the Archdiocese sent people over to pick it up, they used a tow truck. They had already been warned that it had four flat tires and no working battery. By then, it had not been driven for more than a decade. I recall that the Rolls buyer, who knew that he was going to have to recondition the car, even got Dad's original owner's manual.

One of the last rooms to be cleared out was the master bathroom. In the medicine cabinet was a green glass bottle with small granules in it. They were slightly larger than grains of sand. The label was turned toward the wall.

"What's that medicine?" I asked Mama, pointing to the bottle. "Do you need me to pack it up?"

"Oh that!" Mama laughed, "That's the bottle of aspirin my mother gave me when we moved here. We never took any."

I lifted the bottle off the glass shelf and turned it around. The label did say "aspirin" on it. It was not sealed, so someone must have once at least opened the bottle, but the rest of its forty-year-old contents had disintegrated into granules.

In going over Dad's things, Mama found twenty-two cartons of material he had received, over the years, all of which he had carefully labeled as having been sent to him from the New York Mercantile Exchange. I went through them with Mama, verified that they were indeed papers relating to the Merc, but were not likely to be documents she would need later, and then helped her to seal them. She called the Merc to ask whether they wanted these. The Merc sent a "runner" out to pick them all up. I watched, as he carted them away.

Arthur, Mama and I had been investing, as a sort of family council, since late 1994, after Mama took delivery of Dad's stock certificates, retitled in her name. Back then, these were negotiable instruments, once delivered. If you were not going to keep them in a bank vault—and Mama had immediately closed out Dad's bank vault—it was not safe to keep them in the house, unless you had an industrial-quality safe. This Mama did not have, nor did she want to buy one. Realizing, by then, that she wanted to leave Manhasset, she did not want to rent a new bank vault there, either.

At that point, online stockbrokers existed, an investing convenience that had never been available before. We determined that we would deliver our stock certificates to Jack White, the online brokerage we had picked, and the one where I had my account. That way, we would have three different accounts, and each of us could keep the receipts for the original certificates. Whenever we wanted to, we could take delivery of the physical certificates again after we were settled in, in New Mexico, if we found a local broker we liked. It simply was not safe to carry these certificates with us when we moved. If they were on deposit, and there was a paper trail, there would be no danger of certificates being lost or stolen while we were in the process of moving. Meanwhile, we could instruct Jack White where to deliver any dividend checks. Each of us would receive, separately, the dividends our stocks had paid. Mama and Arthur decided to give me power of attorney over their accounts, because neither of them wanted to work on the internet.

After that, I would be responsible for placing all orders. If I was planning to make any major purchases, the three of us met, so they could know what I was planning. Sometimes, Arthur had ideas he wanted me to execute. Mama did not. As with Dad before me, Mama's usual reaction was, "If you're buying some, then please get some for me!"

At a "family council" meeting in 1995, Mama raised a question of whether I wanted to become a Certified Financial Planner, so I researched that possibility. Examining the underlying philosophy of that work convinced me that it conflicted mightily with what Dad had believed, even though the fact that I would be responsible for handling the money made it look superficially similar.

One objection to becoming a certified financial planner would be that financial planners all seemed to be subscribing to the then-newly-articulated "Bengen Rule," published in the October 1994 issue of the *Journal of Financial Planning*,[11] which suggested that retirees who withdrew up to 4.2 percent of their savings each year stood a good chance of not dying destitute.[12] This was not a guarantee that they would still have money when they died, only that they stood a better chance that way than others who took more out.

It had always been Dad's position that you used what you needed and not more. Some years you might need more, some years less, but it was hubris to decide that you knew how long you were going to live at the beginning of your retirement. Financial planners were basing their decisions on actuarial tables, not individuals. Dad did not like annuities, either. Most made no provision for inflation or a greater need one year than another. If you lived long enough, inflation would eat into the buying power of your guaranteed income stream, and if you needed more money in a single year than what you had contracted to get, the company guaranteeing your annuity could penalize you financially.

By the time Dad died, Mama had already been retired for almost fourteen years. If she had followed this new "Bengen rule," she would have had no appreciable amount of her original savings left sometime in the next six years. In fact, if she had adopted this strategy in 1981, the end would have come sooner, because the

---

11 Pages 14-24. Realizing that Bengen grossly underestimated how long many retirees would need to keep making withdrawals, and the inadvisability of making certain assumptions about interest rates and market performance, experts have recently called this "rule" into question. A one-size-fits-all solution, it turns out, was far too simplistic, and in fact might be no solution at all. https://www.marketwatch.com/story/the-4-rule-desperately-needs-to-be-modernized-2018-07-20

12 https://www.investopedia.com/articles/personal-finance/120513/why-4-retirement-rule-no-longer-safe.asp

Mercantile seat figured among her assets, and she would have had to sell that, in order to withdraw four percent of all assets in any given year, after she had exhausted her savings accounts.

Back then, at Mama's age, a certified financial planner, I discovered, would have said that she was doing something "incorrect," because she kept the majority of her assets in stocks. Another questionable asset, from that perspective, was the non-income-producing New York Mercantile Exchange seat. Mama received a pension, but part of it was in an annuity account that paid an invariable amount that remained the same, as it had been when she retired in 1981, regardless of inflation. Between 1981 and 1994, the total inflation rate had exceeded 75 percent. Mama had already discovered that her TIAA annuity was worth less and less each year, in terms of buying power. However, in the financial planning world, one possibility for someone who was older than retirement age was to create an annuity, using a large amount of cash. That would yield a steady income stream, but it would have a limited possibility to increase, and you would have to decide, going in, exactly how much it could be allowed to increase. Mama had already seen what inflation had done to the fixed annuity that was part of her TIAA pension. The only part of her pension that kept increasing was the one based on the stock investments made by CREF. I had a discussion with her about her options.

"You mean it would be limited? If inflation increased, it wouldn't cover?"

"It might cover. But it also might not. No one can tell you what inflation's going to be. It depends on the details of the annuity contract, and also on the insurance company paying the distribution, and how good it is."

"You mean this is insurance?"

"It is."

"You know how I hate insurance companies!"

"Your TIAA-CREF is an insurance company that does investments."

"Well, I hate that, too!"

"Okay, Mama. There's more. I need to tell you about the rest of what I've discovered."

There was a formula, back then, for financial planners to use, to determine, based on age, how much of a person's assets should be in cash. They subtracted the person's age from 100, and the amount remaining was the percentage they believed should be in stocks. Mama was in her mid-eighties, meaning that only about 15 percent of her assets should be in stocks, according to this theory.[13] However, almost all of Mama's assets were in stocks and the dividends from Mama's stocks provided her with the major part of her income. CD rates, then, were running between 5 and 6 percent, far down from the double-digits of the mid-1980s.[14]

Meanwhile, inflation was just under 2.56 percent in 1994. Each year that a finite amount of cash was kept in an account, it would lose at least that amount in buying power, and that would only be if inflation did not rise more than the amount it had risen during 1994. In fact, if the bank interest rate continued to fall, and inflation rose at all beyond where it was in 1994, Mama would lose more than that, and there was no way to predict how much. I explained this to Mama.

"I don't like that at all!" Mama said. "You know how I hate people telling me what I can't do because I'm too old! Besides, I don't want to sit on a pile of cash that's shrinking."

"Then I can't get that certificate. If I do, I'll have to agree to a code of ethics that tells me to tell you to put most of your money into CDs, or a mix of CDs and bonds. And I won't be able to do what Dad did."

"Now I understand. I don't want you becoming a financial planner, then."

Mama made what turned out to be the right decision, for her. The following year, inflation had risen to 2.83 percent[15] and the CD rates had fallen to between 4.9 and 5.5 percent. The pattern of decreasing CD rates continued over the next two decades.[16]

---

13   *https://money.cnn.com/retirement/guide/investing_basics.moneymag/index7.htm* This model is changing, simply because people are now living longer, but Mama would have been among those impacted negatively by the prevailing theory, and I wanted her to understand this could happen.
14   *https://www.bankrate.com/banking/cds/historical-cd-interest-rates-1984-2016/*
15   *http://www.in2013dollars.com/inflation-rate-in-1995*
16   In January of 2012, a 5-year CD yield only paid about 1.16 percent (*https://www.bankrate.com/banking/cds/historical-cd-interest-rates-1984-2016/*). By July 2011,

Meanwhile, inflation continued to rise, at an average rate of 2.2 percent per year. Total inflation between 1994 and 2012 ran to 54.92 percent.[17]

By November 1996, Arthur and I had found an attractive one-bedroom sublet apartment for Mama, in an elevator-and-doorman Manhattan building, about two blocks from our place. I do not recall any parties in New Jersey that year, nor did Mama mention any plans Aunt Louise and Betty had to visit her in the city. I had lunch with her most days, just to make sure she had company.

Arthur Orrmont and Léonie Rosenstiel in Annette's Manhasset home shortly before she moved into Manhattan (1996).
Photo: Annette Rosenstiel.

Meanwhile, Mama had expressed a desire to learn Chinese, another long-term goal of hers, so we started going, together, several times a week, to semi-private classes. The language studio was only a few blocks from Mama's apartment. We walked to and from the tutoring sessions. Mama had fun watching strangers react to hearing us speak what might pass, to non-Chinese-speakers, for Mandarin Chinese to each other as we walked past them on the street.[18]

Arthur and I spent Thanksgiving, Christmas, my birthday and New Year's Day in 1997 with Mama. She seemed to find her furnished apartment extremely congenial. Being in a newer, doorman building on Manhattan's East Side in the 50s automatically

---

shorter-term CDs paid only .26-.44 percent interest (*https://www.bankrate.com/banking/cds/historical-cd-interest-rates-1984-2016/*). However inflation, even if those calculating it had "adjusted" the way it was calculated, and it had slowed down, as a result, was still chugging away at 1.7 percent (*https://www.usinflationcalculator.com/inflation/current-inflation-rates/*)

17 http://www.in2013dollars.com/1994-dollars-in-2012?amount=100

18 Our Chinese conversations likely only sounded like Chinese to people who did not speak that language at all, but they were fun.

meant that almost anything she wanted was nearby. She was even on a high enough floor that the street noise around the corner on First Avenue did not disturb her sleep.

Mama and I were back in Albuquerque in March 1997, looking seriously for homes. Ife picked us up at the Sunport and took us to the Sheraton Uptown. The three of us walked in and approached the reception desk. I gave my name, gestured toward Mama, and said that we had reservations, to which the check-in girl replied, "So, that will be three separate rooms."

I said no, that Mama and I had reserved a double room. She looked shocked.

On the way to the elevator, Ife asked me how I understood what had just happened. The way I saw it, Mama was fair and blonde. I had much darker skin and hair. Ife, part East Indian, part Cherokee and part Jewish, had even darker skin than I did. I suspected that the clerk's prejudice had convinced her that all of us must be checking in and that none of us would want to share a room with any of the others. Ife agreed. Mama was too tired to change hotels that night, but we moved to the Marriott, a few blocks away, first thing in the morning. None of us ever willingly patronized the Sheraton Uptown again.

Mama was delighted that a local restaurateur who then owned the Macaroni Grill across the street from the Marriott, back then, went around the dining room, singing opera arias for his dinner patrons. He did a creditable job, too.

Bruce Shah, our new realtor[19], managed to find exactly the homes we wanted. They were only 1.5 miles apart. In New Mexico terms, that is practically next door. Both were territorial-style. Mama's was all on one level; the one destined for Arthur and me was on three levels. Mama decided that she wanted the one-floor house. She had forgotten her checkbook, so I had to lend her the earnest money. I wanted Arthur to see the photos of our proposed home before we signed. He did.

---

19 He was a broker at a firm called Vaughn Realty, then run by Doug Vaughn. In 2012, Doug Vaughn was sentenced to 12 years in federal prison for running what Forbes Magazine called a "Mini-Madoff" Ponzi-type con, in which 600 investors lost $86 million. Fortunately, no members of my family were involved in this. https://www.forbes.com/forbes/2010/0628/investment-guide-new-mexico-ponzi-vaughan-mini-madoff-case.html#3f7f87b24f24

The first months of 1997 we crammed with errands, as we wrapped up our various activities in New York. Mama happily sold the house for more than ten times what she and Dad had paid for it. Over the last months of her New York residency, Mama sent me on innumerable errands, buying what seemed to me an endless list of things she thought she would need. And, of course, on most days we continued to have lunch together.

Mama led her last book discussion group—on Amy Tan's *The Joy Luck Club*—in Manhasset, in March 1997.[20] I went with her for moral support and because there were a few final details needed to complete the sale of her Manhasset home. By then, Mama was accustomed to a full house at all of her talks. She was happy with the attendance that day, too.

At the end of that session, the librarian announced that Dad's friends would once again be funding the customary annual Raymond Rosenstiel Memorial chamber music concert that they had been offering in his name. The first of these events, underwritten by, as the program notes say, "The Friends and Family of Raymond Rosenstiel," had taken place on Sunday, May 7, 1995.[21] Since I never saw any evidence that Mama contributed to supporting these, and I know that Arthur and I were never asked to do so, I am concluding that Dad's friends paid for them all. The May 1997 concert was scheduled for shortly before Mama left for New Mexico.[22]

One day early in April, I had had lunch with Mama in Manhattan, as usual. She exited the restaurant in front of me, but tripped and fell against a railing. A medical exam revealed that she had torn her right rotator cuff, the same shoulder in which she had twice had bursitis some years earlier. Did she want to delay moving to Albuquerque until the injury healed? Mama would not

---

20 Mama had to get to Albuquerque, to take possession of her new home, so she did not lead a final book discussion, scheduled for June 11, 1997. The six book discussions she had led in 1997 had netted her $875 (just over $1,437 in 2021)—not enough to get rich, but certainly a nice addition to Mama's disposable income.

21 Mama's idea was to choose young musicians who were in the early stages of their careers. The group that performed in 1995 was L'Estro Armonico Trio, which then consisted of Jennifer Tao, Abraham Appleman and Eugene Moye—pianist, violinist and cellist, respectively. Jennifer Tao ended up teaching at Princeton; Abraham joined the Metropolitan Opera Orchestra. Eugene Moye became the principal cellist of the American Symphony Orchestra and a frequent studio musician.

22 These concerts started in 1995, the year after Dad's passing.

countenance that, so we quickly arranged for as much physical therapy as we could fit into the time remaining to her in New York. As was usual for her, she declined to take any prescription analgesic or anti-inflammatory drugs. (The cortisone for bursitis had been her only compromise with that decision, after 1946.)

The Raymond Rosenstiel Memorial Concert was held on Sunday, April 27, 1997, just a few weeks before Mama had to leave. No one who did not already know about Mama's accident ever noticed that she was in pain from her torn rotator cuff. Arthur and I went out to Manhasset to be with Mama that day. We were all delighted to see some of my parents' acquaintances again. They did not seem to come into Manhattan to see Mama, but they had thronged to her book discussion groups on the Island.

Mama had to take possession of her new Albuquerque home in mid-May. So I went out with Mama, got her settled in, made sure her car had been delivered, so she had mobility, then returned to New York to help Arthur do our remaining packing and take care of the rest of our mutual obligations in the city.

Mama called me often, telling me how delighted she was with her new home. The skylights, she said, made it beautiful and light inside, all day. The sunlight cheered her; the past few years in New York had been unusually stormy and overcast. "I'm so glad I got away from all that!" she told me.

Her office, on the east side of the house, had a clear view of the Sandias and the sunrise. From her bedroom, on the west side of the house, she could see the

Annette Rosenstiel leaving her Manhasset home for the last time after signing the sales contract. Spring 1997. Photo: Léonie Rosenstiel

Léonie Rosenstiel and Annette Rosenstiel in the breakfast nook of Annette's Albuquerque home on June 29, 1997. Photo: Arthur Orrmont

sunset over the treetops in her backyard. Mama kept telling me how much she enjoyed living where Dad had said he had wanted to, years before. The dry climate had lessened her arthritis pain, too. Mama started telling me that she wished she would have been able to make this move while Dad was still alive to enjoy it.

Once Arthur and I arrived, Mama and I began attending services on Sunday at God's House Church, on Menaul. The fervor of the congregation seemed to infuse Mama with new vigor. Once, very early in the time we were attending, Mama was having trouble with her arthritis. She went to church with her cane, leaning heavily on it for support. However, when they called for people to approach the altar for healing, apparently, totally unconsciously, Mama decided that she was going to walk up there unaided. When she stood up and started to walk down the aisle, Herbert, Ife and I, who had been sitting together with Mama in the pew, noticed that she had left her cane behind. Herb made signs to me, asking whether he should go after her and give it to her. I smiled and shook my head, "No!"

Mama did not realize she had left her cane in the pew until she came back. Afterwards, at the fellowship meal, she was delightedly telling the lady next to her that she had come to the service today, only able to walk with difficulty, but now she had no trouble at all. "Shh!" said her tablemate to the rest of the people seated with them, "She's giving testimony!" That made Mama even happier.

Arthur and I were just settling in, in mid-June, when we got a phone call. "Welcome to the cul-de-sac!" said the cheery man on the other end of the phone.

He told me that his name was Graham Browne, and he was our next-door neighbor. "Is there anything I can help you with?" he continued.

Mama had already told me that she wanted to make a new will and sign new powers of attorney as soon as possible. In fact, we had all been told that we needed to execute all those documents again, even though we had completed them in New York, only a few years earlier, because we had moved to a new state. So, I said to Graham, "Thanks for asking! My mother, my husband and I just moved here from New York. We all need new wills and other legal papers, too. Do you know a good attorney?"

Graham chuckled. "I'm an attorney! I'm with Sutin, Thayer and Browne, down on Louisiana, in the office building across from Winrock Mall. Do you know where that is?"

I did. Now it was my turn to chuckle. Arthur and I had had to stay in the Marriott for about a week, before we were able to move into our house; it was across the street from the building where Graham had his office. We arranged to see the affable, rosy-cheeked attorney to discuss wills, a week or so later. It was the first week of July, now. We expected the drafts to be ready fairly soon. Graham said he would call us.

Mama called us, over the Fourth of July weekend. Her voice sounded faint and far away. She said she had fallen and hit her back on the bathtub. She could not get up off the floor, but had managed to crawl to the phone and call us. Arthur and I raced over. I called an ambulance, but the EMTs refused to take Mama to the hospital. It was a holiday weekend and Mama was conscious. They were willing to help us get her to our car, so we could take her to an emergency room, but they told us that the ambulance was needed for graver matters.

The ER told us that Mama had cracked three ribs. The doctors wanted to keep her, overnight, in the hospital, for observation because one lung had collapsed from the impact of the fall, but it had been re-inflating, albeit slowly, thereby causing her additional pain. Mama absolutely refused to stay in the hospital overnight. She also refused painkillers.

We called Graham after the weekend was over, to tell him that we were going to put off any will signing until Mama was feeling better. Meanwhile, I hired aides to stay with her, in case she needed something that she could not reach easily. Moving around would be difficult for her, at least for the next couple of weeks. Having had experience with an injury to the intercostal muscles, I could imagine how much pain Mama was suffering, particularly because she would not take any painkillers.

We did not get back to Graham's office until August 25. Or rather to his conference room, with its commanding views of the Sandias. Mama said she was feeling "recovered enough" to talk legalities; she was eager to get these formalities completed, so she did not have to worry about them anymore.

We all started skimming the documents in front of us. We had told Graham that we had promised Dad we would not create any trusts, but each of our wills mentioned one.

"My will has a trust in it!" Mama complained.

"You have to! It saves on taxes and gives you privacy. Estates of this size require you to set up a trust, at least in your will, these days."

"I promised my husband that I wouldn't."

"Well, this isn't a trust that will affect *you*, anyway; it will only go into effect after you pass away."

"I think we should wait outside," I said.

Arthur and I left the room, at that point, so Mama could have a private discussion with Graham.

We sat in the waiting area, to be called only after they had finished. We all talked about our experiences on the way home; it turned out that we had ultimately all agreed to sign on the dotted line, an action that both Arthur and I ended up regretting later. If Mama had realized the unintended consequences of having the word "trust" in her will, even during her life, she would likely have regretted it, too. However, back then, Mama was still recovering from her injury (even though she insisted that she was "fine" again) and she had only a certain amount of energy. She would need to rest for a while after this visit anyway.

Something was odd about the wills we all signed that day; the names of Arthur's relatives found their way onto lists of Mama's relatives and vice-versa. And each of the wills insisted that each of us was to be treated, after we died, as if we had died unmarried, which in New Mexico meant that most of the known relatives were not closely enough related to inherit anything.

The powers of attorney Graham's office had drawn up were fine, in form. But after a few years, during which they served their intended purpose, even they ended up no longer useful.

As soon as Mama felt better, she wanted further therapy for her shoulder. She got a doctor to order some physical therapy, but a few weeks into her series of treatments, that doctor decided to quit private practice, complaining that the insurance companies were demanding that she only spend five minutes, per patient, and she could not practice medicine responsibly that way. She went to work for the State of New Mexico, so it looked as if, at least back then, the state was more generous in allotting time that physicians could spend with their patients. Without a doctor's order for PT, Mama could not get those orders renewed.

Other doctors Mama quickly consulted told her that she was too old to benefit from this therapy anymore, insisting, instead, that she have surgery for her torn rotator cuff. They would be willing to order PT only after the operation. Even then, none of them could promise that any surgery would heal. Mama was furious. Because PT had to be ordered by a medical doctor, I believed that I could not write out those orders in my capacity as a doctor of oriental medicine. Mama demanded acupuncture treatment. At that point, I recommended that she see a senior Chinese practitioner who had some special treatments for this issue. At that point, I was trying to follow the Western model of not treating close family members.

Mama got an invitation, just after this, from the New York Mercantile Exchange. They were setting up an insurance program that would offer long-term care protection to members. A death-insurance policy was required to own a seat, but the medical benefit was optional. Mama never showed me the details, but did discuss the offer with me, in general terms.

"I don't need this!" Mama told me.

"Of course, you don't need it now, but are you sure you don't want protection anyway? Just in case something happens later?"

"My mother died in her sleep. My father died instantly. Your dad was active until the day he died. Besides, I have Medicare. I'll never need something like this!"

She did not sign up.[23]

I had always wondered why Mama demanded perfection of me as I was growing up. Finally, I decided to ask.

"Why were you always so hard on me when I was younger?"

"I wanted to make sure you could survive anything!"

One September day, I went to Mama's home, to take her to lunch. She had unlocked the door for me, in advance, as she often did, so I walked in. Mama was sitting in her favorite red leather armchair, in the den, the one that faced the door. It seemed as if she had been crossing something out on what appeared to be a typed manuscript draft, in her lap, as I entered.

"Hi! What's that you're working on, Mama?"

"They asked to interview me about my Army experience as a Jewish woman, so I did. Now I'm editing the transcript."

Mama got up and put the manuscript on a shelf in the big old dark wood radio cabinet on the wall. She seemed eager to speak of other things. The subject of this interview never arose again.[24]

---

23 There is no way to know whether this offer of a policy survived the take-over of the Merc in 2008, but had Mama had coverage, it might or might not have helped. Some policies require you to have spent time in the hospital prior to needing care; Mama had refused to do so. And later, when she had to stay overnight, she already had home health care, so the need for care was not caused by the hospital admission. My best guess is that the insurance would never have paid her a cent, even if she had taken it.

24 Only long after Mama passed away did it surface that this interview had actually taken place on November 13 and 20, 1989. It runs to 97 pages. The American Jewish Committee placed a copy on deposit with the oral history interviews they gave to the Dorot Jewish Division of the New York Public Library (***P(Oral Histories, Box 355 no. 2). Whatever Mama said was probably conditioned by two things: 1) at that point, Mama and Dad were taking a single course in Jewish mysticism at the Orthodox synagogue's outreach group in Great Neck, and 2) almost certainly,

The fact that Mama was reviewing this interview transcript at that particular moment might have been the catalyst for what happened next, in terms of Mama's connection to the Jewish faith. Or lack of it.

I asked her whether she wanted to revisit her Jewish roots by attending services on Rosh Hashanah and Yom Kippur, which that year, would have been on October 1-3, and again on October 10-11. Albuquerque was home to congregations of most major Jewish denominations. I took Mama around, to look, at least from the outside, at all of them that I could find. She immediately rejected both the Orthodox and Conservative congregations.

Mama said that she wanted to make one more effort to be Jewish. She told me that she thought she ought to try Congregation Albert, a Reform temple on Louisiana, near Montgomery. Paradoxically, she also swore me to secrecy about this, insisting that I tell no one in New Mexico that either of us had any Jewish heritage. She bought tickets to the services, for herself; she wanted to attend, alone. She even gave her part-time aide time off for those hours, so no one would see me picking Mama up or taking her home from the services.

Mama wrestled, once again, with the issue of religion. However, as Thomas Wolfe had so presciently said, many years earlier, it turned out that she could not go "home" again. If, in fact, that had ever been her religious home. She attended multiple services during the holiday period, suffering, it seemed to me, from increasing levels of agitation.

"Do you want to join?" I asked Mama, as she got into my car after the last service.

"Absolutely not!"

"Why not?"

"It's just like New York. All they ever talk about is money! It's disgusting. How can that be a house of worship? I'll never go back." And she did not.

This result probably could have been predicted, given the history of that institution. It was the oldest Jewish house of worship

---

Mama was recommended to the program by my elder cousin. She had worked for many years as a secretary for the American Jewish Committee, in addition to her position in her husband's news organization, Caribbean Network System.

The Failed Great Escape (Darkness Closes In) 29

in New Mexico, having started operations in 1897. After Mama had recovered from her attack of pique, she told me that, while attending services there, she had asked why it was called "Congregation Albert." One of the members told her that the name of the organization had been derived, long ago, from a contest the group ran. They had promised to name the congregation for the member who contributed the most money. His name was Albert.[25] Whatever else she disliked about the group, she did not say. For her, that was enough.

This plaint of the Jewish religion being used as a cash cow in the United States was already an old one. On July 27, 1934, Newark's *Jewish Chronicle* had run an article bemoaning mercenary High Holy Day practices:

"The annual war has started again between the 'vested interests' and itinerant hucksters who try to make a "clean up" during the high holidays…New York State now has a law making it a mild crime to rent an empty loft, fit it out with funeral chairs and hang it out with a sign…[saying] 'We give you the best Jewish services in the city for the best price anywhere. Good singing guaranteed.'"[26]

However, in Albuquerque, it was the established congregation Mama had found mercenary. Although, as I later discovered, Mama kept some of the old Jewish family items out in her garage, she intentionally never had any direct contact with a Jewish congregation or a rabbi for the rest of her life. A few years later, when Mama's commercial guardian wanted to have a rabbi come in to see her, she adamantly refused to see one.[27]

Meanwhile, Mama continued to read any available newspapers—except *the Wall Street Journal*. She complained to me that she had seen an article in *The Alibi*[28] that offended her sensibilities. It suggested that older people were incompetent. Or at least that

---

25 I found this history almost impossible to credit. I had never before heard of a religious organization named after a major contributor. Although that acknowledgement of the derivation of the name of the congregation no longer appears on its website, I do remember being shocked by seeing it mentioned there, back in the late 1990s. Wikipedia, in its article on the synagogue, mentions that Albert Grunsfeld was its first treasurer, but does not make the connection between his given name and the name of the congregation.
26 "Light of New York." Page 6
27 This led Mama's commercial guardian to instruct me to "make" Mama to see a rabbi.
28 The major local alternative newspaper, at that time.

was how Mama understood what she read. She fired off a letter to the editor that was published. Mama fumed when she realized that *The Alibi* was publishing a column by Harry Wilson, whose by-line listed him as "The Old Guy."[29] For some reason, Mama had never before noticed his column (or at least she had not realized that he specifically called himself "The Old Guy"). In fact, he had been writing that column for more than a decade. Mama, however, remained offended that, after she sent them a letter arguing that the author of the article on old people had gotten it all wrong, the paper had not automatically offered her the opportunity to write her own column.

Mama had been the person who chose the musical group to perform at the Raymond Rosenstiel Memorial Concert, between 1995 and 1997. In 1998, she asked me to listen to some tapes, to ratify her decision. In 1999, she said she did not want to involve herself in the decision-making, instead asking me to pick the group.

She had lived in Manhasset for more than 40 years. However, Mama was gradually distancing herself from that part of her life, just as she had earlier distanced herself from New Jersey when she went into the Army, from her Army friends when she lived in New York City, and then from her city friends when she lived in Manhasset. None of them ever visited her in Albuquerque.

During the spring of 1998, *Krippendorf's Tribe*, a then-new movie starring Richard Dreyfuss, played in Albuquerque. Arthur begged off going with me; Dreyfuss was far from his favorite actor. The plot concerned a widowed anthropology professor, pressed to account for his misuse of grant money, the purpose of which was to support him and his family while he looked for a previously undiscovered stone-age New Guinea tribe that, according to modern theory, should not exist. His wild, improbable and sometimes downright silly attempts to cover up his scientific and financial transgressions lead to ever-bigger lies that eventually require the

---

29 Wilson (d. 2010), with his wife, had founded Amador Press and was already well known as a local writer. He had been a columnist for *The Alibi* for years before Mama even moved to Albuquerque. A book of his collected columns, *Duke City Tales*, is listed on Amazon.com as having been published in paperback on June 1, 1993. However, Mama never accepted this fact; she always thought the paper had somehow slighted her, because he had written a letter to the editor about the same article and he was writing a column and she was not.

last-minute efforts of his young daughter to save him from professional ruin. I decided to take Mama. For me, the satirical movie was riotously, sometimes outrageously, funny. But not for Mama, for whom the byzantine plot twists barely raised a couple of half-hearted smiles. Was Mama losing her sense of humor? Now, I suspect that the dishonesty in the movie reminded her of experiences she herself had had that were not funny, but she did not want to tell me about them.

Mama had always loved farce and satire, and this movie had both elements. Back in the late 1970s, when I had first moved to New York City, she, Dad and I had spent a riotous couple of hours, in my apartment, one afternoon, trying to put together an office chair. The in-joke after that, for any task that was unnecessarily complicated was, "Two Ph.D.s and an economist can't manage to put a chair together." [30]

In 1999, Mama and I returned to New York for the Raymond Rosenstiel Memorial Concert. (In 1998, she had deputized Louise, Sondie and Betty to represent the family for that event). Arthur was already having problems traveling, due to his progressing atypical Parkinson's disease. He stayed in Albuquerque. By then, Mama had had a couple of solid years of living in a quiet area with open vistas and clean air and streets. We had reserved a room in a boutique hotel in Manhattan's Murray Hill, but even so, Mama was surprised to discover that she felt confined in New York City. She discovered that she now hated the place.

The morning of the day we were going to go out, by car, to the concert, she turned to me and said, "I don't know why I ever wanted to live in New York. It's dirty. It's noisy. And it's oh, so crowded! Alive or dead, I don't ever want to come back here!"

"Okay, Mama, I'll make sure that you don't."

At the end of that concert, the librarian announced that this had been the last concert in honor of Dad. She did not ask for further contributions. Mama looked relieved. All the more, I am sure, because she did not ever want to see Manhasset again.

---

30 I wondered whether Mama had suddenly lost her sense of humor. Not until years later did I realize that the plot would almost certainly have triggered Mama's memories of the problems she had had getting her Columbia department to accept her descriptions of her experiences with the Motu in New Guinea.

By 1999, the husband of the Great Neck couple with whom my parents had double-dated had passed away. Mama had kept up with his widow, sporadically, by snail-mail, from Albuquerque. Shortly after we had returned to New Mexico after the Manhasset concert, Mama came up to me one day, holding a handwritten letter that she asked me to read. I did. It was the Great Neck widow, asking to visit Mama in Albuquerque so that she could "explore the other side of my sexuality."

"What can I do?" Mama asked, "I don't want that sort of relationship with her!"

"You could tell her to come, but that you're not interested in that sort of relationship. Do you think she'd be offended?"

"I don't think I can do that. Now I don't really want to see her."

"You don't have that many more options. If you don't want to see her, you can answer and say you don't want her to come, but I'm sure she'd be offended at that. The other option is just not to answer at all, and eventually she'll get the idea."

Mama told me later that she had decided not to answer at all. Once that door closed, all of Mama's real connections to New York were gone. Frankly, I was shocked that Mama had included me in this decision. Looking back on this conversation, I do not think that she would have felt that she needed my input at all if she had not already been falling prey to dementia.

After we returned to Albuquerque, I also began to hear from Mama that Aunt Louise and Betty wanted to visit her. They were calling, apparently frequently, on this subject. Mama told me that she did not want to see them, reminding me of what a relief it had been, to her, not to have the predictable anxiety she always had in seeing them on holidays. To my recollection, we had not gathered as a family at anyone's home since sometime in 1996.

"If you don't want to see them, you can always say 'no,' Mama!"

"I can't. She's my sister. I have to see her, even if I don't want to. They want to stay here, in my house, but now they say Sondie and Dottie[31] are coming too."

---

31 My Aunt Louise's girlfriend and almost constant companion for almost all the time I was growing up. She was a fixture at my aunt's holiday dinners. When Dad was still alive, we took Aunt Louise and Betty to lunch on Long Island, one day. Dottie was, uncharacteristically, absent. Aunt Louise had a cocktail (very unusual; she

"Are those too many people for you?"

"I'm not running a hotel, here!"

"You feel like you have to see them, but does that mean you have to let them stay in your home with you?"

"I suppose that I should ask them to stay at a hotel. I think they want things from me that I don't want to give them."

Mama's dining room in Albuquerque, as it looked when Betty called me.
Photo: Léonie Rosenstiel

"What do you mean, they 'want things,' Mama?"

"Oh, I really can't say."

Because Mama did not want to explain what she meant by her last remark, I dropped the subject and went home a few minutes later.

An hour or so after I had that conversation with Mama, however, Betty called me. I was sitting on the couch in the living room, next to Arthur. Because Betty was yelling at me, through the phone, Arthur could hear every word she said.

"Hello!"

"It's Betty. We're coming down, and we're gonna get Aunt Annette out of that hellhole she's living in! New Mexico is a hellhole!"

"What on earth are you talking about? You've never even been here!'

"Mama and I have been going around, seeing old people. We convince them that the people who are taking care of them are hurting them. Then we get them to change their wills, to name us. We'll do the same with Aunt Annette!"

"For one thing, Mama's living in a lovely home, not a 'hellhole,' and it's in a very nice area. For another, she always tells me

---

rarely had anything to drink because alcohol tended to put her to sleep). Aunt Louise started telling us how "adorable" Dottie was and how much she missed her, since her daughter insisted that she move nearer to her and her husband. "Shh!" Betty said, "Stop it, Mama!" I am not sure why, after that, Dottie started traveling around with my aunt again, to visit Mama.

that she enjoys living here. As for what Mama wants—or doesn't want—to write in her will, that's her business, not mine. If you want to discuss it at all, take it up with her!"

After I hung up the phone, Arthur turned to me.

"I heard everything she said. She had no cause to talk to you like that! They're still your relatives. I understand. You can still see them, if you want to, but leave me out of it. I never want to see any of them again, and I don't want any of them setting foot in our home!"

I had been planning a big, festive meal at our house for everyone, if for no other reason than to take the pressure off Mama. But Arthur was right. After that conversation with Betty, it was definitely canceled. Fortunately, I had not yet issued that invitation to Mama's relatives.

Back in May 1998, I had stopped calling my aunt and cousins in New Jersey. After a report about devastating flooding in their town hit the news in Albuquerque, I had phoned them, concerned. They had laughed at my anxiety and hinted that I ought not to bother to call them about "nonsense," so I did not call them again. I thought, briefly, about what might happen if I were not with Mama the whole time the "visitors" were in town. I certainly would not be able to spend twenty-four-seven with them and Mama, just to protect her against their predations. She would have to protect herself, when I could not be there.

I had just reached this conclusion when I got a call from Mama, asking me to take up residence in her home, while the relatives were in town. I could not do that, and told her so. Since she had asked them to stay at a hotel, I was also sure they would be furious if they saw me staying with her instead, when I lived the equivalent of just a few blocks away. Mama was upset, of course. She had been counting on me to run interference. It turned out that her refusal to have the four visitors stay in her home was what seemed to have prompted Betty's agitated call to me.

Mama assured me that she had been firm with them. She had emphasized that she would see them if they came, but that they could not stay with her. They had finally agreed to stay at a hotel during their visit. Not because she lived in a "hellhole," but rather, among other reasons, because she just did not want four guests staying in her home at once. It seemed that Betty simply could not believe that Mama did not want her as a houseguest if there were going to be three other guests at the same time. Betty apparently reasoned that the only explanation for this refusal would be that Mama's living quarters were sub-standard.

We both knew that we needed to prevent any discussion of the "Toy Box Killer" while the visitors were in town. This prohibition put additional strain on us, because the case was still on our collective mind and still in the news because the trials stemming from this sadistic monster's actions had not been held yet.

Back in March 1999, Cynthia Vigil, the granddaughter of one of Mama's home health aides, had escaped from the Elephant Butte torture trailer of sadist David Parker Ray. When found, she was wearing only a dog collar and a chain. Her grandmother had been emotionally devastated by her granddaughter's situation.

The Vigil family had its own stories. Cynthia's grandmother told Mama and me, after Cynthia's escape, that Cynthia was a telemarketer and the press was maligning her. That story did not survive for long. In fact, Cynthia was a prostitute (or, sometimes, she is mentioned in the press and online as a "call girl"). Not until 2012 did Cynthia, now an activist for the rights of sex workers, write, in the *Albuquerque Journal*, "When I was 21 years old, I was kidnapped off the street in Albuquerque and tortured for three days. There are some that might say that was to be expected since I was a sex worker at the time."[32]

Cynthia's' grandmother told both of us later that Cynthia needed to preserve the scars from the terrible burns that David Parker Ray had inflicted on her. Cynthia would get more money for the movie version of her story, her grandmother said, if she had permanent scars. Her grandmother told me that Cynthia's attorney had told her that Cynthia had far more to gain if the scars from her injuries remained painful to look at. And, of course, Mama participated in all these conversations and perhaps a few more on the same subject when I was not present.

---

32 Cynthia Vigil, "Sex Workers Are Human Beings, Not 'Less-Thans,'" *Albuquerque Journal*, December 17, 2012, p. 9

How much of this is true? I have no idea. But then, how could someone like David Parker Ray be living in the midst of a trailer colony for years, torturing (and presumably also murdering) women, apparently at will? The scars remained, but the money never came, even though there eventually was a conviction. David Parker Ray died in custody in 2002, on his way to prison. There has been an occasional follow-up news article since then, but I could never find any evidence that Cynthia ever landed a lucrative movie deal.[33]

While all this was happening, Cynthia's grandmother seemed distracted, which most people would be, in similar circumstances. However, another aide from a different home health service managed to convince me that Cynthia's grandmother had not been making Mama's meals, as she was supposed to. As proof, she took me over to the refrigerator, which was almost empty. Over the past few months, Mama seemed to have been losing weight, but only in hindsight did I realize how many different causes might have contributed to this result. It might have been that marketing might have been on the aide's to-do list and simply had not been done yet. Or, judging from what I saw of the "snitch's" later behavior, she might simply have hidden the food for a while, to convince me of the other aide's malfeasance.

Had I then realized that the aide making this charge had a long history of complaining about other aides with whom she was working, trying to get them into trouble, or even get them fired, I might have reacted differently. But I did not.

The complaining aide insisted that she wanted to be Mama's sole health aide. She said she loved to work "private duty" and swore that she would care well for Mama. She had also involved Mama in this conversation. It turned out that she had been trying to convince Mama to hire her before she ever even approached me about it.

This discussion was already taking place, prior to the arrival

---

33 I cannot find the sole documentary on this subject "The Sex Chamber" on the official database of the movie industry, IMDb, so no major movies seem to have issued from this sensational case. By 2011, Cynthia was back in Albuquerque, raising her three little boys and caring for her aged grandmother. *https://www.newspapers.com/clip/7005818/david_parker_ray/*

of Sondie, Betty, Louise and Dottie. Mama wanted to avoid having them meet any of the aides. I am still not sure whether she was successful or not.

Shortly before the visitors from the East arrived, Mama told me that Betty wanted some of her property. She did not want to wait to inherit it; she wanted it immediately. (In fact, she could not have inherited anything unless Mama changed her will, because Arthur and I were then Mama's only heirs. Mama's then-current will, of which she had given me a copy, specifically disinherited Aunt Louise and her children.) I am assuming that Mama had said something like this to Betty before Betty called me the first time, or Betty would not have told me that the group wanted to come down to Albuquerque to change Mama's will.

According to Mama, Betty especially coveted the portrait that showed Mama as a little girl, holding a 1900s vintage candlestick telephone. Mama told me, quite emphatically, "I don't want Betty getting her paws on that painting!" She said she was going to hide it, in a place where Betty would never see it. She did.

Several years later, Betty complained to Mama's commercial guardian. Mama was not generous, Betty wrote because, when Betty had asked for that portrait, Mama had refused to give it to her, or even to show it to her.

Several times, during their visit, I had lunch or dinner with the four visitors and Mama, at a restaurant. The visitors also insisted on inspecting my office—only half-playfully suggesting, in Mama's presence, that I did not really have one. When it was clear that this was a real office, in a bona fide office building, that avenue of "teasing" was closed to them. But that did not happen until the four of them and Mama trooped into my office to look around. The "visitors" poked around, assuring themselves that I did have supplies in the closet. Mama had already been there many times. She did not need to be "reassured" of anything. Sometimes since then, I have wondered why Sondie's husband did not arrive with the group.

Later events proved that the visitors had been unable to convince Mama to change her will or, failing that, to go back East with them. None of them returned to Albuquerque until December 2003, almost four years later.

Their presence in 1999 exhausted Mama. For her, it was like being stuck, for days and days, in an upsetting marathon holiday meal, just as in years past. I am not certain that Mama ever fully recovered her emotional equilibrium, after they left. Later that summer, I decided to look in on Mama one noontime, when we were not scheduled to have lunch together. As soon as I came into the house, through the side door, I saw blood all over the kitchen.

Mama was standing, facing the wall, a blank look on her face, bleeding. She had accidentally sliced off part of her thumb, trying to make lunch. Except, I did not see any food on the counter. Mama had apparently hallucinated the food that she believed she was cutting. Because she was in a state of mind that enabled her to believe that she was cutting imaginary food, it also had not occurred to her to call for help. She was just standing there, waiting for something to happen.

Fortunately, back then there was a walk-in urgent care clinic close by. I wrapped up Mama's hand and took her there. Mama's wound required 17 stitches. After that, it seemed obvious that Mama needed someone with her at all times.

Also, shortly after the visitors left, I took Mama to a local Applebee's, near my office, for lunch. By then, we had patronized that particular restaurant at least half-a-dozen times. Mama went to the ladies' room. I waited. And waited. And waited. But Mama did not come back. After ten minutes, I went to look for her, hoping she had not fallen or collapsed. When I opened the door, Mama was standing in there, looking confused.

"What's wrong, Mama?"

"I couldn't figure out how to get out of here!"

Visits to various doctors did not offer any help. They all said that Mama was losing brain function and was likely to continue to do so, but this information was of no practical help whatsoever. I tried to watch out for her even more carefully.

Toward the end of 1999, although I did not know this until years later, Mama began to think it was 20 years earlier. A receipt that I found after Mama died is dated by her "1979," but it is for home health aide services provided in 1999.

By early 2000, one of her aides approached me.

"I'm not supposed to discuss these things with you," she said, almost apologetically, "but I haven't been paid in more than a month."

"Really? I'll ask Mama about this. We'll get this solved soon."

I knew where Mama's checkbook was. The next time I saw her alone, I got it and took it to her.

"Mama, I think it's time to pay some bills."

I handed her the checkbook.

"What's this?"

"It's your checkbook, Mama."

"What am I supposed to do with it?"

"You use it to pay bills."

"How do I do that? I don't know how to do that."

Mama just stared blankly at me, not even attempting to open the cover. After that, I made Mama's bank deposits and paid Mama's bills for her, which I could easily do, because fortunately I had long had her power of attorney.[34]

That was when I discovered that New Mexico suffered from a shortage of specialists who could diagnose problems of the sort Mama seemed to have. We made the appointment in March, but could not actually see the doctor until June. Mama asked me to go with her to see John Adair, a University of New Mexico neurologist who specialized in geriatrics and dementia. Mama and I heard the diagnosis at the same time: Alzheimer's. Mama did not want to believe that her problem would not only be permanent, but also progressive. Neither did I.

It had become a security hazard to have bank statements and dividend checks sent to Mama. She had no remaining understanding of money and finance anymore. The Social Security checks could easily be deposited electronically. Checks that could not be deposited electronically, I had sent to my address, so that I could deposit them.

Having aides twenty-four-seven was going to be expensive. Mama still had some cash in the bank, but I did not want to exhaust

---

[34] Today, the same bank would likely not have allowed me to use a power of attorney that was general and drawn up by an outside attorney, only one the bank had created itself, when my mother was sitting in their branch. This undoubtedly would have created a crisis far sooner.

it. Although Mama was not in any immediate financial trouble yet, her cash reserves were shrinking. Fortunately, in 2000 the Merc went through a business reorganization called "demutualization." This would permit Mama to lease her seat and still be indemnified by the leaseholder against any violations of their rules the person doing the actual trading on the floor might commit. Even more positive for Mama's cash flow was the rising price of leases.

Mama asked me to negotiate the Mercantile lease, using my power of attorney; she had no desire to involve herself (nor did she have much capacity to do so anymore, I suspect), beyond having a conversation with the membership department, confirming that she had given me the power to act for her. I signed the first of these leases on April 1, 2000.[35] Given financial events on the Merc, lease amounts were rising fast—to more than $138,000[36], in 2003. One reason was a rumored impending merger between the New York Mercantile Exchange and the Chicago Mercantile Exchange. This projected merger was increasing the value of a seat, too.[37]

Meanwhile, Mama started asking me to hire the one aide who wanted to work on a full-time, private-duty basis. This sent me back to Graham, to ask him to draw up a contract. Another preliminary job I had was to go to the service from which the aide had come, to "buy off her contract." I arrived, checkbook in hand, at the office, only to hear them tell me that, if I did that, they would be unable to hire this lady back later. They wanted to have that right, so they allowed her to break her contract with their firm (which explicitly prohibited her from taking a job to work privately with a client she had had through the home health service). This allowed her to work on a private basis for Mama, and then to pay no penalty at all for it.[38]

---

35 I signed the first lease on April 1, 2000, and had all rent checks sent to my home so that the aides would not see them. The amounts were substantial enough to pay the aides.
36 About 10 percent of its then-current value.
37 The last lease that I directly negotiated, as Mama's attorney in fact, was on October 3, 2003. The monthly rental was $13,500 per month. (Decades 13478-80). Footnotes with names and numbers only refer to specific documents in files offered as part of discovery in Leonie Rosenstiel (PR) v Decades, LLC (et al) D-202-CV-201304646
38 This lady would later claim that I had bought off her contract, or rather that Mama had. That is what normally would have happened. However, it did not. I am

We hired her. She became an employee, and she ended up making about $62,500 per year in salary, plus benefits (that would be about $102,907.41 in 2021). What I had not counted on—and I do not think Mama had either—was that this aide wanted her sons, grandsons, nieces, in-laws and other relatives and friends to do all the work around the house, ranging from roof repairs to gardening.

Whether or not this offer of help was intended in a friendly way, it might take them two or three times as long as other people to get the job done. Until 2007, Mama's commercial guardian continued to use the aide's family to do work around the house. The commercial guardian complained to the court-appointed auditor that, under what might be called "the aide's family must always be hired" doctrine, it had taken "[five] guys two days to shovel snow & paint the interior [of Mama's house]."[39] They insisted that it had been their firm's 'life goal' to "get rid" of that family but that Mama "had very strong opinions" in favor of keeping them.[40] By 2001, it already appeared to me that Mama was afraid to refuse or to allow second estimates, for fear of offending her now-permanent aide.

June 29, 2001 would be Mama's ninetieth birthday. By state law, this meant she would need an eye test if she wanted to keep her license. She had recently been diagnosed with cataracts and her driver's license eye exam was coming up soon. Mama was in denial about her failing eyesight, just as she was about her failing memory. Fortunately, as far as I could tell, her aide had been doing all the driving for at least a year.

Mama might be a hazard on the road, driving a car, should she choose to do that, even if she wanted to and still had her license. Albuquerque driving presented challenges to people without any physical or mental limitations. There is a local joke that most Albuquerque drivers consider the use of a turn signal to be a sign of weakness. I discussed with Mama how important I thought it was for her to see someone more specialized than the oculist at

---

deliberately not giving either the names of the personnel employed by the commercial guardian or the names of the aides. At this point, I have heard of so many other people employed in those capacities who have acted similarly that, to me, all these people are interchangeable. It is almost as if they have all studied in the same school.

39 Decades 24151
40 Ibid

Walmart to determine whether she would be able to pass that upcoming state eye exam for driving, or whether she had to have laser cataract surgery first. Mama refused. Both to see anyone else and to have any surgery, even if it were indicated.

As much as I worried about Mama's vision, I was equally concerned with her increasing inability to pay concentrated attention to anything. Would she be able to realize what was happening on the road in time to react to it, if she did choose to drive?

Rather than seeing an ophthalmologist, Mama contacted one of her aide's relatives who had told both of us that he had considerable political clout. He offered to arrange a protest meeting for Mama, out in Valencia County. A protest against making older people take eye exams to keep their licenses. This meeting was on the verge of actually happening when Mama went for her driver's license exam, which she failed.

I had not been able to go with her that day. Instead, Mama's aide accompanied her. By the time Mama got home, she was angry, blaming me for the fact that she had flunked the eye exam and lost her license. "If you'd been there," she insisted, "I'd have passed."

Fortunately, this also meant that the protest meeting was off. Logically, there would have been no way for me to have affected the results of Mama's eye exam, other than to take it for her. By then, however, any logic was lost on Mama. I chalked Mama's reaction up to her increasing irrationality.

Things soon calmed down briefly, however. I tried to get Mama to take up writing at the computer again, got her a couple of internet subscriptions, and hoped for the best. Knowing that she had done a lot of computer work in New York gave me some hope that she might get interested in and busy with other things. If she found something absorbing to work on, I hoped, in vain as it turned out, that she might be able to concentrate again. I also tried to keep her in the loop about what was happening, financially, but only at times when her aide and the aide's family members were not present.

In the fall of 2001, Mama decided to join Arthur and me in creating High Desert Holdings, LLC, a family holding company. This was, once again, a way to protect vulnerable stock certificates by leaving them in the safekeeping of a broker, and titling them so no one outside the family would have access to trading them. Mama did not want to be bothered with the details, so she asked me to take care of them for her, although in keeping with proper procedure, the broker called Mama to get her oral authorization first. I had power of attorney over the holding company's accounts. Arthur and I were the majority partners, as well as the managing partners of the enterprise. Arthur was trying to get back to writing, so in practice, I was generally the responsible party.

One more protection for Mama would have been if I could have included the ownership of the Merc seat in High Desert. However, the Merc's membership office told me that retitling the seat could only be done either in the name of an individual or in the name of an operating business. It could not be part of a holding company or any sort of trust account, so I dropped that idea.

At that point, the full-time aide started wanting to oversee Mama's finances.[41] Her argument was that she had handled such matters for other clients, even though she really had not the slightest idea what Mama's financial situation was. I had no way to verify her prior experience and thought it was not an appropriate job for her to do, in any case. She began asking me questions about where Mama's money was coming from, how it was invested, and so on. I am guessing this partly was because Mama was no longer feeling independent enough to tell her aide that these questions were inappropriate; she had become too dependent on this person and afraid of her displeasure. I also suspect that, by then, Mama was either unable to answer these questions because she did not understand her own finances, or she simply did not remember the answers I had given her during our private conversations on this subject. Looking back, I am relieved this was so.

It always seemed wise, to me, to preserve Mama's privacy by not involving a health aide in the details of Mama's finances. I simply told her that I had Mama's power of attorney, that I was paying Mama's bills for her, and left it at that.

---

[41] At that time, standards in this industry were that home health aides did not conduct major banking and financial transactions on behalf of their clients. Those ethical standards are still in place. I have little doubt that Mama's aide, who had years of experience in that field, was aware that she was asking for something that was considered improper control of her client.

More and more frequently, I would find that this aide and her relatives were pressing me to get Mama to invest in various "business" schemes. Mama's aide seemed to have concluded that I would not tell her about Mama's finances because Mama needed money. At Christmas, she pushed Mama and me to make wreaths she could sell out of her own home. I do not recall seeing any proceeds from these efforts, although I do remember buying the raw materials.

Rather than seeing Mama pushed to get involved further, I was willing to expend what to me were relatively small sums of money on real estate. I needed a happy aide who was willing to do the work. So did Mama. As it turned out, one of the aide's relatives-by-marriage was a real estate agent. On behalf of a partnership with Arthur and my company, I bought some land in Valencia County from him. In 2002, On behalf of the family holding company, I bought a small, foreclosed building in Albuquerque, in what residents of the area familiarly call "the War Zone"—a community long plagued by gang violence and lack of essential services. Mama's aide was the other partner in that last enterprise, meaning that Mama, through the family holding company, had a business interest in common with the aide. I was aware that this created a conflict of interest, but it was the best available choice at the time.

Even so, the aide asked me to promise that I would never tell her other family members that she was involved in buying this property. "They would kill me for the money!" she whispered to me one day, leading me to worry about these family members associating with Mama, if there was any chance that they might kill someone over about $13,000. The schemes got wilder and wilder, at one time including buying a Spanish rural castle jointly, for the purpose of using it as an inn. (Not that there was much danger of this happening. As I heard this suggestion, I thought of the old French idiom, "*Il bâtit des châteaux en Espagne,*"—which has a recent meaning of "He chases after rainbows," although Mama always used it to mean, "He builds castles in the air"—and tried not to laugh.)

Additional problems were sprouting up in the real estate investments with the aide and her relatives. They did not want any commercial entity to do any of the work on those properties. They knew I had little choice, if I wanted to keep Mama's only aide content. Over a couple of years, their presence cost all of us some $300,000 (this would be $461,370.34 in 2021). And, even though the per-person fee seemed reasonable, this tended to cloak the fact that it generally took more personnel two to three times as long to accomplish any job as other similar workers.

For the past six months or so, Mama had been getting agitated more and more easily. Sometimes, even when nothing was happening and she was just sitting in a chair, she would suddenly get angry for no discernible reason, and her blood pressure might even spike. Labile hypertension, the doctors called it. Mama loved her coffee, which might have contributed to that problem, but there was no way she was going to be dissuaded from drinking it. Once, when she was visiting Arthur and me for dinner, the two of them were sitting at the dining room table. I went into the kitchen to get some food. Mama apparently got agitated, suddenly and for no apparent reason, and threw over a nearby display shelf containing little trinkets Arthur and I had gathered on our various trips, breaking some of them. Another time, we were at her home. Suddenly, she said I was talking to Arthur too much, then threw an heirloom plate on the floor, shattering it.

A psychologist she consulted after that suggested that the inhibitory center of her brain had atrophied. Mama now had less control than normal over her impulses.

I developed some aromatherapy drops that seemed to calm Mama down temporarily, but they were made of essential oils and had to be used in a diffuser. It was impossible to predict when (or where) the problem might recur. The drops worked less reliably when used in a locket.

One of the aide's relatives-by-marriage, hearing about the drops from her, and believing that he had adequate political clout to get this done, suggested that he could get a contract for me to make these, to be secretly used in New Mexico prisons, to calm down the inmates, and he wanted a cut of the action. I said it would not be ethical for me to do this. You cannot dose people—particularly captive individuals—with anything that can remotely be classified as "experimental." And you absolutely cannot do this "secretly." He got angry.

Another proposal, from the aide herself, made to me in Mama's presence, was that I make these drops the basis for a multi-level marketing company. I had already had some experience observing her business schemes, so I balked. I made a quick trip to Graham's office, to gather arguments against doing this. They convinced me, but angered the aide.

Meanwhile, the aide's friends in Mexico also wanted me to join them in various business ventures. One, who operated a market in Juarez, tried to interest me in importing essential oils. She offered me no way to verify the purity or actual content of the liquids in those bottles, or any way to know where they had been made. Besides, I did not want to get an import license. Another of the aide's friends from Juarez, this time a dentist, wanted to use the Albuquerque building partially owned by High Desert, to hold a dental clinic. The aide arranged it so Mama acted as a witness to all of these discussions.

The dentist, urbane and intelligent, kept delaying in showing me his New Mexico dental license. I could not accept his ability to charge Delta Dental Insurance for his work; he had it because he owned a large dental clinic in Juarez. Finally, I called the New Mexico Board of Dentistry, only to learn that they had never heard of him.

Once I told him I knew he had no license, he started promoting a friend of his, a Mexican medical doctor, to use the building. I quickly discovered that the friend was not licensed in the U.S. either. The community where the building stood was an area in need of medical care, but as I told them, there was no way I could help to provide it this way without losing my own license and possibly going to jail. According to a notation in the commercial guardian's files, the dentist later was arrested, charged with practicing dentistry without a license.

Mama's aide then tried to convince me to buy a trailer so that I could take Arthur and Mama to Mexico with me. In this, she told Mama and me that she had the support of the Mexican dentist, who suggested that he would put together classes on traditional

Chinese medicine for me to teach, once I arrived. His idea was that Mexican doctors and dentists might find these techniques useful with their patients. I did not think the long trip in a trailer would benefit Mama at all. Nor Arthur. Because I declined this invitation, and never bought that trailer, I never knew whether this was a bona fide offer or not.[42]

Around 2002, Mama started talking to me about discussions she had started to have, again, with Aunt Vicki, her youngest sister. She and Uncle Tad were still living in Charlotte, but now in a retirement home. Both of them were becoming increasingly incapacitated. Concerned, Mama told me they were having financial difficulties and asked me for some money to send to them. I gave it to her, from her bank account, both in check form and in cash. Arthur and I also contributed. A court-appointed observer (formally called the Court Visitor) later quoted one of Mama's aide's sons as saying that he saw Mama putting money into an envelope to send to Aunt Vicki.

A year or so later, the court observer, who apparently never spoke with either Mama or me about this action, made it seem as if both Mama and I were doing something wrong in sending Aunt Vicki money. When I spoke to Aunt Vicki for the last time, in June 2003, Uncle Tad had just passed away. Aunt Vicki herself had already suffered a series of strokes. During that conversation, she seemed resigned to the prospect of dying soon herself.

She did die within weeks of this conversation. I was with Mama when Betty called to say that she and Aunt Louise had arranged for Aunt Vicki's funeral. None of her personal effects was sent to either Mama or me, by which I mean that any cards or letters we had sent her either were discarded or taken back home by Aunt Louise and Betty. Mama had a very difficult time accepting that her "baby sister" had passed away. To the best of my knowledge, she did not have any idea about the funeral until after it had already happened. If I had not been standing with Mama when the call came in, and if she had not put the call on speakerphone, I might not have known about this event at all, at the time.

---

42 There were no educational standards at all for the practice of Chinese medicine in Mexico, prior to 2006. In 2016, a limited, church-based program in auricular acupuncture, used for stress, was permitted. *https://www.kvia.com/news/residents-in-violent-juarez-mexico-use-acupuncture-to-cope-with-trauma-/55645601*

Mama must have been concerned about me worrying about her problems. She decided to give a class at the Bear Canyon Senior Center to prove that she was still mentally sharp. She kept saying, "I'm as 'with it' as ever. I'm going to prove that at the lecture."

The aide insisted that I attend. In all my life, I had never seen Mama so anxious before a class. Listening, I understood why. Mama had forgotten what she had known about anthropology, and even with huge cue cards, held by one of the aide's family members, Mama still could not remember what she was going to present. How shocking to discover that I recalled more anthropology from my undergraduate college courses than Mama did, after teaching the subject for more than forty years!

Mama said, "In earlier times, people used to get married much older than we do now. They were thirty or thirty-five."

The lady sitting next to me looked to be well over seventy. She turned to me, angry, and growled, under her breath, "She doesn't know what she's talking about! I was born in Sicily and they married me off when I was fourteen!" I was hoping that Mama had not heard, because if she had, I was afraid she would come over and start a fight with this attendee.

During the break, I went into the administration office, told them that Mama was suffering from dementia and begged them please, please, not to allow her to give another class there. Mama was lucky this attendee had not challenged her directly; the next time, someone might. I could imagine the headlines now, "Elders duke it out at the Bear Canyon Senior Center." Or maybe "Catfight at the Senior Center."

When I was done in the office, I spent the rest of the break thinking how ironic it was that, for many years, Mama cited the Talmud and sometimes the *Jewish Encyclopedia* as the source of her authority on Jewish life. In 1906, the *Jewish Encyclopedia* acknowledged the Talmud as the source of its authority in stating that anyone remaining unmarried after age twenty was considered "cursed by God."[43] Some rabbis counselled marriage at puberty. "A man who refused to marry after he had passed his twentieth

---

43 *http://www.jewishencyclopedia.com/articles/10435-marriage-laws*. Accessed January 17, 2020.

year," the *Encyclopedia* reported, "was frequently compelled to do so by the [Rabbinical] court."[44]

Mama used to know this. So did her parents. That her own parents did not enforce these precepts speaks more to their own disregard for them than to any lack of knowledge. Grandpa Julius was famous for having read all the volumes of the Talmud through, three times. Mama knew a lot about Sicilian practices, too, from the Sicilian family who were friendly with her and her parents. I could no longer doubt that Mama was losing her mental faculties. Even information from long ago seemed to have evaporated.

Despite the wild inaccuracy of what Mama had said at the senior center, a number of people, all of them located in one section of the room, on the side furthest from me, near where Mama's aide was sitting, were wildly enthusiastic after Mama's talk. The others sat on their hands. It turned out that there were six members of the aide's family that Mama's aide brought along as a claque. They were the ones clapping. Mama (or perhaps her aide, acting in her name?) had also invited them all out to lunch afterwards and expected me to pay, both for the lunch and for their presence, as I recall, $25 each for being there.

Mama and her aide at that point both realized that I had doubts about Mama's competence. I did not have to say a word; I could not hide it. The look on my face would have been enough.

Over the previous five months, Mama had had several hospitalizations—in January, for the flu, and twice during the spring for pneumonia. Another hospitalization in June, this time for jaundice stemming from a blocked bile duct, resulted in Mama again refusing any surgery. It also led me to the realization that the aide's family was taking Mama over. There were four of them, crowded into Mama's hospital room when I arrived, and they only reluctantly allowed me in to see her.

The hospitalist called me, later, to say that Mama had been seen, in the nude, chasing her aide angrily around the hospital corridor. That doctor admonished me that I had better take the measures usual for advanced dementia, "Your mother needs a guardian." she insisted.

---

[44] Ibid.

I duly called Graham, to ask for guidance, repeating what the doctor had told me. "Will she testify?" he asked.

Getting her back on the phone was a difficult undertaking. And useless. "I'm just a hospitalist!" she insisted. "No one will listen to me in a courtroom anyway. You need a specialist. I just wanted you to know, so you can do what's needed."

"How can I do what's needed if I have no one to support me?"

"Ask your attorney. I won't testify."

I called Graham, very upset at what I had just experienced and, even more than before believing that Mama needed protection. He referred me to Cristy Carbon-Gaul, a large, take-charge attorney who was then the specialist in his firm on the subject of guardianship.[45]

Meanwhile, Mama had been having second thoughts about her aide. "When you're there, she's so sweet. But when we're alone, she's nasty to me!" Mama complained.

"Remember, you wanted her to be your only aide?"

"Yes, but she's not nice anymore."

"I don't have many choices, here. My house is on three levels. Arthur needs the bedroom on the main level, and you can't do stairs. If I fire her, you're going to have to stay somewhere else, while I look for another aide." I did not say to Mama that I was afraid of what the aide would do, since, even though she was under five feet tall, she had told me that she was a former security guard and had a gun. Regardless of what I thought, I knew that it would not be safe for Mama to stay alone anymore, even for one day. A regular hotel was out of the question. She might wander off, or forget how to get out of her own room. Someone had to check on her frequently.

Over the last six months, the aide had become increasingly dramatic when relaying to me her on-going state of agitation about Mama's health, often calling me in the middle of the night if Mama awakened with a minor complaint, demanding that I come over immediately. The aide's anxiety, in turn, agitated Mama further. At one point, Mama told me the aide had warned her that she would die if this particular aide were ever taken away. I tried to reassure

---

45 As of 2019, Ms. Carbon-Gaul became the Probate Judge of Bernalillo County, running for office unopposed.

her, but realized that, as long as the aide remained at Mama's side, reinforcing this suggestion, I had little hope of changing Mama's mind. There had been, of course, several times when Mama had in fact needed hospitalization over the past year, but all of those had happened during the day.

As I recall, it was one day late that spring that I received a call about 9:30 one night. It was the aide. She seemed hysterical.

"They're going to arrest me! You have to come now and treat me!"

"Who's going to arrest you? And why?"

"The police. The fire truck wasn't supposed to be in that lane. It was their fault! Your Mama's alone! I was on my way back to her when it happened."

"Where are you?"

It turned out that the aide was at the corner of Wyoming and Academy, about three blocks from where Arthur and I lived. This was when I discovered that the aide had had someone else staying with Mama (and had not told me that she had planned to) until the time when she was expecting to be back, but that person had left about half an hour earlier. Mama was alone, and I knew that I could not stay with her myself.

I grabbed a bottle of ylang-ylang essential oil and got myself out there. I found the aide easily. She was standing on the sidewalk, screaming at the police.

"If you don't stop this, we're going to arrest you!" the officer in charge said.

"Come here, now!" I said to the aide. "I have something I'd like to treat you with."

This distracted her, and the oil calmed her down a bit. She had seen me use oils before, to help Mama.

"Why are you yelling at the police?"

"In my country you have to protest, and loudly, too, or they are sure you're guilty."

"It's not a good policy to do that here. If you do it again, they're going to arrest you. Who will stay with Mama if you're in jail? You can protest later, in court, if you want to."

The second time Mama was hospitalized for pneumonia, she asked to spend another day in the hospital. I could not decide whether it was out of a feeling that she was still too weak to go home or for fear of being alone with her aide.

Shortly after that, the aide came over to me one day when I was visiting Mama.

"Did you know your mother was Jewish? I found a menorah in the garage."

"Jewish? I don't know. In the garage, you say?"[46]

By the time we reached Mama's birthday on June 29, 2003, the tense situation had become a crisis, with Mama continually complaining about her aide to me and refusing to believe that moving in with Arthur and me would not be possible. After taking her out for lunch on her birthday, I drove her to Montebello, one of the nicest assisted-living establishments in town—and one with what appeared to be the best security, too, in case the aide decided to follow Mama. I had gotten information from the place, including the explanation that if people did not agree to stay there voluntarily, only a court-appointed guardian could sign them in. According to what they told me, even if we had been co-trustees in a family trust, I still could not have signed Mama in there against her wishes.

The baby grand piano in Montebello's wood-paneled library did not convince Mama that living there for a month or so until I found another aide was not "putting her away like Aunt Lucy." (Lucy was a much-loved paternal grand-aunt whose family had put her in a retirement home many years earlier.) Mama still wanted to stay with Arthur and me, which was impossible since both she and Arthur now had unpredictable periods of violence and anger.

Mama clearly needed an attendant, all to herself, but Arthur had forbidden me to allow anyone in the house other than the two of us, and the exterminator who came once a month. He might have relented for Mama (providing she stayed either upstairs or downstairs), but not for the professional attendant Mama needed. Arthur also did not want me telling anyone how serious his condition was,

---

46 Considering Mama's extremely negative reactions to Jewish ceremonies, congregations, and rabbis that I had witnessed even when I was growing up, I did not really think so. In any event, this menorah only existed in pieces by the time I saw it again, after Mama died. It must have been destroyed at some time during the commercial guardian's tenure.

thereby making it very difficult for me to tell anyone anything much. I was concerned that, if I told Mama, even swearing her to silence, if this same aide were still caring for her, then the aide would find out eventually.

The aide quickly managed to get Mama to tell her about visiting the assisted-living facility, after which Mama's aide jumped to the incorrect conclusion that I wanted Mama declared incompetent so that I could to take Mama's home for myself. The next time I visited, she took me aside and offered to "disclaim" her own interest in Mama's house, which she told me now belonged to her, by law, if I would stipulate to Mama's competence. And of course the court would never recognize me as a psychologist or psychiatrist able to attest to anyone's mental competence anyway. What led her to say this? It turned out that the "ownership interest" had nothing to do with Mama changing her will, which in fact Mama had not done. Instead, the aide believed that she had acquired it because of all the time she was spending with Mama, much of it in Mama's home, entirely ignoring the fact that she had always been an employee, not a domestic partner.

I had already started toying with the idea of installing a "nanny cam" in Mama's bedroom to monitor the aide, just to make sure she was not abusing Mama. However, Mama was mobile then. A camera in the bedroom would not disclose something happening elsewhere in the house, or in the car, or in a restaurant.

Graham had given me intermediate solutions, along the way, including the creation of High Desert. While useful for a while, none of these had worked long-term to completely insulate Mama from the consequences of her worsening dementia. I was getting desperate.

Cristy first made me list all Mama's assets, which is still a court requirement. Then, she said she knew exactly the right experts to hire to take care of Mama properly. The next thing I received was a faxed list of fees for a court visitor. But other required fees would eventually be needed by a *guardian ad litem*, and a medical expert. I would have to pay the court visitor; the others would be paid for if the court agreed that Mama was not competent to manage her own affairs. I could not use one of the doctors who had previously examined Mama because he refused to make house calls. As with a maiden grand-aunt for whom Dad had been the guardian more than thirty years earlier, this case also had to be captioned as me suing Mama to force her to prove her competence, which I knew she could not do. I also knew that she would be upset if served with court papers, and asked if it could be handled any other way, but there was no longer any other way. On July 18, I filed the necessary paperwork.

Cristy insisted that the only way I could protect Mama, prior to the guardianship hearing, was to create a trust in Mama's name, with myself as trustee. So, I retitled Mama's home and car, and created a new bank account in the name of the trust. There was no way, however, to retitle the Merc seat as well. Once again, the membership office said this could not be done in the name of a trust. They asked me whether, as Mama's power of attorney, I wanted to authorize them to sell it. Considering that the rental from that seat constituted the largest single source of Mama's income, I said I did not. So, Mama's pension money went directly into her checking account, as did her Social Security. The rest went into the trust account.

At that point, I had never met anyone, except attorneys and my father, who had had experience with the court-administered guardianship system. Dad had found his experience very painful, despite all his financial training. Of course, it was in a different state. If the situation between Mama's caregiver and me had been difficult over the past several months, once Mama was served with the papers, it became close to impossible. She kept Mama away from her own home, most of the time, in order to prevent the court-appointed experts from seeing her. I even got a call from her, threatening to take Mama to Mexico to prevent her from being declared incompetent. Many years later, I realized that Mama was then in a well-recognized stage of Alzheimer's disease—stage four, where the inability to handle financial and personal affairs accompanies both volatility and an adamant unwillingness to admit to needing help.

The way the court papers are written in any suit, I can understand that this looks like an adversarial proceeding. All court cases do. Unfortunately, I can understand why my attempts to tell Mama that I was trying to protect her were hard for her to credit. I do not really know whether the aide truly believed that I was trying to take Mama's home away from both her and my mother, to take away what the aide now seemed to believe was her rightful inheritance.

Graham called me in mid-August 2003. "Just wanted you to know. I'm going into the hospital next week for some roto-rooter," he chuckled. "Had the same thing done three times before. Piece of cake! Cristy will take good care of you and your mother."

I wished him a speedy recovery.

Graham died on the operating table on August 22. He had told me, before, that Cristy was the best his firm had to offer in this area. Looking back on what happened later, I believe that he truly thought he was telling me the absolute truth. Cristy had been his protégée at the firm, in fact, one of his many protégés at the firm over the decades he had spent there, and he had confidence in her.

Eventually, Mama decided to see the court-appointed experts. One of them mentioned that she had showed him the outline of a book she was working on, its subject the loss of autonomy by elders. This still exists, and is almost certainly a part of the outline for the position piece she had written with Dad more than ten years earlier, which itself was derived from a college course Mama had offered on ageing at William Paterson College shortly before her 1981 retirement.

The court-appointed expert had no way to know the provenance of this document, and he never inquired into it by asking me about it, thereby making it seem that Mama had a bit more competence than she actually had at that point. Her claque had convinced her that she could easily prove that she was competent. The experts, however, realized the same thing I had a year or more earlier—that, although superficially Mama could often cover for her lack of ability to think clearly, any sort of lengthy or deeper conversation led her to confabulate extremely improbable stories. For a year or more, those stories had seemed increasingly unlikely to me. Now, some of them at least had become unbelievable, even to total strangers. Their reports to the court, insofar as they were accurate, reflected this.

The court visitor's report cherry-picked specific statements and chosen facts, some of them invented. In any event, when I eventually got to read it, it seemed to lack adequate context. The visitor had spoken with me several times, assuring me, each time she did, that her only goal was to improve my relationship with my mother. She simply did not ask me for documentation of what I was saying, or accept any I offered to show her. Not about the genesis of High Desert. Not about the fact that I had been handling Mama's financial affairs for almost ten years before the guardianship proceeding, and definitely not for the fact that the aide was fomenting trouble between Mama and me.

Instead, she decided to take the aide's word for actions and events, even when very little research on her part would have shown the aide's statements for the fictions they were. One of the oddest examples was the aide's contention that she, personally, had assets of well over $1 million in Albuquerque real estate (more than $1.4 million in 2021). This notion could have been dispelled by simply checking the real estate rolls. Even back then, they were open to the public in Bernalillo County.

Another fiction in the court visitor's report was the aide's contention that she was my personal business partner, as a consequence of buying, together with me, the building that High Desert had bought with her. Meaning that, if the court wanted to interpret that building as creating a conflict of interest for me, because I owned a share of it, then the aide had an equal conflict of interest, and should have been dismissed immediately, on that same basis. I offered to show the court visitor the deed, but she refused to look. She seemed to have decided that she did not have to accept my deed as proof of what I was telling her, at least not if she did not want to. The county real estate records contained exactly the same information I told her they did. The county clerk, like other county clerks, kept careful records, for tax purposes, of exactly who owned each piece of real estate in the county, including the names of all owners.

"I know your mother better, now, than you ever could."

"How is that possible? You've only spent an hour or so with her. I've known her for more than half a century."

"Because I'm a social worker. We're trained to know these things. You can't possibly know as much as we do! But please understand that all I want to do is improve your relationship with your mother."

"There weren't any serious problems before Mama's dementia and the aide's meddling."

"We can talk about that at the hearing."

Why did I want to believe her?

I did have a phone conversation with Mama, some weeks before the hearing. Betty, she said, had advised her to retain a separate attorney. A cousin-by-marriage of the aide knew Chuck Reynolds (Charles A. Reynolds) who, I was concerned to discover, was the same attorney who had defended the New Mexico priests who had been accused of sex abuse dating back to the 1990s. That scandal continued well into the new century, with Chuck Reynolds generally acting as spokesperson for the Santa Fe Archdiocese.

Once the hearing date was set, I got a call from Betty. "I want to know what I can do to stop this. My aunt is perfectly normal!"

"You haven't seen her since the summer of 1999. That's more than four years. A lot has changed. Mama needs help. Three experts agree with me that Mama needs help."

"I talk to her every week, on the phone. I tell you, she's fine! What are you trying to do to her?"

"Being able to talk about the weather, or to listen to you talk about it, isn't the problem. Mama covers quite well on that level, but that doesn't mean she's fine. Even if you were here, you couldn't stop this process. And, if you're the one causing all the current upset, and making Mama think that I'm trying to hurt her, then I never want to hear from you again."

I hung up. I never heard from Betty, or any member of her immediate family or their longtime friends again, so I concluded that Betty was, at the very least, assisting the aide in revving up Mama's level of agitation.

Chuck Reynolds' billing records say that Mama visited his office on October 14, 2003. A notarized document from that date shows that was when she revoked the powers of attorney she had given me back in 1997. The health aide's records, however, say that Mama saw Chuck Reynolds at 10 AM on October 13 and was nowhere near his office the following day. Is that really her signature on the revocation document? The aide carefully choronicled everyone Mama saw on any given day.[47]

The competency hearing date arrived—October 28, 2003. Mama and I had not seen each other in weeks. Cristy had just been telling me that Mama hated me. This was news to me, although I was sure Mama was very upset that there was a hearing in the first place, particularly after listening to others trying to interpret my actions in a profoundly negative way.

Mama, Chuck Reynolds, the court visitor, Cristy and I were all seated at the same table, in the middle of the large hearing room. What Chuck Reynolds and the court visitor might have been saying to Mama before I arrived with Cristy, I can only guess.[48] Mama fidgeted in her hard-backed chair; I felt agitated too, but tried not to move. After some prompting by Chuck Reynolds, Mama said, "I want to go back to being just your mother again."

That comment took me on a whirlwind emotional tour of all the times that the person named on legal documents as my mother had not acted particularly motherly. I blurted out, "You were never my mother. Grandma Bessie was my mother!"

As if on cue, someone coming from the direction of the judge's chambers opened the door to the judge's bench area. Apparently, she was the judge's clerk. "Judge Baca is indisposed," she said. "The hearing has been postponed until next week." Mama started in her chair, as surprised as I was. The others present remained impassive.

Cristy gave me the impression that my actions that day made Mama revoke the power of attorney. I felt guilty for years as a result. In any event, Cristy did not complain that this revocation

---

47 Rosenstiel(2)019996, 34066-34067, 26474, 26476, 26488. The billing records show Mama had either seen Cristy in person or she was present via phone more than once prior to the competency hearing.
48 Years later, I learned that the "playbook" of people who are seeking guardianship is to convince elderly parents who are suffering from dementia that they are a terrible burden on their children and it would be much kinder to the children to have a neutral outsider "help" them instead. By presenting a guardianship as "help" and not a "takeover of their affairs," often they can convince an incompetent person to go along.

had taken place after the experts had found Mama incompetent, which would throw into question Mama's judgement (and how easily she might be subjected to undue influence) at the time. Furthermore, this revocation was never questioned at the ensuing competency hearing.[49]

Because of the close relationship between Mama's health aide, the aide's cousin, and Chuck Reynolds, I still have more than a vague suspicion that Mr. Reynolds was, in fact, seeing to the interests of Mama's aide at least as much as he was representing my mother. In any case, Mama was paying him.

Standard practice in New Mexico competency hearings then was to keep all but the most closely involved people, known as "interested parties," from entering the hearing room in any initial competency hearing. Even when a prospective ward is about to try to preserve autonomy and wants to waive that "privilege" of maintaining the secrecy of the initial hearing, the judge often enforces it anyway.[50] Aunt Louise was Mama's sister. She might have been considered an interested party. Had Betty wanted to attend Mama's hearing, since she was not directly an "interested party," theoretically she might have been denied access. Everyone left property in a will might be considered an interested party, but Mama had specifically disinherited both of them in her 1997 will.

Before the November 3, 2003 hearing, the two "sides" waited on different sides of the courtroom. Cristy turned to me.

"You don't want your mother upset by having a hearing in open court, do you? It would be so much better for her if we did this in the judge's chambers."

The medical expert did not come to the hearing. His report spoke for him. So, all the rest of us—Judge Baca, Mama, the court visitor, the guardian ad litem, Chuck Reynolds, the court reporter, Cristy and I all piled into an eight-by-ten-foot room that served as

---

49   I thought that I had an attorney, whose job was to represent my interests.

50   Even as late as 2017, Peter Grotte-Higley was unsuccessful in his attempt to get the judge in his guardianship case to allow reporters from the *Albuquerque Journal* to attend one of the hearings in his case. When they appeared, Judge Denise Barela-Shepard said she would not hold the hearing until she determined whether she was allowed to open the hearing, even though the journalists had been invited in by the ward. *https://www.abqjournal.com/1072313/reporters-presence-prompts-judge-to-postpone-hearing.html*

the judge's chambers. With all those occupants, it seemed more like an overcrowded jail cell. Cristy and I sat on the same side as the court reporter, to the judge's left. The judge had one end of the room to herself (and her desk). Mama and Chuck Reynolds sat on the back wall. The guardian ad litem and the court visitor sat to the judge's right. Cristy told the judge that she was representing me.

At that hearing on November 3, 2003, Judge Baca offered Mama the opportunity to speak at some length.[51] Mama had brought with her some of her publications, the newest of which dated from 1982. She had Chuck Reynolds show these to the judge. Mama spoke about having visited a reservation "yesterday" and being treated as an honored guest. However, her health aide's own handwritten notes—which I only saw after Mama's death—show that Mama visited that reservation on October 8, about a month prior to the hearing.[52]

One of the themes of Mama's presentation was how hard she had worked with Dad to build a "financial empire." I looked on in shock as the woman who had made fun of Dad all those years for his efforts in the financial arena was now claiming at least some credit for the results of his (and later my) efforts. Mama confabulated repeatedly during that hearing.

When Mama told Judge Baca that she had "spent time at the Court of Versailles" I could not prevent my tears from starting to flow, although I tried to be absolutely silent to avoid disturbing the proceedings. There had been no royal court at Versailles since the French Revolution in 1789. Mama had spent years studying French history. Had she been halfway competent, she would have instantly corrected anyone making such an assertion. Mama, had she been herself, would never, ever have said anything like that.[53]

Judge Theresa Baca decided that Mama, having voided the

---

51 For reasons understood only by the New Mexico Supreme Court and the New Mexico Legislature, this material remained sequestered, even years after my mother's death.
52 Decades 26524..
53 A week or so later, the court reporter called me. "Did your mother really say she'd spent time at the Court of Versailles?"
"Yes, I'm afraid she did."
Oddly, that further proof of incompetency never made it into the court record.

powers of attorney, had said she did not want me taking care of her. The court visitor had stated, during the hearing, that she thought I should have end-of-life decision-making capability, but should not be allowed to become Mama's day-to-day guardian, given what she termed my conflict of interest with Mama stemming from her fiction that I was in a personal business partnership with the aide. Cristy put her hand on my knee to prevent me saying anything to object to this story, just as she had looked daggers at me to prevent me from saying anything to correct Mama's and the court visitor's earlier inaccurate statements. She did not object on my behalf, either.

Frankly, having later learned how families are routinely disregarded in such proceedings, I think that the court would likely have listened to the court visitor, even if I had complained. She was a person who had invented quite a few readily-disprovable stories in her report to the court. But only if the court had wanted to listen to both sides. It did not.

The way the judge presented her situation to Mama at the hearing, her guardian and conservator were only there to "help." The conservator would be in place to help Mama manage her accounts. The guardian would help Mama to take care of health-related matters. At no time during the proceedings was the suggestion made that they were being placed in a decision-making capacity by the court. The court visitor became both guardian and conservator, with what soon turned out to be the temporary proviso that I had end-of-life decision-making ability. Much later, Mama, in a lucid moment, told me that she had been advised before the hearing that, if she said she did not want me taking care of her, the judge would send her home and all would be as before, meaning that she would continue to run her own life and make all her own decisions.

Mama left with Chuck Reynolds. I saw them meet the caregiver in the hall. She would be driving Mama back to her home.

As we waited for the court elevator, Cristy turned to me.

"Now you and your mother are divorced. You can come back to collect the money."

"What do you mean? I never asked to be divorced from her. I promised Dad that I'd take care of her."

"Isn't the money all you're interested in? I mean, aren't you Jewish?"

"No, in fact, I'm not."

CHAPTER II

Lies and More Lies

During the first month of the guardianship, someone closed out an investment account I did not know Mama still had.[54] When they drilled into Mama's vault later, they discovered that she had owned 2690 shares of Federated stock that later was renamed Macy's. Only 345 Macy's shares were deposited in High Desert in 2001. These additional shares had remained in the previously unknown account. The stock had closed at $18.85 per share on July 18, 2003, worth a total of $50,704.50 ($72,988.43 in 2021), as of the date I filed for guardianship.[55]

The medical professional and the court visitor did discuss with Mama, before the hearing, what they called Mama's own needs for "help," even though she continued to attempt to deny them. She had told them both that she was in the process of writing a book about older people losing their autonomy.[56] Among the papers the

---

54 Decades 17853-17867
55 According to the docket later posted on the internet, this was not filed until July 24, 2003. https://finance.yahoo.com/quote/M/history?period1=1058486400&period2=1058572800&interval=1d&filter=history&frequency=1d Accessed January 20, 2020. Mama's commercial guardian was well aware of the value of these assets. A copy of a letter to Mama from Sutin, dated April 1, 1998, discussing them, was among the Discovery documents the guardian produced. Mama was still in command of her faculties at that time. She deliberately did not choose to change her estate plan at that point. Decades 12122-12124.
56 I believe that the outline for a book that the guardian ad litem thought he saw is simply an outline of the article Mama and Dad had worked on, years earlier, more or less on this subject. (Decades 03294)

commercial guardian firm kept from the early days of their tenure was an ironic bit of printed doggerel.

Just a line to say I'm living
And not among the dead,
Though I'm getting more forgetful
And mixed up in the head.[57]

At the end of this long poem, which describes the many tribulations of age, Mama has handwritten "HA HA HA HA HA HA!"[58]

"It'll be far easier for me to fire your mother's aide than it would be for you," my mother's about-to-be-appointed guardian had told me, when we met in person before the hearing. She had assured me that she would start the severance process gradually, by arranging at least four hours each day when someone else was relieving that aide. This, the commercial guardian said, would enable me to re-establish my relationship with Mama, at times when the aide was not there. That aide had, by then, fomented so much hostility that we both knew that I should not visit Mama when the current aide was there.

The hearing had upset both of us. In Mama's case, her upset took the form of physical symptoms. Her aide called me the next day, asking for my help.

Having been told that her guardian was only there to assist her, Mama had no real understanding of what being the ward of a commercial guardian meant. She thought that she could have her aide call me, to get me to prescribe herbs and treatments, not realizing that all of us would need the prior approval of the court-appointed guardian, even more so because the aide said that Mama wanted me to do this by phone only, which would (at that time when telemedicine was not the norm) have been unethical for me. I had to refuse. Mama was angry and puzzled about why, to her, it seemed that I was not willing to help her.[59]

---

[57] The internet attributes this poem, called "A Little Mixed Up" to Faeza Gilani https://www.poemhunter.com/poem/a-little-mixed-up-2/

[58] Decades 31213 (To reproduce the poem would violate copyright; please refer to the link above.)

[59] Rosenstiel(2)016252

Later, the guardian suggested that I give the commercial guardianship firm treatments to give Mama, but secretly, so Mama would not know who the doctor was. They were not going to allow me to see the patient. This would have been unethical, too, so I could not do it. In addition, if I accepted that arrangement, I could no longer tell how many people stood between the patient and me; there were too many opportunities for misunderstandings. If Mama's condition worsened, due to an improperly administered treatment, it would be my fault. On November 4, 2003, I emailed the guardian, telling them that I could not provide any health-related services under the current conditions.[60]

November 3, 2003 had been a Monday. Face-to-face, the head of the commercial guardian agency had promised to fire the aide soon. However, on November 6, 2003, I got an email from her that said, in part, "As I noted in my report...we are in the process of evaluating the entire caregiving situation. No promises or determinations have been made about anything yet." The aide, she told me, "remains at 24/7 without any paid relief."[61]

Meanwhile, hundreds of items on Mama's premises belonged to me. She had told me that keeping them around made her feel "young again." Like the passport I had had back in the 1960s. While she was in full possession of her faculties, Mama had always readily acknowledged that they were mine.

Almost immediately after the hearing, I got a call from Mama's guardian, asking for a list of everything on Mama's premises that was mine. By November 12, I had provided a list of most of those.[62]

On November 12, the order creating the guardianship was signed. After that, the commercial guardian told me that Mama was balking at returning my things. I have no way to know whether this was true. After that, I did not see my passport and some of my college ID cards for more than ten years.[63] Even if I had proof of having bought an item myself, there was no possibility that I could

---

60 Ibid
61 Rosenstiel(2)016253
62 Rosenstiel(2)016255
63 Early in 2020, while going through some of the last of the remaining boxes, I found a folded-up, bulging mailing envelope, under some shredded papers, where Mama had hidden it. She had written on it "passport." It contained the missing identity documents—Mama's, Dad's and mine.

convince the guardian that it was mine unless Chuck Reynolds, stating that he was acting for Mama, who had just been declared incompetent, concurred.

Soon, the commercial guardian had created a pitched battle with me over material that belonged to me and was part of my decades of research and writing activities. They denied these items belonged to me because they were located in Mama's garage. On November 25, 2003, I emailed the guardian, asking, "Would you accept the fact that I wrote a published book on each of these people as some sort of 'proof' that the reference materials now housed in my mother's home and a few boxes in her storage locker are mine?" The email is nothing more than a howl of pain. They kept telling me that Mama hated me.[64]

"I have to 'step into her shoes' and decide things as closely as I can to what I can guess she [Mama] would have decided," one of the partners wrote to me on December 16, 2003.[65]

Cristy said she was representing me, but she never objected to this situation. This "change of ownership" even extended to over 100 letters in a box that was stored in the shed in Mama's backyard. They were all addressed to me. Mama, Chuck Reynolds said, did not want to return them to me. Years later, the next time I was allowed to look in the shed, the box was still there, but it was open and empty. All the letters had vanished.

Ironically, now that Mama had been declared unable to manage her own affairs, the commercial guardian had decided to give her total control over deciding who owned which item. My firm belief is that she very likely did not remember, and so might have followed visual or verbal cues given by whomever was asking her a given question. Of course, I cannot prove what happened, because I was not there. However, it makes a great difference, when dealing with a vulnerable person who might be easily influenced, whether you ask, "You don't want to give this item away to that nasty woman who hauled you into court, do you?" or if you ask a neutral question like, "Who owns this item?"[66] And even so,

---

64 Rosenstiel(2)016266 . Eventually, the guardian allowed me to take file cabinets containing some of these materials to a storage locker.
65 Rosenstiel(2)016288
66 This matter of division of property often nets commercial guardians many hours of fees, even when people do not actually take them to court over prized

the court had just decided that Mama was no longer able to recall details. Is a long list of items not a set of "details?"

"Maybe in the future we would be able to negotiate a transfer without a court order, but right now I think this would be impossible," wrote one of the commercial guardianship's partners to me on December 2, 2003.[67] In the next paragraph, she wrote, "I think you could initiate a court order."[68] But then she said that she did not recommend that course of action. Did Mama have any understanding of this situation? Even she, in her state of confusion, would have known that letters addressed to me were mine.

Years later, I discovered by talking to other family members of people placed under commercial guardianship, that this sort of drama was part of a standard playbook. Getting family members upset enough to sue would later give the commercial guardian the right to complain about how difficult that person was. The exact reason why specific family members sued varied, but the attempt to get family members feuding seemed like standard operating procedure. However, if that had been the guardian's intention, it did not happen in my case.

"...My job is to protect your mother's possessions and person...I am considering meeting with your mother and her attorney to discuss the list of possessions you claim," one of the partners wrote to me on December 15, 2003. That was how I discovered that perhaps not much had really happened for the past month in this regard, even though the firm had told me more than once that they were trying to help. I wrote her back the same day, "I am unclear how... it would harm either Mother's possessions or her person for me to remove my old files of correspondence and photos and books..."[69]

Meanwhile, I had been getting requests for information from a researcher in another country who was writing a book about my first fiancé. He wanted Mama to confirm the relationship, since she was the only person still alive who knew about it. Because I could not see Mama, I could not confirm it at that point. Nor would the guardian allow him to phone Mama. There was no legal way

---

family heirlooms. I refused to participate in a court squabble over these items, even though I had my doubts that they all would survive intact. Many of them did not.
67 Rosenstiel(2)016275
68 Ibid
69 Rosenstiel(2)016284

that he could call Mama without the permission of her legal guardian; being a ward (now called a "protected person" in New Mexico) then entirely deprived a person of autonomy in regard to activities, visitors, calls and any other associations, although I noticed, in going over the documents during discovery, that for years Mama's original aide continued to ignore this legal requirement.

In addition to my first fiancé's biographer, other researchers had contacted me, seeking access to my research materials from the years when I was writing books on Nadia and Lili Boulanger. These documents were still housed in Mama's garage. Now I had several requests, from scholars thousands of miles away, all trying to finish projects on deadlines. I had no assurance that the original items would remain safe. The commercial guardian would not allow me any access to them, either.

The commercial guardian and Mama's aide were telling me that Mama did not want to see me or talk to me. At one point, the commercial guardian said I could call Mama. I said hello to her once on the phone before her aide took it away. Looking back on these statements after a suitable intervening period, I wonder whether I gave too much credence to what others, particularly those who were supposed to be "experts," told me. The fact is that I was kept away from Mama, whether in person or on the phone. My interpretation, back then, was that she did not want to see me. However, she was entirely dependent on her aide and her commercial guardian, and incidentally on what they might have told her.

Wondering when (or whether) the commercial guardian was going to use the current home health aide less, I contacted the guardian weekly, asking whether, finally, they had found someone to relieve the aide so that I could see Mama again. I had become convinced that the current aide was doing her best to increase the emotional distance between Mama and me. There was a hole in my life, after seeing Mama almost daily for the past seven years.[70] I can only imagine what Mama might have been feeling.

---

70   During 2014, in the course of discovery for a lawsuit Mama's estate conducted against the commercial guardian, I discovered that it had not been much easier for that firm to loosen the aide's grip on my mother than it had been for me. She kept finding fault with her relief aides. In fact, it took almost four years (until 2007) before the commercial guardian actually managed to fire her. (Decades 26805)

Lies and More Lies

I still believe that what I told the commercial guardian on November 20, 2003, is the absolute truth. The aide and her family, who had not allowed me to see Mama alone, had also controlled her for at least the six to seven months prior to the guardianship. "She has been a hostage all this time and has adopted the attitude of her captors," I wrote them.[71]

After Mama died, I discovered that the court-appointed guardian had had great difficulty getting the aide to loosen her grip even a bit. The documents prove that they found this aide as hard to manage as I ever had. The commercial guardian eventually amassed a 638-page file documenting much drama and upset relating to this person in the years before they finally fired her. How much extra money this cost Mama for the "professional" time the commercial guardian billed her for as a result of all the trouble this employee created, I have no idea. In that time, she took Mama to doctors without telling the guardian, took her to the hospital without permission, agitated against her relief aides[72] (and, of course, against me), and finally accused one of the guardianship firm's male minions of making advances to one of the other female aides.

The next emotional assault was the commercial guardian's contention that, because they wanted me to believe Mama hated me, and had been making considerable headway in leading me to believe this, that she must always have hated me. The guardian next asserted that Mama had never given me a gift in my life and did not ever want to, so I had to disprove that. Mama might never even have known about these noxious exchanges between the guardian and me.

Did they say the same sorts of things, to Mama, that they said to me? I certainly did not tell Mama later about my conversations with the guardianship firm on this subject, because I was convinced that knowing would upset her.[73] On January 5, 2004, I wrote to the guardianship firm, "I have now come across back check registers

---

71 Rosenstiel-02704
72 Decades 26417
73 Rosenstiel-02704-07. What I do know is that, sometime during the commercial guardianship, someone changed the attribution on one of my books so that Mama was listed as a co-author. It had never been listed that way between 1982 and 2004, and that is certainly not how the publisher's contract is written.

and a couple of checks for Mother, showing a pattern of gifting going back to the 1990s."[74] Of course, most of Mama's records were in her home, where I now had no access to them. Had she not given some items to me, years earlier, I would never have had them to disprove the commercial guardian's statements.

Not until December 1, 2003, did the guardian manage to hire a second aide to relieve the first. She was contracted to spend four hours per day at Mama's house.[75] But I did not get this information until later. And I think this hiring was conditioned more on the fact that Aunt Louise and Betty were arriving on December 7 to visit Mama than on anything else.[76]

On December 22, 2003, Betty faxed the commercial guardian a copy of a long letter that she had previously sent to Chuck Reynolds, stating what she thought Mama should do, have, and be. In it, she referred to a meeting that was going to take place in Chuck Reynolds' office that day. She thought that, based on the time differential, the letter would reach the guardian's office before that meeting. It did not.[77] A later invoice from the commercial guardian describes this meeting as purely financial in scope.

One of the guardianship's partners attended that meeting with Mama, after which she typed up a full-page, single-spaced report on it. "I met with Chuck Reynolds and Dr. Rosenstiel today regarding financial matters," she wrote. After the meat of the discussion, about High Desert, Mama's bills and her income, Chuck mentioned Betty's letter. "Chuck," the partner wrote, "showed us a letter from Betty Singer, regarding multiple issues... . We did agree that these questions were not really Betty Singer's business." It did not seem that Betty's letter made Mama happy.[78] "Dr. Rosenstiel seemed to feel well during the meeting up until near the end," she reported. In fact, from her description, Mama became agitated and combative right after the group's discussion of Betty and her letter. Years later, the guardian tried to suggest that a different partner had

---

74 Rosenstiel-02756
75 Decades 33042-33044
76 Rosenstiel(2)016283
77 Rosenstiel(2)017323-25
78 Decades 12079

been there, witnessing Mama writing, in her own hand, a "Values History."

In addition to Mama's dementia issues, the commercial guardian firm seems to have kept her confused and feeling isolated, a ploy that I later discovered was part of the profession's standard playbook. Far from interpreting their actions as a sign of respect, Mama took many of them as disrespectful, even insulting. Mama did not even know the correct name of the guardianship firm. After Mama died, I found an undated, handwritten letter written in Mama's style. It also shows her waning mental powers. Mama detailed her complaints, and the guardian put a copy in her file and provided it during discovery. I found the original in Mama's home, after her death:

> Dear DeKay
>
> I demand respect in my relationship with my employees. This includes all professional employees including caregivers. It is unforgiveable for a caregiver to pat my head every time she passes by me. I shudder not because I suffer from an aversion. Frankly, it's unnecessary to touch my back, my neck, rub my face. I pay for them to work, to do their job, not to fawn on me. It can become repugnant.[79]

The guardian firm must, however, have noticed that Mama disliked extreme familiarity engaged in by people she barely knew. Eventually, they instructed every caregiver to call Mama "Doctor." (Except the original caregiver, while she was still working there. She was the only person to address Mama as "Lady-Lady.")

Creating this sort of formality raised yet another issue by placing perhaps an extreme emotional distance between Mama and her caregivers to replace the former excessive familiarity. Simply

---

[79] I found this item, still in a notebook in Mama's home, after she passed away. I also found a copy of Mama's separate, later complaint that the home health aides had taken her keys away. Rosenstiel(2)017363-(2)107364. As late as September 2006, Mama was still able to write.

calling someone by name is not necessarily insultingly familiar and demeaning, the way that patting them on the head is. Some people—and particularly those who have suffered physical abuse as children—are simply not amenable to the random touch of strangers, however well intentioned.[80] I had tried to warn the commercial guardian about this reaction of Mama's from the outset, but they automatically discounted whatever I told them; this matter was no exception to the rule.

Aunt Louise and Betty arrived in Albuquerque to visit Mama within a few weeks of the guardianship coming into force. The commercial guardian told me they were in town, but gave me no idea of their schedule. Given their degree of hostility, I could not visit Mama until after they left. Now, from my point of view, not only was there the question of the hostile aide to contend with, but there were also extremely angry (at me, at least) relatives staying with Mama, with the blessing of the guardian, relatives who wanted Mama to believe they thought that she was still in full possession of her faculties. Relatives who had not stayed in Mama's home in 1999, the last time they were in Albuquerque, because Mama had not wanted them there.

The guardianship firm, of course, met with them, informing them of its function. Betty, I discovered years later, told them around that time that Mama was an Orthodox Jew. She continued to insist this was the case until Mama died, and her actions caused innumerable repercussions for the rest of Mama's life.[81] I am not certain whether Betty told the commercial guardianship firm that I was also an Orthodox Jew, but I was shocked to see, from documents that came to light during a partial audit in 2010, that the commercial guardian told this to the Protestant chaplain for a hospice that was caring for Mama, and who was then attending

---

80 I had made sure to apprise the commercial guardianship firm of Mama's status as an abuse survivor, so that they could plan accordingly. They ignored what I told them because, they said, I could point to no specific court records documenting that abuse, either for Mama or for me. Just for the record, this sort of abuse of children by family members in the early 1900s, and even as late as the 1950s, was almost never documented, much less prosecuted.

81 Only one health provider's records reflected that Mama was not a practicing Jew. Dr. Morgan, the doctor who took over for Dr. Leech in 2009, placed this notation on the form she transmitted to Hospice of New Mexico, the day Mama died. Rosenstiel(2)017515

to Mama's spiritual needs. They told him that, for that reason, he should never meet me, because I would be angry that a Protestant chaplain was attending my mother. However, the guardianship firm never discussed my religious beliefs with me.

After the relatives had left, according to documents divulged during discovery, Chuck Reynolds and the guardian met with Mama to speak about her finances.[82] They cautioned her not to speak about money matters with either her aide or with her sister and niece. Considering that Aunt Louise and Betty had already left Albuquerque by then, and that both they and the aide had been speaking with Mama over a period of months, if Mama had remembered enough to tell anyone anything, she would already have done so. Or she would simply have shown them her copy of the court documents, as filed. She was served with copies of all of them.

After Mama died, I found several years of financial reports in the top drawer of her bedroom bureau. One of them had the original aide's handwriting on it, so the aide had to have examined it, regardless of what Mama's guardian told her. What is interesting is that these reports do not accurately state Mama's net worth—they lowball it, sometimes by a factor of ten. So, both Mama and her aide were being misinformed.

After a period of weeks, I theoretically had the right to visit Mama any day between 1 PM and 5 PM. However, things did not work out that way. As I wrote to the guardian on December 24:

"Please note the time (3:15 PM). This is the fourth time in the past 2 weeks that I have gone over to Mother's home between 2 PM and 5 PM and found no car in her driveway and no sign that anyone is in the house...You also told me that you were encouraging Mother to stay home in the cold weather...so she doesn't get the flu. It certainly doesn't seem that she is taking your advice..."[83]

Finally, the guardian firm told me there would be a relief aide on duty the day after Christmas, between 1 PM and 5 PM. I even received a call from Mama, asking me over for a visit at 3 PM.

---

82 This is the same meeting that the functionary from the guardianship wrote up. Reynolds' invoice describes it the same way.
83 Rosenstiel(2)016299

Her demeanor seemed to suggest that all was fine and none of the drama I had recently witnessed had ever happened. I went over to Mama's house, believing the relief aide would be safely in place, only to discover that the original aide was still there and showed no signs of leaving. Mama herself was welcoming.

Instead of letting me visit with Mama undisturbed, the aide kept demanding Mama's financial information from me. Fortunately, I was able to refer her to the commercial guardian, but that was the only aspect of the hostile situation between us that was anything other than baneful. Regardless of what the guardian had told me about a relief aide being on duty in the afternoons, I now realized that I could not trust these representations.

During my post-Christmas visit, the aide also demanded a set of keys to Mama's car, which of course I did not have with me, in part because Mama's car had not been driven in quite a while.[84] Nor, as I informed the guardian after my visit, would I give them to the aide because Mama no longer had insurance for driving that car because she had already lost her license. In fact, Mama had not been using the car recently. "I'm currently awaiting Cristy's instructions on what to do with the car papers and for your instructions…on where to deliver the car keys," I wrote them on December 28.[85]

Given the level of this aide's hostility and the fact that she had told me she had been a security guard and had a gun, I was convinced that, if I returned while the original aide happened to be there, she would physically attack me or at least start screaming at me, which in turn was bound to upset Mama. I did not return to Mama's home without a member of the guardianship firm being present for as long as they continued to employ that aide.

Only on January 7, 2004, after I met the guardian and Chuck Reynolds at Mama's home to remove some of the archival material, did I realize that no one had so far shown Mama the longer list of my items that I had delivered to the guardian firm weeks earlier. Being presented, suddenly, with this enumeration of items, Mama got predictably upset.

---

84 Rosenstiel(2)016301
85 Ibid

Lies and More Lies

Finally, after waiting for months, I gave them a deadline of two weeks to get Mama to look over the list, a deadline that I eventually extended indefinitely in order not to take Mama's guardian back to court over my possessions.[86] "This list was already presented to you some weeks ago," I wrote to the guardian on January 7, 2004,[87] in response to yet another request for the list of items I had sent back in November. In fact, it was into February before Mama even saw the list I had sent in November.[88] Each time the subject arose, the commercial guardian either did not seem to know or did not quite believe that I truly needed my property.

Now that the other anxiety-producing activities were winding down, the commercial guardian started demanding access to the broker who was handling the High Desert account. Of course, I gave them his contact information, but Mama had never been a managing partner. The only information he had was about the very few times he had called her because her direct authorization had been required for a purchase for her part of the account. By 2003, that had not happened for quite some time.

The guardianship firm as it turned out, had no actual power to buy and sell for Mama within that account. Arthur and I had always been the managing partners, just as I had always told them. We controlled the entity because we owned the vast majority of the High Desert assets. Mama was simply a minority partner. They were not able to convince Arthur and me to vote to dissolve High Desert. There seemed no reason to do so, and the by-laws of High Desert did not make any special provisions for a partner coming under guardianship. Nor were they able to get me to meet weekly with them to discuss my trades, simply because I was not doing a lot of trading and I refused to see them that often, knowing that paying the guardian for a weekly conference during which I would say, "There's been no change since last week" would be a waste of Mama's money.

At that point, I advised the guardian that, in the current circumstances, High Desert was obliged to sell the property it owned

---

86 Rosenstiel 02761-02765
87 Ibid
88 Rosenstiel(2)016255

in common with Mama's aide. There followed two years of wrangling, as the aide refused to cooperate, ultimately obliging High Desert to sue her, requesting that the court order the property sold. Eventually, High Desert settled, selling the aide its interest in the property at a loss.

The guardian, in an effort to gain direct control of as many of Mama's assets as possible,[89] took over the final decision-making for the Merc lease and started having the monthly rental checks sent to them, rather than to me. It took until the spring of 2004 for the Mercantile Exchange and the leaseholder to recognize this change. They did not seem to like it, but at last they agreed to send the check to the guardian instead of me.

Early in 2004, after seeing multiple documents proving that Mama had indeed given me gifts over the years, the guardian firm decided to give a monetary gift on Mama's behalf, but to Arthur, instead. They were, I gather, shocked when he said he did not want a gift from Mama. "You're her daughter," he told me. "If they're giving gifts to anyone, they ought to be giving them to you, not me!"

Eventually, I managed to convince him that he might be irritating the guardian further by continuing to refuse. The guardian persisted and eventually Arthur gave in. Then, after all the *sturm und drang* about saying that Mama hated me and did not want to give me anything, they decided to continue with annual gifting to both of us. During discovery I could find no indication in their case notes that anyone had ever discussed the guardian's contemplated or actual financial decisions with Mama.

Did this have anything at all to do with Mama and her wishes? I have no idea whether this was the guardian's independent idea or whether they said anything to Mama about it. I gathered later, in speaking to the family members of other wards, that monetary gifts might sometimes be used to create jealousy or envy among

---

89 This is called "marshalling the assets" and I found it quite disagreeable, even though sanctioned by law. At this point, I suppose, Arthur and I were, in fact, technically defying the guardian by keeping Mama's assets in High Desert. However, those assets were verifiably safe and untouched. The "gifting" to Arthur was accomplished simply as a book entry, transferring some of Mama's assets in High Desert from Mama's High Desert account to Arthur's. Had the assets been sold, it would have cost a lot of money for the guardian's time in transferring cash between outside accounts.

other family members. If that is what the commercial guardian had tried to do with Arthur and me, again it did not work.

Late in March, I got a request to meet with the commercial guardian to discuss Mama's budget. It turned out that they wanted cash from High Desert, which would have required me to sell at least some of the stocks Mama had originally contributed. This, in turn, would have triggered a dissolution of High Desert, under the terms of the operating agreement. I rebelled, asking why this was necessary because they had immediate access to that huge monthly check from the Merc lessor (the annual lease amount would soon rise to $167,250 for the year), plus Mama's several pensions and annuity income (totaling another $71,640.46), in addition to whatever might have been in her checking account(s).[90] I refused to sell.

By March 24, I had been scandalized by Mama's proposed "budget" that her guardian showed me. I emailed them:

"...if you wish to liquidate any portion of Mother's interest in High Desert, you will need a court order to do so. And I am still mystified by how a single individual who is not doing extensive first-class traveling and expensive entertaining, or suffering from multiple chronic illnesses for which she must take expensive medication that is not covered by Medicare can continue to spend upwards of $20,000 per month while under the oversight of a qualified conservator. If you could explain the need to spend more than $20,000 per month to me, I might feel different about the current request for funds...Perhaps we can go over the budget on Monday, if you're free."[91]

Sometimes, during the early months of Mama's guardianship, no one was in the guardian's office when I delivered that five-digit check for the Merc rent. "...no one was in your office [on March 4 when I was supposed to deliver the check], so I put it in the mail slot and left," I emailed the guardian firm on March 24, 2004.[92] However, it took quite a while and some persistence on my part before the firm admitted it had received that money.

---

90 Rosenstiel(2)013800
91 Rosenstiel(2)016376
92 Rosenstiel016377

For reasons best known only to the guardian and REDW, my then accounting firm, REDW, started copying the guardian on correspondence sent to me and showing the guardian my husband's and my tax information. They also made available to the guardian the monthly brokerage statements that they demanded I have sent to them, because otherwise the broker would keep them confidential. (During discovery for the 2013 case, I also discovered that REDW had provided the commercial guardian copies of some information from High Desert, and that the guardian had obtained information on Arthur's account and mine. I had no idea they had done this and certainly had not authorized them to have them.)[93] I assumed that REDW would automatically redact the information for Arthur's and my part of High Desert, since that seemed to be standard practice.

By April, the guardian firm absolutely demanded $40,000, in cash, which I sent them. Fortunately, Mama had enough cash in her High Desert account that this would not trigger the dissolution of the entity. At that time, I reminded them that, "Mother's income from the Mercantile seat and her pensions is over $200,000…I disagree with some of your financial projections also. I think the expenses are estimated too high."[94]

Mama was in the hospital about that time. I had managed to have brief phone conversations with her twice, once on April 12 and again on the April 13. Mama sounded confused; she was not able to recall and relay anything to me about her condition. The guardian did not give me any information. Despite having a court order saying that I had end-of-life authority, I would not be getting any information from them. They did not allow me the right to see Mama in the hospital. I have no idea whether Mama's trips to the hospital during the spring of 2004 correlated, in any way, with the visit of my aunt and younger cousin. However, the usual anxiety Mama suffered in my aunt's presence might have made this slightly more likely.

By mid-May 2004 the author writing about a former fiancé of mine was about to reach the publisher's May 31 deadline

---

93 Rosenstiel(2)016398 (The purposes were so I could have access to my own possessions still in Mama's house and to my correspondence and other documents)
94 Ibid

for submission of his manuscript. For some reason, the idea of a deadline was anathema to the guardian. "We have engaged in a long and costly negotiation, lasting about 6 months," I wrote to Cristy on May 14, "in which both of my primary purposes have been entirely frustrated in advance."[95]

I still believed that Cristy was representing me, because that was what she had told the court during the November 2003 hearing, and thereafter.[96] And, of course, because the court records refer to Chuck Reynolds as Mama's attorney. Mama's commercial guardian, meanwhile, had retained attorney Judith Schrandt, to represent them.[97] The fact that I saw Judith Schrandt's signature on legal documents, signing, sending and accepting legal documents on the guardian's behalf,[98] unfortunately sufficed to convince me that she was the guardian's attorney and Cristy was my attorney. Wrong![99] I continued to pay Sutin for work done through mid-2005, so I assumed it was not simultaneously working for the commercial guardian.

All three attorneys—Judith Schrandt, Chuck Reynolds and Cristy Carbon-Gaul—I discovered after Mama died, were now being paid by Mama. And there was yet a fourth attorney, the second one at Sutin Thayer & Browne, Maria Montoya Chavez, who was handling some details of the Mercantile lease. She was paid as well, her activities billed for separately on Sutin's invoices. Even though their specific jobs were redacted from the invoices I saw during discovery, the initials of the lawyers clearly showed when Christy was performing services and when Maria was. Mama now had four attorneys to pay.

On May 24, a colleague of mine who also knew Mama's original aide and had visited the aide's home that day, told me that she saw Mama sleeping on the couch in the aide's home that afternoon, at a time when the guardian had told me that the relief aide should be with Mama, in Mama's home. If the purpose of establishing the

---

95 Ibid
96 Rosenstiel(2)020452 and p. 1 of posted court docket for D-202-PQ-200300170
97 Rosenstiel(2)020438
98 Ibid
99 I was surprised to see emails I exchanged with Cristy described as "confidential" by the defendant during the discovery process.

guardianship was, in part, to wean Mama away from the aide's influence, this certainly was not the way to accomplish it. Why did the relief aide not report to the guardian that her charge was missing? Did she simply leave, then go and collect her check for Mama's care, despite the fact that Mama was not there?

Neither Arthur nor I had ever thought of charging Mama money for managing her investments. Given how difficult, time-consuming and exhausting we found dealing with Mama's guardian, however, Arthur and I started asking to be compensated, at the then-prevailing rate of a total of 1 percent per year, for managing Mama's High Desert assets.[100] Strangely, we met with little resistance. Money, they understood.

I was still asking Cristy about getting permission to see Mama, which I needed prior to visiting her. Cristy casually commented to me in June that Mama's condition had worsened considerably, and that she might even be dying. She had also made a suggestion to me that the original aide might be replaced two to three days per week. When I contacted the guardian about this, it led to Cristy saying that I was blowing things out of proportion. I never heard, again, about the substitution of another aide until years later, when the aide was fired.[101] "I realize that I was not allowed to see her [Mama] the last two times she was in the hospital," I wrote the commercial guardian on June 12, 2004. "Being out of the loop on these things is distressing...I'd appreciate getting bulletins, as appropriate, on Mother's condition and her household status."[102]

"When I pass Mother's home on my errands...there is no car in her driveway," I wrote the guardian on June 14. I asked the guardian whether Mama was, once again, spending her afternoons in the original aide's home.[103] "I don't sense that your mother is dying," the guardian replied...If you are interested in again trying to visit with your mother, I think it would be best to wait..."[104]

---

100 This possibility to take payment for our management work had always existed, even in the original operating agreement, except that Arthur and I had never before asked for payment or reimbursement of any sort. Rosenstiel(2)016407
101 Ibid
102 Rosenstiel-02851-02852
103 Rosenstiel(2)016410
104 Ibid

Mama, it turned out, was back in the hospital. Which branch of which hospital? They did not say. Being so far out of the loop on Mama's condition was the main reason I felt compelled to forego any remaining "medical authority." While Mama was under guardianship, I never really had any. If reminded about the court order, the guardian always said that Mama did not want me to do what the judge seemed to be saying that I should do.

It was useless to remind them that a court order was supposed to rule in these circumstances.[105] The guardian would simply counter that Mama's condition was not yet terminal, and leave it at that. The original order said that the guardian would make day-to-day medical decisions and I would make both emergency and end-of-life decisions. Is not a trip to the emergency room an emergency medical situation?

Not until reading the guardian's annual report to the court, a report that was months late in the filing, did I discover that Mama had been taken to a hospital three times during that annual reporting period. Not only had the guardian not advised me that any of those trips to the hospital was imminent, but the guardian did not allow me to make a single decision at any time during Mama's hospital stays.

Whether Mama did not want me there on a given occasion I will never know. Just for the sake of argument, if she ever did say that, was she aware that what she was saying violated a court order? It is difficult to believe that the commercial guardian would have tried to inform Mama of the court order. If so, how did they frame the question?

Despite the commercial guardian's assurances that they had asked Mama frequently about visits, these questions are documented on only a few occasions, and then generally in unsigned, computerized notes I first saw in 2014. There is no way to know exactly

---

[105] It took years before I realized that the order stating that I "may" obtain emergency treatment for Mama was not at all the same as saying that I "shall" obtain such treatment for her. Then, too, the original order gave no definition of what end of life care and "extreme" treatment really meant. It only seemed as if I was being given end-of-life authority and emergency care authorization. Believing I had those powers mollified me at the time but really, those words ultimately meant nothing. (Decades 24410)

when they were written. Not until after I contacted the commercial guardian in June 2004, about there being no car in Mama's driveway, were they willing to admit that Mama had been hospitalized. Her condition, I was told, had stabilized. They did not make clear, at that time, exactly when she entered the hospital, or why.

Theoretically, Judge Baca had given me both emergency and end-of-life authority over Mama's medical care. However, it seemed that the commercial guardian had carte blanche to ignore this. They mentioned one hospital admission to me during the year; the others they only disclosed in their annual report to the court.

Documents produced by the guardian during discovery provide conflicting information on Mama's hospital visits that year— April 12-14, for pneumonia; May 9, for probable gallbladder pain; June 14-18 for an infection, and a final visit on September 23 for possible pneumonia show in their report to the court.[106] Notes kept by the commercial guardianship show different dates for these hospital visits—an ER visit on April 11, an inpatient stay on April 12-14, another on May 2-4, another on May 9, and another ER visit on September 1, 2004.[107]

For the June visit only, which does not even show in the firm's internal notes,[108] I was allowed to contact Mama's doctor, but not Mama herself. I still find it shocking that Mama made other visits to the hospital that I did not find out about until after the fact

Given the unusual timing of Mama's June illness, I now wonder whether there is some connection between it and the stipulated order that was agreed to on June 16, 2004 (although not finalized until December 2, 2004). It did not take effect until August 4, the date when Judge Baca signed it). This document, in addition to relieving me of any responsibility for Mama's medical decision-making, not only formalized the gift to Arthur but also ordered me to terminate the trust that Cristy had created in Mama's name on September 10, 2003. All of this was completed on June 16, 2004.

Did some discussion of this matter by the commercial guardian upset Mama? Did Mama want to make sure that she only saw me when she was in perfect condition, so that I would not think of

---
106 Decades 03553-03554
107 Decades 03278-03281
108 Decades 03279

her as being less than perfect? Both are possibilities. However, it is equally likely that they told her nothing. On June 18, the guardian wrote to me that it would be "best to wait until she is back at home and strong...to see if visits can be possible again."[109]

The stipulated order removed me from participating Mama's health care, including end-of-life decision-making. However, it seemed to me that the commercial guardian had already done that unilaterally, and certainly made it impossible for me to have information on Mama's day-to-day health issues long before any court order directed them to do so. Henceforth, the court-ordered guardian assumed all power, except over High Desert and, for a few years, over the Mercantile lease, which I continued to negotiate, at their command, but behind the scenes, deciding on the amount while Maria Montoya Chavez took the public actions required to finalize the details.

Judge Baca's order also allowed the guardian to change the High Desert Operating Agreement to give more of the income to Mama than she had gotten before. I agreed to this reluctantly, at Cristy's insistence. The suggestion was made that, if I did not, they would have the court destroy High Desert altogether.

Usually, the percentage of ownership determines the income; the guardian, however, demanded that the division of income be made, instead, in a manner that favored Mama and gave her more income. They changed the way High Desert was run so that, from an accounting point of view, it resembled more having three separate accounts, under my management and Arthur's, rather than a partnership. Well, at least they did not go to court and force me to sell everything...

According to New Mexico's court rules governing wards, the commercial guardianship firm owed the court a report within a month of the first anniversary of their appointment. Back in mid-October 2003, I had written to the commercial guardian, asking why Mama's expenses were so high. In unsigned, typed notes, there is the following notation: "I responded that we would be providing an annual report in December..."[110] That deadline would

---

109 Rosenstiel (2)016415
110 Decades 03314

have arrived on December 14, 2004. No such document was forthcoming, however, until July 22, 2005.[111] The "first year" conservator report did, however, end with information, including Mama's net worth as of November 14, 2004.

In December 2004, my aunt and younger cousin visited Mama again. Betty was delighted to write to Mama's case manager on December 21, 2004, "We had several excellent and productive private conversations with her [i.e., Mama]…"[112] Betty's report led the guardianship firm to redouble its efforts to make sure no one got any private time with Mama, not even Betty, the relative whom they most favored.

Meanwhile, the commercial guardian had been telling me things about Mama aimed, it seemed, at driving additional emotional wedges between us. Among them, a partner there reported that Mama was saying that my husband and I were not married. Mama had been a witness at our wedding, so I was shocked. However paradoxically, I still hung onto the hope that the commercial guardian was accurately reporting to me what Mama said. It took me quite a while to let go of that notion. We tend to be trained to listen to the "experts." Normalcy bias is an insidious beast.

The commercial guardian's social report required by the court was no more factual than some of the statements the court visitor had made in 2003. "Mrs. Rosenstiel has reported to the case manager that she bought [the caregiver's]…contract from Kelly Home Health in order to retain [her] service fulltime."[113] Here, the guardian had not bothered to check the veracity of Mama's statement, either with me or with the home health aide service. The partner signing this report, while transmitting incorrect information, managed to deny responsibility for the accuracy of that information, first, by saying that her firm never checked the veracity of Mama's statements, and then, by using this "information" to misinform the court about the nature of Mama's relationship with her aide, by making the statement an indirect quote from Mama herself.

The commercial guardian also wrote, in that first annual report, that Mama's memories "have never included negative, deprecating

---

111 Decades 0356
112 Decades 25066-25067
113 No one ever checked with me or asked Kelly Health to verify this statement, which as I have already said, is untrue. (Decades 03570)

or malicious comments."[114] I disagreed with their evaluation, particularly in regard to the statement they had attributed to Mama, that Arthur was not my husband.

On May 10, 2005, my aunt and cousin were in the process of paying another visit to Mama, in Albuquerque. Mama "wanted to laid [sic] down and rest," the aide wrote. Her sister went to bedrm [sic] to talk with her." (Excuse me, but when someone asks to be left alone, to rest, does this mean it is fine to follow her into her bedroom, so that she cannot have the respite she seeks?) I would never have seen the aide's notes without getting the records as the result of a subpoena. They would have been considered "privacy-protected" under HIPAA. Otherwise, I would have believed that the commercial guardian was wholly responsible for this fabrication:

"Betty & I stayed in the Kichen [sic] to talk alone & I learned a little more about Dr R a[nd] her daughter." The aide wrote. "Apparently there was never a real close relationship between them. Even before they moved to N.M. Betty stated that the cousin saw less of her Mother, than they did!...[the original aide says] they want to take Dr R back East with them at that time [when they visit in December 2005]. And not just to visit, but to live!...So, as usual, I'm not sure what is really going on! [The original aide] said that they (she and Dr R.) saw Dr. Rosenstiels [sic] daughter drive by the house. And it upset Dr. R"[115]

Periodically, my aunt and cousin seemed to try to find some way to get Mama to go back East with them. How interesting that this relief aide's sense of never quite getting the whole story and always feeling emotionally off-balance mirrors mine. As to the charge that during 2005, I had had the temerity to drive by my mother's home, actually I had not done so. I had not driven past there since that fateful visit just after Christmas in 2003. Two blocks away was Layton, a street that I sometimes used to take a shortcut to my office. However, there is not a direct line of sight between that street and any room in Mama's home, although it is possible to glimpse her driveway from one intersection. Unless Mama was standing in her own driveway, looking away from her home at exactly the right angle, I would have to conclude that

---

114 Decades 03571
115 Decades 26190, 26192

Mama "saw" my car the same way she "saw" the invisible food on her counter that she had tried to slice a few years earlier.

As for that "estrangement" tale, most likely, Betty had retailed this story to the future commercial guardian, prior to the initial hearing in 2003. She had also had access to all other court-appointed experts as a sort of stand-in for her own mother. This monster of a story grew legs and perpetuated itself for the rest of the commercial guardian's tenure. It came back, at intervals, to attack me in various contexts. I never knew why everyone was saying that I was "estranged" from Mama until I found that document among the 40,000 unearthed during discovery.

The aide who wrote that report (not Mama's original aide) had no particular bias; I have no reason to believe she was doing anything other than reporting what my cousin was saying. For the first thirty years of my life, I would have seen my aunt and cousin whenever either of my parents did. I did not officially move out of my parents' home until I was thirty years old. After I was already living in New York City, when Betty and my aunt were on their way to another appointment nearby, a few times they stopped in Manhasset to see my parents. My parents told me about those visits. Aunt Louise and Betty reached Mama before I did after Dad died, but they did not stay with her.

Once, after Dad died, Betty also helped my mother with a car lock problem. Betty would certainly have been a more logical person to call, since she had credentials as a locksmith and I did not. However, I must confess that I still cannot think of a good reason why Mama would have called Betty, in New Jersey, in preference to calling the AAA or the local Acura dealership.

Perhaps Betty interpreted the fact that I got my own apartment in New York City, at age 30, as some sort of abandonment of my parents. (I had been spending increasing periods of time traveling and doing research, after I entered graduate school, anyway.) Betty's life journey, as an Amway distributor, locksmith and Naval reservist was very different from mine, and also from that of her own elder sister. Even though Betty traveled, she remained rooted in her suburban town for life. After she graduated from college (during those years, she seemed to go back to her parents' home on most weekends) and spent two years in the Navy (during which time, family legend had it that she also spent most leaves at her parents' home), she moved back to her childhood home, permanently. My elder cousin left even earlier than I did. After college, she never lived in her parents' home again. When I learned about this document, I started to wonder whether there might be some element of self-justification in Betty's condemnation of me.

The commercial guardian's 2004-05 report, submitted on December 22, 2005,[116] less than six months after the first, said of Mama, "She recognizes family and friends seen frequently, but requires cues with individuals she does not see on a regular basis."[117] I had not seen Mama since early 2004, so this statement sent me to those old publications known as phone books, and then to recheck on the internet whether any of Mama's relatives had in fact moved to New Mexico and might have been seeing her on a regular basis.

No one had moved to New Mexico from the East Coast. Aunt Louise and Betty visited twice a year, for a few days each time. According to what I was hearing, Betty called every week to ten days. But, back then, there was no Skype, so Mama was not "seeing" either my aunt or Betty, and Mama no longer had any idea how to get onto the internet anyway.

Prior to the guardianship, Mama did not have any local friends, other than my friends (who did not see Mama at all during the period 2003-07, when I could not see her either), so these people could not have been visiting her. (My belief on this subject was confirmed, during discovery, when I saw the aides' notes.)

By "friends" did the guardian mean the relatives of Mama's caregiver who should not have been part of Mama's life anyway? Their names do occasionally figure in the original aides' notes, but only very early in the process, and at times they were doing work, for money, in Mama's home. I also wanted to know what the commercial guardian meant by "frequently."

Perhaps the guardianship company wanted the court to think that Mama was having as much of a social life as possible under

---

116 Decades 03578-03585
117 Decades 03580-03581

the circumstances. The firm reported to the court a social life that would seem almost normal, but even with the limited information I had, this did not appear to be the case at all.

The judge, of course, only considered the information the guardian gave her and it would then have been considered improper for me to write, personally, to the judge to lodge an objection to the commercial guardian's report[118]; back then, that was the function of the interested party's attorney. From what I could see, Mama was isolated with her caregivers (and the family members of her initial caregiver), a situation that seemed designed to increase her emotional dependence on them. As I later learned, someone from the guardianship firm attended doctors' appointments and was in the room with Mama at all times during those meetings, so she would have had no privacy during these visits, either.

The commercial guardian's report was supposed to contain facts. To me, this one did not seem to describe Mama's social situation accurately. I contacted Cristy, telling her I wanted her, as my attorney, to register a formal objection to the parts of the guardian's report that I knew to be inaccurate and asking that she not approve the guardian's first report. "I've already signed it," she said.

"How could you approve it before I read it?"

"I approved it on your mother's behalf. I'm her attorney too."

"How can you be both my attorney and Mama's attorney? Isn't that a conflict?"

Almost immediately, Cristy sent me an email. She complained that she did not know how to satisfy me as my attorney, so she was resigning from the case. The email did not acknowledge that she had already had a conflict of interest for a couple of years.

Cristy's resignation did not mean that Sutin Thayer & Browne resigned from the case. Maria Montoya Chavez continued to handle aspects of the Mercantile Exchange seat lease (until 2008). My query to the firm about whether someone else there could represent me elicited the information that no one could. Now that I

---

118 SB 395, allowing interested parties to write directly to the judge, in guardianship cases, passed the New Mexico Legislature in 2019. See: *https://nmlegis.gov/Legislation/Legislation?Chamber=S&LegType=B&LegNo=395&year=19*

had identified that there was a conflict, I needed to find another attorney.

After my conversation with Cristy, I knew that I would need a new attorney, a person who was representing only me. I found Debbie Gonçalves, an attorney with a soothing manner and an objective ability to assess what could, practically speaking, actually be accomplished, given the then-current statutes and legal climate. On August 24, 2005, Debbie Gonçalves wrote to Judith Schrandt, with copies to Charles Reynolds, Cristy Carbon-Gaul, the guardianship firm and me, "Judy, I'm substituting in as counsel for Leonie Rosenstiel...I'm attaching a copy of my Entry of Appearance and Substitution of Counsel which will be filed today or tomorrow..."[119]

An unsigned agreement in the discovery documents the commercial guardian produced shows that the Sutin firm was aware of a conflict of interest in continuing to assist, even with negotiating the Merc lease. Whether the guardianship firm ever signed a copy of this agreement is impossible to tell. If it was signed, that document does not seem to have been produced, by the guardianship firm, during discovery.

Based on the firm's reports to the court, it seems that the commercial guardian subscribed to the theory of deficit financing. During discovery, the guardianship firm was required to supply us with its ledger and any printouts. The firm listed Mama's net worth on February 29, 2004 as $2,927,432.57. Of this amount, only $1,218,232.57 showed as being truly liquid assets, and Mama's loss for the month, even with all her income, showed as $8,007.56.[120] The Merc seat was not liquid unless Mama wanted to forego the income from it, which she badly needed, given the guardian's high level of spending. The guardian's first report to the court gave Mama's income as $339,337.54, with disbursements of $297,802.32. This is still a fair-sized expenditure for a single person who, as I have already said, is not travelling, is not buying designer clothes and really is not socializing.

Mama had a checking account at First State Bank that the guardian had opened, and another at Wells Fargo, that she had

---

119 Rosenstiel-02966
120 Decades 04239

had prior to the guardianship. This money was exclusive of whatever money was in the trust I had created at Cristy's urging. The guardian's internal records show that Mama only had a balance of $4,489.30 in the First State Bank account and $6,232.68 in her Wells Fargo account on February 28, 2004. They also said Mama still had a balance of $5,465.30 in an account at H & R Block, but other documents indicate that this account had been closed in December 2003.[121] Where was that cash? The guardian's internal ledger said that there was a balance of $1,202,045.29 in something called the Annette Rosenstiel Revocable Trust. That was her interest in High Desert.

I had always thought of the Trust as the cash account I had set up in Wells Fargo, and that consisted of several months of Merc lease checks I had deposited there, along with the title to Mama's home and car. When I "liquidated" the trust (i.e., handed over the contents of the Wells Fargo Trust account to the commercial guardian), it had the same approximately $37,000 cash in it that it had always had from the time the guardianship was created.

On that same "Statement of Net Worth" page, they had already listed the value of the home separately, and the value of "other assets" separately, by which I assume they meant Mama's car. So, they were double-and-treble-counting Mama's initial assets. This page is interesting. At the head of the page is the printed date "3/18/04." The heading says, "Statement of Net Worth As of February 29, 2004." Fair enough.

The guardian insisted that Mama's "extra" expenses were my fault, for asking so many questions. They did not, however, tell me how much of their billable time was likely spent both traveling to and visiting Mama in various hospitals during those emergency room trips and hospital stays. Someone from the guardian's office was legally supposed to sign and agree to any treatments Mama received. All their self-generated arguments in favor of gifting stock to Arthur took hours, as did their attempts to make me do things that would have forced the dissolution of High Desert. They

---

121 The last statement included in the commercial guardian's discovery is from January to March 2004, but in June, one of the firm's partners opened an account in Mama's name, naming herself as the guardian, apparently transferring Mama's assets into that account. (Decades 17853-17866) There were no further statements for that account among the discovery documents.

reported to the court that they had walked away from the first year with $52,670.36 ($74,135.39 in 2021) in fees.[122] The attorneys, they stated, earned another $31,389.23.[123] If those expenses had all been incurred during 2004, then these services, in 2021, would have been $74,135.39 and $61,425.27, respectively

Mama only had about $1.2 million in truly liquid assets, back then (if the guardian's figures are to be trusted), so the fees associated with the first year's guardian's fees and legal expenses amounted to just over 6.99 percent of Mama's liquid assets. Yes, Mama's home could theoretically have been sold. However, then she would still have to pay to live somewhere. Besides, the guardian firm said it was going to keep her in her home. It also insisted that it was not going to sell the Merc seat, either.

The guardian claimed $746,563.60 in expenses during 2005, and additional payroll liabilities of $42,791.83. About half a million of those expenses resulted from the guardian's estimate of the value of stock journaled to my husband. So, in one year, Mama's expenses had mushroomed by $491,553.11.[124]

That second year, Mama had had far fewer medical expenses because she made no hospital visits. The Merc lessee was now sending his checks directly to the commercial guardian, so I had little to no interaction with the firm, outside of email. In all fairness to the commercial guardian, they reported that Mama paid them only $22,202.47 that year.[125] "Mrs. Rosenstiel...has a history of poor judgement in that area [i.e., financial] and requires a conservator to monitor her resources,"[126] Mama's guardian reported to the court in their report hand-dated November 14, 2004, but not filed until mid-2005.

Notes in the guardian firm's file showed their on-going concern with having enough of Mama's money (for themselves) during any given year. One page said that their direct compensation for being guardian and conservator amounted to $42,221.80 between May

---
122 Decades 03558
123 Ibid
124 Decades 03584
125 They did mention, in their first report that I was unable to make any visits, but attributed that to fulfilling Mama's wishes that I not see her. I now doubt much of what they told me; I wanted to believe them then because the commercial guardian was supposed to be an expert and I was not.
126 Decades 03555

2004 and April 2005. Of course, that was not the reporting period, so it was possible to apportion that amount partially to the period May to November 2004 and list the rest as part of the 2005 report, thereby making it appear lower than it really was.

In preparing the firm's report to the court, the guardian chose to include increases in the value of the Mercantile seat and theoretical profit and loss in High Desert in Mama's income. This is not wrong, from an accounting point of view. However, if those assets had actually been sold, Mama would have lost much of the gain to taxes and ended up with much less "income" than the guardian was suggesting to the court that she had. Had they actually made these sales, after that, Mama would no longer be getting the needed income on those investments, thereby triggering repeated rounds of selling that would have further depleted both her assets and her later income.

The guardian had insisted to me, at the beginning of the firm's tenure, that the life expectancy of wards was only about three years, which, in itself, was upsetting enough. This sort of cannibalization of assets might have been a tolerable situation for a short while if Mama's life was truly about to end, but I refused to believe that, even when the "experts" told me it was true. And, that is definitely not what happened.

Although, at the beginning of the guardianship, Mama was eating out with some frequency, she was generally going, with her aide, to moderate-priced restaurants like Golden Corral and Sweet Tomatoes. Mama's credit card charges also reveal that she was never eating in the most expensive places in town. By the time the second report was filed, the guardian admitted that Mama was already eating out less often.[127]

Mama had always refused to take flu vaccine. Because there is no mention of any flu shots in Mama's medical records while she was under guardianship either, I am assuming that the guardianship firm allowed her to continue to refuse them. However, the guardian discouraged Mama from going to public places during flu season, so for about five months of the year Mama did not go out much. In fact, when Betty and Louise visited in December 2005,

---

127 Decades 03553

a time when people are generally out shopping, socializing, eating in restaurants and preparing for the Holidays, the guardian wrote to them, "It would be in the interest of her [i.e., Annette's] health and safety, if you avoided crowds."[128]

Years later, Mama's commercial guardian told the court-appointed auditor that Mama was spending some $300 per week ($422.26 in 2021) on groceries during that same period, expenses that often were paid for with gift cards and could not be documented. And they did not jibe with the amounts for "food" that the guardian reported annually to the court.[129]

This level of expense was either unlikely or impossible unless Mama was feeding others, in addition to herself, most of the time. On this subject, the commercial guardian gave different answers at different times. At one point after Mama died, the guardian firm told Baca & Redwine, then the court-appointed auditor, that they believed that Mama would have wanted to pay the bills for others. They meant her aides, declaring that it would have been uncivilized not to feed Mama's aides (and presumably also the aides' family members) as well. At another, it told the same auditor that a different caregiver had been discharged for the impropriety of buying groceries for herself on Mama's credit card.[130]

The guardianship firm later admitted to the auditor that it had allowed one of Mama's aides[131] to make numerous long-distance calls from Mama's landline phone over a period of several years. Again, the excuse was that Mama would have wanted to allow this. In my experience, the same aide always had made such calls from her own cell phone, or from her home phone, prior to the establishment of the guardianship.

During 2003-2006, Mama could manage to get some privacy by closeting herself in her office during the time when her primary aide

---

128 Decades 25093
129 The guardian told the auditor that it considered the $300 per week to be for groceries, which would mean that Mama spent $15,600 per year on groceries. However, in 2004, on their report to the court, they claimed $4,651.83 (Decades 03575); in 2005, it was $7,958.46 (Decades 03584); in 2006, $10,868.94 (Decades 03592).
130 The auditor made no attempt to reconcile this contradiction and, in fact, refused to address the entire question of whether any expense paid by the commercial guardian might have been either unjustified or excessive.
131 Decades 24138. The guardian told the auditor that the original aide was considered "part of the family" and so any expenses were allowed.

was on duty. The aide's notes show that Mama banished this aide at times when she was supposed to be working.[132] I have no doubt that Mama believed that she actually was working, but Mama had been unable to concentrate while at the computer, even before the guardianship was created.

Mama's old typewriters were already long in storage, so the computer, which I had, delivered and hooked up in 1999, could only really be used by one of the aide's children or grandchildren, when they were there. A children's picture book, describing a highly fictionalized version of our long-ago experience in a German zoo, later produced by the commercial guardian during discovery, and complete with computer illustrations, had to have been done, at the very least, in that sort of collaboration.[133] Mama might have dictated some of it. She could not have input the text; there was absolutely no way that she could have created (or even copied and pasted) those digital illustrations. The only reason I can accept this document at all is that Mama had to have told some version of this story to someone for it to end up in a computer file. However, I am equally convinced that a number of other documents purporting to have been written by Mama, on the computer, during the earliest period of the guardianship, were outright forgeries. Generally, I believe this because I have found drafts of them, written in the very distinctive handwriting of Mama's original aide. They were also signed with Mama's name, but that is not Mama's handwriting in the signature on the bottom of the page.

By September 2004, the home health care service started complaining, vigorously, about the original aide. "Annette," the anonymous report-writer said, "...has become extremely dependent on [the original aide] and is losing her independence each day as she allows [the aide] to run her life and house for her...she [the aide] is quite controlling of Annette and also threatened by our presence."[134] The aide, of course, disputed these claims.[135]

---

132 Decades 26442
133 Decades 26527. This "book" most likely took shape on October 15, 2003, when the aide's notes say that the original aide's granddaughter spent time with Mama, in Mama's office, using the computer.
134 Of course, I had made the same observation more than a year earlier. It was one of the problems I had originally thought that going through the painful guardianship process might correct. Decades 26809
135 Decades 26811

In June 2005, Betty wrote the commercial guardian a letter, attempting to make funeral arrangements for Mama. Her letter was supposedly addressed to Mama, I am sure knowing that it would end up in the guardian's hands. Betty, saying in the letter that she had done research at Mama's request, had already contacted a funeral parlor and a cemetery.[136] The firm took no action at that point.

By 2006, the commercial guardian required Aunt Louise and Betty to stay at a hotel. In other words, it took the experts several years to get to the point Mama herself had reached, back in 1999. It seemed that Mama paid the bill for all these hotel stays, the guardian speculating that my relatives needed money, but I never found any indication of these payments in the invoices the guardian produced during discovery. They certainly were not separately reported to the court. I cannot recall any time in my life, for the many decades during which Mama was in full possession of her faculties, and even when Dad was alive, when either Mama or Dad paid any travel or living expenses for my aunt or her relatives.

For my aunt and cousin's late February and early March 2006 visits, the guardian's attorney, Judith D. Schrandt, wrote to my aunt, "Once again, we would respectfully request that you reframe [sic] from discussing either medical concerns, financial concerns or legal concerns with Dr. Rosenstiel as due to her dementia it is more confusing than helpful and therefore stressful to Dr. Rosenstiel."[137]

On August 17, 2006, Mama complained of severe pain and difficulty breathing. The aide on duty took her immediately to Lovelace Hospital—a good call (from my point of view, at least), as it turned out. Mama had a pulmonary embolism. Although the aide had gotten no prior permission from the commercial guardian to take Mama to the emergency room, it was most emphatically an action in Mama's best interest. However, it earned the aide a reprimand from the commercial guardian because she had had no legal authority to sign Mama in for treatment without their prior permission. (How the aide could be certain of reaching someone in authority instantly, they did not explain. Any delay might

---

136 Rosenstiel(2)017041-42
137 Decades 25062

have cost Mama her life, had the aide been delayed in getting the required pre-authorization.)

No one told me about any of this when it happened; I learned about the embolism in the guardian's report to the court some months later, and about the aide's severe scolding in documents produced during discovery after Mama died.[138]

The doctors kept Mama overnight, after determining her diagnosis. She was still on the blood-thinner Coumadin, and being monitored on an outpatient basis, when the commercial guardian filed the 2006 annual report. Mama continued taking Coumadin for the next few months. During the guardianship, Mama's original aide had been taking her for treatment to a doctor of oriental medicine in Albuquerque, often more than once per week, as the guardian told me "for social reasons," and sometimes without the guardian's permission. He was quite charming, when he wanted to be, and Mama enjoyed his company. Mama paid for all these sessions, whether it was simply a social visit or not.

Now that Mama was on Coumadin, she might have uncontrolled bleeding from the use of an acupuncture needle. Her medical doctor forbade the use of either herbs or acupuncture that might cause adverse reactions when employed while she was taking the Coumadin. At first the aide defied these instructions, but finally she complied. Given the way the guardian's reports were set up, it is hard to know how the payments to this doctor of oriental medicine were folded into the medical expenses, just as it is difficult to know where the money they paid for Aunt Louise and Betty's expenses were shown on the Annual Reports. However, they might be the "Other" category listed under "Medical" in the 2005 report, for $2,174.00.[139] That is likely because the category "Other" is only $988 in 2006,[140] which would correspond to Mama discontinuing treatment with him in August, after she started taking Coumadin.

Mama was apparently becoming weaker (at least according to the commercial guardian's report to the court; I did not have any way to verify this because I had not seen her since early 2004). However, the performance of the Mercantile investment was

---
138 Decades 03592
139 Decades 03567
140 Decades 03592

beyond robust. As of November 2005, the lease that I had negotiated was bringing in $16,250 per month ($195,000 for the year).[141] By 2006, it reached, briefly, $18,000 per month.[142] However, the same changes at the exchange that had greatly increased the value of the seat itself brought with them problems, inducing the lessor to demand a rent reduction, granted in the fall of 2006, from $18,000 to $10,000 per month.[143]

At the same time that the income from the lease decreased, the value of the seat skyrocketed, as avid investors anticipated the Merc having its Initial Public Offering on the NASDAQ, sometime during 2006. As it turned out, the IPO came within days after the end-date of the period covered by the guardian's 2006 report.

In 2005 and 2006, purchases for which Mama paid included a chaise longue and a recliner. The recliner, which never seems to have found its way to Mama's home, eventually cost Mama over $1600, factoring in paid hours for one of the guardian's minions to travel to Rio Rancho, a distance of some 30 miles, to pick it up.[144] The chaise longue, bought in 2005, was nowhere to be found after Mama passed away, either. However, the empty shipping box for this much cheaper item of furniture was still in Mama's garage, with the delivery stickers intact, after she died. The granddaughter of one of Mama's aides was getting married in 2005, so perhaps the chaise longue was a wedding present for her, authorized by Mama's guardians. I will never know. There is no discussion of this item, specifically, in their records.

I have a vivid memory of attending a conference in Judge Baca's chambers; I think the year was 2006. I attended with my then-fairly-new attorney, Deborah Rupp Gonçalves.[145] For some reason, the fact that this conference took place is not revealed in the on-line case docket. Because it was a conference, not a hearing, there was no court reporter present. Debbie, on my behalf, raised objections to the huge annual expenses the guardian claimed. As I

---

141 Decades 13469
142 Decades 13468
143 Decades 13466
144 The only recliner in Mama's home, after she passed away, was the red leather one I had gone to Ethan Allen with her to buy in 1999, and for which I found the receipt still among Mama's papers.
145 Debbie had entered her Order of Appearance, formally substituting for Cristy Carbon-Gaul on August 24, 2005.

recall, Judge Baca said, "This estate is hemorrhaging money. It has to stop!" It did not.

In my opinion, Mama herself had been unable to understand financial matters since before she became a ward. The Mercantile Exchange reported the prices of seats publicly each time one was sold. By November 14, 2005, the last sale, which also coincidentally happened on the court-imposed deadline of November 14, which would have been the end of the guardian's reporting period, the Mercantile seat had a reported value of $3,775,000, up from its initial value of $1,625,000 at the time the guardian took over in November 2003. However, the guardian's 2005 report listed a value for it of $2,500,000.[146]

Unlike truly liquid assets like shares of stock in well-known public companies that may trade in the millions of shares per day, the Mercantile Exchange seats traded one-by-one, sometimes with days or weeks between sales. The price of a NYMEX seat on November 10, 2006, the sale nearest to the end-date of the guardian's reporting period, had risen to $6,000,000, and now included 90,000 shares of stock in the IPO. At that point, the stock was restricted, meaning it could not be sold, except if the seat was also sold at the same time. The guardian's 2006 annual report, however, listed a value for the stock-plus-seat of $9,800,000. Again, that report was filed seriously late. The NYMEX did list a sale for that amount, but it occurred two months after the cut-off date. The report the commercial guardian filed on December 14, 2006, gave the value of the seat at $2.5 million.[147] If the values of Mama's assets were supposed to be reported to the court accurately, as of the end-dates of the reporting periods, this was not happening.

Why did the judge not realize that the guardian's reports were not being restricted to the reporting periods specified in the rules and statutes? If she did realize that the guardian was operating in some sort of time warp, why did she not take any action to correct things? The guardian's 2006 report specifically mentions other events that occurred on December 8, 2006, almost a month after the reporting period ended.[148]

In that report is the following footnote:

---

146 Decades 03584
147 Decades 03591
148 Decades 03590

"Please note this unrealized gain [of $7,300,000 in the NYMEX investment]...represents the current value of the asset that was the New York Mercantile Exchange Seat." It then goes on to cite a value for the seat, not as of the cut-off date of the report, which would have been November 14, 2006, but rather a value from January 2007.[149] The correct value on the cut-off date, as I have already said, would have been $6,000,000.

Mama's original aide continued to pose myriad on-going problems for the commercial guardian, just as she had for me. When that aide was not too late or too early returning from her time off, she was trying either to dismiss or argue with the other aides, or according to the guardian's records, she was saying things specifically designed to get other aides fired.

At her annual review on January 17, 2006, the commercial guardian firm placed a report in her file, attesting to their dissatisfaction with her performance, although not for her actions in zealously guarding her charge. They complained about her getting unauthorized treatments for Mama, demanding that she have anything of that nature pre-approved by Mama's guardian. They also insisted "There will be no more than five minutes of crossover time [i.e., time when both aides are present, between the time one aide goes off shift and the next one comes on]."[150] The commercial guardian gave the aide strict instructions that, when Aunt Louise and Betty visited that spring, they were going to be required to stay at a hotel—on Mama's dime, of course, although they did not specifically tell the aide that they would be paying for this.

Once again, this hotel expense was never broken out in the guardian's annual report, and they never told the court they were paying our relatives' expenses, so it is impossible to know what Mama spent on their lodging and food, and perhaps other charges during their visits. When the guardian produced documents during discovery, not one shed further light on the payment arrangements for this, and future, sojourns. It seemed to me that this document, with its fulsome and substantive complaints, could only have been produced by an organization that was about to fire someone and wanted to suit-proof itself.[151]

---

149 Decades 03619
150 Emphasis theirs. (Decades 26436)
151 Decades 26699- 26701

An undated and unsigned set of notes regarding the "possible undue influence" of Mama's original caregiver mirrors my own concerns, dating from before the guardianship. At least eight months had passed before a professional could document the problem I had mentioned to that firm a year or more earlier. "It has been clear for some time," the anonymous writer states, that this caregiver "has an impact on Annette Rosenstiel's thoughts. Recently, we have been concerned that this impact is greater than just a normal caring friendship as well as a caregiver relationship." The author wondered whether this resulted from the caregiver's "over-identification with Dr. Rosenstiel."[152] Just as Mama had concluded that her relatives belonged in a hotel, while visiting her, it had again taken quite some time for Mama's commercial guardian to see the same problems in Mama's relationship with her caregiver that I had described to them, back in 2003.

Imprecision seriously infected the guardian's 2006 report to the court. The firm told the court that Mama had 180,000 shares of NYMEX stock rather than the 90,000 shares she did own as a result of holding the single Merc seat.[153] If Mama had owned double the number of shares, that would have meant that her Mercantile seat and associated stock were worth at least $20 million.

I nearly fainted when I read this part of my copy of that annual report. I still wanted to believe what I was told, but the NYMEX was then paying generous, publicly announced dividends that absolutely did not gibe with the guardian occasionally still saying that Mama needed money from the stock she still had in High Desert. Mama could not possibly own all that stock and still need cash. In 2005, Mama would have been getting just over $100,800 in dividends from the Merc stock. By 2006, this had jumped to just over $339,000. If, on the other hand, Mama had twice that number of shares, she would have been getting more than $200,000 in dividends the first year and more than $670,000 in 2006.[154] The annual report certainly did not reflect the latter figures.

---

152 Decades 26442
153 Decades 26435
154 NYMEX Holdings, Inc. Annual Report 2006, p. 58. See: *http://investor.cmegroup.com/static-files/473dd6bf-a00c-499c-9906-4855045cdb7a*

By 2007, however, the Merc dividends had been greatly reduced, to a total of $1.36 per share (a total of $122,400, and at a time when the revenue from leasing the seat was drying up as well). Having refused to sell any of the tranches of stock, as they became unrestricted, the commercial guardian seemed to be getting extremely anxious. I was having trouble making what the guardian said match, from one discussion to the next and there was no one else I seemed to be able to ask to get a reliable story.

It appears that the last time the guardian showed Mama any financial documents was back in early 2007, covering the receipts and disbursements for 2006. They had told Mama, years before, not to tell her original aide anything about her financial affairs. However, that aide's distinctive handwriting is all over this document.

There is no mystery about how that aide managed to get to read it (and almost certainly the other printouts as well). When I was cleaning up after Mama's death, I found that print out and the two that had preceded it in a neat pile in one corner of the top drawer of Mama's dresser, a place all of her aides could have accessed easily, since it had no lock. Nevertheless, there was likely no reason to worry; I do not believe that any of these reports gave an accurate statement of Mama's net worth. And they did not seem to me to be all that accurate about her income and expenses.

Despite the warning that she knew had been placed in her personnel file, Mama's original aide continued acting in ways that upset the commercial guardian. I, of course, knew nothing about the details of what was happening, although I had warned them, in advance, of the aide's machinations, which I had also told them that I observed myself, even before the creation of the guardianship.

How I wish that the court and the commercial guardian had accepted the truth in the first place. This aide had only worked full time for Mama for about two years at the time when the guardianship was created. Before that, she had simply been one of half a dozen aides provided by two different home care services, serving in rotation. If they had believed the truth, I would have hoped that they would have behaved differently toward that original aide.

There is no guarantee that they would have, if only because it seemed the guardian wanted to recognize, with no proof of this fiction, a long-standing relationship between Mama and her aide. In so doing, they created on-going problems, both for themselves and, ultimately, for Mama.

When I learned about all the dramatics after Mama died, I wanted to say, "I told you so!" But by then the aide's antics had brought in a lot of money to the guardianship firm. Each time Mama's original aide acted up, Mama had to pay for the commercial guardian's time to resolve the latest issue. Eventually, they would pay for the services of a specialized attorney to advise them on how they could fire this aide without provoking her to sue them.

By November 17, 2006, the date of the actual NYMEX IPO, Mama's shares had a fair market value of $136 each (a total of $12,240,000, for all 90,000 shares, and another $600,000 for the "trading right" that was once called a "seat"). At any time before the stock was released in lots of 30,000 shares at a time, the guardian could have sold Mama's Merc seat and the shares as a unit. If they had sold the entire holding on the date of the IPO, obtained the fair market price for the stock, and invested just the proceeds from the stock in CDs, the prime rate would then have been 8.25 percent. The $600,000 for the trading right ought to have paid for some of Mama's care for a while, too.

Investing only the stock proceeds in CDs would have netted Mama $1,009,800 in annual income. If they kept 50 percent uninvested, reserved for paying taxes, and invested half that amount, they would have gotten a little over $500,000 in income from the interest, in addition to about $150,000 from Mama's various pensions and annuities, leaving the principal intact. "What on earth do they want?" I wondered. How did they not consider this potential income stream "enough" to take care of Mama? And the principal would not be touched, either.

Once during that period, they even told me they "couldn't" sell because Mama had told them that she did not want them to. "What are you talking about?" I asked, shocked. "Mama has been unable to handle even her day-to-day finances for at least four years! We all know that. What sort of an authority can she possibly be, now, on high finance?"

After Mama died, the guardian produced an envelope with the return address of the Mercantile Exchange, on which someone, writing in a hand that looked a little like Mama's, had written, "I don't want this account to be touched by anybody!"[155] I am not altogether certain that even is Mama's handwriting. In any case, the Mercantile asset was not an "account," in any normally understood meaning of this word. There was still a seat, which belonged to Mama, not the Merc. The guardian had already obtained proof of her ownership from the Merc.

The Merc stock had always been on deposit with Computershare, a transfer company on the East Coast. That was where the stock was, not at the Merc. Any lease payments came from the lessee, directly to the guardian, and the transfer company sent any dividends directly to the guardian. Only the annual 1099 tax form mentioned the name "New York Mercantile Exchange," and then only on a form that made clear that Computershare had issued it.

This would be exactly the same thing as owning AT & T stock held in a brokerage account. The annual tax form shows that the dividend money came originally from AT & T, but the 1099 has the broker's name on it and you cannot sell that stock unless you give instructions to the brokerage firm that actually has custody of those shares.

Although Mama had not yet been re-evaluated by a psychologist or psychiatrist, even the 2003 evaluations showed that she had no real understanding of her assets. How can someone who does not understand her assets be considered able to discuss the disposition of them? Even if this were truly Mama's handwriting, what was written on that envelope made clear that whoever wrote it had no understanding of what that asset was. It also seemed to me that the partners in Mama's commercial guardianship firm had little understanding of it themselves, and perhaps did not want to find out. How more than passing odd! Really?

At her March 1, 2017, deposition, the head of the guardianship firm was describing her work history, under David A. Garcia's questioning:

---

155 Decades 12580

Q: And what was your next job?
A: Then I was the reservation manager at La Posada here in Albuquerque.
Q: And what time period was that?
A: 1984 to 1986.
Q: And, what was your next job after that?
A: I was working as a broker.
Q: And who did you work for as a broker?
A: Corless & Winslow.
Q: That's one name—Corless & Winslow is the name of the firm?
A: Yes. So, Financial Investment Network Corporation is the broker-dealer.
Q: And what was your title there?
A: Financial planner.
Q: And did that title change over time?
A: No.
Q: How long did you work for Financial Network?
A: Nine years.
Q: So, approximately 1986 to—
A: 1995.[156]

Over the course of a year or so, as 30,000 shares at a time were released from restriction and could be sold, I started worrying that Mama had a seriously over-concentrated asset in the NYMEX because that holding was now worth more in the neighborhood of $12,000,000. I tried, repeatedly, to talk to the commercial guardian firm about its logical options—either hedge the stock, or sell it and invest the proceeds in something that would produce enough income to support Mama. Debbie and I met with two of the guardian firm's partners. To no purpose at all, as it turned out. They insisted that Mama had $400,000 in cash and had no need of generating any more for at least two years. To the best of my recollection, this conference took place late in the summer of 2006.

I had not heard a single hint, in 2006, that the head of the

---

156 Deposition of Nancy Oriola. Albuquerque, New Mexico. March 1, 2017, p. 20, ll.5-20.

guardianship firm had been a stockbroker in her earlier years. However, she was not anymore. Because she was not licensed, there was nowhere to go and no one to complain to that she was not acting responsibly with Mama's stock holdings. Other than to Judge Baca, that is.

Had I known, back then, what I learned later about the excuses guardians routinely give for losing the money of wards, and the veracity of the opinion leaders in that field, I would have expected what was going to happen. However, I now realize that I was hopelessly naïve. Not until three years after I sued the guardian for the millions of dollars in losses Mama had suffered while under their control, did we arrive at the deposition stage of the legal process.

Mama's commercial guardianship firm had hired Texas attorney Terry Hammond, a bespectacled witness with what appeared to me to be the personality of Rev. Jim Baker, to testify as their expert on guardianship.

He was famous. In a *New York Times* article published on April 20, 2004, he had been described as "a lawyer often appointed as a guardian for abused and neglected adults."[157] Mr. Hammond, who had been the Executive Director of the National Guardianship Association between 2006 and 2010, had been giving talks for years, all over the United States—describing what an accomplished guardian and conservator he was. Hammond lectured all over the country about the time he had spent as the California court-appointed conservator for Brian Wilson of the Beach Boys. He even posted a PowerPoint on this subject that he continued to update, the last time I am aware of, in 2018. Hammond took credit for getting both Wilson's life and his art on a solid footing again. At one point, Hammond had had his picture taken against the background of hundreds of old LP recordings in a bookcase. The posted slides show what appear to be three separate lawsuits on this subject.[158]

---

[157] "Texas Agency for Elderly Under Fire Over Neglect," by Ralph Blumenthal and Barbara Novovitch. *https://www.nytimes.com/2004/04/20/us/texas-agency-for-elderly-under-fire-over-neglect.html?searchResultPosition=1*
[158] The most recent updating of this lecture occurred on May 18, 2018. What purports to be a transcript of it is posted at: *https://prezi.com/mzddajfrejle/love-and-mercy-the-conservatorship-of-brian-wilson-broward-county-may-2018/* Slides 29-32 appear to document the existence of three separate suits.

During Hammond's daylong deposition, he made clear that the guardianship industry had some favored buzzwords and terms used only in that profession. They conflicted with most legal terms in the field, and were somewhat counter-intuitive. Hammond advocated what he referred to as "progressive guardianship." This, in turn, had a variety of meanings and consequences, but its definition was, at best, and perhaps even when defined by the person I assumed had invented the term, somewhat hazy.

One word the commercial guardians wanted scrapped was "ward." They rejected it on the basis that it was insulting, making those so described seem as if they are unable to make their own decisions. Which, from the point of view of most people, is the major reason why anyone ever tells a court that any adult needs guardianship anyway. To the best of my understanding, this is a last resort after a person has been making decisions harmful to himself or herself for a while, or if that person does not seem able to make decisions at all. Instead, they wanted the ward called a "protected person." In addition, any protections, Hammond insisted, should be minimal.[159]

The commercial guardians, Hammond said, also wanted the word "incompetent" eliminated. However, that is what the judges' orders say, when they give someone a guardian or conservator. Trying to examine what he is saying from a logical point of view, why would anyone want a guardian appointed unless another person is challenged in the area of decision-making?

Commercial guardians wanted people to believe that "incapacitated" is a more accurate description, because there are so many degrees of incapacity. This, of course, makes it almost impossible to say that the guardian should not have allowed the ward to do a given thing. Since people are often placed in mental institutions for doing things that are harmful to themselves, I found myself listening, incredulously, because his position seemed to contradict that entire mindset.

A final term he expounded on for quite a while, and that the commercial guardians wanted people to know about was "substituted judgement." This meant that guardians (or conservators)

---

159   Some states, including New Mexico, have already reworded their statutes, at the behest of the guardianship industry, to change "ward" to "protected person."

would act in ways they believed the ward would have acted, even if this might have resulted in death. In one example he cited, the ward had previously said, "no invasive medical procedures," leading her guardian to follow her wishes by allowing her to die when she contracted gangrene.

Hammond insisted that, according to the guardian's current code of ethics, any objective opinion of the logic of a guardian's actions was impossible because the guardian could always use the justification that "substituted judgement" had been governing either that guardian's action or that guardian's inaction. No benchmarks truly existed, according to Hammond.

In Mama's case, the guardian had chosen to make judgements they later claimed to have been those Mama herself would have made, had she been competent. The problem with this argument was that they had never met Mama at a time when she was fully competent. Everything they knew about her behavior or wishes dated from a period when her mental processes were already seriously enough impaired enough that all the experts who examined her agreed that she needed both a guardian and a conservator.

In all fairness to Mr. Hammond, the guardian's attorneys gave their experts documents to examine and those were the only ones each expert saw. Mr. Hammond does not seem to have examined Judge Baca's second order, the one issued in August 2004. He never mentioned that document during his daylong deposition. The commercial guardian had always been Mama's only conservator, but Judge Baca's second order gave the guardian "plenary" status *as a guardian*. In other words, only the guardianship terms had changed slightly, to allow me to withdraw from responsibility for end-of-life decision-making, and then only because the guardian was giving me no reliable health information about my mother.

Because the laws in Texas call a conservator a "guardian of the estate," it is unclear whether this particular "expert witness" understood what he was saying, in terms of New Mexico law, which this Texas attorney repeatedly stated that he had not studied prior to testifying.

The time of that 2004 order was when the guardianship firm and their attorney stipulated that Mama gift Arthur a lot of stock, thereby greatly diminishing Mama's stock holdings in High Desert and changing both her own and Arthur's percentage interest in High Desert. The judge had approved this change, as had Cristy, acting as my attorney, and I had at last agreed. To me, this suggested that, regardless of any promise the guardian later said had been given at the November 2003 hearing about keeping the "structure" of Mama's investments intact, it had already been radically changed.

At one point, the guardian told me that Mama had approved the gifting. I have never found any proof of this in the discovery documents, but if the gifting directly violated Judge Baca's original order, which everyone in authority claimed honored Mama's wishes, why did the judge approve the violation of her own order less than a year later? After this happened, the guardian went right back to adamantly stating the position that the structure of Mama's investments could not be changed. After that, from my perspective, it seemed as if the guardian's position was subject to radical change on any given day.

But, back to the Hammond performance. During his deposition, Mr. Hammond said that the guardian firm also wanted to allow wards to continue to make decisions, both personal and financial, even if a neutral party or the guardian him/herself knew those decisions would be harmful to the ward. In practice, I believe that I have seen guardians maneuver the ward into making decisions that are not in that person's best interest and might even be harmful.

Hammond lectured for the National Guardianship Association on May 17, 2013, just two weeks before I filed suit against Mama's commercial guardian, in my capacity as personal representative of Mama's estate. The blurb for his talk included the promise that Hammond would be explaining to an audience of guardians and conservators "how the guardianship/conservatorship process returned [Brian] Wilson to a healthy and productive lifestyle and musical career."[160] At the time of his deposition, The National Guardianship Association website listed Hammond as their Executive Director. Hammond claimed he had not acted in that capacity

---

160   NGA 2013 Colloquium on Guardianship, p. 1. *http://lcius.com/wp-content/uploads/2013/02/Colloquium-Brochure-2-15-13.pdf (now no longer posted)*

since 2010. Whatever the truth of that listing may be, he was and as of 2020 still served on their board of directors. (In 2021 the website was changed so that no names of directors or officers appear there.)

Hammond gave his deposition via a video hookup, on June 27, 2017. Patricia G. Williams, one of my lead attorney's co-counsels, was asking the questions. Hammond admitted to having "fewer than 20" wards over all the years he had been serving as guardian. He described the National Guardianship Association as "a voluntary association, really, of anyone with interest in guardianship. I don't believe that the NGA has a threshold [i.e., set of professional requirements] for membership…" As for the organization itself, "They have not had an executive director since 2010."

> Q: Are there licenses that you held in the past that you let lapse, Mr. Hammond?
> A: I don't believe so.
> Q: I noticed when I was doing research that it appeared you were licensed as a fiduciary in California. I am not exactly sure what that is.
> A: Oh, yes. Yes, I—in 2008, and this is a sort of a very personal issue. In 2008 my daughter—I have one child—developed a very severe eating disorder and we could not get treament for her, competent treatment anywhere in Texas. I had to go out with her to California, and this is when she was in La Joya [sic] and she went to Los Angeles. And during the time I was in California with her I did become licensed as a professional fiduciary in California. I never carried any cases as a California professional fiduciary and once that situation was largely resolved, I did not renew my California fiduciary license…Had to take an exam, a competency exam…I never actually served as a conservator in California…
> Q: …In New Mexico, Mr. Hammond, do you know what the duties of a professional guardian are?
> A: You know, I would have to look at the statutes to respond to that question with any Accuracy…
> Q: And that is not something that you did in order to prepare your opinions in this case, look at the statutes to determine—

A: I'm sorry...

Q: So if a ward gets up and says, "I would like to go to the casino, put all my money on black on the roulette wheel." Do they have the right to do that?

A: They can... What came to mind for me was a case I am familiar with generally in Utah where a court appointed a guardian for a federal judge and the guardianship was limited in a way—retired federal judge...the guardianship was in effect in the daytime but at nighttime the Judge could go out and play the casinos. That is the way the court structured the guardianship...

Q: Okay... How much have you charged to date?

A: ...I believe it is in the range of about $80,000.

Q: Have your expenses for the care of someone [while you have been that person's guardian] been comparable [to those charged by the commercial guardian and conservator in this case]...600,000 [sic] or so a year?...

A: I have not had a case where I served as guardian where I have had those kinds of expenses... [161]

Another little nugget from Hammond's deposition was that a ward could eat only graham crackers, if that was what the ward wanted to do. Might this diet be ultimately harmful?

When Hammond gave his deposition, the entire case was under a strict gag order. I wonder whether, if the case had not been sequestered at that point, he would have been as forthcoming about that court in Utah. Or about the real meaning of "substituted judgement." And of its sometimes-fatal consequences. Or about a guardian perhaps feeling entirely ethical in allowing a ward to eat a diet restricted to graham crackers.[162]

My questions: Why did Hammond avoid any mention of the case for which he is best known? Moreover, why did he deny having been the fiduciary (conservators are, after all, fiduciaries) in California for anyone other than his own daughter?

---

161 Skype and Telephonic Deposition of Terry Hammond, June 27, 2017, pp. 13ff (Mr. Hammond was in Texas; Ms. Williams was in Albuquerque.)
162 Ibid. p. 86, l. 1-p. 89, l. 10

Lies and More Lies

Hammond kept insisting that he would not judge the appropriateness of the spending levels of Mama's commercial guardian. That job, Hammond said, was going to be saved for one Shay Jacobson, a nondescript-looking blonde colleague of his on the board of the National Guardianship Association, who was the commercial guardian's second expert witness. While being deposed two days later, she described herself as "a registered nurse and expert witness" by occupation, even though she testified under oath that she had only been deposed three times and testified at trial once.[163] In any other cases, she said, her work had been limited to writing a report.

Unlike Mr. Hammond, whose work seemed to be on a boutique level by comparison, Ms. Jacobson's Illinois company claimed to be the guardian and/or conservator for 200 to 250 wards per year, although the titles they are given for performing this service vary from state to state. Her firm had offices both in Illinois and in Colorado. David A. Garcia deposed her on June 29, 2017, which would have been Mama's 106th birthday, had she survived.

Ms. Jacobson concentrated on presenting the concept of what she called a "person-centered" care plan at every possible opportunity. As David deposed her, it seemed there was no way to find any objective means by which to evaluate this guardianship practice:

> Q: In this case, though, you're using that—that term of art again, that person-centered care plan. In this case, it would be—a person-centered care plan is, say, on the one hand. What would be on the other hand? A person-centered care plan as opposed to what?
>
> A: ...They [the wards] aren't incompetent, but they have a level of incapacity that they need help and assistance and guidance from a guardian. So, what is important is a guardianship of—the concept of person-centered guardianship is that the guardian takes into account the wishes to the ability the client is able to express them, that they use substituted judg-

---

[163] Skype and Telephonic Deposition of Shay Jacobson, June 29, 2017, p. 5 (Mr. Garcia was in Albuquerque, New Mexico; Ms. Jacobson was in Chicago, Illinois.)

ment, which is honoring what the client would have wanted to do if she was so able to do that, as long as it's safe.[164]

Ms. Jacobson's description of the National Guardianship Association differed greatly from Hammond's:

> Q: ...Can you tell me what the National Guardianship Association is?
> A: The National Guardianship Association is a professional organization that sets standards and practices and sets ethical guidelines for individuals, companies, [and] family guardians to serve in their role as guardian of a ward.[165]

Ms. Jacobson admitted that she had no idea who had filled out a values statement for Mama. "When I look at this value [statement], I don't know if somebody has answered the question and written it for her [Mama] or not."[166] She did not find it at all hard to believe that perhaps several people had participated in writing it for Mama, since it contained more than one sort of handwriting.[167] Regardless of who filled it out, or whether the presence or absence of other individuals might have influenced Mama while it was being filled out, she said it should be accepted. "My job here was to evaluate the guardian's view of the client,"[168] she claimed. She said nothing about having asked any questions about Mama's ability to write at the time the Values History was supposed to have been written. Had she, she would have known there was no reason for someone else to fill out the form for Mama, back in 2003.

There was the matter of how many people it took to change the position of a patient:

> Q: Right. Does it take two people—two trained people to turn and reposition someone that weighs 105 pounds?

---

164 Ibid, pp. 76-77
165 Ibid, p. 131.
166 Ibid p. 53.
167 Billing records show that the guardianship company did not bill for services related to writing the values statement on that date—December 22, 2003. Rosenstiel(2)014691, Rosenstiel(2)014693
168 Skype and Telephonic Deposition of Shay Jacobson, June 29, 2017, pp.58-59

> A: So there's two parts to that question. Does it take two people? It can be done with one person…What I disagree with— if it could be done gently and as pain free as possible, it would take two…
>
> Q: …But wasn't the staffing reduced to two caregivers in the daytime and one at night?
>
> A: My understanding what happened with the care is that they had two caregivers, and then they reduced the professional caregiver at night. Is that the change of which you speak?
>
> Q: That's exactly the change.[169]

I was amazed. One of the former guardian's "expert witnesses" propounded allowing a ward to die of gangrene or lose every penny in the casino, while the other said the ward should be allowed to do only things that could not result in harm. And both of them claimed to be associated with or using the standards of the same organization. If there is no standard that can be used to judge a guardian's conduct, then in fact, the guardian can do whatever the guardian pleases to do. At least the situation sounded that way to me.

As for my own expert witness, Susan Wright, also a guardian and nurse, the diminutive brunette said that she believed only one aide was necessary. Greg MacKenzie, one of the commercial guardian firm's attorneys, took her deposition on May 11, 2017. That would have been the birthday of my paternal grandmother:

> Q: So on the last page [of your report, it says], "If Dr. Rosenstiel's condition was so tenuous as to require continuous eyes-on supervision and another attendant to complete household chores, she would have met the definition of being unsafe at home." So what is the consequence of that characterization? If a person is defined as being unsafe at home, then what?
>
> A: Typically the individual would be placed in a facility that could assure that person's safety until they improve to the point that they could be cared for safely at home.
>
> Q: Like a nursing home.

---

169 Ibid, pp. 111-112-According to Mama's health records, this had been happening, sporadically, long before the court had agreed to any changes.

A: Potentially, or a rehabilitation facility.

Q: So is it your opinion that in a nursing home, a person would get more supervision—or Dr. Rosenstiel could have had more supervision than she would have at home?

A: It's not just limited to supervision. It's the idea that it might take two people to safely and comfortably turn a person. It might be that there are equipment and supplies available in a facility that wouldn't typically be available in a home. I'm coming at this strictly from a home care perspective. I'm not trying to comment on the rules of guardianship here. In my experience in home care, safety is the priority. Physical and mental safety of the patient is always the priority. And if you cannot provide for that in a typical one-on-one environment, then that person typically is not considered to be safe to be at home.

Q: But [the commercial guardian] was able to provide for that with double coverage, isn't that right?

A: I don't think so. I don't think the double coverage was necessary.[170]

The guardianship firm seemed to think in the same illogical, non-intuitive, non-linear way as its experts, and also to charge at the level of Mr. Hammond.[171] But I had no idea of this between 2003 and 2013. For years, I had the feeling that I was Alice in Wonderland, watching things shrink and grow unpredictably, as they also appeared and disappeared, seemingly at will. Now, at last, I understood that everything had seemed totally arbitrary because it was totally arbitrary.

Is the National Guardianship Association a voluntary organization of people who do not necessarily have any credentials, but have an interest, however vague, in the subject, or is it a professional organization? Different levels of certification—Associate,

---

170   Susan Wright Deposition, Albuquerque, New Mexico. May 11, 2017, pp. 122-123

171   Between 2003 and 2012, when Mama died, the hourly charges rose from $75 per hour to $125 per hour, with the highest amount being charged for "post-death services." These extended to June 2013, more than a year after Mama passed away, even though I had already been appointed personal representative of Mama's estate during June 2012. Rosenstiel-22376

Guardian and National Master Guardian—always existed. Two witnesses, both of whom were under oath, and both of whom were then serving on its board, disagreed it seemed, on the basic nature of their main national organization.

Does substituted judgement mean a guardian is justified in allowing a ward to die of gangrene because the ward did not foresee a particular medical issue? That does not jibe with Shay Jacobson's statement that a guardian can only use substituted judgement if the client is not harmed. If allowing a ward to die when that can seemingly be avoided is not considered "inflicting harm," then what is "harm?" To a guardian or a conservator, what does the word "harm" mean? Did it "harm" Mama financially to lose millions of dollars, or is the guardian or conservator the final judge of whether it might have somehow been good for her to lose this money?

It was not until 2010 that I realized that most people whose loved ones were swallowed up by the guardianship system suffered from similar sets of conflicting standards and practices. I would suspect that having to deal with inconsistency on a daily basis could not have done Mama's mental state any good either.

Arthur and I had continued to send Mama cards, which, between November 2003 and March 2007 were almost our only contact with her. Mama did sometimes receive cards and flowers we sent. I saw a few documents giving evidence of this in the commercial guardians' discovery documents.

Toward the beginning of the guardianship (I am not sure whether it was Thanksgiving or Christmas in 2003), Mama managed to escape from whichever aide was on duty long enough to call me, "Thank you for the beautiful flowers..." she said, her wistful voice trailing off and sounding as if it also implied the questions: "But where are you? Why don't you come to see me anymore?" Hearing Mama's voice on the other end of the phone shocked me. The guardian had consistently told me that Mama did not want to have any contact with me. I was silent for a split second. I did not even have time to reply before the standard "click" let me know that someone—I assume not Mama, since she clearly wanted to talk to me—had hung up the phone. After that, I have no idea whether she received most of our cards and flowers.

Mama never called me again. Considering how carefully some of the minutest details of Mama's life are documented in the guardian's records, I was amazed to find no mention of this phone call when I reviewed all the aides' notes that the guardian produced during discovery. Perhaps that is because Mama's action does not support the commercial guardian's contention that Mama did not want to see or speak with me. Or maybe the aide who was with Mama that day was afraid of discipline or dismissal if the guardian discovered that she had allowed Mama to contact me.

Complaints abound in the 638 pages that constitute the file on Mama's original caregiver. Problems she said she had with other caregivers. Problems they reported having with her. In late January 2007, there is a set of handwritten notes in which one of the later aides is describing recent events to someone from the guardian's office (the notes are not signed). The original aide, the later aide said, was coming back to Mama's home on her time off, picking Mama up, shaking her and yelling at her.[172] These notes never made it into printed form, and they were not cited later. Considering what violent shaking does to vulnerable children, I wonder whether it similarly affects fragile elders, damaging their brains. I knew nothing of this until discovery.

On February 19, 2007, one of the guardian's minions, who was then Mama's case manager, emailed me to say that Mama's original aide had finally been fired "effective this morning." She continued, "We have arranged for a new, unlisted telephone number that will begin at 6 PM tomorrow. Should you want to call your mother before that time, please call and let us know first as we have turned the telephone ringers off in the home until the new number is in effect..."[173]

They had told Mama, they said, that her primary aide was on vacation. Or so this email says. This is typical of their thinking in such matters: "it goes without saying that you would not inform your mother of the termination. We will determine the appropriate time and manner in which to share the termination information with your mother. We will inform all other interested parties..." I never found out whether or when they did so inform Mama.

---

172 Decades 26416
173 Rosenstiel-03040

In examining documents produced by the commercial guardian during discovery, it turned out that apparently stones thrown by someone shattered the windows in Mama's garage shortly thereafter. At that point, the commercial guardian took the same sort of action that I had wanted to take back in 2003, when I had planned to fire the same aide. They hired a Brinks guard to protect Mama against what they called the "uninvited" return of her former aide and/or her former aide's family. When I saw the $11,000 charge for those first three weeks, it occurred to me that the $6,000 for one month at Montebello, at the time the most elegant of assisted-living facilities in Albuquerque, had been a good deal, and Mama would have been entirely out of the line of fire. The records show that the aide and one of her sons did attempt to get back into Mama's home after she was fired, but the Brinks guard prevented this intrusion. No charges were filed.[174]

There was likely even more to the original aide's firing than the file divulges. After Mama died, the guardian returned Mama's heritage collection of liquor to the closet under the wet bar. I know that closet was empty initially, because I opened it a couple of days after Mama passed away, at which time the shelves were empty. I recalled unpacking those bottles for Mama in 1997 and stocking the wet-bar's closet shelves with them. However, the second time I opened the closet after Mama died, I found the shelves filled with the ancient liquor bottles my parents had used mostly for display, on the wet-bar of their Manhasset house.

Many of the bottles were now partially empty. Because Mama only drank an occasional bit of Jaegermeister if she had an upset stomach, she would not have been responsible for opening and draining these bottles. With the bottles, under the wet bar, I also found a sheet of paper. It inventoried the bottles as of a date late in 2006, and also contained complaints about some of the aides drinking on the job. Mama's original aide wrote the inventory and one set of complaints. I recognized her distinctive handwriting. The others were in Mama's handwriting. The original aide, to the best of my knowledge, did not drink at all; she had long ago told me that, if I am recalling that ancient conversation correctly, she had been raised a Seventh Day Adventist.

---

174 Rosenstiel(2)17576

At the time that this inventory was created, I was not being allowed to see Mama at all. I do not think that the drinking stopped after that, because sometimes I would get out of my car in Mama's driveway, only to be greeted by a strong smell of beer. Because I had no proof, never saw any beer bottles, cans or kegs, and could not identify who might have created that situation, I could not think of an effective way to get anything done about this issue. There is documentation that at least once Mama's original aide complained about other aides drinking while on duty.

How were my offers to visit, over the years, extended through the commercial guardian or one of Mama's aides? Might their own negative attitudes have colored them, the negative attitudes toward me that they seemed to want to inculcate into Mama? There is a page of handwritten, unsigned, jumbled notes in the guardian's file that purportedly shows someone saying that there was no point in Mama seeing me because she had her money and I had mine. To me that simply is not something my mother was ever likely to have said. Unless, of course, someone had recently planted in her susceptible mind the thought that any visit from me would be about money, even if that had never been true before.

By February 26, 2007, Betty had written the guardian firm a multi-page, single-spaced letter. It purported to convey both Betty's and Aunt Louise's concerns for Mama's health and well-being, now that her long-time aide was gone. Betty advocated for Mama getting chiropractic care. Mama's father, Betty reminded them, had been one of the first chiropractors in New Jersey. They ignored her. Mama had not had any chiropractic treatments since Dad died. She had never attempted to find a chiropractor in Albuquerque. More to the point, on the subject of "substituted judgement," Betty wrote:

"We know that, in the past, when my aunt has been taken to the hospital, she has been asked to sign a 'do not resuscitate' order. She has always been against this. We also know that it is common practice to encourage the signing of a DNR. Such pressure is very intimidating to her, and grossly unfair, particularly when she is ill and weak..."[175]

---

[175] Decades 03248. In fact, the commercial guardian's own records noted that Mama wanted "Full Code!" as of July 6, 2004 (Decades 24311).

The commercial guardian suddenly said I could call Mama once a week. Meanwhile, when I called Mama, trying to re-establish contact, I was stuck trying to pretend everything was fine while Arthur lay dying in a room across the hall. It was the guardian's position that I must not upset Mama in any way. Arthur passed away on April 10, 2007.

Although the commercial guardian still said Mama must not be upset, they offered to take her to Arthur's funeral. I demurred. To me, this offer was far too much of a logical disconnect because Mama supposedly had no idea that he had died. We agreed that I would not tell her, either, unless and until she asked after him specifically, which she had not done since I had been speaking with her again.[176]

On April 25, the boyfriend of the fired aide called me. He said he had been trying to call Mama, but the phone had been disconnected. He asked whether Mama had died. I said, "Not as far as I know." The original number had been changed, of course. However, he would have had no reason to call Mama. His obvious motive was to glean some information for his girlfriend and her family. He would only have had a reason to call his girlfriend, the aide, at Mama's home, but it was clear that he knew about her firing. He told me that his girlfriend "used to work for your mother," so he was already aware that she had been fired.

Immediately, I contacted the guardian and my attorney. The guardian "had security in place for a time," my attorney told me, in a letter copied to the guardian. Apparently, everyone else knew a bit more about events than I did.[177]

Shortly after Arthur died, Debbie petitioned the guardianship firm, trying to get its permission for me to resume visitation with Mama, who by then was my only remaining close relative. It had not seemed to me that Mama was upset by talking to me on the phone, although I was, knowing that the current aides were always listening in. After a few such monitored calls, the guardian relented, allowing me to see Mama, starting in May, but only if her caseworker was also present.

---
176 Rosenstiel(2)15886-15887
177 Rosenstiel(2)015889

We finally fixed the time when I could see Mama again, for the first time in three years. I arrived at Mama's home at the appointed time, 11 AM on Saturday, May 19, 2007.[178] Mama's caseworker and the aide on duty were also there, so Mama and I had an audience of two.

Mama, thinner and paler than I had ever seen her, was sitting in a wheelchair, at her kitchen table, an oxygen cannula in her nose. I sat next to her, in a chair. "Topics of conversation were general, with some memory sharing, and seemed pleasant," the caseworker wrote in her report. She left for a while because Mama was out of the protein powder they had been using to keep their ward's nutritional needs met. As the caseworker wrote, "I did leave them alone for about 20 to 30 minutes while I ran to Wild Oats. When I returned everything was fine."[179]

As soon as her caseworker left to get the protein power at Wild Oats, Mama had leaned toward me until she was, at most, a foot from my right ear. "What about that book?" she whispered. "Can I do anything to help with that now?"

I turned fully in her direction, so the aide could not see my lips. "No, Mama," I whispered back, "The book's already been published."

I did not want to tell Mama that I believed her commercial guardian would be dead set against her cooperating with the author anyway. That would only have upset her, and I had been warned that, should Mama become upset for any reason, the commercial guardian would unilaterally terminate my visitation rights. A primary function of the aide sitting across the room from us, now that the caseworker was out running an errand, was clearly to look for signs of any agitation or upset.

Mama was whispering again, "What about Arthur? How is he?"

I turned to face her again, so that the aide could not see my lips, still concerned that maybe she could lip-read. "He died last month, Mama."

"I knew he wasn't well last time he was here." Her eyes started to fill with tears. So did mine.

Mama had known Arthur almost as long as I had; he had been

---

178 Rosenstiel(2)15895
179 Ibid

part of her professional as well as her personal life, because he had also been her literary agent. Out of the corner of my eye, I could see the aide staring at us. Any tears that fell would definitely have been reported to Mama's caseworker, who would surely be back any minute.

"You can't cry, Mama," I whispered to her. "If either one of us cries, they'll stop me from seeing you ever again. They told me so."

She leaned in, again, whispering, "You'll remember that I want to be cremated!"

"I'll remember, Mama."

"And that I never want to go back to New York?"

"Yes, Mama."

Somehow, both of us managed to control ourselves, but when I turned around again, I could see the aide looking intently at the back of my head.

Mama and I went on to discuss other things. Safe topics. By the time her caseworker returned, the major areas of serious concern had long been dealt with, so all was sunshine and unicorns again.

"The visit lasted two hours," Mama's caseworker wrote, "as every time I suggested that we leave, Dr. Rosenstiel said that we did not have to leave just yet. She also told Leonie she was welcome to return for a visit 'any time'...I felt the visit went well and hope that Leonie did also."[180]

Once Mama got over her initial upset after the 2003 hearing (and I am convinced that would have happened far sooner had the trouble-making aide not been present, and had meddling relatives not stoked the fires of anger), I have no doubt that any visit I might have had with Mama would have been similarly positive.

That same day, I wrote the caseworker, explaining that I had told Mama about Arthur in answer to her question.[181] I mentioned nothing about the book (an issue the guardian firm had considered a potentially upsetting matter for Mama), since I had received no instructions on that subject. And I saw no reason to discuss funeral arrangements, either, because I already knew that this was a job that fell to me, under the terms of Mama's will. Clearly, Mama had not been upset by the visit. On Wednesday, I received another email

---

180 Ibid
181 Rosenstiel(2)15898-15899

from the caseworker, saying she had consulted with the guardian and "she agreed with your visiting without [the guardian's] staff present."[182]

How does the insistence that Mama never be allowed to become upset—even when tears might have been a normal, human reaction to loss—jibe with the guardian's prior offer to allow Mama to attend Arthur's funeral a month earlier? I cannot imagine. Would they have faulted me if Mama had returned home, crying, from Arthur's funeral? Might that fact, alone, have led to me being banished again?

There is no way to know whether Mama spontaneously remembered the first two very emotionally fraught subjects she raised the first time I saw her in 2007. She had not mentioned either of them in our prior phone conversations. Did seeing me again remind her of these "loose end" situations? In that case, her mental condition, at least in the emotional sphere, would have truly been a whole lot better, at least for occasional, short periods of time, than the guardian had told me. However, it also might have been that, because I then was "scheduled" for these visits, rather than being able to see Mama at will, someone might have prompted Mama, just before I arrived, to be sure to ask these questions. Might this have been done in the hopes of getting us both upset so that I could be banished from her Mama's life again?[183] Given what I later learned about the commercial guardianship field, this is a distinct possibility.

Later, I was beyond astonished to find the guardian reporting to the court that Mama could no longer tell the difference between

---

182 Rosenstiel(2)015901

183 I would later learn that commercial guardians had told family members of other wards that their charge's mental condition had deteriorated to the extent that their loved one did not remember them anymore. There are documents to that effect in the guardian's file for Mama. In another case I discovered later, a wife was told that her husband would no longer recognize her, so there was no point in her visiting him. She insisted on seeing him in the nursing home to which the guardian had taken him, effectively separating the couple. When he saw her, several family members who had been there reported to me that he said, "There's my beautiful wife! She's come to take me home!" Unfortunately, the ward's wife, who was beyond delighted to know that her husband had recognized her, had no legal authority to sign him out of the place; he remained institutionalized until he died because that is what the commercial guardian wanted. Of course, recognizing a relative is not the same thing as being able to understand finance.

me and any of her aides. At one point, Mama had referred to me as her sister. The guardian believed this was proof Mama did not know me. Having been with Mama, many years before, watching the movie *Chinatown*, and given our mutual history of abuse at the hands of her father, I took that statement as an acknowledgement from Mama that she remembered the abuse that had happened, so long ago.

The other issue that might sometimes truly have prevented Mama from knowing who was with her had several parts. Mama had been diagnosed with cataracts back in 2001. Her distance vision was bad enough, then, even with distance glasses, to induce the state to deny Mama the right to renew her license. Looking at Mama's medical interventions shown in the guardian's documents produced during discovery, I learned that these cataracts had never been treated; they had not yet even gotten her stronger reading glasses. I know that, in 2010, Mama could not see, when attempting to read, type smaller than 40 points (a little more than half an inch) high, even with her reading glasses. I had taken over my laptop to show her the proofs of Arthur's co-authored and about-to-be-reissued book. I had to keep increasing the type size of the text until we reached that huge headline size. By then, there were so few words per line that reading it strained Mama's eyes; I ended up reading the proofs to Mama.

Mama's problems with distance vision would have been similar, although I did not see that the guardian ever got Mama distance glasses. If Mama had no distance glasses, and was looking at someone standing, perhaps 15 feet away, I am almost certain that she would have been unable to make out the person's facial features. Another point of confusion was that Mama's aides almost never wore nametags. Of course, even if they had, Mama would not have been able to read them because the size of the type was too small. Then, too, some of the aides were similar to me in size and shape.

Having recently been taking graduate courses in public health, I had become increasingly aware of safety concerns. More so, perhaps, than the average person. One of the first course assignments I had had consisted of evaluating safety hazards for various sorts of buildings and room configurations. There were no ramps at any of Mama's doors, which meant that Mama, now that she needed a wheelchair, had no safe means of escape in the event of an emergency.

After realizing this, I raised the issue repeatedly with the commercial guardian. First, they said Mama did not need ramps. Then they said they had already installed them. However, I was visiting Mama daily at that point. Periodically, I checked her doors and found no sign of a ramp anywhere. Finally, I made the ramps an issue in a legal complaint that I filed. Eventually, the court ordered the guardian to install them, and the guardian agreed to do so, but that did not actually happen until many months later. In total, it took over a year from the time I first requested that three ramps be installed until there was one single ramp in place. The guardian never installed the other two relatively inexpensive ramps. Several years later they did install a second ramp made of concrete. Along with the other modifications they insisted on making to Mama's backyard at the same time, the second ramp ended up costing over $20,000.

During the spring of 2008, one day I was invited to accompany Mama to a podiatrist appointment. I arrived in time to see Mama get there, in a hired handicapped van that could accommodate her wheelchair. With her was a functionary from the guardianship firm. Mama sat in the waiting room, looking over a magazine the firm's representative had given her. It featured landscaping photos. "What do you like?" the functionary asked Mama.

"This one!" Mama said, pointing to a simple, almost austere photo.

"Oh, no! You don't want *that* one. It's too empty! It's *ugly*! What you really want is *this* one!" The functionary pointed to another photo, showing a landscape crowded with plants.

This little incident would not have much importance, except that the guardian's representative later told me that "Mama" had personally chosen the new landscaping for her front yard, which turned out to be a replica of the one pushed on her. I realized this after I saw it in place. The guardianship firm also reported to the court that it cost $30,000 to re-landscape Mama's front yard in this fashion, although the property so redone was only approximately

1/8 of an acre. Later, the commercial guardian claimed that bulldozing the backyard reflecting pool (which had somehow been considered part of this work) had eaten up $20,000 of this cost.[184]

"Why did you bulldoze the reflecting pool?" I asked.

"It wasn't being maintained," a representative of the commercial guardian answered, as if this lack of upkeep had somehow been the fault of the pool. Who else should have been responsible for its maintenance? Demolishing a feature like this lowers both the aesthetic value of the landscaping and the value of the property.

Whatever the commercial guardianship firm thought about Mama's deteriorated mental state, with me she still exhibited flashes of clarity, at least in the emotional and relationship sphere, although I certainly would not have followed her financial advice. Well, I would not have done that even when she was not under guardianship.

Although the guardian had explicitly authorized me to see Mama without anyone else present, I would find the aide on duty refusing to leave us. I later discovered that they had been issued strict instructions to monitor even my phone calls.[185] The guardian would later deny that it had ever instructed the aides to require advance notice of my visits, but that is definitely not what the guardian's discovery documents say.[186] To my mind, these seemed to be more manipulations, an attempt by the commercial guardian to make the aides the bad guys (or bad gals) so that the guardian could be made to seem to be cooperating and helping. Having the aides staring at us during our visits between mid-2007 and early 2008 was beyond intimidating, but we did manage to exchange some important and useful information by sitting close to each other and whispering, which always irritated the aide on duty mightily.

Almost immediately after I started seeing Mama again, the guardian began demanding that I sell Mama's share of High Desert

---

184 Decades 03648 claims $45,179.72 for "landscaping" during the 2008 annual reporting period. Of this amount, I was told, when I asked, about the division of expenses described above. Rosenstiel(2)02693 is the estimate, asking for $40,195.69
185 Decades 24790
186 Decades 24787

because they insisted that their ward needed cash. "What do you mean?" I asked. "A few months ago, you told me that Mama had enough cash to last for two years." I absolutely refused to comply. The guardian was not pleased. If there had been any way they could have gotten into that account, I suspect that they would have liquidated it themselves, regardless of the taxes Mama would have had to pay.

Judging from what the aides were actually doing, the commercial guardian had instructed them to listen intently to my conversations with Mama in the hopes of hearing me say something I was not supposed to say (and if they could invent something I might have said that the guardian would not like, that would be fine, too). That would have given the commercial guardian an excuse to bar me from visiting Mama again.[187] To say that my visits with Mama were tense, for me, because of the constant hostile surveillance, is the understatement of our century. Whatever the aides might have been told about me, I already suspected that it had not been good. One day, one of the aides, a youngish, petite brunette who seemed to have a special rapport with Mama, took me aside as I was leaving. "You're the first relative I've ever seen who got back the right to visit. I worked at one house where the son wasn't even allowed to travel in the same car with his mother. If they allowed him to go out for lunch with her, she and her aide traveled in one car, and he had to follow in another."

"That's horrible!"

She said the guardian had told her (and the other aides) what

---

187 Years of contact with other family members of the wards of commercial guardians have shown me that this sort of tactic is part of what I would regard as *The Commercial Guardian's Playbook*. One daughter of another ward was standing there when the guardian accused her (falsely) of stealing $1,000,000 from her mother, who was also standing there, leading her mother, the ward, to burst into tears. I was told that this accusation was placed in the court record, but there is no way to prove it, because the case was sequestered. The son of another ward told me he had discovered, by looking at court papers, that he had been barred from being his mother's guardian because a court visitor had (again falsely) accused him of saying that he planned to put her into a nursing home. Fairly soon after the hearing, the court-appointed guardian did place her in a nursing home. Why do courts insist that their appointed "professionals" have no conflicts of interest? Is it a conflict of interest (because they are going to get an on-going income stream), spite, lust for power, or simply a hatred for families, in general, that motivates such people?

a terrible person I was, and furthermore, that I had threatened to kill my mother.[188]

"I don't understand."

"Seeing you together, I don't believe it anymore. I just wanted you to know. They're probably going to fire me for talking to you, if anyone finds out. When I finish with this case, I'll never work with these people again!"

"The other aides don't talk to me. I'm not going to say anything that could hurt you. Thanks for the vote of confidence."

"If you're going to sue them, I can only testify if you subpoena me because I'm still working in this field." At that point, I had not yet decided to sue the guardian.

When that aide was fired in 2008, after Mama suffered a hip fracture, I lost my only ally at Mama's house, but not before she told me that the aide on duty when Mama broke her hip had been bragging to the other aides that she had dropped Mama, but that she knew that she was going to waltz away without consequences. Apparently, she did.

All the aides back then kept daily handwritten notes. When I got copies of the aides' notes, first during a preliminary audit in 2010 to 2011 and then during discovery, the aide's notes for that day had been suppressed and a word-processed statement from the home health agency substituted. The agency's version of the story was that Mama had gotten out of bed by herself and fallen while the aide was out of the room. Having broken her hip, Mama did not even cry out, so the aide did not know anything had happened until she happened to walk into the room, sometime later. However, Dr. Kincaid, who admitted Mama to Lovelace Westside Hospital, wrote into the hospital record, "The patient today was being assisted in transfer when she fell."[189]

When I visited Mama at her home, the hatred of all but the one aide was palpable.

Soon, I realized that Mama had only the companionship of the aides, except for once or twice per month, when someone from

---

188 Estate Response to the First Set of Interrogatories, p. 18-19.
189 Rosenstiel(2)019292-01293

the guardian's office visited for a while. I asked her whether she wanted more people around. "Yes! You know how I like people. I want people to come around and ask me things. They always used to do that."

When I brought this issue up to the commercial guardian, I got a verbal dismissal. "She has plenty of companionship! She has the aides. And she also has *our* company."

A follow-up request to the commercial guardian to allow me to take people to see Mama at first produced only the demand that, if I planned to take anyone to see Mama, that person had to be at least as old as Mama herself.

"That's ridiculous!" I countered. "How many people are there all together in Albuquerque who are as old as Mama? And how many of them can travel easily? We all know that Mama herself can't, not anymore. But I can take over some of my friends to see her."

At first, they said they would take some of their other wards to visit Mama. It occurred to me that doing this would absolutely violate the iron-clad privacy restrictions the courts seem to advocate. They claimed that they could not find a service they could pay to come and read to Mama either. We had several go-arounds on this subject. Eventually they relented. But that did not happen without the intervention of my attorney. I had to sue the commercial guardian first and get a court order in December 2007 that explicitly permitted this.

Before I saw Mama again, the commercial guardian had told me that I would find Mama looking the same as the last time I saw her. It did not seem that way to me. In 2004, Mama had been walking on her own and breathing on her own. When I visited Mama in 2007, it was the first time I had seen her in a wheelchair and on constant oxygen. Walking had become too painful. Mama's caseworker emailed me on May 23 to say that the visiting nurse was going to request physical therapy for Mama's legs,[190] but did not tell me whether or when the doctor had granted that request.

On May 24, I replied to the caseworker, concerned that Mama

---

190 Rosenstiel(2)015903

was not eating very much. While I was there, she had had only some of a protein shake, a tablespoonful of cereal and a quarter of a slice of toast. As I wrote in my email to the caseworker, if this was Mama's new "normal," then her condition had declined quite a bit since I had last seen her. She was too weak to lift a teacup to her lips, instead spilling the tea but not reacting at all to the spill. I got towels and cleaned up the lukewarm tea. Mama's cannula did not fit and kept falling out of her nose. Her mind was wandering badly. Even given Mama's dementia diagnosis, her new problems might have been partially due to the twin facts that the cannula was out of her nose as much as it was in and that she had had so little of what I would think of as mental stimulation for years.[191] At that point, the matter of whether I would be allowed to see Mama alone, and if so, when, had not yet been decided.

The caseworker warned me that my relatives would be in town on June 6-8, staying at a hotel and seeing Mama for part of each day. Although they were supposed to leave on the eighth, they were still in town and showed no signs of leaving. I had called on the twelfth, to see whether I could visit Mama and, as I reported to my attorney, who forwarded my email to the guardian:

"Mother was, according to her aide, 'completely exhausted' and wanted to lie down but my aunt and cousin had told her they were coming back again this afternoon, and to be ready, so she was attempting to sit up and wait for them anyway...It is now 2:15 PM. By 5 PM, Mother will be too tired to see anyone anyway.

"From what the aide said to me, Mother wishes my aunt and cousin would not make her spend so much time with them. The aide even told me that Mother wishes that they were not coming back...[however] she apparently feels obligated to comply with their demands. This situation doesn't surprise me because their presence always exhausted Mother...[Does the guardian] know whether, when they are visiting Mother, whether Mother really wants to see them as much and as intensively as they apparently want to see her?"[192]

As for Mama's formerly beautiful home, it had undergone a very bad interior paint job, which I later discovered had been executed

---
191 Rosenstiel(2)014904-(2)014905
192 Rosenstiel(2)015907-(2)015908

by members of the family of Mama's former aide. I wrote Mama's caseworker that it was "really bad in the rooms I saw (breakfast room and den). There, paint from the baseboard is smeared on the walls above it. I wonder whether the rest of the house is similarly treated. I understand that you are putting the yard-work out for bids; after the recent rains, we are sure to see even more weeds than those currently there, so I hope you find someone soon."[193]

The guardian delayed in getting a new landscaper, inducing a neighbor to write a hate-filled, handwritten note to the homeowner. This piece of real estate was, the complainant wrote, a disgrace to the neighborhood and was going to bring home prices down for everyone. When the guardian produced this document during discovery, it was photocopied in such a way that the signature could not be seen. I was told that there had been more than one complaint to the city of Albuquerque about the property being an eyesore. Later, I met someone who had lived in the neighborhood during that time. She told me that the neighbors were concerned that Mama's home and grounds were in such a state they were afraid that the place had become a drug house.

I happened to arrive at Mama's home one day when the physical therapist was trying to get Mama to walk. Mama was screaming in pain and begging the woman to stop as she put Mama into a contraption that looked like a leash with a harness and tried to get her to walk. Mama's aide was sitting calmly in a corner, acting as if what was happening was an everyday occurrence. Maybe so. The harness was a larger version of what some parents use for their toddlers. By then, Mama seemed to have had no synovial fluid left. Her knees were bone-on-bone. Knowing what a stoic Mama had been all my life, I realized that, to provoke such an extreme reaction, the pain must have been intolerable for her.

Mama's pleas seemed to leave the therapist unmoved, judging from her impassive expression. Other than, "Hello! I'm Annette's daughter." I said not a word to this visiting professional. However, the look on my face turned out to have been enough to make her quit. The documents the guardian produced during discovery

---

193 Rosenstiel(2)015903-015904

show that she tendered her resignation after that encounter; she simply was not going to risk me being there again. That is what her resignation document says.[194] I did not know at the time why I only saw her on that one occasion until I reviewed the documents during discovery. I am going to venture a guess that her absence saved Mama some serious pain.

The guardian firm made a great deal out of my refusal to sell Mama's stake in High Desert which, because they had transferred so much stock out of Mama's account and into Arthur's was only worth about $600,000. At the rate they were spending then, even if I had liquidated all of her stock, after taxes, this would have netted them about $350,000 to $400,000, enough to last "Mama" for only a period of months.

However, on May 24, 2007, almost to the day when I was allowed to see Mama again, 30,000 shares, constituting the first tranche of NYMEX stock, were released from restriction. The fair market value of those shares on that date was $3,690,450 ($123.015 per share). Even after she paid the taxes on her gains, and even if those taxes were assessed at the highest possible rates, Mama would have ended up with almost $1.5 million. Selling the whole NYMEX investment of course would have yielded much more.

Reminding the guardianship firm's partners of this brought only glares in return. During the summer of 2007 institutions offered some of the highest CD interest rates in recent history, over 5 percent. Investing in a better-paying asset might have netted Mama even more, perhaps enough to keep her very comfortable for the rest of her life, without eating up her principal. I began to get an odd feeling that the guardian was trying to ensure that Mama's assets evaporated.[195]

---

[194] Decades 32951. The resignation is dated July 17, 2008.
[195] On reflection, some of these developments seem to illustrate the mindless application of the theory of financial planning that I had first encountered in 1995. You had to take at least 4 percent of the total assets out of an estate annually, after retiring. If you lived longer than the actuarial tables said you should, then you had to take much more out, to make sure you ended up with nothing by some date of the conservator's choosing.

CHAPTER III

Money Takes Wing and Truth Flies out the Window

Given the extreme secrecy with which guardianship cases have been handled in New Mexico, a couple of documents that surfaced during discovery shocked me. For Mama's ninety-fifth birthday, her commercial guardian seems to have been discussing having a big party and inviting the press (although, apparently, not me, since no one ever contacted me about this). Some years later, they arranged for one of their wards to have an interview with the press so that he could express his appreciation about how much better his treatment was under them than under his previous guardian (who is now in jail). They sometimes ignored their own instructions to others to observe strict secrecy to avoid exposing wards to press coverage when they thought the results might be favorable to their interests.[196] I am relieved that they did not use Mama that way.

Mama had been taken to several different primary care physicians between 2003 and mid-2008. By May 2007, Mama's aide wrote in her notes, "Dr. Rosensteil's [sic] knees are buckling when she tries to transfer and walk. Please be very vigilant with transfers."[197] On September 17, 2007, Ronald Sauter, MD, the practitioner she had been seeing the longest, had prescribed that the guardian use a device called "a Hoyer lift," which would transfer

---
196 Heild, Colleen, "Guardian Hearing Delayed after Reporters Try to Attend," Albuquerque *Journal*, October 2, 2017, pp. 1-2.
197 Decades 24962. Emphasis is the aide's. Rosenstiel(2)019900-(2)019901.

Mama to a wheelchair mechanically, in a sort of sling contraption, to prevent her from placing too much weight on her painful knees. Why? "Transfers are more difficult." He wrote, "She has had 2 episodes where she has fallen while being transferred."[198] Neither of these falls is mentioned in the discovery documents that the guardianship firm provided.

Mama, her guardian told me, did not want to use the Hoyer lift. Mama herself never said this to me. I am assuming that, using "substituted judgement," they decided that she had a right to reject using it, even though this greatly increased her danger of falling.

They did not keep a Hoyer lift on her premises for a period of time to try to accustom her to it gradually, either. After that, every time Mama got out of bed, with an aide helping her, there was a greater danger that she might start, when she felt a sharp pain in her knees, or collapse from the pain. In either case, Mama might fall. When I asked the commercial guardian about this hazard, the answers always translated into the following: "Old people always fall." Certainly, this happens frequently, but is there any reason to create a situation where it is more likely to happen?

It now seems as if attempts to upset me neatly coincided with financial events in Mama's life or with other events (sometimes as part of a legal maneuver) the commercial guardian had engineered or tried to engineer. However, the patterns only showed after the fact, during discovery, when many of the relevant documents became accessible.[199] These confluences of events happened during the guardianship even when I had no idea of what the commercial guardian was trying to do at the time. Occasionally, I tried to find patterns so that I could discover some underlying logic to events, but these were uninformed, at best, without access to the documentation. Mama herself had to have been unaware of these too, at least on an unconscious level.

The commercial conservator seems to have stopped giving Mama any financial information when her original aide was fired, because I did not find any of those annual printouts in Mama's

---

198 Rosenstiel(2)019900-019901
199 Often, I wonder about those family members who never had the benefit of discovery. How do they make any sense of their lives during those chaotic years during which a loved one is under commercial guardianship or conservatorship?

dresser for the years after 2006. They would later say that Mama became totally incompetent only in 2008, when they had the same psychologist who had examined her before the first hearing re-examine her. Based on the evidence I saw, I still believe that she had lost what financial acumen she had long before the first hearing. Interesting, because the conservator kept appealing to what the firm described as *Mama's instructions to them* on money and investments when trying to justify making decisions that I believe seriously harmed her, financially.

Despite all the hours they billed Mama for their work, as far as I could see, they acted as if they had no idea what to do with the Mercantile Exchange asset. They filed their annual report almost on time, on December 22, 2006. (It had been due on December 3.) Then, according to the case docket published on the internet,[200] in January 2007, Mama's guardian wrote to Judge Baca, asking to amend that report. The company filed the first amended report on February 13, 2007, just as the guardian was in the final stages of planning to fire Mama's original caregiver. Of course, because the reporting period had already ended, they made no mention of this pending firing. Then, they filed a second amended report (it seems without asking prior permission from the judge this time) on June 21, 2007.

The commercial guardian fired Mama's original aide in mid-February but this firing was not mentioned in any of those reports, even the one filed in June 2007, again because the reporting period had ended in November 2006. Social and medical data did not change from report to report. However, the numbers in the report changed radically from one version of the report to the next. The first report claimed Mama had an estate of $20,499,511.29.[201] The one in February said $16,300,000.00, with an asterisk and a footnote, explaining that the conservator was not sure what Mama's estate was worth because the value kept changing.[202] That is true of any particularly volatile, concentrated

---

200 Back then, the docket was kept secret. I did not find out they had asked for permission until May 2017, when I was able to look this up in the then-newly-released dockets on the internet.
201 Guardian and Conservator Report, p. 9 (TOC file)
202 Amended Guardian and Conservator Report, p. 7 (TOC file)

stock position, so the fact that the guardian seemed surprised by the situation suggested to me that whoever wrote the report knew nothing about that asset. Strangely, it later turned out that the partner who signed that report was a former stockbroker. The second amended report, filed on June 21, stated a total estate value of $11,499,511.29.[203] From claiming in the December 2006 report that Mama had 180,000 shares of NYMEX stock, the firm changed the second amended report to read that Mama had 90,000 shares.

Watching the commercial guardian change the figures more than once, in rapid succession, and by such astonishing amounts, I saw any confidence I might once have had in that commercial entity's ability to manage Mama's finances evaporate. I am glad that Mama herself did not have to see this; I think she would have been hysterical watching all that money first appear, then disappear, over the span of only a few months. There is no evidence that the guardianship firm ever showed Mama any of its annual reports to the court. For most of the rest of 2007, I tried to remain in contact with the guardian about the NYMEX asset, attempting, in vain, to force myself to trust anything they said.

At the time, I was not following the day-to-day fluctuations in the value in Mama's NYMEX holding; I had long ago realized that to do so would lead to more intense frustration than I already felt. However, elapsed time affected its value. With many IPOs, after the initial rise in price, there is often a dip, sometimes a steep one.

If Mama's financial memory had been functioning at all, she would have remembered at least some of Dad's many warnings against continuing to hold an unprotected, over-concentrated asset. Or my own actions in 1999, when I liquidated a highly concentrated position in my own Intel stock by selling two-thirds of the shares and diversifying the profits by investing in other securities before the tech bubble finally burst.

Although the financial confusion created annoyance, Mama's safety came first. I had been agitating for the guardian to install handicapped ramps from the first time I realized that Mama needed a wheelchair. Interesting that, even though no ramp had

---
203 Second Amended Guardian and Conservator Report, p. 9

been installed, neither the guardian ad litem nor the psychologist appointed by the court to examine Mama seemed to care that she was using a wheelchair but there were no handicapped ramps at any of her doors. I would have thought that one of the first things that a GAL, charged with protecting someone, would notice was whether the place where the person she was charged with protecting was staying was safe for the ward to exit in the event of an emergency.

Meanwhile, I assume on orders from the commercial guardian (if only because this memo is conserved in their files on Mama's case), I got little information. The home aide service instructed its aides, "When talking with family members of Dr. Rosenstiel, including her daughter Leonie, we have been asked to keep information...to a minimum."[204]

A little professional jargon, a few friendly operatives cooperating, and the guardianship firm would be able to create a situation congenial to them. "We'll all work together, and we'll teach this dumb family member her place." That was the gist of the message I got every time I tried to advocate for Mama.

One day, during that emotionally supercharged summer of 2007, Mama and I were sitting at the kitchen table when Mama leaned close to my ear and whispered, "I want you to take care of me!"

I whispered back, into her ear, "I can't, Mama! You have a legal guardian now."

"I want you to take over," Mama whispered, repeating, "I want you to take care of me."

"I'll try," I whispered back.

The only way to accomplish this would be to go back to court to petition the judge to transfer the current guardian's and conservator's authority to me. Suing would make the already-strained relations between Mama's commercial guardian and me far worse. Could I withstand the emotional fallout, so relatively soon after Arthur's death? I still felt emotionally fragile and was not at all certain that I could.

After agonizing over this question, I reminded myself that Mama was my last remaining close relative. If this was what

---

204 Decades 24787

Mama said she wanted me to do, then I decided that at least I had to try. Debbie filed the required papers. Until I met members of other families who had not tried to get the guardianship returned to family members, I thought that everything that happened later resulted from my attempt to do so. For almost three years, I blamed myself, unnecessarily as it turned out, for having aggravated Mama's commercial guardian.

If a family member has the guardianship, I later learned, sometimes a commercial guardian wants to come in and take over, and, if there is already a commercial guardian serving, the only guardian the courts seem to want to substitute for one commercial guardian is another commercial guardian, unless the ward has become destitute. The courts seemed especially partial to appointing commercial guardians for wards who had money. Back in 2007, I thought this applied only to people with money, by which I mean assets in excess of $500,000.

But I was wrong about that. By 2017, Paul Donisthorpe and Susan Harris were separately indicted in state and federal court in Albuquerque, for fraud in the millions of dollars. Along with her partner from the guardianship firm, Harris was eventually headed to jail. So was Donisthorpe, for defrauding the accounts of his many conservatees and those for whom he served as trustee. Most people were shocked to realize that even the professional guardianship/conservatorship of people who are relatively poor is also big business. I wonder whether it is a total accident that the recently-retired chief executive officer of the Second District Court of Bernalillo County started a guardianship and conservatorship firm after he retired.[205] In 2017, I discovered that Lorraine Mendiola, one parent who wanted to take over the guardianship of her son (a son who suffers from mental illness) was not even given notice so that she could arrange to attend the hearing being held for that purpose after his original commercial guardian had been criminally indicted, and later pleaded guilty.[206]

---

205   *https://veritas-athena.com/about/our-staff/*; Scott Sandlin, "Court executive officer says goodbye," *Albuquerque Journal*, February 20, 2015, p. 16; and "Business Outlook," *Albuquerque Journal*, May 28, 2018, p. 16.
206   "Concerning New Mexico," KANW, January 20, 2020. She also said, on that program, that she was violating a gag order to speak about her son's case, which was then still on going.

What I could not predict was that Mama would be unable to follow up on what she had to do, in order to, as I thought at the time, make it possible for me to take over her care. She found herself unable to complain about the current commercial guardian to the guardian ad litem appointed by the court or to the psychologist appointed by the court, or to request specifically from them that the court change her guardian.

The GAL and psychologist seem to have seen her, together, at a time when I was not present. (It is unclear to me whether a representative from the commercial guardian's office accompanied them, but one of the aides they employed would have been in Mama's home at that time.) Then they gave the impression that I had not wanted to attend, necessitating a complaint from me, and a request that they return to Mama's home to talk to me, which they did with Mama present. They seemed annoyed that I had bothered them. At another time, Mama's guardian sent her to a different psychologist. They allowed me to sit in the room with Mama and a representative of the guardian's office, but asked me to leave after a few moments, so I have no idea what went on after I left. I noticed that, while I was there, the guardian seemed to do the question answering for Mama.

Afterward, when I was able to talk to Mama privately, I asked her about why she had not said anything to them.

"I can't take over, the way you asked me to."

"Why?"

"Remember those two people who came to talk to you from the court?"

"Yes."

"You didn't tell them that you wanted me to take over as guardian."

"I was afraid. I was scared of what they'd do to me."

"I understand, Mama."

I did. By then, I was terrified of the commercial guardianship firm myself. And of anyone associated with them. I considered them all quintessential bullies. Beyond that, they were bullies who had the court's ear and attention and respect. They seemed to act with the court's blessing. Quite the contrary, the court appeared to consider me an inconvenience, to be neutralized. Not a good situation. Before one of the hearings, Ruth Pregenzer approached Debbie and me, as we were about to sit down at "our" table in the hearing room. "You put her on the stand, and I'll destroy her!" she snarled. At that hearing, there had been no plans for me to testify. After that bit of psychological warfare, I wondered whether I would have been able to. We were clearly playing chess with a grand master in the Russian tradition.

Theoretically, even though I was a bit shaky, when the hearing ended, I was able to walk out of that courtroom and care for myself. How much more frightening would it have been, I wondered, to be like Mama, entirely dependent on the commercial guardianship firm and their hirelings, waiting for a court hearing under their "protection," perhaps for a month or more, after speaking out against them, or even simply in favor of wanting me to care for her instead?

After Mama found herself unable to speak out, she started spending more time in bed. For the first couple of weeks after that, when I arrived to visit Mama, the TV was on, and was playing Protestant evangelists. Consistently. At this point, based on the "information" in their records that Mama and I were both Orthodox Jews, I assume that the aides had been told to do this to anger me. (I would love to have seen the emails that circulated on their private server during this period. But, of course, I never did.) Why, if they believed that Mama was an Orthodox Jew, would they not think hearing a Protestant preacher all the time would anger her? But, of course, it did not. Did they think they were punishing her, or me? Of course, this tactic did not work because Mama was definitely not an Orthodox Jew. She generally did not make that assertion anymore, unless she felt required to, for some reason.

The same sort of attempt to make me furious came from one of Mama's aides. She could sometimes come across as very sweet, but I soon realized it was a false sweetness. One day, we had the following exchange:

"I made your Mama the most delicious seafood paella for dinner last night!"

"Did she like it?"

"She loved it."

"I'm glad she liked her dinner."

The aide looked disappointed. I am assuming, only now, that she had been tasked with making me angry that day. Which I certainly would have been, if I had been an Orthodox Jew. Orthodox Jews are not supposed to eat shellfish at all. Perhaps all of the aides were tasked with trying to anger me, whenever possible, so that the commercial guardian could eventually find a way to stop me from seeing Mama. Probably, the guardian's secret server could have enlightened me on this point, but I never had access to those communications. And then there was Betty's letter, complaining that Mama had eaten seafood and warning the guardian not to let that happen again.

Indeed, during discovery, grocery receipts attested to Mama's aides buying pork and seafood.[207] Given the guardian's "inconsistent" oversight practices, where they could both claim that Mama would have wanted to feed her aides and their families as well, and then fire an aide for buying food for herself, I cannot know how much of that was likely bought for the aides, personally. However, I would be shocked if at least some of that food did not end up on Mama's plate. Examining the list of Mama's menus, produced during discovery, proved that at least some did.

Between 2007 and 2010, I believed that I was alone out there. All guardianship cases were kept secret in New Mexico. Back then, they were so secret that even the case dockets were not posted. If you did not know about a hearing, you could not even find out from the court schedules listed on the internet. Any interested party absolutely had to retain an attorney, because often interested parties without attorneys did not seem to receive any notice of hearings. I only intuited that at the time; later I learned, from other victims, that it was true.

From January 2007 to May 2012, I hosted a public-access TV talk show, "Healers, Health and Healing." Arthur had always wanted me

---

207 A few examples, both pork and seafood, from different times: Decades 07456, 07942, 08395, 08472, 08474, 25019, 29936, 29968, 30588

to host either a TV or a radio show. I had resisted his wishes on this subject for years. Over the summer of 2006, knowing that he was slowly dying, I got my certification to produce shows on what was then Channel 27, the local public-access television station, so that I could let him see that I was following his wishes, at last. And I used a professional studio, not the tacky one down at the station (now long closed). The first season of shows went "in the can" toward the end of 2006.

Out of my terror of the guardian taking away my visitation rights, I both refrained from ever discussing any subject relating to guardianship on the air and from attempting to syndicate the show, although I was soon offered the possibility of airing it over some PBS channels, outside New Mexico. Thinking about this promotional idea, I decided that I simply could not; to do so might place Mama in jeopardy. People want all sorts of information on public figures. The TV episodes satisfied Arthur, but if they were syndicated, they would definitely anger the commercial guardian. I decided not to promote the episodes, either. I never spoke to the commercial guardian about the show.

Simply in the normal course of communication, the commercial guardian told Debbie frequently that my behavior was aberrant. Their attitude communicated their position that everyone else loved their work.[208] They were saintly people. I did not quite agree, so clearly, I was wrong. In any case, theirs was a for-profit firm, so earning money had to be part of their underlying plan. The gist of their message to me was twofold: Why did I not love them as I ought? And, what was wrong with me? At times, their

---

208 After the dockets were posted on the internet, I was a able to document the following evidence of complaints against Mama's commercial guardian by their wards and the families of their wards before the estate's suit against the guardian settled: Reports not timely filed (8 wards); request for initial public competency hearing denied (one ward); this commercial guardian sued to remove a prior guardian (one ward); confidentiality orders imposed on interested parties (six wards); order prohibiting evidentiary hearings in a case (one ward); visitation restricted, banned or curtailed (12 wards); complaints of lack of due process (two wards); ward separated from significant other by guardian (three wards); estate distributed out of the guardianship, in some cases with gag order (five wards); motions for replacement of guardian due to objections to their actions (18 wards); complaints about fees or costs/demands for an audit (12 wards); notice of hearing not provided to next of kin (two wards).

tone got so acerbic that I started worrying that, if I were not careful, they would come after me and have me forcefully examined, against my will, so they could perhaps make me their ward. Was I looking for conspiracies here?

(Beginning on May 23, 2017, when case dockets were no longer secret, I discovered what looked to me like the guardian coming back, a year or two after guardianizing one member of a family, to take over one or more relatives. Even considering that posted dockets might be misleading, I still think I was reading these correctly. So, I continue to count myself lucky to have retained at least some of my freedom, during and after Mama's commercial guardianship.)

Oddly, the guardian was monitoring me in various ways. I was then serving as the secretary of a non-profit supporting a public-health-related bill in Santa Fe. Not surprisingly, the guardianship firm was in favor of a competing bill. I discovered that accidentally, when I attended a statewide meeting of public health people in Albuquerque, only to see someone I knew from the guardian's office at the table of a competing program's bill. Some months later, I ran into the same person. She did not bother to greet me.

"Well, your bill didn't pass!" she sniffed, contemptuously.

"Yours didn't, either," I answered, hoping not to sound too irritated.

The secrecy of guardianship cases in New Mexico made it impossible for me to know what was happening to other families most of the time Mama was alive. I concentrated on complaining about things I thought were ultimately important, like whether Mama had a safe escape route and whether she was going to have enough money so she would not become a public charge, no matter how long she lived. The whole idea of becoming a public charge would have been anathema to Mama. That is not my guess at what Mama wanted; Mama often used to say, while she was entirely mentally competent, "I never want to be on the public dole."

Perversely, the commercial guardian helped me by making sure my emails went through my attorney first. Paying all that money to an attorney did discourage me from complaining unless I felt obliged to lodge a protest.

One of the major differences between me and other family members of wards came from my years of financial apprenticeship with my father. Other families of affluent wards with whom I am familiar seemed to have had trust funds or investment accounts with professional money managers heading them. Generally, the parents and spouses did not feel obligated to teach their heirs to manage substantial sums of money. Even a family member who might have been named as a trustee might not have had any real background or sophistication in finance, before assuming that trusteeship. A professional could haul these people into court and dice them up in front of a judge with half their brain tied behind their back.

They really could not do that to me. At least not as easily. All I had done for Mama financially was make money for her. I had been doing it for almost a decade, by the time the commercial conservator took over. Because Dad hated trusts, he had trained me to handle large sums of money without going through a "professional money manager." I was not the standard "trust fund baby" at all. And, if someone else were doing a bad job of handling money, I would notice that, too.

Another major difference: I have always felt driven to understand what is happening. After I cry about something that is painful, I start amassing information, trying to understand why it is happening. Figuring that Mama's situation could not possibly be unique, even though the facts about other families in New Mexico were then hidden, I wanted to find out more about guardianship, as an institution in society. I went back to school online, and over a period of a few years graduated from Walden University, with a new master's-level degree, in public health. (This would be my sixth master's degree, so I guess that makes me different from most family members of wards in other ways as well, because most of them were not academically inclined to this extent.)

Once I realized how large a social issue dementia already was, and that it had been projected to become an enormous issue over the next decade or so[209], as Baby-Boomers aged, I also realized that I was looking at large and growing business/industrial interests. It did not matter whether a commercial guardian operated a for-profit or non-profit corporation. Both sorts of entities need to bring in money to survive. All the ancillary professions—home health, medical devices, visiting medical services, bankers, attorneys, etc., that the guardians and conservators used to care for wards, also benefit when the industry continues to run smoothly.

That knowledge relieved me of the necessity to take personally the guardian's insults. By 2006, I had realized that commercial guardians were simply part of an interest bloc, using some sort of institutional playbook. Their industry's interest lay in doing whatever was necessary to preserve and expand their sphere of influence. The law encouraged them to think of themselves as being an extension of my mother. In fact, they sometimes told me that they *were* my mother. In the eyes of the law, they were supposed to "stand in the shoes" of the ward. However, it seemed as if they did not see me as another human being. They seemed to see me, instead, as some sort of non-human collateral damage, to be discarded, if possible.

July 23, 2007, would have been another excellent time to sell Mama's "bundle," which then included 60,000 shares of stock and the trading right. On that date, the bundle alone was worth $8,400,000. If Mama truly had an emotional attachment to the NYMEX, she could still have kept the last 30,000 shares, which had a fair market value of $4,054,500 on that date. All Mama had to do was pay the applicable tax on her gains from the assets she sold. All the remaining cash could then have been used for Mama's care. And certainly, any "excess" cash could have been re-invested. The

---

209 As of January 20, 2020, Rick Black of the Center for Estate Administration Reform (CEAR), speaking on "Concerning New Mexico" (KANM) estimated that guardianship would become a $14 billion industry by 2030. According to his estimates, there are currently about 9,000 individuals under guardianship in New Mexico. At about $50,000, which in my experience is the least guardians usually charge, per year, without conservatorship fees, that would add up to $450,000,000 annually. It is big business. In addition, there are only about 30 guardianship firms in the state. If the pot were divided equally, that would be $15 million per guardianship business, per year. For the larger firms, it is probably more and for the small ones, likely less.

guardian, however, kept arguing that Mama should not be forced to pay taxes. Instead, they wanted her to keep everything, awaiting they said, the date on which there would be a "stepped-up basis."

That "stepped-up basis," which would have ratcheted higher the cost-basis of this investment, resulting in a lower tax bill to the person selling it, however, would not have taken effect until after Mama died. Waiting for a "stepped-up basis" is often used as an estate-planning technique. However, there is absolutely no logical way that holding any asset for this reason would have benefitted Mama herself in the slightest. I had no problem with them selling some of the stock and using the money for Mama's care, if Mama needed that money. Or selling the soon-to-be non-productive seat and using the money for her care. Instead, they decided to sit on the problem, as if incubating an egg. Even if they chose to incubate the problem, that "egg" would eventually hatch. A merger was pending between the newly-IPO'd Merc and the Chicago Mercantile Exchange (CME).

When Mama had accepted having a trust in her will, back in 1997, it was already clear that the seat would be sold on her death. This fact I had reconfirmed in 2003, when I tried to retitle that asset in the name of the trust Cristy had set up, but the Merc would not permit it. Cristy (and, therefore, Sutin) knew this. Mama's guardian had a copy of Mama's will in their file. We had all stipulated to its authenticity at the beginning of the guardianship. The commercial guardian and conservator also had free access to the NYMEX Membership Office, to discuss anything they wished about Mama's seat, including what the Exchange did and did not allow, in terms of titling a seat. I believed that their entire argument about having Mama hold onto the seat so that I could inherit it was bogus.

The commercial guardianship firm kept arguing that they wanted to keep all of Mama's NYMEX holdings, both the trading right and the stock. It also seemed to me that, no matter what I said, they would say the opposite.

A few months later, they told me that Mama had told them something she never, ever said to me before she became a ward—that, despite a will that would have left everything she had to Arthur and me, she did not want to conserve her assets for any heir.

They would theoretically have been able to "conserve" free-trading stock if they wanted to, so I could inherit it, but not the seat itself anyway. Occasionally, I reminded them that they had never known Mama when she was in possession of her faculties. Mama's will had been drawn up when she was competent. Anything she might or might not have told the commercial guardian (and I am not at all convinced that Mama said what they told me she did) would have been said after she had lost most of her reasoning ability, and perhaps after the guardian or someone else had just said something negative about me, or Arthur, or even both of us.

Once more, Mama paid for my aunt and my younger cousin to visit Albuquerque. Or rather the guardian did, in Mama's name. No suggestion of this payment shows in the financial records the guardian produced as part of discovery; the payments are mentioned only in correspondence, leading me to wonder where the account was out of which the guardian took this money.

The commercial guardian, because of my younger cousin's favored status, always seems to have allowed my aunt and cousin to talk to Mama privately over the phone, without supervision. On the basis of what I saw of Mama's condition after our relatives left town, I now suspect that they had promised Mama, in advance, that they could get her freedom back for her on that trip. And perhaps having Mama state, whenever possible, that she was an Orthodox Jew, might have been one of Betty's requirements for her continued friendship.

My guess is that Mama was left, crushed and monumentally depressed, when she realized that Betty could not free her from her commercial guardian. I had never observed that spending concentrated time with those relatives had done Mama any good, anyway. I had never promised Mama that I could spring her from the guardianship because I knew it was not possible. Even if I had been able to take over, she would still have needed to be under guardianship. Except that I would have that responsibility, rather than the commercial guardian. For a few days, at least, Mama and my visiting relatives had likely joined in a mutual delusion club. Now reality must have looked even worse to Mama than before.

I knew nothing about my relatives' goals before I saw the

guardian's discovery documents, but I certainly did observe the effect of their visit on Mama. Mama remained exhausted for weeks after my aunt and cousin left, and the friendly aide was complaining that she had started refusing food and oxygen.

Worried, after they left on June 12, several days after they were supposed to end their visit, I wrote to Debbie, who transmitted these complaints to the commercial guardian, "Mother rarely gets out of bed anymore and is eating almost nothing...Three weeks ago this was not the case. Then, I sat with her at her kitchen table... [and] we had a conversation for about 2 hours... [She] has been weak and totally exhausted ever since you allowed my aunt and cousin to come down and spend unlimited amounts of time with her. Mother complained to the aide but felt herself powerless...it is clear that [the guardian] didn't do anything to protect Mother. The caregiver told me that she also complained about that situation at the time...You even allowed them to stay for two additional days...In my opinion both [the guardian] and my relatives showed a reckless disregard for Mother's needs."[210]

At the time, I never guessed that the best explanation for Mama's behavior was that she was exhibiting signs of severe depression. Why did not the guardian explain her response? Perhaps because Mama wanting to escape their control made them look a little less than perfect. The guardian would have known why Mama would have been extremely depressed, but once more the firm was not forthcoming. Ironically, the commercial guardian was resolutely attempting to keep me from finding out something I already knew—namely that Mama was unhappy under their guardianship.

The guardian had instructed me not to contact Mama at all while our relatives were in Albuquerque, to avoid provoking any sort of confrontation with them. After I knew that they had left, I called Mama. As I wrote to the guardian, "...the first time I spoke with Mother after they left, she asked why I didn't call. She complained that she had not heard from me in a long time (it was actually about 6 days, although I had spoken with the aide on Sunday)..."[211] I had called on Sunday because the commercial

---
210 Rosenstiel-03070-03071
211 2008 Hearing Documents, Decades 0442

guardian had told me that the relatives would be gone by then, but they were not. I did not call back again until I knew that they were safely gone.

Recently, the guardian had taken some photos to inventory Mama's possessions, at my request. They had taken Mama out of the house during the expedition because they said this process would upset her. Debbie and I went through the premises with Ruth Pregenzer and a partner in the guardianship firm, who took the pictures, except, for some reason, in Mama's closet. As we arrived, I heard this exchange:

"Hi Ruth! I hear you're on the short list for a judgeship. Can't think of a better person for the job."

"Thanks."[212]

Opposing attorneys traditionally treat each other collegially. It is expected. Ruth Pregenzer, however, did not get that appointment.

The commercial guardian sent the resulting photos to me, to compare with another set they had taken toward the beginning of the guardianship. For reasons known only to the guardianship firm, and not related to the trip the group of us had made through Mama's home, on another occasion, they had forced Mama to display some of the costume jewelry, so they could photograph it. Mama does not look at all happy. Why involve her? Any person designated by them could have entered that closet and taken those photos without using Mama as a model. Or we could have done that while we were already there, photographing the premises.

Mama had a bit of a win, here. Apparently, she feared certain jewelry would be taken. She hid some, including one earring from each of several pairs of her favorite earrings, in ways I will not describe in case another ward uses this tactic. Like the Claddagh ring Dad had given her, I found them after her death, hidden in locations apparently only I would search. The distinctive, serpentine solid gold chain that had once held the medallion given her by her NYU class was gone, however. Apparently, Mama had not found the right hiding place for that.

Some photos and artwork now seemed to be missing. At the same time, I warned the guardian about the computer in Mama's

---

212 Information on the applicants also appeared in The Albuquerque *Journal*, "15 Apply for Court Vacancy," August 20, 2007, p. 9.

Annette Rosenstiel, grudgingly holding costume jewelry in her Albuquerque home (2007).

study. Because they did not allow me to spend time in any rooms other than the kitchen, den, and living room, and somewhat later, Mama's bedroom, I did not even know whether the old desktop with its already-outdated Millennium edition of Windows still held its original contents. Back before the guardianship, it had contained financial files that were not password-protected. I had been trying to get Mama interested in her accounts, back then. By mid-2007, there was no knowing who might have seen those files.[213]

I copied Debbie. I had accidentally sent the email to the guardian firm's secret internal server (the one from which they gave us no documents during discovery). That email was returned, so Debbie re-sent it to the guardian. This was back when I was still allowed to email them directly.

One of the problems with Mama remaining in bed for long periods, I discovered by looking at the new "inventory" shots the

---

[213] Decades 00376-77. As for the old computer, it was still there after Mama passed away. However, the financial files were gone. Oddly, the children's picture book the commercial guardian said Mama had written was not on it and it was not on the discs in her study, either, suggesting to me that Mama did not have much to do with inputting that manuscript.

guardian had sent me. Photos of Mama's birth family, of her maternal grandparents and of her paternal great grandfather, along with a blown-up photo of a grown-up Aunt Louise, now filled the wall nearest her bed. There was also an ornate silver-colored frame on that wall. It held a blown-up photo of Betty. Mama had never before kept any photos of either Louise or Betty that I could see. For some reason, Sondie's picture had been neglected. It was not there. These photos replaced the Egyptian bark paintings Mama had originally hung there, and which I never saw again. The large photo of Aunt Vicki and Uncle Tad, dressed for their formal wedding, hanging on that same wall, was the first tip-off I had ever had that they had not simply eloped one day. (If Mama already felt depressed by not having managed to get her freedom back, the sight of Grandpa Julius, her father and her original abuser, looking down on her whenever she opened her eyes, was unlikely to cheer her up.)

A snapshot-sized picture of Dad had been relegated to the bureau on the other side of the room, as had a two-by-four photo of me as a young child. Both of us, in photos so small, Mama probably could not even see at that distance, given her failing eyesight. The relatives whose photos hung on the wall near her bed were people Mama did not want near her. How she lived her life, and all the additional evidence I have found since, testifies to this fact.

The commercial guardian's discovery documents revealed that Betty had made these prints and sent them to the guardian, so that they could be placed on that wall. Other than one photo of my maternal grandfather and one group photo of my maternal great-grandfather and two of his sons (now relegated to the den), Mama had never displayed the "newly-sent" photos anywhere in our home as I was growing up. (We did have a few photos of Dad's relatives on display, but none of them had found its way into Mama's bedroom.) Mama never even put up a photo of her own mother in the Manhasset house during the almost half-century of her residence there.

In fact, not until after Mama died, did I discover that the whole time I was growing up Mama had hidden away quite a few photos of her family, including most of the ones Betty had sent. And others that perhaps no one had seen since they were taken. Had she denied she had them to make Betty—who had constituted herself the "family historian" many years earlier—feel more important? Had she denied to the commercial guardian that she already had these photos, because the evidence shows that she had hidden them away because she did not want to see them? Had she forgotten she had them?

Mama had kept these family photos of hers secreted, for half a century, or more, in boxes. Those boxes she securely taped shut, then buried in the bottoms of other, larger cartons, with junk placed on top, so no one else would ever see them. No one did, until I came across them after I became Mama's personal representative. It then seemed as if Mama had been attempting to insulate herself from these people, because otherwise she would not feel emotionally able to live her life. But she still felt that she did not want to deny entirely her connection to their world, so she did not discard the photos themselves.

Although Mama often spoke with respect about how brilliant and accomplished her relatives were, which certainly seems to have been true, she nevertheless seemed to have avoided seeing them as much as she could, and wanted me to do the same. Now, they peered, most of them stoic-faced, at her twenty-four-seven from their vantage points on the wall. Her commercial guardian followed the rule that you needed to keep dementia victims connected to their earliest memories. Now Mama, who had spent most of her life trying to escape from her early, painful memories, was confronting them, day and night. Cornered, she had no way of avoiding dealing with whatever she remembered. Knowing the guardian required her to speak well of her relatives, she did.

Once, after I had started to see her when she was in bed, I asked Mama whether she wanted to praise her relatives, as I had heard her do, occasionally, over the many years I had known her.

"No. You change how you feel about people, over time."

"Do you like having those photos on the wall?"

"No choice."

In speaking with Kathy Becker, the accountant at REDW who was handling Mama's taxes, and had, for years, been handling Arthur's and mine as well, I told her about my expectation that things were about to change for the worse with the Merc seat. "Leonie recently mentioned to me that Annette's income from the Mercantile Seat was going to decrease significantly,"[214] Kathy wrote in an email to the guardian on June 18, 2007. So, it is not as if they were unaware that the income stream from the seat was about to dry up. I did not see this private email between Kathy and the guardian until the guardian presented it as one of the exhibits for a court hearing the following year.

Looking at the photos of Mama's home that the guardian sent me, I discovered that many of Mama's possessions either had disappeared or become damaged during the years when I had not seen her. Eventually, it turned out that a few of them had been moved and no longer showed in the photos, but many others were now gone. Who took them? No witnesses would be coming forward; there was no way to know exactly when this had happened.

From the time when I first saw Mama again, I had never known who might have told her something that might upset her, or something negative about me. And if I happened to call or visit her afterwards, the commercial guardian might interpret her state of mind to have been caused by me. Later, I discovered that this was such a feature of the operation of commercial guardians—maligning one or more family members either simply in order to alienate the ward from them or to try to make the ward feel closer to different family members—that it is hard for me to think, that it did not happen in my case also, and far more frequently than I have any documentary proof.

At one point, an aide left her ring binder open, on a table. The page that showed was the set of instructions for visitation. Betty was to be given complete freedom. On the other hand, I was to be scrutinized carefully. If Mama was upset before, during or after our visits, the aides were instructed to blame me for her state of mind, and to report that "incident" immediately to the guardian's

---

214 Rosenstiel-03073

office. There were months when no one knew exactly what time I was going to visit. How could Mama possibly be upset by the prospect of a visit she did not know was about to happen? No worries! Just blame the designated target.

Any information I did get was confusing and sometimes contradictory. On any given subject, Mama would often tell me one thing, the aides another, and the guardian a third. Sometimes, if I spoke with the guardian or one of the guardian's employees twice, I would get two very different explanations for the same situation.

Mama's caseworker, from the commercial guardian's office, had told me that I should not believe anything Mama told me, including if she said she did not feel well or if she was angry because she thought the guardian was ignoring her. Anything she might have said that might in any way be construed as being at all negative about me, however, should be accepted and interpreted to put me in the worst possible light, even though Mama welcomed my visits. This lack of logic had been going on for a couple of months. On July 7, 2007, I wrote to the guardian, pleading for some clarity: "My request to you is that, at this point and to avoid further miscommunication and misunderstandings, we need to share information on the details of Mother's true condition—mental, emotional and physical—or there is no way I can react in a reasonable manner to what I'm told by Mother's aides and to what Mother herself tells me."[215]

In late June and July, we continued discussing what could be sold to generate adequate cash to care for Mama. On July 22, 2007, the NYMEX stock was worth $131.11 per share. This meant that the 30,000 free-trading shares were then worth $3,933,300. I wrote to the guardian and the accountant: "Are any possible measures being contemplated to reduce expenditures? What cash does Mother currently hold and how long will that suffice for her needs? When Barb and Cathy (the accountant who worked on Mama's financial records and tax planning at REDW) and Deb and I had a conference a few months ago…Mother had in excess of $400,000 in cash.[216] If that was true about two months ago, why is more cash suddenly needed urgently now?" Eventually, with the

---

215 Rosenstiel-03145-03146
216 Rosenstiel-03154

help of Mama's accountant, we determined that Mama would net about $450,000 if she sold the seat. Nothing happened. We later got an email from the commercial guardian, stating that Mama really did not need any more cash at that moment, but they would revisit this subject later, if necessary.

The guardianship firm said my criticisms made them feel threatened—particularly ironic because I had felt threatened by their behavior from the beginning, and recently all the more so. After Mama died, I discovered Mama's own numerous failed attempts to get away from the guardianship firm, realizing, then, that she had felt very much the same way. By mid-August, by the commercial guardian's request, I was communicating with that firm only through my attorney, by writing letters to Debbie and having Debbie transmit the gist of what I had written to her, to Ruth Pregenzer, the commercial guardian's attorney-of-record.

This tactic, I thought, was designed to drain Mama and me of money because, each time an attorney read a letter, had a conference with a client about its contents, and then had to write a reply letter, it cost the client money.[217] Mama was considered the "client" on that end, so Mama would have had to pay both Ruth Pregenzer and someone in the guardian's office each time the guardian sent me (or rather Debbie) an email or letter. Debbie, of course, was now my attorney, so I was responsible for paying her.

This "dueling attorneys" arrangement left me feeling emotionally drained. Even though I am sure the guardian firm did not tell Mama about it, I worried about how much it was costing her. Within a few months, the guardian added at least four additional expensive attorneys to the mix, but I did not find out about them until much later. Looking at the documents relating to these people later, I concluded that the commercial guardian primarily needed them because the firm did not understand the Merc asset.

Chuck Reynolds had disappeared off the scene, after billing Mama in August, September and October 2008, when Mama

---

217 I am not complaining, here, about the fees Debbie charged me. I absolutely needed her to run interference with the commercial guardian. Later on, only her intercession gave back me the right Mama had given me in her will, to take care of Mama's funeral arrangements; the guardian kept trying to pre-empt that function.

herself could not possibly have directed him to do anything.[218] (Of course, I knew nothing about who was billing, and who was not, until either the guardian filed an annual report or discovery). Reynolds did not re-emerge, to start billing Mama again (and being paid out of the "trust" account the guardian had established in Mama's name), until after Mama's death.[219] Reynolds did not charge for seeing Mama during 2007-08; all his charges stemmed from requests made by Mama's guardian.

When Mama was not kept on her prescribed oxygen, she became extremely disoriented. I tried to remind the guardian that it might be a good idea to keep Mama on oxygen.

For months (except when our relatives from back East were visiting), I had been seeing Mama daily. When I asked Mama what she had been doing when I was not there, she would say, "Nothing!" very emphatically, which led me to suggest to the guardian that Mama might be bored and perhaps might profitably be given more of a chance to interact with other people. Those people would normally have included her aides who, when I arrived without an appointment, were often playing computer games or working on their laptop computers rather than speaking with Mama, although I did not offer this last observation to the guardian at the time. I was sure that the company would have interpreted this as criticism and started calling me names again. And, without supervision, there was little likelihood that they could monitor, in real time, what was happening in Mama's home anyway.

Months before, the guardian had bought Mama expensive hearing aids. Several thousand dollars each. They insisted she could hear nothing without them. One day, I entered her room and, without thinking, started talking to her, at my normal distance from her bed, and in a normal, conversational tone. Mama asked appropriate questions. However, when she turned her head, I could see she was not wearing her hearing aids. I looked around for them. They were on the dresser.

"Do you need your hearing aids, Mama?"

"No."

"Can you hear okay?"

---
218 Decades 34140
219 Decades 34146

"Sure."

"Why do you have hearing aids?"

"If they think I can't hear, I'll find out who my friends are."

During that period, they did not lock the side door to Mama's home, which allowed me to enter the den and then wait until Mama was available. I simply suggested that the aides might interact more with Mama. As far as I could see, nothing ever came of my suggestion.

The aide's job was to provide "companionship" as well as practical help. However, these aides had little in common with Mama. Their written entries in the log say that they provided companionship on any given day. It depends on whether you consider combing someone's hair, painting their nails (when in fact Mama had rarely polished her nails before), or washing them "companionship." No one, except a functionary from the guardian's office who came once or twice a month for an hour or less, ever seemed to supervise them.

A few of them did interact with Mama, even occasionally advocating for her with the guardian (knowing that they might, at any time, be risking their jobs to do so). One made it her crusade to stop the other aides from smoking right outside the door to Mama's room and dropping their cigarette butts there. The fugitive smoke, wafting in, could not have done someone on oxygen any good. A flying spark might cause a fire. A big sign hung over the head of Mama's bed, saying "No Open Flames" because she was on oxygen. Even on the front door, the guardian had posted the traditional warning sign, "Oxygen in Use." The other aides simply put in their time and collected their checks, feeding Mama some Hamburger Helper or pepperoni pizza along the way.

After some months, the guardian assured me that I did not need to call anymore before visiting Mama. One day after that, I appeared and the aide refused to let me in. She yelled at me, through the door, that I had to call first. I called on my cell phone. She refused to answer the house phone. I rang the bell. She refused to answer it. Even if the doors had been unlocked, at that point, I could not have gone in without being considered (by that aide, at least) to be trespassing. So, I went home. I emailed the guardian immediately, through my attorney, but of course, the visit for that day was canceled because my email could never go through the vetting process that quickly.

The guardian eventually promised that Mama and I would have privacy during our visits. Sometimes we did. Often, we did not. Sometimes, aides kept coming in and out of the room. On other occasions, they sat in the room and glared at us. Were they, perhaps, daring me to try to evict them? If I even so much as mentioned a court order, particularly the one that had guaranteed me privacy during visits to Mama, I knew they could complain to the guardian that I had been speaking about "forbidden subjects."

Mama was in a wheelchair, then, and the house still had no handicapped ramps, so I could not safely take Mama outside. More and more often, Mama was in bed for our visits. The guardian had placed a baby monitor on the nightstand at the head of Mama's bed; I finally got express permission from the guardian to turn it off during my visits.

Many of the aides had been with Mama a long time, which means they had likely heard negative things about me both from my relatives and from the guardian and/or the home health service for which they worked. In all fairness to these relatively poorly paid aides, if you have heard that an adult child has threatened to kill her mother, would you want to leave the two of them alone together? Most of the aides were in no position to evaluate what the guardian or their immediate employer told them. Looking back, it is a bit easier to understand why they might have decided to ignore the change when the guardian rescinded the command to be in my face. At least the guardianship firm told me they rescinded that order. They might just as easily have countermanded it on one day and reinstated it the next.

At times, the aides did not follow instructions not to talk to me. That was when I learned that not all of Mama's aides were the most stable individuals. One told me that she could hear spiders walking on the ceiling in other rooms while she was sitting in Mama's bedroom. She also said that the birds outside the window were singing Bach backwards.

"Really?" I asked.

"Everybody knows that!" she insisted.

Another time, an aide told me that she had broken all her fingers, on both hands, by slamming the knuckles in the garage door at the house where she used to live, and then she drove herself to the hospital. I had had two broken fingers. Even though they healed relatively well, if you looked carefully at my hands, you could see that those fingers were not quite shaped like the corresponding fingers on the other hand. However, when I managed to get a good look at her hands, her fingers did not seem to have suffered the sort of damage that her story suggested. Particularly not the crushed knuckles she mentioned. Not only that, but she had suffered no apparent loss of function in either hand. Highly unlikely.

Then, an aide told me that she was a moonlighting television reporter. Even though I had pretty much stopped watching commercial TV after I saw the second tower of the World Trade Center come down, and so would not have known who was on those shows after that, I seriously doubted her story at the time, and still do.

The next tranche of NYMEX shares would be released for sale on November 21, 2007. Between late May and September, it seemed to me that Mama's guardian had declared emotional war on me. As I continued to push the guardianship firm to diversify Mama's still extremely vulnerable and highly concentrated NYMEX asset, if they told Mama anything about what I was actually doing, she never spoke to me about it. However, I sensed that she had at least an inkling that the emotional climate had changed. On November 26, the CPA who was then nominally Mama's guardian wrote to Kathleen Winslow (who had become the principal in the investment firm Corless & Winslow, with which she had worked for many years), "I have a client that has an interest in the New York Mercantile...This is a very contentious family situation..."[220] A note on the printout states, "Heir is pushing for diversif[ication]."[221] Well, yes, I certainly was.

---

220 Rosenstiel-08808
221 Ibid

Mama's guardian still took no action at all. The NYMEX stock simply sat in Mama's Computerserve account. During discovery, however, I saw documents showing that they had asked for information about lending out the released stock, which would have brought them some income. They did not discuss this information with me at the time.

Regardless of whatever information they received, or who offered it to them, they took no action on it, seemingly paralyzed by the magnitude of the transaction. If I am not stating the irritatingly obvious, it should be axiomatic that, if you suffer from meganumerophobia, then you should not take on this sort of obligation in the first place. And, if you have taken it on, but it is too much for you, you should seek to resign and find a replacement.

All the commercial guardian needed to do, to get a hearing with Judge Baca in 2004, was to ask and wait a few weeks. So, I saw no reason why, if the commercial guardian believed that the judge needed to be involved, they could not have requested a hearing anytime between early 2006 and the fall of 2007. However, they did not do that, either. Nor did they say that they wanted to.

Nominally, Mama's actual guardian within the firm at that point was a CPA. The senior partner in the firm had delegated Mama's guardianship to her. I would have expected more financial savvy from a CPA than from someone off the street. Unfortunately, she admitted, at her deposition in 2017, that she had never had any expertise in dealing with stocks.

The discovery documents show, however, that she kept the senior partner in the loop on what she was doing. The senior partner, as she admitted during her own deposition, had actually been a stockbroker for years before co-founding the guardianship firm. Amazing. She had always seemed so contemptuous of financial matters that I would never have suspected this prior occupation of hers until it surfaced during the discovery process. She was not licensed as a stockbroker while the firm was caring for Mama, but that did not mean she had forgotten everything she had ever known, did it?

As was customary, the head of the guardian firm's first day of deposition was taken after my own. She testified before her own experts did. We—two of my counsels (David A. Garcia and James E. Dory) and I—met with her side—three attorneys and Mama's former guardian—at a private room used by my head attorney's court reporter in Downtown Albuquerque on March 1, 2017. David, asked the questions. One of the three attorneys on the other side (Greg MacKenzie's associate), spent her time looking at her laptop screen, eating nuts and dropping the shells on the floor.

Some months prior to setting a hearing date late in 2007 that was later canceled, the one friendly aide had told me that the guardian was looking for something to tax me with, and I could certainly feel hostility increase exponentially over the summer, in the way the other aides treated me during my daily visits. I noticed in the discovery documents that they complained I stayed too long, even on days when Mama kept asking me to stay (the same way she had, the first time I was allowed to see her again, back in May 2007). And on other occasions—generally when Mama looked tired, or seemed about to fall asleep, or if I arrived when she was asleep and I did not want to ask them to wake her up—the complaint was exactly the opposite, that I did not stay long enough. Looking at the documents, it seemed that they had been instructed to complain about something. Anything.

The supposed agreements the commercial guardian made in 2008, not to prevent me from seeing Mama, did not stop the firm from attempting to create events that might prevent me from seeing Mama. If, that is, they had been true.

Discovery also brought to the surface an email, in which one of the partners in the guardianship firm asked Ruth Pregenzer to find a reason to keep me from seeing Mama. Shortly after that, Debbie received an email from Ruth Pregenzer, detailing two supposed "episodes" during which I must have done something awful, because Mama was upset during my visit.

The first accused me of visiting Mama against Mama's wishes—which, of course, was a bogus complaint. Pregenzer also said, in her letter, that Mama was not able to explain her reason for not wanting to see me. She went on to speculate that I was paranoid and delusional because I reported to the staff the concerns Mama was voicing to me.[222]

The second supposed "event" was that I had left Mama's room, told the aides she needed something, and then not gone back into Mama's room with them. They said Mama was upset and it had to be my fault. They concluded that I must have been bringing up subjects that upset her.

The only problem with this well-written letter is that its assertions are false, just as every attempt to characterize what I was doing or saying is critical of me. I must have been doing something wrong if they can just sense what it was. And, of course they can, because they are omniscient.

In both cases, the guardianship firm got an incomplete and misleading report—or created one, out of extremely inadequate information. One of Mama's aides had been watching a violent show on TV. As I walked in the door to Mama's bedroom, the aide got up and started to walk out the door.

I heard an explosion. (It was coming from the TV.) Immediately, I saw Mama jump from the noise.

"You can't stay!" she said.

At that point, the aide who had been watching the TV walked out the door of the room,

"Why not?"

"Because this place will blow up at two o'clock."

"No, Mama, that's a show on TV. You're watching a TV show."

It was before 2 PM when I arrived. I am assuming, from what Mama said, that there had been some dialogue in the script that mentioned an explosion that was supposed to happen at that hour. In her current mental state, she could not distinguish between reality and a TV show. I stayed until well after 2 PM, trying to prove to Mama that the place was not going to blow up, and that neither Mama nor I was in any danger. Or, if we were, at least it was not going to come from an exploding bomb.

The aide could plausibly deny that she had heard the rest of our conversation. Maybe she did not, but it was clear to me that Mama's fear was the spawn of that TV show, and perhaps she had

---

222 Decades 24741-24744

heard the aides talking about the fact that aides had been smoking, just outside her door to the backyard, as testified to by butts I had seen in that area. Mama's anxiety had nothing to do with wanting me gone; instead, she wanted to save me from the fictional bomb.

On the other occasion, Mama kept asking me to help her get out of bed. The guardian tried to convince me that no one else had ever heard Mama say a word about wanting to get out of bed; they absolutely prohibited her from even trying. No matter how I tried to change the subject, Mama kept coming back to it, because getting up was obviously on her mind. When I left, there were tears in my eyes, which the aides saw. Of course, they assumed I had said something mean to Mama that had upset her. Yes, I suppose that I did; I told her the truth—that she was not allowed to get up and I did not have the authority to countermand the guardian's orders. That was the day I was forced to tell her that I was not allowed to help her in this effort, regardless of how long she begged for her freedom.

During discovery, I realized that multiple caregivers, including nurses,[223] knew that Mama wanted to be able to get up, and had been forced to refuse Mama's requests to be allowed out of bed, on firm orders of the commercial guardian. On April 12, 2008, an aide wrote (knowing the commercial guardian would read this), "Leonie making remarks re-Dr. A wanting to go outside to Dr. Leach [sic]."[224] One aide wrote on May 27, 2009, "She threw the covers off and really tried to get out of bed—got frustrated because she couldn't—calmed her down... Dr. [Annette]has made several requests to get out of bed. She said "I'm well!" over the last mo [sic]"."[225] Ruth perhaps did not know about what the aides were reporting, but the guardian did. Aides' reports were faxed to them weekly.

The guardianship firm had obviously started amassing supposed "evidence" of my malfeasance after sending Ruth that email, and then accused me of the worst possible motives in interpreting these very partial and misleading facts.

Not until I saw the request from Mama's guardianship firm that their attorney find a way to prevent me from seeing Mama did

---

223 Rosenstiel-04793
224 Decades 28314.
225 Decades 28247 (other entries also attest to Mama's fervent wish for freedom.)

I feel absolutely validated: Had there been no discovery, I might have continued forever to debate whether excuses were being fabricated to manipulate Mama, me and the situation.

I had always had doubts about what the guardian said. One of the first things witnesses are usually asked is whether they have ever been deposed before:

> Q: My name is David Garcia...We are here today for your deposition. Have you had your deposition taken before?
> A: No.[226]

After the New Mexico guardianship dockets were released and posted on the internet in 2017, I decided to see whether I could figure out why the head of the guardianship firm and the court reporter seemed so friendly when I saw them meet at my deposition. It turned out that on April 3, 2015, a certificate of deposition was filed, presumably indicating that she had had her deposition taken in another guardianship case.

This witness appeared to have been deposed before, as the guardian in another case, and the deposition had been listed on a now-released court docket.[227]

Did depositions given in sequestered or gagged cases—excuse me, cases with "confidentiality orders"—not count (because no one could ever find out you had given them)? Or, perhaps that deposition had been canceled or postponed, just as my initial deposition had, but given how friendly the head of the guardianship firm was with the court reporter, I doubt it.

Because the friendly aide had told me that all the aides had been warned that I had threatened to kill Mama (I am still incensed by this egregious lie!), I tried to refrain from actually touching Mama at any time when an aide was watching.

Many months of inconsistency when the aides prevented me from seeing Mama, or did not allow me to see her privately,

---

226 Nancy Oriola Deposition, March 1, 2017, p. 6
227 D-202-PQ-201000104 IMO Bob L. Turner, Caselookup Case Detail, p.3, https://caselookup.nmcourts.gov/caselookup/app?component=cnLink&page=SearchResults&service=direct&session=T&sp=SD-202-PQ-201000104 accessed May 31, 2020

eventually culminated in some temporary satisfaction and relief. On December 11, 2007, Mama's then-current guardian within the commercial firm distributed an email to the rest of the staff, saying, "We have a stipulated order [now] that says that effective immediately, Leonie has open visitation with her Mom. Leonie can bring friends of hers to visit if she thinks it's appropriate."[228]

Over time, after the stipulated court order went into effect during December 2007, I brought at least half-a-dozen different friends to visit Mama. Theoretically, the court order gave me carte blanche from the commercial guardian to bring along anyone I liked, without the guardian's prior approval.[229] However, I did not introduce them to the aides who, with only one real exception, would not speak to me in a civil manner, anyway. In the guardianship world, this "liberal" visitation situation shocked the aides. In order to get it, however, I had had to agree to drop my own petition to become Mama's guardian and conservator.

At one point, when Mama and I had some privacy, I asked Mama about her aides.

"Are there any aides you particularly like?"

"Doesn't matter."

"Why do you say that, Mama?"

"I can't get attached to anyone."

"Why not?"

"Because they're all going to leave anyway."

Two or three of Mama's dozen or so aides had any sort of relationship with her that I could see, so I figured the best thing I could do for Mama, at that point, was to get her some interesting and varied company. That would be better for Mama than worrying over who had a court-bestowed title and who did not.

Sometimes, having company seemed to bring Mama back to her old self.

One counselor friend of mine whom I took along to visit Mama spoke to her about anthropology, which my friend's daughter was then studying.

---

228 Nancy Oriola Deposition, Exhibit #165
229 A few years later, I would learn that such general permission is highly unusual; typically, a commercial guardian demands to know, in advance, all about anyone who is going to see the ward.

"What do you think of Margaret Mead?" my friend asked.

"Oh, she always wanted to keep people close, so she could control them," Mama answered.

My friend, the counselor, had noticed the glares of Mama's aide that day. Just after we left, she turned to me. "How do you stand this?" she asked. "That aide was glaring at you as if she wanted to kill you."

"I know. She probably does. But if I stop visiting, Mama won't have anyone to talk to at all. She needs company."

Another friend, a social activist, asked Mama, "How do you like the food?"

"They make it specially for me," Mama answered, "but I don't like it."

Only years later would I see all the Hamburger Helper in the pantry and hypothesize that at least some of the expensive food that showed on the grocery receipts I saw during the discovery process must have been ending up in someone else's home. This hypothesis was confirmed when I saw the receipts from cheap Chinese take-out places and pizza from local pizza parlors. At one point, one of Mama's aides had told me that Mama loved pepperoni pizza. That would be a new taste for Mama; she never ate it when I was growing up, although she used to be fond of margherita pizza.

In 2010, another invited visitor, an acquaintance of mine who was then helping me unearth material from my garage for use in a new edition of one of the books Arthur had written, went to see Mama. He was an engineer. Arthur's book dealt with World War I and the Russian Civil War.[230] Mama talked to the visiting engineer a little about being a young girl at the time of the Armistice.

After I dropped my petition to become Mama's guardian and conservator, the commercial guardianship firm instantly dropped its contention that I was dangerous to my mother's safety and stopped trying to force me to get a psychological evaluation, which they had been claiming I needed because I was so dangerous.

If on Tuesday, they considered me so much of a threat to Mama's personal safety that I needed a psychological evaluation

---

230 *Last Train over Rostov Bridge*. London: Thin Red Line, 2010. Arthur had co-authored it with a distant relative of Mama's visitor.

Money Takes Wing and Truth Flies Out the Window

before seeing her (after seeing her, daily, for months), how on Wednesday, did it suddenly become perfectly fine for me to see Mama with no restrictions on visitation, and without needing their advance approval to bring anyone I liked?

This makes no sense. If they had really thought that I posed any sort of threat to Mama, their duty, as Mama's guardian, would have been to go to court to prevent me from having any access to her, not to make any sort of agreement with me. However, they might have had to prove some sort of evil intent on my part if they went to court. I still cannot imagine how they could have done that, since none existed.

On January 20, 2020, Rick Black of the Center for Estate Administration Reform made the point that it is not the law, as written, that is at fault. Instead, the enforcement of those laws by the "courts of equity" (both family court and probate court, which includes guardianship) do not work properly. Judges, attorneys and commercial guardians pick favorites for the purpose of their own convenience and do not offer fair hearings.[231] That has certainly been my experience, too.

In practice, the professionals seem to favor family members living out-of-state or far enough from the ward so that visits are rare and there is plenty of notice before they arrive. Shades of the mythical villages of Potemkin. (Among the documents in the guardian's discovery production were a couple from just such a family member from out-of-state, begging the guardian to get dental care for the ward and groveling to them as being the only people onsite to provide information. It seems that was how they liked to work. I do not think those got in among the guardianship firm's discovery production by accident; they were designed to show how other family members trusted the firm. Were they right?)

The stipulated order left me with absolutely no respect for the commercial guardian whatsoever. However, that is how these cases seem to work. One person makes an absolutely wild, unsubstantiated charge. The other side makes an offer. Then the first side makes some accommodation, and the situation is considered "resolved." From a legal point of view, perhaps this is true.

---

231 "Concerning New Mexico," KANM, January 20, 2020.

To me, the only truth of the situation was that Mama remained in a house with no safe escape route in an emergency, and her money seemed to be evaporating rapidly. At least, now I could give her some variety in her visitors.

If I had persisted, I had little doubt that they would have interpreted whatever results they got on any psychological test as meaning that I should be kept away from Mama anyway. The only way I could "win" the right to continue to see Mama was to lose the legal battle to become her guardian. Now, on the basis of the experiences of half-a-dozen other people who wanted the guardianship of loved ones, I have finally concluded that, had the case been heard by the judge, there would not have been any way Judge Baca would have named me anyway; Judge Baca would simply have appointed a different commercial guardian with a philosophy similar to the then-current one. That was what I later saw happening to other families I met who, for one reason or another had to have a change of guardian, or conservator, or both.

Not until I subpoenaed Winslow's records in the probate case, did I confirm that Mama's commercial guardian knew the outcome of the hearing long before we entered Judge Baca's courtroom for the March financial hearing. On February 1, 2008, Winslow's Customer Service Specialist sent the guardianship firm what she described as "paperwork to open the Pershing [they were then the clearing firm for Winslow] account for Annette Rosenstiel...Additionally, we will need a copy of the court document establishing the Guardian/Conservatorship..."[232]

Elizabeth Church, the blonde, anxious-looking guardian ad litem appointed by the court, for the purposes of the two 2008 hearings the commercial guardian eventually requested from Judge Baca, had even said in her report that she thought the current guardianship firm should withdraw from the case because it could not function effectively. However, she did blame this on me, because I was so critical of them.

I could probably point to a dozen or more statements of hers with which I took issue or which conflicted with the facts. Not the least of which was her contention that Mama evinced no signs of

---

[232] Rosenstiel(2)0111341

dissatisfaction with the commercial guardian. On some other subjects, the GAL repeatedly appealed to what Mama had wanted in earlier years. Yet even the questionable Values History that figured so importantly in the 2008 hearings suggests that Mama was not happy under the guardian's control. Under "What are your goals for the future"? the answer was "to appeal the guardianship."[233] The GAL never reported to the court or acknowledged this statement.

Several other bits of information she apparently felt obliged to include, but buried in the inner pages of her twenty-eight-page report and did not emphasize to the judge. Chief among these were that she never told Judge Baca that I had taken legal action to fulfill Mama's request to take over as her guardian. The guardian absolutely forbade me to speak to Mama about it and the GAL misinformed Mama of the purpose of her visit. "The GAL," Church admitted, speaking of herself in the third person, "did not reveal that a petition had been filed by Leonie Rosenstiel to remove [the commercial firm] as guardian and conservator and to substitute herself."[234]

No need to mention the emotionally-fraught words "law suit." If I had been the GAL, I would simply have said, "I'm here because your daughter has volunteered to take care of you for the rest of your life. She says she has the time. She says that you would not be imposing on her and that she wants to give you whatever you need. How would you feel about her taking these functions over from the people who are handling it now?"

Had Church levelled with Mama, Mama might have answered Church's questions differently. When asked about me, Mama nevertheless referred to me as "a doll."[235] Mama said she did not want to "burden" me by having me take over. "She worries that her daughter is too busy and does not want to take too much of her daughter's time," Church observed.[236] Would Mama have worried about this if she had known, in advance, that I would not consider this work an imposition?

One other consideration: Mama had a baby monitor in her

---

233 Rosenstiel(2)014413
234 Report of the Guardian ad Litem, January 15, 2008, p. 2. This was her "first" report; she ultimately filed two supplements.
235 Ibid
236 Ibid

bedroom. Church interviewed Mama in her bed; she does not mention its presence, but Mama certainly would have been aware of it being there. Church does not mention either seeing it or turning it off. So, Church was supposedly having a private conversation with Mama when, the whole time, any aide in the house would have heard every word. Church ignored this fact.

Other family members of wards have complained about what a guardian ad litem has had to say about them. It still does no good to complain; in New Mexico, guardians ad litem have total judicial immunity. Regardless of what they said about someone involved in a suit, there is no legal recourse.[237]

After Mama died, I learned that Elizabeth Church and Ruth Pregenzer had graduated from the University of New Mexico the same year. Pregenzer was summa cum laude in English and philosophy; Church was getting her JD.[238] Ruth, of course, went on to get her JD as well. Church, it turned out, was an aspiring novelist. She had wanted to be one throughout her entire thirty-year law career, as she later admitted in various internet posts. Finally, she quit law to write fiction full time. A few years later, as Church was honing her novel-writing technique, she says that she turned to Ruth Pregenzer for advice on the early drafts of her first novel, *The Atomic Weight of Love: A Novel*.[239] "If you weren't writing," one interviewer asked her, "you'd be…" Church answered, "Still miserable, practicing law."[240] Had her husband, like her father, not died young, Church wrote in an essay entitled "Exquisite Adaptations," "I would likely not have been able to call an abrupt halt to one career and so that I could pursue my dream of writing."[241]

At this point, I suspect that what I then considered the strange

---

237   The New Mexico Civil Rights Act of 2021 (HB7), does not affect judicial immunity and the immunity of guardians ad litem.
238   University of New Mexico Board of Regents Minutes for May 13, 1983, pp. 14 and 139 Accessed January 27, 2020 from: *https://digitalrepository.unm.edu/cgi/viewcontent.cgi?article=1844&context=bor_minutes*
239   Church, Elizabeth J. *The Atomic Weight of Love: A Novel*, Chapel Hill, NC: Algonquin Books, 2017, Acknowledgements.
240   "Books By My Bedside: debut novelist Elizabeth Church," by Farhana Gani. *https://www.readersdigest.co.uk/culture/books/meet-the-author/books-by-my-bedside-debut-novelist-elizabeth-church* , accessed May 31, 2020.
241   Accessed July 1, 2020, from: *https://www.bookbrowse.com/author_interviews/full/index.cfm/author_number/2815/elizabeth-church*

events of December 2007 were not an accident. I do not think Debbie was involved, but I do think the commercial guardian had probably arranged all this in advance.

While my petition to become guardian was active, Marty Brown, another commercial guardian in town, theoretically was being considered to take over. She initially said that she wanted to be at least co-guardian with me, while I was to take over as conservator. Knowing what I do now, about how the families of wards are manipulated, I have come to believe that there was never the remotest possibility that the court would have allowed me to take over either of these functions for a still-affluent ward. They would likely have used Betty's antipathy to me as an excuse, arguing (as they did in another case) that I would likely prevent my relatives from seeing Mama if the judge gave me the guardianship. Not that it was true, in the least, but I am convinced that this would have been their argument.

Meanwhile, I kept hearing that someone in Marty Brown's office was insisting that she already knew me. When I heard the woman's name, it was entirely unfamiliar. I remember saying, several times, "I've never met this person before!"

Finally, the date of my appointment to see Marty arrived. I got to her office. The functionary with the unfamiliar name was there, too. As I recall, she was a petite, middle-aged, non-descript woman with pale white skin and frizzy blonde hair. Another social worker.

"Good to see you again!"

"Nice to meet you, but I've never seen you before."

She kept insisting that she knew me and asking why I was denying it. When we were about done with several go-arounds of this discussion, we got on with the meeting.

"How do I know that you won't spend too much money, trying to keep your mother alive?" Marty asked.

"If I have that responsibility, I'll make decisions based on the circumstances. I don't know what they're going to be."

I decided to try a new approach with the social worker I had not met before.

"How long have you been working for Marty?"

"About a year. I saw you when you came to the house."

"You left the guardian's office at the end of 2006. I did not see Mama between mid-2004 and mid-2007. If you were in Mama's home when I wasn't seeing her, then I couldn't possibly have met you there."

"I guess I must have met your cousin Betty. But tell me the truth!" she said, smiling broadly with what seemed to me like false solicitousness, "When I kept saying that I knew you, didn't that make you feel as if you were crazy?"

"No. I knew I'd never met you before."

I left, feeling manipulated and monumentally unsatisfied. In terms of how they treated people, there really did not seem to be much difference between one commercial guardianship firm and the other. Was it "bait and switch," or "Meet the new boss, same as the old boss"?

Before our meeting, Marty Brown had promised that Debbie would receive a report and her offer to take over in a letter before the deadline of December 31, 2007. Instead, she went out of town over Christmas, apparently remaining incommunicado until after the New Year dawned. Therefore, we had no one specific to present to the judge as a substitute. From what I know now, that does not necessarily matter at all. Just as the judge could pick someone's name without that person being there at the first hearing, she could have done (and did do) the same later, except that I assume that she would have needed some indication, in advance, that the person would accept the appointment.

On May 9, 2017[242] the one remaining partner, who had by then taken over the commercial guardianship firm, was deposed by David. He asked about the email sent around on December 11, 2007:

> Q: Okay. At the inception of Annette Rosenstiel's guardianship, were there any restrictions on visit—imposed by [the guardian] on visits by Leonie Rosenstiel to her mother?
> A: Only that we asked that when she visit with her mother, that she remain positive and upbeat.
> Q: Okay. And did that happen? Were there any instances where she did not remain positive and upbeat?

---

242 Volume 2 of 2. May 9, 2017. P. 29

A: I don't recall right now.
Q: Was there a time when Leonie Rosenstiel visits with her mother became restricted in any way by [the guardianship firm]?
A: No. Oh, restricted in any way?
Q: Restricted in any way.
A. Well, I see reference to a monitor.
Q: Okay. And can you explain the monitor?
A: You know, I can't recall fully why there was a monitor.
Q: Okay. Was there a requirement at any time that Leonie Rosenstiel needed to call ahead before visiting?
A: I don't recall a requirement for that.

In September 2007, the guardianship firm had submitted hundreds of pages of email printouts as exhibits for the hearings in Mama's guardianship case that took place in 2008. They had petitioned Judge Baca for instructions relating to both Mama's guardianship and her conservatorship, and of course, the judge ended up doing exactly what they asked of her.

During the years that this firm had been Mama's commercial guardian, the partner in that firm whom David A. Garcia deposed in May 2017 had either authored or been copied on well over 100 emails referencing various visitation restrictions, my frustrations with them, and my attempts to get those restrictions lifted. In fact, she was the same person who had written to Ruth Pregenzer, asking that attorney to find some way to prevent me from seeing Mama.

After conducting my own analysis of the discovery documents, and listening to the way my lead attorney had structured his and his colleagues' depositions of the guardianship folks, I finally began to understand why I had felt like Alice in Wonderland for the past fourteen years. I hated having to conclude that all this emotional pain had been part of a carefully-structured pattern, but there was no longer any way I could continue to believe that the commercial guardian's actions had been anything other than deliberate.

The first hearing the commercial guardian had requested, on March 6, 2008, dealt with finances. It went on pretty much all day.

The transcript ran to 134 pages. Easy to see where the guardian's and the judge's priorities lay. Mama was still in her home without a handicapped ramp that I believed would have cost only a few hundred dollars to install, and they wanted to discuss the money first.

Theoretically, the commercial guardian had "solicited" financial plans from four different money managers. However, the one they picked to do the job was the one with what I considered the worst plan. The guardianship firm had brought on, as its financial expert, Kathleen Winslow, the remaining partner in the brokerage firm for which the senior partner in the guardianship firm had worked as a stockbroker for a period of almost a decade, years earlier.[243] As Ruth Pregenzer told Judge Baca in her opening statement, "(W)e are going to be asking you to approve the placement of the asset with Kathleen Winslow & Associates, and then allow Ms. Winslow to actively manage that asset...I can either move immediately to have Ms. Winslow, or..." [244] Judge Baca cut in that she wanted to hear what Debbie had to say. I was beginning to hope that the judge was open to learning something about Mama's major asset and how it might be managed for her benefit.

The senior guardian who had once worked for Winslow did not show up at the hearing. The CPA who was nominally Mama's guardian at the firm did. This provided the impression that Winslow's proposal to manage Mama's account had always been what is called an "arm's-length transaction," picked dispassionately by the commercial guardian, as, in its expert judgement, the best submitted. Disinterested money managers might have submitted the others. This one, somehow, did not seem to be, although until the deposition I did not know of the long association between the head of the guardianship firm and Winslow.

Again, I was Alice in Wonderland, hearing Winslow pontificating, as the expert, saying, in response to Ruth Pregenzer's questions and as if it were new information, exactly what I had been saying for a couple of years already:

Q: What is your understanding of the duty that the conservator has to its ward?

---

243 I did not find this out until after Mama died.
244 Rosenstiel(2)020515

A: ...I was going to say that it depends on whether there's a trust or not, but there's obviously not a trust when you have a conservator. But the conservator is bound by the prudent investor rules, it's kind of like what they say about obscenity, that you can't exactly define it, but the closest any entities have come to defining it is saying what a prudent person would do...there's a further explicit provision that at some point you have to obtain diversification ...there is an obligation to take heirs into consideration...[245]

Winslow, warned in advance, that I was "litigious," felt obliged to denigrate what I had been doing in High Desert. I was, she said, no better a manager than any random person off the street. Besides, she was sure that I was only listening to my friends when I made investment decisions.

Winslow went on to describe to the judge what I wanted. This witness who had never spoken to me said that she knew what I wanted. How was that possible?

She had been saying these things under Ruth Pregenzer's questioning, and while under oath. I sat next to Debbie, fuming silently.

On cross-examination, Debbie had this exchange with Winslow:

Q: Ms. Winslow, you've never talked to Léonie Rosenstiel. Is that right?
A: That is correct.
Q: So you've never had a discussion with her about what her position is about capital gains tax or anything of that sort?... And you're saying that there's an email where she says she won't pay capital gains tax?...And [in making that statement] she wasn't talking about herself...she was talking about, if at all, an asset that was owned by her mother..."
A: Yeah...[246]
Q: ...I'm just asking if there's something here [in the emails] that indicates some reference to capital gains tax [by Ms. Rosenstiel].
A: No...but that is the most pressing concern for people...

---
245 Hearing Transcript, March 6, 2008. Rosenstiel(2)020543
246 Rosenstiel(2)020620-21

Q: You made an assumption?

A: Right.

Q: Okay. And there's nothing in here that talks about her concern about capital gains... [247]

On that day, Judge Baca decided Mama's (and much of my own) financial future, without having consulted either one of us. Not until March 28, 2008, did Winslow even approach the commercial guardian, proposing that she meet me. "I think it's time for me to get to know Leonie, and discuss how she feels about the various issues at hand," she wrote them in an email.[248]

Only after Mama died was I able to understand what happened there. Fortunately, Mama's will had named me both her sole heir and her "personal representative," the term used in New Mexico for the function other states call "executor/executrix." This gave me the legal power to open a probate case and subpoena the records kept in the back office of Kathleen Winslow, going back to the very first contact from the commercial guardian, asking them to submit a proposal to manage Mama's assets.

Those records, however, were held at Invest, a separate business, in another state. As the broker who cleared the transactions placed by Winslow's firm, and in fact oversaw the conformance of Winslow's firm with applicable investment regulations, it was legally required to keep all related documents for six years. That included all notes and correspondence relating to any given account. The guardian had approached Winslow during late 2007. Mama had died in mid-2012, and we had instituted the suit during May 2013. A few months later, and we would have missed receiving the early documents showing the original discussions between Winslow and the guardianship firm. As things turned out, we got all of them. At least I think we did.

The subpoenaed correspondence from Winslow's back office showed the commercial guardian's tendency to make negative statements about me to everyone with whom they dealt. Prior to the March hearings in 2008, this notation appears in Kathleen Winslow's notes on a conversation she had had with the head

---
247 Rosenstiel(2)020625-6
248 Rosenstiel-18953

of the commercial guardianship firm: "Eliz. Church=GAL. [GAL] knows that Leonie=lunatic."[249] Who—other than this same guardian of Mama's—might have told her that? This was certainly also true in their court pleadings, which never stood the test of any evidentiary hearings, but I had not expected all their statements that I was crazy, that my mother never trusted me and that she did not want me involved in her affairs.[250] Most commercial guardianship firms are populated mainly by social workers; the head of this guardianship firm was a social worker, too. A number of other social workers were either on staff or contract workers. This allowed the firm to claim some expertise in psychology.

The newly appointed guardian ad litem interviewed the guardian first. I am assuming that this led her to form the opinion she expressed to the court that my cousin had always been closer to Mama than I had, now and in the past, and that I was the equivalent of a mad dog walking around on two legs. And of course, Winslow spoke with the commercial guardian months before she met me, and seems to have based her opinion of me on what they told her. The documents showed that they had told Winslow that Mama had never trusted me to handle her finances, and that I was extremely volatile and unstable. They had fed Winslow her now graven-in-stone (or at least in the court record) opinion that I did not have any special knowledge of investments. Rather than acknowledge that my father had some special knowledge of investments, it looks as if they never told her about his certificate from the American Institute of Banking. She simply referred to him, in her court testimony, as if he were an ordinary off-the-street investor who happened to get lucky. In fact, a letter of instructions to Winslow from Pregenzer, on behalf of the commercial guardian, requests that she render a similar opinion of me. My expert had not charged for his proposed investment plan. Winslow charged Mama $11,617.76 ($14,192.25 in 2021) for her opinion.[251]

Winslow had admitted to the court that Mama's financial investment account would be at the "upper end" of the accounts she managed. When she started trying to transfer Mama's holdings

---

249 Rosenstiel-08699
250 Ibid
251 Rosenstiel-18797

into the account the guardian set up, she discovered that her back office would not allow her to authorize the transfer of amounts over $1,000,000 without special authorization. So, in 2007, Mama's NYMEX asset, with a cash value of between $8 to $9 million (down from the more than $12 million or more it had been worth a year or so earlier), would have been worth, perhaps eight to nine times the values of accounts she had been authorized to manage without further question from her back office. *That* she did not tell the judge. Nor did she tell Judge Baca that her firm never handled individual stocks, only mutual funds. This would be her very first time handling the stock of a single company—and a great deal of it. I would not have known, either, if Mama's estate had not subpoenaed the back-office documents in the probate case. Winslow had emailed her associates on February 13, 2008 that they might need "third party managers for that asset, since we do not do individual stocks."[252]

Nor did she tell Judge Baca that her proposal essentially risked Mama's assets. Within months of implementing her strategy, Winslow started receiving complaints from her compliance department about the investments she had chosen. Each of her mutual fund purchases worried that group. Its concern arrived in the form of "alerts" covering each of her early mutual fund purchases, each one of them stating, "client's risk tolerance not consistent with this mutual fund purchase."[253] Instead of being contrite for exposing Mama's account to all that risk, Winslow attributed her decisions to the fact that "she [Mama] is elderly—way past life expectancy...She has a very high risk tolerance because she has way more assets than she needs."[254]

Not until the day of that first 2008 hearing did anyone show me what they afterwards called the "Values Document,"[255] purporting to state Mama's wishes not to conserve her assets for any heirs. At the time, I did not think it was Mama's handwriting and asked

---

252 Rosenstiel-19266
253 Mama was then 97 years old. Winslow's compliance department was complaining that Mama did not have a long enough life expectancy to benefit at all from the chosen investments and that they were exposing her to too much risk. Rosenstiel-14988-15001
254 Rosenstiel-14989
255 Rosenstiel(2)014407-(2)014415

whether she had had a stroke between the time the guardianship was declared and the date, about a month later, when (according to the date the person who signed as a "witness" dated it) she supposedly wrote this document. No one would give me that health information.

Ruth Pregenzer then represented to the court that Mama had written this document. She told Judge Baca, "This is a Values History Form that was prepared by Annette Rosenstiel in her own handwriting a month after the guardianship began."[256] The judge entered it into the court record on that basis. The guardian's attorney then proceeded to discuss a DNR:

> MS. PREGENZER: ...and she [the guardian] wants to go ahead and put a 'do not resuscitate' order in place... because this was a point of ambiguity...we're asking for approval as well.
>
> THE COURT: All right.[257]

During the 2013 to 2017 discovery process in the estate's suit against the commercial guardian, I would find out that no one from the guardianship firm had billed for working on the values document with Mama that day. They had billed for a number of other activities, but not that one.

During her sworn testimony, Shay H. Jacobson, answered David Garcia's questions about this same values history:

> Q: Just looking at page 1 [of the Values History], does it look— like if you compare the handwriting on page 1 with the handwriting on page—the seventh page of the values statement, does that look like the same handwriting to you?
> A: ...I don't know if somebody has answered the question and written it for her or not...So I don't know whose writing is even on the first page...
> Q: ...In terms of your general review of the medical records in this [case] and your general knowledge as an expert in

---
256 Rosenstiel(2)202663 (March 13, 2008, Hearing Transcript, p. 23)
257 Ibid , p. 24

this case, would a person in the medical condition reflected in the records...be more or less subject to coercion or undue influence in filling out a form like this?[258]

Jacobson never gave a coherent answer to this question, on the basis that she had never interviewed Mama. Considering that, some years earlier, one of the commercial guardianship firm's minions wrote up her worries about Mama being subject to undue influence from her caregiver, the question does seem relevant. When was this document actually written? Considering that one of the items in that document says, "I am an Orthodox Jew," it sounds as if it might have been written under someone else's instructions, perhaps Betty's.

Back in 2008, however, I did not have any way to reach an informed opinion about whether Mama had written it, but I thought she had not. To me, none of those different handwritings that appeared in that document really looked like Mama's. My statement did not go into the court record. Ruth Pregenzer's did. Interesting, however, that Pregenzer was not under oath when she made the claim that Mama had handwritten the entire document.

With twenty-twenty hindsight, I probably should have jumped up and objected to introducing this document into the official record, since I was about 90 percent sure, even back then, that Mama had not written it. Having it there caused trouble later. Would Judge Baca have listened to me? I doubt it. I wonder whether she would have simply ruled me either out of order or in contempt of court and insisted on accepting the document anyway.

I had invited my own stockbroker, Erik Gallegos, to serve as my expert witness, to offer a counter-plan for managing Mama's assets. Although I did not know this until years later, Ruth Pregenzer actually preferred his plans to Winslow's, on the basis that all three of his scenarios cost Mama much less. "At first blush, the exchange fund looks like an awfully good and cheap deal," she wrote Winslow on February 25, 2008. In the second scenario, Erik had recommended bonds. "It appears that with the second scenario, Axxant is reducing its fees...Is this something Winslow

---
258 Shay H. Jacobson, Skype and Telephonic Deposition, June 29, 2017, pp. 25-26

and Associates would consider..." As for the third scenario, Erik had proposed, she warned, "in order to be competitive, we need to show why Axxant's proposals are not the best way to invest Annette's assets..."[259]

The bailiff swore Erik in. Debbie and Ruth Pregenzer asked him questions, only to occasion this eventual comment from Judge Baca:

Her [Winslow's] proposals are being heard today...I can consider some of her testimony with the expert testimony of another financial manager, which is being done, but I just want to make it real obvious to everybody that this is not an audition for a job, and it is not a motion to change conservator at this point, okay."[260]

There was no way Winslow could conclude that High Desert had been in any way mismanaged because Mama's assets had doubled during the time that I had been managing them. In fact, Winslow was forced to state, for the record, that she was not making any complaints against my management. However, she kept insisting that my success was just a matter of luck, because I clearly knew nothing about what I was doing.

This hearing resulted in the commercial conservator taking the (to me) weird step of making me sign an indemnification agreement. The conservator agreed to split Mama's assets, so that I would handle and manage all those within High Desert, and they would not meddle with my management. However, if I lost Mama's money within High Desert, I had to promise not to sue the conservator for not preventing this from happening.

Winslow's written report to the court had mentioned AT&T stock, which she said had belonged to my father, and that he had bought it because he essentially had better financial judgement than I did. In fact, Dad had never owned any AT&T stock. However, Arthur had held shares of that company for years. Dad and Arthur had had an on-going joke about Dad not being as savvy about the ultimate worth of this stock as Arthur, who had owned the original stock before it split up in 1984 into all the little "Baby Bells."

Brokerage firms maintain absolute privacy for their clients. I knew Erik would never share copies of our statements. Outside of

---
259 Rosenstiel-19240
260 Rosenstiel(2)020592

Arthur and me, the only entity capable of having given those financial statements to the commercial guardian was REDW, because as High Desert's accountant, it received copies of the monthly brokerage statements. There was never any reason to keep Mama's monthly High Desert financial reports from her conservator. However, normally, if an accountant is going to show something that has private information in it, the private information must be redacted first. They had a list of each holding of each of the partners. Ethically, I assumed that they would have redacted Arthur's information and mine before showing the statements to the conservator and Winslow, or they should have asked the managing partner(s), for permission to show the whole statement. But they did not. They had divulged private information without permission.

Expert witnesses get their documents from the entity for whom they are testifying, which meant that the commercial guardianship firm must have had the monthly statements from High Desert's accounts. Greg MacKenzie revisited this matter at my second deposition on March 22, 2017:

> Q: At any time did they [REDW] represent you, do any work for you individually?
> A: They were doing work for me individually up until the hearing in 2008. After the hearing, I moved my accountant to be another person, and that was Dick [Satter].
> Q: And is there a reason for that?
> A: Yes.
> Q: And what was the reason?
> A: When I was going through Kathleen Winslow's report and listening to her in court, she said something about my mother's stock in AT&T that had been a legacy of my father. My father never owned any AT&T stock, but my husband did. So the only way that Kathleen Winslow would have known that there was AT&T stock in that account was if she had access to records she should not have had access to. And so I withdrew my account from REDW at that point.[261]

---

261 Deposition of Leonie Rosenstiel, Vol. II, March 22, 2017, p. 405, lines 4-20

My whole family had used REDW since we moved to Albuquerque, back in 1997. REDW had knowingly given the commercial guardian access to privileged information for both my late husband's account and mine. I was not even sure for how long this had been happening. Perhaps they had been doing it for the length of the conservatorship. After reading Winslow's report, I went to talk to Kathy Becker, who had been handling the High Desert account, to tell her that I would no longer be using REDW as my accountant, and to explain why. She said, "Well, we knew that we had a conflict of interest there." I answered, "Now, you don't anymore."

Ironically, at the time I became aware of this ethical lapse, REDW was running an ad campaign emphasizing how ethical the firm was. Every time I heard that ad, I could not help smiling, ruefully.

The guardian-conservator introduced letters from experts in estate planning whom it had consulted, stating that Mama had already exceeded her allotted length of days, as expressed in the actuarial tables and that, therefore, she should already be dead. Based on this expert opinion, they were essentially stating that the guardian-conservator would be entirely justified in taking more than 4 percent of the total value of her estate out and spending it annually. Just because it could. Assuming that Mama had $8 million in disposable assets, that would be $320,000, in addition to the $90,000 or more that Mama received annually in pensions and annuities. If she had $9 million, then she could withdraw more than $360,000, and her $90,000-plus in pensions and annuities.

How, I wondered, could they possibly dispose of such a large amount of money if Mama was not able to travel anymore, was not frequenting expensive restaurants, was not taking expensive medication, was not buying designer clothes, and simply was not personally spending that much money? Within months, I deeply regretted asking that question, even if silently, to myself. If I had been allowed to speak, at all, during that part of the hearing, I might have said something extremely impolite.

Even though the guardian ad litem had suggested, in her report, that the commercial guardian-conservator might want to withdraw from the case, and the fact that Judge Baca always had the power to appoint a different guardian and a different conservator, or even one entity, again, to serve in both capacities as she sat on the bench during that hearing, the judge decided to endorse the one currently in power. That was her final word.

No matter who managed the account, if any broker acted under the orders of a conservator who followed the mandate to spend down Mama's assets at the rate of at least 4 percent per year, the result would have been inimical both to what I believed were Mama's interests in conserving capital, and to mine. Any commercial conservator would likely have the same "professional" attitude as the current one, if only because the current conservator would bring them up to speed on this account. Normalcy bias in the professions being what it was, and still is, I had no hope of convincing any new conservator to adopt a different management philosophy. After all, the current commercial conservator was a professional in this field. I was not. I was just a family member.

This led to, among other things, an email Debbie received from Ruth on April 8, 2008, after I inquired whether, if I met with Winslow, she would charge either Mama or me for this privilege. "I feel like we are already lapsing back into discussing details about information that is beyond the purview of Leonie's role as Annette's daughter,"[262] she wrote. My question, itself, now drew censure as inappropriate. Considering that the commercial guardian had already made all relevant decisions, I did not see much value to having a meeting with Winslow. I did not want Mama to suffer financially because I cared about her finances. It did not appear to me that anyone else did.

The guardianship "instructions" hearing on March 13, 2008, upset me equally. Mama would have been angry, too, I am convinced, had she known about it. That hearing only lasted one hour and thirteen minutes, producing just 48 pages of transcript. Judged by the time spent, considering a ward's welfare is unimportant when compared to the amount of time spent discussing their money. The GAL and the guardian presented some convoluted arguments, many of them unnecessary, I thought, given the fact

---

262 Rosenstiel-18931

that we already had a stipulated order regarding visitation, which had been one of the major issues between us.

The guardian wanted to redraw the visitation agreement, to prevent me from bringing any sort of sound recording or photographic device onto Mama's premises. Again, this was their reaction to me not wanting to be misquoted. Some months before these hearings, the guardian started accusing me of saying things they did not want to allow me to say. They claimed that the aides had been "reporting" me for doing this.

(During discovery, I realized that this had started after the head of the commercial guardianship firm asked Ruth Pregenzer how she could stop me from seeing Mama. No correspondence from the guardianship firm attests to this, as a policy, but of course, other emails sent through their secret server, phone conversations, or even in-person discussions might have taken place that would have fallen under the rubric of "attorney-client privilege." If that had been true, then even during discovery, I would never have seen any additional documentation on them.)

After quickly realizing that a hostile aide could "misunderstand" or "mishear" just about anything I said, I had started taking along a tape recorder to protect myself. Interesting, how these bogus claims stopped entirely once the commercial guardianship firm knew that everything I had said was already on the record. Then, their complaint to the judge was that it had cost them too much to make copies of the tapes I had recorded. Well, I saw Mama daily, sometimes for hours at a time. What did they expect? Perhaps they were simply disappointed that, in all those recordings, they could find nothing that showed me to be guilty of anything.

Elizabeth Church found a particular complaint I lodged with the guardian so ridiculously trivial that she used it to demonstrate to the court what a chronic complainer I was. The problem, on August 16, 2007, had been that, when I arrived, I had seen Mama's food from lunch left out on a kitchen counter, with Saran Wrap over it. They clearly planned to feed the leftovers to her later. Those leftovers remained on the counter for about three hours while I was visiting Mama. Mama and I sat, talking, at a table right next to the counter all that time. No one moved the food while we were there. I had arrived at 2:30 PM (when the air temperature outside was 91.9°F at the airport, and likely higher in the Northeast Heights, where Mama lived) and left at 5:30 PM (when the temperature was also 91.9°F at the airport).

That day, the 38 percent humidity meant that Mama's swamp cooler that served that part of the house could only lower the temperature by about 20 degrees, if operating at full power. If the outside temperature was about 92°F, then the inside temperature could not have been lower than 72°F. So, by the time I ended my visit, those leftovers had been sitting, unrefrigerated, since Mama finished her lunch, perhaps as long as five hours earlier, at a temperature of approximately 72°F. Good food handling practices say not to leave hot food out at room temperature for more than two hours. (David, who during an earlier part of his career had inspected restaurants for compliance with health codes, immediately understood why I had complained and was as shocked as I was that Church had found this specific complaint of mine so deserving of censure.)

To the GAL, however, only a nasty, picky person would make such a stupid, unnecessary complaint. Why, it was entirely unworthy of an attorney's time in writing a letter![263] To me, it was a health issue. Mama had been complaining to me of stomach upsets recently, and what I had just seen suggested to me one reason why she might have been having problems. Those stomachaches, I reasoned, might easily be avoided by simply instructing the aides to put leftovers in that shallow plate into the refrigerator after half an hour. I was in no position to tell Mama's aides what to do, but the guardian certainly could have. Clearly, the GAL did not agree.

To me, this is of a piece with the GAL denying that a person in a wheelchair might need to have a ramp to exit her home safely, in case of an emergency.[264] Church seemed to be so busy justifying the commercial guardian that she refused to notice the obvious ways in which the ward was not being protected.

That entire second hearing, it seemed to me, had been designed to show how saintly the commercial guardian had always been, in

---
263 Rosenstiel(2)020647-(2)020650
264 Rosenstiel(2)020954. One door had a 5-inch step; aides had suggested some concerns about getting Mama out the door, should that become necessary.

trying to put up with me, and conversely how absolutely awful and intolerable I was. After writing one long report, and then an addendum to that report—at a total cost of $20,712.39 to Mama,[265] the GAL ended up asking the judge to reconfirm the commercial firm's guardianship and conservatorship authority. Which the judge did. As a result, the guardian agreed to provide me with medical information, which, after that, they actually did for a few months.

Judge Baca appointed a "permanent" guardian ad litem, Gerard Lavelle. The designation "permanent" turned out to be wishful thinking because, about eight months later, he was appointed to a judgeship in the Second District Court, resigned, and vanished off the scene. I did not realize he had left until I read about it in the paper. At that point, no one was there to enforce court orders. Well, that is not entirely true. The commercial guardian could, at any time, have hauled me back into court, on Mama's dime, if the firm could have found any evidence that they thought I had violated one.

During discovery, I learned about Betty's letter to the commercial guardian about resuscitation and how much Mama wanted to avoid signing a DNR. Betty complained that each time Mama had been taken to the hospital by her guardian, whoever was with her had tried to force her to sign such an order, against her will.[266] The commercial guardian made a point of stating, during the March 13 hearing, and despite the notation in their own records to the contrary, that Mama had never wanted to be resuscitated. They asked for—and got—the judge's express permission to post a DNR (Do Not Resuscitate) order. They said, for the court record, that Mama had told me the same thing, but never allowed me to confirm or deny this.[267] Of course, Mama had never told me any such thing; she had told me that any decisions depended on the circumstances.

With great trepidation, I had agreed to visitation without any way to document what was being said. As Debbie managed to tell Judge Baca:

"And while she [Léonie] feels very vulnerable by agreeing not to tape at this point, her options as she perceives them—and I hope

---
265 Guardian and Conservator Report (2008), p. 10
266 Decades 032448
267 Rosenstiel(2)020664

I'm not misstating—are to agree to the not taping or essentially having to give up visiting her mother for fear that she will essentially go and have some accusations lodged against her that might even result in her having some criminal issues...but I've encouraged her seriously going forward ...The visits she has not taped... are those visits when she's taken a visitor with her, because that person could backup what occurred....It's clear that she and her mother benefit from these visits, and there is probably very little time left for these visits, and so I think it's critically important that they continue..."[268]

Again, money and credit determined the guardian's decisions. The commercial guardian was willing to have me continue to manage Mama's part of High Desert, the smallest asset Mama owned. The firm was even up for allowing me to file an independent annual report to the court on Mama's interest in High Desert. However, they expressed distress to the judge about anyone calling me a "limited conservator."[269]

No practical aspect of my management of High Desert had changed. Was there some problem with the legal definition of what to call my management of High Desert since the inception of the guardianship that explains this kerfuffle over titles? If so, why had I not heard about it before? It cannot be explained by a wish to deny public credit, because Mama's had always been a sequestered case, so secret that you could not even find this hearing listed with the other cases in the online court calendars.

Judge Baca summarized her understanding of the resolution of this issue as follows: "I do not think there's any need to come back to a full blown [sic] court hearing again."[270]

In March 2008 the handicapped ramps I had requested the guardian to put in, back in the spring of 2007, had still not been installed, despite the fact that they had already been charged for on the 2007 annual report, at about three times what they were worth. When I had Debbie notify the firm and GAL Church about this, the guardian backtracked, saying they had accidentally mistaken a

---

268   Rosenstiel(2)020671-2
269   Rosenstiel(2)020678-(2)020681
270   Rosenstiel(2)020686

plumbing repair for the ramps. Eventually, they installed only one, and then not until after the second hearing.

After the 2008 hearings, the guardian started spending, in earnest. By the time they were finished, they had spent over $70,000 "re-landscaping" Mama's approximately quarter acre of ground. (Paved areas and the house itself occupied the rest of the property.) They, of course, instantly disposed of all the plants we had lovingly collected in the wild, from the properties of friends, early during Mama's time in New Mexico.

Although the commercial guardian would later say it was my fault that they had had such high legal expenses in 2007, and that they were for the March hearings, most of the attorneys were not engaged until May and later. (Of course, I did not find this out until discovery in 2013 to 2017, and so for years I blamed myself for causing Mama this expense; those later documents showed that it was the guardian's lack of knowledge about the Merc asset that caused them to seek advice from more and more expensive experts. On the annual report, the expenses showed, but not the date when they were incurred.)

During that year, the guardian spent over $100,000 on the attorneys who were advising them on the Merc asset. These details show only in the documents subpoenaed from Winslow's back office, because the guardian redacted all the subject-matter indicators from those lawyers' invoices. No serious context for this spending came from the guardianship firm's discovery documents. If I had not been the personal representative of Mama's estate, and able to subpoena those back-office records, I do not believe that I would ever have seen them. Multiple people from the guardianship, in addition to a half-dozen legal firms, billed for repeated briefings because the conservator simply did not have the background to handle Mama's investments. How many hours? A few hundred? A thousand? More?

On April 3 Ruth Pregenzer asked her client why Kathleen Winslow had not started managing the trading right.[271] Not until June 2 did Winslow email all concerned that her compliance department would not allow her to advise the guardianship firm

---

271 Rosenstiel-07938-07939

on the seat itself.[272] Not on the lease and not on whether to keep or sell it. (Why did she not know this prior to the hearings?). On June 30, 2008, an email from the firm placing the collar on Mama's stock informed Winslow that she was not allowed to make decisions on the collaring of stock (which had also been part of her management proposal to the court).[273] They split their commission with Winslow.

Winslow supplied information and pocketed half of the commissions when a collar was made. Technically, she did not make the actual decisions. These decisions, everyone then kicked right back to the guardianship firm, which then had to sign an agreement stating that they had done their own research and were acting out of their own expertise. However, no one told me (or the judge) this during the hearing. Nor did this arrangement ever show transparently in the guardian's annual reports.

A single commission on placing the collar (suggesting that only one would be placed), which was the way Winslow had described the situation to Judge Baca, became, in practice, a single commission every time a collar was placed. Examining the collar documents, after I became the personal representative of Mama's estate, I quickly realized that collars were placed, with increasing frequency, over time. Commissions were paid on the value of the collared stock. As the value of the holding decreased (which was what happened), the only way to keep the same dollar amount of commissions stable was to make more trades, which was what was happening, regardless of the excuses given for doing so.

Winslow, who had testified as the commercial guardian's expert witness at the hearing (even though she never explicitly told the judge she was testifying as an expert witness), certainly had not admitted to the judge that this would be the first time in her professional life that she would be responsible for handling a collared stock account. On February 11, 2008, she had written to a senior colleague, urgently requesting advice and information about this sort of investment transaction, and information on what to say in court. Why did she need this? "I haven't initiated a collar before..." she wrote.[274]

---

272 Rosenstiel-07764-07765
273 Rosenstiel-07799-07801
274 Rosenstiel-07988-07989

Winslow, the discovery documents in the probate case showed, had no authority to transfer large amounts of money.[275] Anything over $1 million went beyond the scope of her authority—rather like a teller who cannot accept deposits over a certain amount without a counter-signature. Her back office rejected her first attempt to transfer Mama's account to her firm from Computershare, the transfer agent then holding the Merc stock, for this reason. Not a good sign.

More than $4 million in value had evaporated from Mama's NYMEX holdings before Winslow even took over. The guardian and conservator had allowed more money to disappear because of their almost two years of inaction than Winslow did, later, by what I considered to be her repeated bumbling.

After the hearings ended, Kathleen Winslow suddenly wanted to talk to me. I had agreed, during the hearings, to speak with her about the purchases she had told Judge Baca that she was planning to make for Mama's accounts.

When I went to see her, I felt as if I had walked into a Halloween party. On a hot spring day in Albuquerque, everyone on the staff (except, I suspect, the person with a masculine-sounding name whose business card was displayed on the reception desk, but whom I never saw) seemed to be wearing ankle-length, long-sleeved black dresses. The fabric looked like heavy wool. Some of the women had long, green-enameled fingernails. Everyone seemed glum.

After I sat down in her office, Kathleen Winslow herself began by telling me that she had started out to be a scientist, but there was discrimination against women when she graduated.[276] She

---

275 Eventually, there were two cases progressing. I had to act immediately to file for probate because stock firms, in accordance with FINRA and SEC requirements, keep records for six years and then discard them. As it was, I barely got some of this information before the deadline. I filed for probate immediately but did not have enough evidence to file suit for the estate until 2013, after I had reviewed those documents. To get that information, I subpoenaed documents in my capacity as personal representative, from within the probate case. If someone else had been named trustee or PR, that person might or might not (most likely would not) have allowed me to do this.

276 This assertion seems questionable. I discovered later that Winslow was one of the first female attorneys in New Mexico. According to Stanford University's Women's Legal History Biography Project, she was an attorney for years after obtaining her degree from the University of New Mexico Law School in 1974. https://wlh.law.stanford.edu/biography_search/biopage/?woman_lawyer_id=11158

could not get a lab job, she said, so her current occupation was essentially just a back-up option. She had to support herself somehow, she whined.[277] Her monologue did not inspire me with the confidence I wanted to have that she loved what she was doing and would perform well in caring for Mama's account. Judging from the letter she sent the guardian afterwards, it had been her intention to interview me extensively about my life and goals, rather than to allow me to ask her any questions, but the last person I was likely to allow to grill me was precisely someone in the employ of Mama's guardian. And particularly since she seemed to be perfectly happy to tell the court, before ever meeting me, that she knew as much as she needed to about me.

After that, it seemed that her only intention in setting this appointment was to grill me about my investing experience. Since she had already testified to what that was—when she obviously did not know—I thought that it was a question she should have asked me prior to March 6. Now, in my opinion, it was none of her business. I said I had gone there because she had told Debbie she wanted to discuss Mama's accounts. I reminded her that she was not my investment advisor; she was Mama's. Winslow told me that she had no authorization to tell me anything about Mama's account, that the commercial guardian was her client, not me. I got up, said my goodbyes, and left. Winslow wrote an email to the guardian afterward, emphasizing how unreasonable I was.

Were these next events integrally related? Did one flow naturally out of the others? It seems so, in hindsight.

First, I saw Gerard Lavelle, who was at least nominally the permanent guardian ad litem, giving him a list of my concerns. He said he would consider the items but never got back in touch with me about them.

After the hearings, the guardian started consulting estate experts, trying to get a new will blocked out for Mama. They had not mentioned doing this at either recent hearing. A few months earlier, they had gotten the psychologist to state that Mama could not make decisions anymore, so any new will would have to be

---

277 She never mentioned to me, during that conversation, that she had ever been an attorney. However, she was acting for Mama as an investment advisor, not an attorney.

their fantasy of what Mama would have done, had she been competent. Would this be another incidence of "substituted judgement"? A primary reason they gave to the expert they picked for doing this was that they wanted to make sure I did not inherit "too much." They even told Debbie and me the same thing. How much is "too much" and who decides?

The commercial guardian said not a single word to me at the time they were doing this, which made the timing of their proposal when they submitted it later, all the more shocking. Of course, they were not doing this superfluous "work" for free. They were billing Mama for every minute they spent, as were any other experts they hired.

Of course, I would have objected, loudly, had they told me when all this was going on, and they knew it.

The one friendly aide confided to me that she had recently become very much concerned. Not only was she worried that someone had seen her talking to me, meaning that she might soon be fired, but she also said that guardians sometimes arrange for "things to happen" to their wards, when it might be convenient for them. She said she thought that Mama might be marked for "something to happen" soon. No way could I get her to be more specific.

That was when I stopped sleeping well. When I did manage to sleep, I had nightmares. I did not sleep well again until almost ten years later, when I had almost finished the first draft of this manuscript. Since I could not see anything that had changed, and I did not know any other victims at that point, I had no way to evaluate what the aide had said, except that I suddenly felt impelled to go looking for a litigator. At this point, I had heard and seen a bit too much not to at least consider suing the guardian later.

Debbie was not a litigator so, with her blessing, I went out searching. It was no secret to anyone that I was extremely dissatisfied with the situation. The guardian also expected me to sue, eventually. I found such notes in a fair number of discovery documents because they told this to most of the people they hired.

Shortly thereafter, another aide, not so friendly, told me that the guardian firm generally called her in when a client was "about to pass." That little conversation terrified me and I started asking the commercial guardian, through my attorney, of course, whether there had been a change in Mama's health status. They insisted there had not been.

One day, early in July 2008, I arrived at the side door of Mama's home to the sound of Mama screaming in terror, so loudly that I could hear her, all the way down the long hall, through the closed door and out onto the patio. I quickly slid open the sliding door, which back then they did not lock, and ran down the hall into her bedroom, to find Mama, face down in the covers and hanging halfway off the bed. Mama's aide was holding her down by pressing on her waist. Her aide that day was the same one who said she was called in when clients were about to die.

"What happened?"

"She was getting up and she fell." (She said this, despite the fact that Mama was face down on the bed, not face up. Almost certainly, she would have been face up, had she been trying to get up.)

"What are you going to do?"

"Hold her. Wait for my relief aide."

"When's she due?"

"In about an hour."

Mama would not be able to keep her head up that long. I figured that she would have been smothered by the covers by the time an hour was over, so I said:

"I'll help you raise Mama up and put her back on the bed. Probably shouldn't wait for an hour. Let's do that now."

We did. As soon as we got Mama onto her back, she stopped screaming, breathed a deep sigh of relief, and started to relax.

I informed the guardian about this incident, through Debbie, as soon as I got home. The firm disputed that Mama had "fallen." Apparently, this sort of situation has a special name that I had not used, "assisted fall." It was "assisted" because someone was there to "catch" her. Score one for them; I had given the guardian another opportunity to tell me how ignorant I was. Not that it matters much what you call it, if it ends in the ward being smothered.

Right after this happened, and after drawing several blanks in my search for a litigator, I prayed, then went on the internet. By then, I was pretty sure that I was going to sue these people at some point. Useless to call the police or the fire department or the DA's office. The fire department had already refused to examine the premises to confirm they were hazardous for a person confined to a wheelchair, for as long as they had no ramp. I had tried all that before filing my petition for guardianship. They had all said, "You have to go back to court. This is a guardianship case." The police told me to contact the DA, who could order an investigation, but the DA refused even to return a call.

I found Micky Barnett's legal office, through its internet listing and, the first week in August, I took over some documents to him, so he could see at least the monetary hemorrhage that the conservatorship had become. There was almost no chance that I would be compensated for my pain and suffering, or Mama's for that matter; but money, the law generally understands.

Mickey, his then-partner David A. Garcia, and their paralegal, Jane, met with me. At the time, nothing seemed imminent, but I wanted to get Mickey together for a conference with Debbie, which happened quickly. Within days, as I recall. They agreed, easily, on a division of labor.

Years earlier, Betty had sent the guardianship firm a set of detailed instructions for Mama's funeral and burial. The commercial guardian told me nothing about this. Up until that point, they had done nothing about them. During discovery, I would find out that, while these other events were happening during 2008, after the second hearing, the guardian had suddenly, simultaneously started arranging for both a new estate plan for Mama and for her funeral. I found emails and letters and phone messages back and forth to a funeral parlor in New York. They had been discussing this for weeks. Had I known that while it was happening, I would probably have gone ballistic, given what was happening otherwise, and what the aides had been saying. Judging by the documents I saw after Mama died, by early August the commercial guardian and the funeral parlor seemed to be just on the verge of signing a contract.

Almost a month, to the day, after I found Mama face-down on

the bed, screaming, I got a call from the commercial guardian. It was the morning of August 8, 2008. Mama was in the hospital. Her hip was broken.

Those were the facts everyone agreed on. After that, the stories about what happened diverged radically. The hospital admission records state that Mama was being "assisted in transfer" when she fell.[278] Meaning that the aide was helping her get out of bed. I later learned that the aide who had accompanied Mama to the hospital was the aide who had reported the incident in the first place, the aide who had been on duty when it happened. Presumably, she was the person who was doing the reporting because Mama herself would not likely have used a phrase like "I was being assisted in transfer." By the time I reached the hospital, the original aide had gone off-shift. Not knowing that, I blamed the relief aide for this event.

In 2008, every aide was still producing handwritten notes for each shift worked.[279] However, when we got the discovery documents from the guardianship firm, the notes for that day had mysteriously disappeared and a typewritten letter from the service that supplied the aides replaced them.[280] That letter stated that the aide was in another room when Mama fell, that side rails were still up on Mama's bed, and that Mama never cried out or complained, so the aide had no idea that anything was wrong. A while later, when the aide decided to go in and check on Mama, she found Mama on the floor.

The problem with accepting this story is that there was a baby monitor in the room. The same baby monitor that I turned off when I visited, because of a special dispensation from the commercial guardian. Otherwise, it was always on. The sound of someone falling or moaning (even if done quietly) would have echoed throughout the house. Any major effort expended to climb over

---

278 Rosenstiel(3)01929323
279 Now that most home health care firms (and health-related professions, in general) have gone to computerized record keeping, they just check boxes that say "companionship," or "toileting." Everything is standardized, which means that anything out of the ordinary that happens cannot satisfactorily be notated, and they cannot testify to it because it is technically "not in the record."
280 Decades 30447

the rails would have caused Mama to make some sort of noise, if only heavy breathing. Mama would not have had to cry out loudly at all. I knew that monitor; it was so sensitive that it could pick up the sound of Mama moving around in bed, providing that she had been able to do that unassisted.

In fact, in an addendum to that report, the home health service felt obliged to say something about the monitor. "The baby monitor [receiver] is located in the kitchen area, which can be heard in the kitchen, den and living room...Typically, when Dr. Rosensteil [sic] needs assistance, she will call out."[281]

Then, there is an additional problem that the aide who was friendly to me told me that, at a group meeting after the event, the aide who had been on duty had gloated that she had been the one to drop Mama. It sounded as if some sort of assignment had been given to everyone and she was taking credit as the one who had completed it. I certainly hope not! The aide who told me this seemed terrified even to tell me this much, as if some sort of ethical compulsion made her admit it, even though I could not really do anything about it because I could not prove anything, and neither could she.

Before leaving for the hospital on August 8, I called Gerard Lavelle's office, to ask what part he planned to play in the new situation. He said that he had not been told about Mama's hip fracture and asked whether I wanted him to go to the hospital. I said that I did. He seemed surprised. As I recall, he got there the next day.

I had a major argument with the guardian over whether Mama should have surgery. With her compromised respiratory system, leaving her in need of oxygen under normal conditions, I was concerned that the sort of general anesthesia used in major surgery would stop her from breathing altogether. I had already spoken to Mama's orthopedist at the hospital, and he agreed with me. He advised against the surgery.

Gerard Lavelle, fortunately for Mama, inclined in the direction of accepting medical advice. The guardianship firm seemed angry. As David C. Leech, who at that point had been Mama's primary

---

281 Decades 28449

care doctor for only about a month (and later admitted that he had only seen Mama once before her hip fracture), wrote in his notes, "The orthopedists [sic] opinion is that the patient would not significantly benefit from a hip surgery and the surgery would likely be more dangerous than allowing the fracture to heal on its own."[282]

While Mama was in the hospital, I had a chance to talk to her about whether she liked the busy environment of the hospital better than the quiet environment in her home.

"I like to have people around."

"Do you want to go home, or to a place with more people?"

"More people. I want to have people to talk to."

I spoke with the hospital's social work staff. They did not see any reason why they could not recommend rehab for Mama and then, seeing how she reacted to it, whether a longer time near more people might benefit her. The problem was that the staff at the commercial guardianship firm primarily consisted of social workers also. The hospital's staff social workers could only make suggestions to the guardian; hospital personnel could not countermand what a court-appointed guardianship firm, headed by a social worker with special credentials as a guardian, too, wanted to do. And the guardianship firm, if challenged, could always produce that bogus "Values Statement," with what they claimed was Mama's request to stay in her own home written into it.

Mama was 96. The commercial guardian assured me that she did not have long to live. Old people with hip fractures, they said, do not live more than a matter of weeks. While I had seen that happen with my grandmother, who was 80 when she broke her hip, I told them that I did not think Mama was going anywhere for quite some time. They laughed in my face. They brought up the Values History on the subject of Mama staying in her home and said she did not know what she was saying when she asked to go where there were more people.

Did Mama need a convalescent facility, at least until she got a little rehab for her injury? Might it do her some good to be with others? The commercial guardian refused. Refused to allow Mama any time in a facility. Mama was going home, on hospice, they

---

282   Rosenstiel(2)019434-(2)019435

insisted. At that point, I had no standing to object. Nor did the hospital social workers.

This matter came up, again, during my second deposition, with Greg MacKenzie leading the legal team defending the commercial guardianship firm:

> Q: So at some point they began to discuss discharging her from the hospital, correct?
> A: Yes.
> Q: And you were involved in those conversations, correct?
> A: Yes.
> Q: And your position was that institutional care would have been preferred rather than home care, is that IO fair to say?
> A: It's not quite accurate in that I'd had conversations with her [Mama] while she was in the hospital. And she had said to me that she wanted to see more people. She had not realized that saying she wanted to stay in her own home meant that she was gonna be in her own home but she wasn't gonna be able to get out of it. And now she realized she wasn't gonna be able to get out of it, which was pretty true at that time. She couldn't move. So I started discussing with various people from [the guardianship firm] and the hospital what that meant, and they basically said that she could be in a rehabilitative facility for a period of time and with other people and see how she felt, and then go home because she could if she wanted to. But that did not happen.[283]

One thing about Mama's hip fracture worked in her favor, even though I did not know it at the time. It placed on hold the firm's attempt to arrange Mama's funeral, which I gather that they would otherwise have finished arranging, in accord with Betty's instructions.

After I found these documents in the course of discovery, I started to wonder whether, if the commercial guardian had signed a contract with the New York funeral home the day before Mama broke her hip, I would have been bound by it, as

---

[283] Leonie Rosenstiel, Deposition, Vol. II, Albuquerque, New Mexico, March 22, 2017, lines 2-25.

her personal representative. The figures they had been bandying about with the funeral parlor were in the $50,000 and up, range ($63,703.25 in 2021). And Mama would not have had her original wishes honored.

At my urging, Gerard Lavelle attended the group meeting we had at Mama's home on August 14, 2008, the day Mama was brought home from the hospital. (Ironically, it would have been my parents' 65th wedding anniversary, had Dad still been alive.) Again, the GAL seemed surprised that I wanted him involved at all. Having him there, as a witness, seemed to me to afford me a little protection. Debbie was going to be there as well. She and the GAL were not supposed to be opposed to me. Otherwise, everyone else in the room—the doctor, the hospice representative, the representative of the home health aide service, the head of a nursing service the guardian was about to engage, a representative of the guardianship firm, and Ruth Pregenzer, could all be presumed, in advance, to be hostile parties. And they were. Six people on the guardian's side. One—the GAL—supposedly on Mama's side. Debbie and me on "my" side, whatever that meant, since I did not think "my" side was anything other than supportive of Mama's side. The gathering still seemed a bit unbalanced to me.

David C. Leech, D.O., told the group that he had only seen Mama once before her hip fracture. He had not been allowed to see Mama in the hospital because he was not an attending physician there. He did not really know Mama very well before her hip was broken, and he did not know me, either.

Whatever Leech had heard about me had not been good. While I was sitting there, he instructed Hospice de la Luz that they were there to take care of the needs of the staff, including the guardian's staff, and his own needs, but definitely not mine. I was simply a supernumerary and not to be considered. I can wholeheartedly attest to their scrupulous attention to his instructions. Meanwhile, the number of aides needed to attend to Mama depended, he said, solely on how much she was able to pay. That discussion had nothing to do with medical necessity. Since she was a private pay patient, there was no need to attest to any medical necessity, he said. According to him, Mama could have as many attendants as she could pay for. Maybe Mama was lucky she did not have an even larger bedroom. They could only fit two attendants, comfortably, in there.

Doctor Leech gave Mama a prognosis of three weeks to live, maximum. When I suggested that my sense of the situation was that Mama would survive for quite a while, he got a look on his face that suggested he had already been told how crazy I was, and now he knew it was true.

Greg MacKenzie asked about this discussion at my March 22, 2017, deposition:

> Q: Was there any discussion about levels of care?
> A: It was a rather unusual discussion in that what I discussed was I was concerned to make sure that she [Mama] got whatever level of care she needed. And I did not get great clarity on what that was from him, but it seemed clear that she needed somebody to dispense medication periodically, and it would not be clear how often, probably for a couple of weeks, until they saw what her reactions were.
> Q: Was there any question or any discussion about the number of people who would be hired—sorry—any conversation about the number of people who would be hired to provide that care?
> A: There seemed to be a concern on the part of hospice that because narcotics were going to be on the premises, that normally they have relatives administer them. And that was not going to be possible in this case, and so someone needed to be on the premises who had the right to administer narcotics if called for. With precision, I don't recall being there for having to have somebody on the premises 24/7, but there needed to be somebody who could administer medication if needed.
> Q: Such as a nurse?
> A: Such as a nurse. And, in fact, hospice ended up coming a number of times to administer medication because some one with a license was not present.[284]

---

284 Deposition of Leonie Rosenstiel. Vol. II. Albuquerque, New Mexico, pp. 435-438

Originally, they told me that this staffing would be true for a few weeks. (I realize, now, that that was when they expected Mama to die, but she refused any narcotics most of the time, and she lived.)

The commercial guardian was paying for a licensed individual to be present, even if no one appeared, as ordered. What sorts of controls did the guardian have in place to monitor whether personnel actually appeared and worked? Apparently, none. If an invoice arrived, they paid it. Because of various electronic ways of checking in, including calling from Mama's land line, either the number could have been spoofed and the employee checked in when not at Mama's home, or the person could sign in, then skip out, then return in time to check out, via phone, again. Later, I saw people sign in, then skip out.

When Hospice called to complain that they had had to send someone to administer narcotics because the nurse was nowhere to be seen, the guardian did not seem to have any idea that no one with a license was there. If a nurse was not present, and the nursing service was billing for a nurse, that would be anywhere from $46.97 per hour for an LPN, on up to $130 per hour for an RN on a holiday, that the guardian was paying, needlessly.[285]

Expenses rose rapidly, to somewhere between $1,153.04 to $3,120 per day ($1,439.75 to $4,766.43 in 2021) for a licensed person, which was what they initially contracted to spend, just for the private-duty nurse. The few weeks of this they mentioned was certainly warranted, but continuing at that level might use up all Mama's income and force her to invade her principal, which up until then, although that principal had been shrinking in value rapidly under the conservator's control, did not seem to have been tapped into at that point.

Knowing Mama's resilience, I believed firmly that Mama was going to survive for a long time, perhaps for years. I felt compelled to try to protect her principal so that she would not end up penniless. She and Dad had both worked hard. Throwing money away

---

[285] That was not the only occasion when the specified personnel were not present. The hospice nurse complained also about some time in 2009 when no one was there to help with medication. (6/18-21/2009 and 6/22/2009). Rosenstiel(2)019062; Rosenstiel(2)019574-(2)019575

was not going to help her much, that I could see. I knew, in advance, that the commercial guardian would try to make me feel contrary and stupid for my efforts, but I felt obligated to try, anyway.

Who is it, by the way, trying to convince everyone that it is going to be less expensive to keep an elder (alone and isolated?) in that person's home instead of an institution? Less expensive than what? In 2007, it had cost me about $4,636.21 per month during the time Arthur was in a nursing home and that included everything he needed. However, the fee was $11,000 for a single home health aide, twenty-four-seven, for a month, after he was home on hospice that same year. And that second amount did not include any other supplies or services. (Those amounts would have inflated to $5,954.02 and $14,126.66, respectively, by 2021.)

Now, marry Dr. Leech's "medical instructions" to the financial "guidance" given by the commercial guardian's estate-planning attorney Kenneth C. Leach (and yes, their names only differed by one letter) during the financial hearing in March 2008. Leach had written, in his "expert report" that the guardianship firm could withdraw more than 4 percent of Mama's net assets, per year, if they felt like it. A heady mix, indeed. The later records produced during discovery showed what looked to me like a sort of wild scramble to spend money had ensued. For all but six weeks of the next almost four years, the documents kept secret from me at the time proved that, except for the first few weeks, it was almost all unnecessary. And even then, most of the extra expense could have been averted by doing what Mama told me, during her hospitalization, that she wanted. She wanted rehab. In that sort of facility, a nurse would always have been available to dispense medication, at no extra charge.

Over the summer, the guardian had been in discussions, repeatedly, with expensive Wall Street attorneys, trying to decide what to do about the Merc asset. These sets of recommendations they often passed on to other, local attorneys, for comment, thereby incurring additional fees. Someone from the guardian's office had at least monthly meetings with Winslow and emails back and forth, in the interim. Everything was charged to Mama. Mama and I knew nothing about this, at the time. I assumed that Winslow was handling everything, just as she had given Judge Baca the impression that she would. No, I need to correct that statement. Winslow did not simply give Judge Baca the impression that she would. While on the witness stand, under oath, she told the judge, and everyone else in that courtroom, that she not only could, but would.

All they told me was that, per the guardian's instructions, Mama was supposed to have at least two people on duty, at her bedside, twenty-four-seven. I was later to discover, through complaints filed by Hospice de la Luz, that often workers did not show up for their shifts at the appointed times; they did not have a clue how to raise and lower the head of Mama's hospital bed; sometimes the sheets were full of crumbs for a week (suggesting they had not been changed in that long); and so on.[286]

I never saw the sheets under Mama's blankets, but given the filthy wall-to-wall carpeting that, even when cleaned commercially and repeatedly, showed up as filthy again within a week or two, I concluded that the days of pristine cleanliness, back when Mama had the first aide who had thought the house would one day belong to her, were gone forever.

Hospice apparently believed that their orders would be respected. "TV is only to be on @ Dr. Annette's request," their supervisor wrote to the staff on August 24, 2008, "to watch the news, etc. Please turn TV off when Dr. Annette has visitors."[287] Had they followed her instructions, some of the problems I had later would never have happened, because Mama would never have been upset by what she saw on TV.

One new aide, who apparently had not heard yet that she should not talk to me, congratulated herself on the "easy duty" she had at Mama's home. "At the place I used to work, I had to flick roaches off the client's drinking cup," she said, quite matter-of-factly. Another new aide said substantially the same thing, but she added that, at Mama's, she was glad that she did not have to "walk on roaches in the hall all the time."

---

286 Rosenstiel(2)019556 The nurse on duty also complained about this on March 16, 2009. Rosenstiel(2)019473 December 20, 2008.
287 Decades 33133

Both of those wards had, these aides told me, said they wanted to stay in their own homes. They owned those homes, which meant they were not indigent. On the other hand, on questioning, these aides admitted that no one ever visited those other wards. The only difference I could see between those clients and Mama was that Mama had me visiting daily and the other clients were all alone in their homes, except for the aides.

Before the 2008 hearings, I had already discovered that the state did not monitor guardianship situations in homes where there were fewer than three "unrelated" residents. No inspections. No standards. Many people ask to stay in their own homes. They are even encouraged to do so, to remain in familiar surroundings. It is supposed to be good for them. Dementia patients favor familiar surroundings and schedules, we are all told. I wonder whether elders realize that, if they do not have frequent visitors, and if the people caring for them are not monitored carefully, they might end up living under truly deplorable conditions. What those aides told me scared me.

I got a good chuckle, during discovery. An email surfaced, from among the documents my attorneys received from Winslow's back office. The commercial guardianship firm wrote to Winslow and Ruth Pregenzer. "Why don't we just ask Leonie what to do?" was the gist of that email. Ruth Pregenzer quickly emailed them back. "We have recently had a long court battle, one consequence is to free [the conservator] from obtaining prior approval from Leonie...In my opinion the decision regarding the lease of the NYMX seat should be one of those issues."[288] Years later reading this correspondence, it seemed to me that the conservator had no clear idea what to do with its ridiculously expensive freedom of choice.

It turned out that what the actual guardian wanted to do, instead of asking me, was even stranger. "Please ask Steve if he has any thoughts on this,"[289] she wrote to Maria Montoya Chavez on March 19, 2008, not yet two weeks after the second hearing. Steve was the person leasing the seat. Did he not have, at best, somewhat conflicting motives here, since there were times when he seemed to want to buy the seat himself?

---
288 Rosenstiel-18981
289 Rosenstiel-19005

Only a few months earlier, they had asked Judge Baca to issue an order telling me to stay out of management decisions, except for High Desert. At least they eventually acknowledged that I was the only one around who knew how to navigate these particular shoals, even if they did not want me to find out they could not.

Hospice, as hospice usually does, wanted to keep Mama from feeling pain, and so they urged her to take morphine and other painkilling drugs. Mama had always hated medication. She considered it poison. She was very weak during her early days at home. Speaking cost her more effort than she wanted to expend, but I could still communicate with her by getting her to draw pictures. Mama had been looking very worried for the first couple of days.

"Is there anything you want me to know?"

Mama drew a picture of Gael, her long-ago pet who had been poisoned with cyanide

"Is that Gael?"

Mama nodded.

Thinking about all the drugs they told me that they wanted to give Mama, and how one of Mama's aides told me they had given her morphine not too long ago, I thought I would ask Mama whether she thought she was being poisoned. It would have been all but impossible to ask that question in the presence of staff, so I simply asked her, "Are you Gael now?"

Mama nodded, weakly. None of the aides gave any indication that this conversation had any meaning to them. Apparently, Mama had not mentioned Gael to those aides.

After that exchange, I started making as much noise as possible about no one pushing any drugs on Mama, that she did not want to take them. I did manage to get them to stop, albeit reluctantly. Once they did, Mama did not have that look of perpetual concern anymore.

Mama had acquired bedsores in those few days she had spent in the hospital, even though the guardian had paid an aide to be with her twenty-four-seven, and theoretically, the aide should have been making sure Mama did not stay too long in any one position. The guardian would later deny that Mama ever had any bedsores.[290]

---

290 Between mid-August 2008 and late October 2008, 18 documents provided by

Now that Mama had two people on duty at all times (or at least the guardian said she did), she still had bedsores. One of the people present during the day was supposed to be either an LPN or an RN. They were waiting for Mama to need medication. And Man, were they expensive! For the first couple of weeks, Mama was too weak to eat by herself; by law, the aides could not put medication into her mouth, only food, but the nurses could.

One thing that had terrified me during the meeting with Dr. Leech was his statement that I firmly believe that I recall on the subject of blood clots. Mama had had a blood clot before. If she seemed to be developing one again, so that she became short of breath, the way she had been several years earlier, when she ended up in the ER at Lovelace, Dr. Leech said she would be given a heavy dose of morphine, and it would make her stop breathing. As I recall, he said the injection would prevent her from being in pain. He would train the aides so that they could easily administer the shot.

I tried to object, but got nowhere. The judge had given the guardian plenary power and the guardian said they would be bowing to the doctor's judgement.

During discovery, I later found one aide's notes, stating that any shots must be administered to make it look as if Mama had given them to herself.[291] Come on now. Mama was in no shape to administer a shot to anyone, let alone to herself. Call the doctor and then administer the drug, the notes said. So, now they would be allowing home health aides to give Mama a lethal injection and pretend she had given it to herself? Really?

At least figuratively, I held my breath and prayed for the next year or so, that Mama would not get a serious blood clot. She did have a couple of small ones, induced by all that bed rest, but readily controlled by hot applications. Another physician replaced Leech, and hospice was discontinued, when it became clear that Mama was not going to die, on schedule.

Hospice de la Luz show various incidences of skin breakdown. Considering that Mama always had an aide with her when she was in the hospital, I wonder whether there should have been any, in the first place. See: Weekly Wound Assessment & Care Sheets, 8/15/2008-10/23/2008.

291 Comfort Keepers Caregiver Activity Log, October 29, 2008. The guardian did not provide this during discovery. "If a nurse isn't present we can give injections of Roxanol that are pre-drawn & in a bag…If this happens, Dr. Annette will have shortness of breath… ." Rosenstiel(2)019946

Fortunately, for the time that Leech was her physician, Mama did not have a blood clot that made it necessary to see whether Dr. Leech's plan would have been put into operation. Do the judges know what sort of power they are giving these people? Do they care?

In 2016, the New Mexico Supreme Court ruled that even assisted suicide was not allowed in New Mexico, for terminally ill patients.[292] Assisted suicide remained illegal in New Mexico until 2021. Normally, a patient has to show volition and clear-headedness in making a decision to commit suicide for the law to accept it. Mama's guardian had recently sworn to the court that Mama did not have those qualities. Not being an attorney, I am not sure whether court orders giving guardians end-of-life power over wards allow them to make these sorts of plans, even now. Is this something people ought to be discussing?

I was deeply sorry, then, to have given up "end-of-life" decision-making power, back in 2004. However, by 2008 I was sure that some coalition of the guardian and the medical community would tell me exactly what they wanted me to hear and I would not get a straight story out of any of them anyway. By then, my one friendly aide had been fired, too, so I was alone in hostile territory.

The day after Mama returned from the hospital, Debbie got a letter from Nell Graham Sale, who had taken over Mama's account at Swaim & Schrandt. Because Debbie was my attorney, I still cannot say exactly what she said to me or what I said to her about Sale's letter, without compromising the famous "attorney-client privilege," but the email she forwarded to me appended the commercial guardian's proposal to change Mama's will. The guardianship company wanted to create a nest of trusts, to make sure that I had only a stated amount of money every year, for ten years. "It fixes the amount that is distributable to Leonie," Sale wrote.[293]

Although admitting that, by the terms of Mama's current will, I had the right to exhaust the funds in any trust during my lifetime, Sale nevertheless insisted that I should "name" the relatives who

---

292 Retrieved on June 25, 2020 from: *https://www.governing.com/topics/health-human-services/tns-new-mexico-suicide-doctors-ruling.html*
293 Rosenstiel-10829-10831

would inherit whatever remained after my death. She ended up proposing the creation of three trusts. Not only did she want to alter Mama's will, she wanted to look at my will, also.[294] I already knew what it took to keep up the single trust Arthur had left me. Since they did not want to allow me to administer the trusts they proposed to create, I saw this proposal as a good way to exhaust whatever funds Mama might still have.

The August 15 letter said this plan had been in process for some months, so it had not just been cobbled together after Mama's accident. We discussed the proposal, of course, although estate planning was not anywhere near my top priority at that point; I was busy trying to support Mama in her recovery.

This "estate-planning letter," in its timing, really did appear to have been created in response to Mama's accident. Nevertheless, the documents I saw during discovery proved that the commercial guardian had started these discussions with attorneys about changing Mama's will earlier, just as Sale said. However, the date when the attorney chose to send that letter remains just about the most insensitive one that anyone might have picked. Winslow's notes on her conference with the commercial guardian's, estate-planning attorney Ken Leach and Sale on May 29, 2008, make clear that Ruth "was not an estate-planning attorney."[295] Ruth had left Schwaim & Schrandt, but not yet set up her own firm. Sale had taken over for her at Schwaim & Schrandt (albeit, as it turned out, very temporarily). On May 14, 2008, Sale had written to the others, "Why are you meeting with Ken Leach? Why are you discussing estate planning for Annette?"[296]

Reading Winslow's notes on that meeting,[297] it seemed that Ken Leach and Nell Sale sat there insisting that non-existent "heirs" would have some right to the putative "remainder" of Mama's trust, when in fact there should no longer have been a trust.[298] No one, apparently, consulted the files showing who Mama's relatives were, nor do they seem to have understood her will, which

---

294 Rosenstiel-11319
295 Rosenstiel-11317
296 Rosenstiel-18824
297 Rosenstiel-11317-11321
298 Judge Clay Campbell dissolved Mama's trust as part of the probate case, on July 18, 2013. Dad was right; the trust should never have existed in the first place.

showed that she had explicitly disinherited every one of those relatives still living, except for me.

Mama had made her will, back in the 1990s. In 2003, the guardian had agreed that she had done so when she was of sound mind, and the will was valid. Mama had named only Arthur and me as her beneficiaries. Contrary to the way Sale wanted to read Mama's will, Mama had never named any other beneficiaries, nor did she intend to. Arthur—who would have been the only other beneficiary—had already passed away, leaving me the sole remaining beneficiary.[299]

Impossible, however, to say no immediately. We asked a few questions first. Sale replied: "The only way to work this out might be to have a co-trusteeship with [the commercial guardian] and Leonie over the revocable trust during Annette's lifetime...I have always joked about how it is estate planning lawyers who are the ones with the sirens on our cars, rushing to the hospital [to take care of estate matters]."[300]

Maybe this is a "correct" way to arrange things, using some sort of one-size-fits-all template. However, Sale did not seem to know anything about the dynamics of my relationship with the commercial guardian. Anyone who had done a little research would have known that, for the previous five years, they had wanted everything I did not want and I had wanted everything they did not want. Perhaps Sale did know, but maybe she had decided to ignore the reality of the situation, in favor of adhering to some theory then current among estate-planning attorneys.

Apparently, their legal status gave all these people the belief that they "ought" to change what Mama said she had wanted. We had both promised Dad never to name a charity as beneficiary in our wills. Now the guardian wanted to create a "charitable remainder trust" with Mama's money, and get me to agree.

If I concurred with the guardian and helped the firm make these changes, and hauntings were possible, I was sure that Mama would come back to haunt me, she would be so angry. I tried to

---

[299] This was exactly how the impartial probate judge read Mama's will, and then decided to dissolve the trust itself. Retrieved June 4, 2020 from: *https://caselookup.nmcourts.gov/caselookup/app?component=cnLink&page=SearchResults&service=direct&session=T&sp=SD-202-PB-201200284*
[300] Rosenstiel(2)004209

think how I would have felt, had I been in her place. I would not want some stranger coming in from the outside and deciding they knew better than I did what I wanted. I figured Mama's will should be her own will, not her guardian's will. I refused to sign off on changing Mama's will. I did not think I had a right to ignore Mama's wishes. We sent my absolute refusal back to Sale almost immediately.

Usually, hospice sends a harpist when they expect someone to die soon. Only a matter of days after Mama came back home from the hospital, the commercial guardian arranged to have a harpist come and play for Mama. In preparation, they asked me to make a list of some of her favorite music, which I did. On it were some French Christmas carols, "Belle nuit" from the *Tales of Hoffman*, and a couple of other things I knew Mama loved. I was waiting, out in the breakfast nook, the list in my hand, when the harpist arrived. Another non-descript-looking lady, dressed in drab clothes, carrying a small harp case.

"You wanted me to make this list?" I handed it to her.

"I'm not going to play any of that stuff! I'm just going to let Spirit lead me."

"You know, Mama was a trained musician. She has strong emotional reactions to music."

"I'll trust Spirit."

A representative of the guardian's office was standing there with me, so I did not want to make myself too unpleasant. I was hoping that Spirit would lead the harpist to avoid pieces Mama hated, or works that upset her for one reason or another.

Bach's "Jesu, Joy of Man's Desiring," her first offering, was definitely not Mama's favorite piece, although it sounded great on the harp. As I listened, I was standing across the room, watching Mama. Given the state of Mama's eyesight at that point, she probably could not see my face. Her expression was neutral.

The harpist then launched into a fairly long arrangement of Beethoven's "Ode to Joy," which most people find inspiring. Mama did not. It reminded her, predictably, of the many arguments she had had with her sister Louise's husband over the years, primarily about his involvement with the Masonic Order, which Mama hated, and to the close relationship between that piece and the Masonic Order. In addition to which she had never liked that "too massive" music. Mama always said the singers screamed. Even though there were no singers that day, I could see that Mama could still hear them, in her memory. Mama's face started to turn dark.

Beethoven's contribution to the afternoon's entertainment having come to an end, the harpist apparently decided to end the recital on an up-note. I suspect that she had not looked at Mama's face at all as she played, even between the numbers.

The harpist from Hospice launched immediately into a spirited rendition of "Daisy Bell (Bicycle Built for Two)." Mama started looking actively angry, screwing up her face as if she was about to scream. Had the harpist asked me in advance, I would have warned her not to play this. But she did not want my input; she, like the guardian, knew better.

By the time the harpist had finished, Mama was holding her breath and her face had turned red. Why? That song was one of my paternal grandmother's favorites. She used to sing it all the time. She had died after breaking her hip, even before the stage after the event that Mama was in now. Mama had interpreted it as the harpist telling her to die, and she really, really objected. So did I.

How can some people totally ignore what is right in front of their faces? The harpist noticed none of this. She approached Mama's bed, smiling broadly.

"Wasn't that great? Would you like me to come back?"

"Do you have to?"

After that, the guardian asked me to give Mama a record player and some records that I knew she would like. Even though there were shelves and shelves of albums in Mama's garage already (but of course I did not know that at the time), and she had a record player, as well. To the best of my knowledge, the commercial guardian did not invite the harpist back. Some of the albums I gave Mama, at the guardian's behest, I never saw again.

On September 10, 2008, Gerard Lavelle called the commercial guardian. They made three separate charges related to his resignation from the case as of that date. I did not know he had resigned and wondered why I never heard from him again. Not until the *Albuquerque Journal* listed him among the applicants for one of the two then-open Second District Court judgeships did I realize that he had only served a few months as the GAL and was now leaving the case.[301]

Back in December 2006, a truck had rear-ended my car, leaving me with a couple of nagging physical symptoms and a nasty concussion that had erased my entire memory of music. Over time, it had started to return a bit, as I realized on listening to the harpist, but I did not recall how to play any instrument by the time Mama had her hip fracture.

One of Mama's LPNs, after she returned from the hospital, said he played the violin. He had heard that I did, too, and started trying to insist that I play for Mama. I said "no" as politely as I could. I told him Mama was very critical of my playing, which was certainly true, although she might not be of his. I am sure he thought I was mean, not to want to play for my own mother, but I absolutely could not risk the guardian finding out about my concussion. I was so terrified of them that I was sure the moment they did, they would start guardianship proceedings against me, just to get even. Later someone told me that the LPN had played for Mama, but I only heard that once. Maybe he did not play for her again. Maybe he had played music Mama did not like. Maybe Mama was critical of his playing, too. He never mentioned the matter to me again.

As Mama strengthened, and her memory of the harpist's recital receded, she looked much more cheerful. One sunny summer afternoon, a week or so after she got home, Mama started talking again. I mean whole sentences, not the occasional few words. The aide and the nurse were out of the room. The monitor was off. Mama clearly wanted to tell me something.

"One of us has to tell the story," Mama said, slowly, and with some difficulty. "I know it won't be me. You have to do it. Promise?"

"Okay, Mama. I promise."

Mama, who had been leaning forward a little, sank back into the pillows of her hospital bed, exhausted, a slight smile briefly playing on her face before she started to doze off. The rays of the

---

301 "Judge Seats Draw 25 Hopefuls," Albuquerque *Journal*, October 28, 2008, p. D2

desert sun streamed in through the window. I looked at Mama's porcelain skin, remarkably unlined given her ninety-seven years of life. Her now-long hair flowed free, pure white, against the pillowcase. Ever since she had graduated from high school, Mama always told me she had kept her hair short. She hated having long hair. Always said long hair gave her headaches when she was growing up. Her commercial guardian never seemed to cut it anymore.[302] I sat by her bed for a while.

When she woke up a few minutes later, Mama realized she had forgotten something:

"One of us has to remain standing to do this."

"Yes, I understand."

Almost as soon as Mama was home from the hospital, the guardian's minions had started importuning me, demanding that I force Mama to see a rabbi. They said that they had asked her but that she had adamantly refused. Normally someone in Mama's situation would want the "consolation of religion," they reasoned. They wanted Mama to want to be part of the religion Betty had told them she belonged to, but Mama herself would have none of it. I told them more than once, "If Mama doesn't want to see a rabbi, then no one should force her. I know that I won't." In return, whomever I was speaking with at the time would shoot me a nasty look. I got the impression that they were angry with me, once again. But then, no matter what I said or did, they always seemed to be angry with me.

Whether this conversation resulted from something Betty said to them, I do not know. What they might have told Betty, after that conversation, I have no idea. I found no documents relating to Betty's conversations with them on this subject, although I suspect there were some. After Mama's hip fracture, Betty never visited Mama again. I would have known if she had, because I would have received a formal communication from the guardian, barring me from Mama's premises until after she left.

The commercial guardian did not tell me when Aunt Louise died. I arrived on September 4, 2008, to find Mama's eyes filled with tears, but she was not able to tell me what the matter. At

---

302 To me, it seemed that they did not cut it at all between the time Mama's first aide was discharged in February of 2007 and the day she died, in 2012.

the time, I worried that the guardian's minions would blame me for Mama's sadness. In fact, I was surprised when they did not.

Years later, I discovered her sister Louise's obituary on the internet. That was the day she had died. Someone had clearly told Mama. If the guardian had only told me at the time, I might have been able to do something more specific, to console Mama for losing her last remaining sister.

Although Mama had absolutely rejected the idea of seeing a rabbi, she had eagerly accepted the offer to have the Protestant chaplain from Hospice de la Luz visit her. Rev. Angus Smith, a Scottish-born-and-trained Presbyterian, I know only from his pastoral notes. (I now wonder whether he reminded Mama of an early Scottish beau.) Rev. Smith died in August 2010. I would not have dared to attempt to contact him before Mama died, for a talk, even though I had seen his name in documents before that. His obituary, however, names the good qualities I identified in his notes: "a thought-provoking and highly intelligent preacher and a man of unfailing compassion"[303] it said. I have always wanted to thank him for his efforts on Mama's behalf. (Mama's guardian refused her any other social services; the social worker from Hospice de la Luz felt obliged to mention this on every report he wrote, and to attempt to explain why, because he seemed to see something odd in their refusal.[304])

The good chaplain documented the absurdity of some of what he was told; given his high intelligence, I suspect that he intuited that this information would later be useful to someone.

By the time I learned of his existence, it was 2010. Both he and Hospice de la Luz were long gone from the scene.

The guardian told everyone I was an Orthodox Jew. This "information" was made part of the hospice file, so that they advised Rev. Smith to visit in the morning, because Hospice "remains concerned about Leona [sic] Rosenstiel's response to a Christian clergyman at her mother's bedside."[305]

At times, Mama would say she was an Orthodox Jew. I heard her say that a couple of times myself, after a letter from Betty

---
303 "Obituary for Smith," *Albuquerque Journal*, August 29, 2010. Retrieved June 4, 2020 from: *http://obits.abqjournal.com/obits/print_obit/208697*
304 Rosenstiel(2)023951-(2)23956, and all other months during Hospice service.
305 Rosenstiel(2)024372

arrived, containing detailed instructions for the celebration of one Jewish holiday or another, and an aide had been discussing it with her. Is this coercion? Leading a vulnerable person, perhaps? She did once say that to Rev. Smith as well. However, I do not have documentation of the exact circumstances surrounding that conversation. Perhaps that statement, too, followed a letter or a call from Betty. Or someone else discussing Judaism with Mama. I do not think Mama was trying to lie; I think that she was taking great pains to tell her visitor what she thought that he wanted to hear. She once said she had grown up in a Chasidic community; in fact, she had grown up in a solidly Roman Catholic area.

Rev. Smith was an extremely talented observer. During his first visit, after Mama's aide brought in the studio photo of Mama to show, "Dr. Rosenstiel looked at it dispassionately," he said "and then turned it around to show me. I smiled and nodded, studying the face in the image. "I see a woman much loved by her father," I said. She looked surprised, reclaimed the picture for another look, then her eyes became moist..." Unfortunately, I think that he misinterpreted Mama's reason for crying.[306]

On December 2, 2008, during another of his visits,[307] Mama admitted to him what she had admitted to me, back in August, about how lonely she was. "I thank my fates that you have come," he quotes her as saying, "I stare and stare at the walls." Asked about her caregivers, she replied, "They are very good, but they leave me in peace. Oh, so very *much* peace!" After a bit more conversation, Mama felt much more positive, "Indeed nobody has stolen my imagination. I stare at the wall, through the wall to the next room, into the room beyond and so on, right out into the world!"

For reasons I cannot understand, the chaplain described this December visit as, in part, to console Mama for the recent death of Aunt Louise. According to my aunt's obituary, she had died on September 4, 2008. Had the guardian been late in telling Hospice?

Mama spoke with him of her love for New Mexico, just as she always did with me. "I am so glad that I moved here all these years ago. I love New Mexico. I love the sunshine, the weather, the short

---

306 Rosenstiel(2)024370
307 Rosenstiel(2)017132

winter."[308] To me it seems that Mama was more comfortable and open with Rev. Smith than with anyone else, except me.

If not for Rev. Smith doing his homework, I would have had no idea to check Amazon.com, to see why he had said, in his notes, that Mama and I had co-written a book about Nadia Boulanger.[309] The good reverend had apparently looked Mama up online prior to his visit. Someone had managed to change the attribution of that book so it listed Mama's name as a co-author. I ignored this and went on with life.

By January, he started to worry about seeing Mama, because she was supposed to be Jewish. Out of a sense of ethics, he explored this matter with someone from the guardian's office, whom he quotes as saying, "Ms. Rosenstiel is an unusual person, who has had no connection over her lifetime with her faith community."[310]

On Thursday, July 16, 2009, Rev. Smith was concerned about Mama. He had been told that she had refused lunch. He wrote that he had found Mama "wakeful but listless, her usually lively eyes lusterless, unresponsive to my greeting as to my presence at her bedside." It took him a while to bring Mama back into the world again. The Thursday aide, Rev. Smith wrote, "...tries on Thursdays to cook sufficient nourishing food for a week...to spare her charge commercial frozen dinners." He was worried enough about Mama's demeanor when he arrived to take this matter up with his supervisor. The hospice supervisor told him that, as Rev. Smith wrote in his pastoral notes, "...the regular Wednesday caregiver is somewhat intrusive upon Dr. Rosenstiel's life, which causes her to withdraw into herself."[311] Considering that Mama could not move unassisted, and needed everything done for her at that point, how much more "intrusive" must someone be to provoke that sort of reaction?

Eventually, Rev. Smith began to wonder why Mama was not seeing a rabbi instead of a minister. He worried about how well he and Mama got on and how much Mama obviously enjoyed seeing him. He worried that someone (me?) might see him as proselytizing Mama. If the guardian did not tell me about him, I am

---
308 Ibid
309 Rosenstiel(2)024375
310 Rosenstiel(2)017535
311 Rosenstiel(2)024362-(2)024363

even more convinced that they did not tell Betty. When Mama was discharged from hospice in October 2009, he simply disappeared from her life, after hospice decided to discontinue his services. They had considered telling him not to see Mama again as early as August 20, 2008, on the grounds that Mama no longer was speaking, an assertion that, according to Rev. Smiths' notes and my own observations after that date, was totally untrue.[312]

At one point, I saw one of Mama's aides take some matzo out of a box Betty had sent her, and ask Mama, "D'ya want some Jew bread?" At another point, another aide stuck some Hebrew in front of me and demanded that I read it. She said that her priest knew Hebrew and he had taught her enough so that she could say whether I was doing it right. He had told her what to listen for. I demurred. I had no idea when or where he had learned his Hebrew, whether it was before or after certain elements of pronunciation changed, but I did not want to get into that whole question. Besides, I had never learned much Hebrew.

When faced with a situation that seemed to call for religious intervention, Mama did not want to have anything to do with a functionary from the Jewish religion. Nor did she wish to have any contact with Jewish observance. However, Mama did have and enjoy real discussions about religion with Christians. Finally, I realized that her attempts to adopt Jewish positions in these discussions might well be holdovers from her days as a professor. Mama had always prided herself on being able to argue any subject, from any point of view. If she was discussing things with a Christian, she wanted to speak from the point of view of a different religion, and the most accessible to her was Judaism. Years before there was any suggestion that Mama might be falling prey to dementia, she had given me very different instructions about after-death arrangements than Betty had sent the guardian, despite the detailed instructions the guardian sent me that purported to be hers, covering her burial.

Mama had already complained to Rev. Smith about her loneliness. He wrote, "She talked about her experience, bedridden, in terms of a form of imprisonment." He quoted her as saying, "I remember the days when I could do things, and select some

---

[312] Rosenstiel(2)024372

cherished events in order to relive them"."[313] Seeing that made me feel sorry for Mama, but vindicated. Mama was not just saying that because, perhaps, she thought I wanted her to. She really felt that way. And she was right. If one person sits by your bed and plays computer games, you are still essentially alone. If two people do that at the same time, are you twice as alone?

As to Mama being certified, and then recertified periodically for hospice care, discovery revealed contradictory documentation. Rev. Smith's notes quote real conversations. However, the LPN evaluating Mama's mental status for Hospice wrote, at about the same time that Rev. Smith was quoting, verbatim, intelligent discussions, that Mama "smiles, laughs & shakes her head but does not respond appropriately to any questions."[314]

Is this about money? If Mama improves enough, she cannot stay on hospice, meaning hospice cannot be paid. From a financial point of view, however, Medicare will pay hospice, no matter who its clients are.

However, a different explanation makes more sense for me. As with Mama using her hearing aids as a way to find out who her friends were, she might have decided that the only way she could have any level of control in her life would be to refuse to communicate with certain people. I discovered that when I first met Elizabeth Morgan, who replaced Dr. Leech as Mama's primary care physician on her discharge from hospice. One day, I was standing in Mama's room when Dr. Morgan walked in. Immediately, she started asking me questions about Mama. Did she like this? Had she been feeling that?

"Your patient is right here. Why don't you ask her?"

"Oh, does she speak to you? I've seen her a few times, and she never speaks."

"Mama speaks to me all the time. We were just talking when you came in."

Then I realized that Mama had not said a word after Morgan entered the room. If Mama could do that in 2009, she could have done the same in 2008, with the hospice nurse.

---

313 Rosenstiel(2)024366 (He had conversations with Mama over the summer of 2009)
314 Rosenstiel(2)024119

As I predicted to Dr. Leech, Mama simply refused to decline. Eventually she had been discharged from Hospice because she refused to die.

By early September 2008, the commercial guardian finally informed Debbie that the firm was in the process of making funeral arrangements for Mama, the arrangements the discovery documents revealed they had actually started to make, back in June. I told them to stop, that this was my prerogative as her personal representative. They responded by sending me the instructions Betty had sent them, years earlier, and other instructions they said had been written by Mama, but after the guardianship was in force. These were supposed to have been Mama's instructions, except that they contradicted what she had told me when she was mentally competent. However, they did agree with instructions Betty had sent to them. I would more trust Mama to tell me what she wanted than I would trust anyone else—particularly one of these people.

We eventually resolved this dispute with a stipulated order, stating that the guardian would permit me, as Mama's personal representative, to make funeral arrangements for my own mother. How generous of them! That was what Mama's will had always said, anyway. With all the various fees that had to be paid, on both sides, to get that stipulated order blocked out, it cost me another few thousand dollars, to ransom back the power that Mama had clearly given me years earlier, when she was able to express her own wishes.

In October 2008, the guardian paid for an independent "Lifecare Plan" for Mama, to be completed by Ronda St. Martin, R.N., a Certified Lifecare Planner at the Albuquerque office of Broadspire, a disability management firm.[315] Everyone, except me (because I was not part of the care team, I assume), met at Mama's home on October 21, and St. Martin interviewed the members, separately.

The verdict: Mama no longer needed skilled nursing care, nor did she, at any time, require two attendants, anymore, on a single shift. This report cost the guardian about $2,000. Did this mean

---

315 Shay Jacobson, Skype and Telephonic Deposition. June 29, 2017, Exhibit 17

that the commercial guardian followed those recommendations? Did this mean that they informed me that Mama had improved so much that she did not need all that care anymore? Not on your life! They kept all the redundant personnel employed, which, practically speaking, meant that they could continue to spend more than 4 percent of Mama's net assets per year.

I tried to get the guardian to allow Mama out. Out of her bed and out of her room. Dr. Leech at first said it would be acceptable to take her out of bed, and then he backtracked. I always wondered whether this resulted from some instructions from the commercial guardian, but no documents provided during discovery prove anything, one way or the other. They certainly gave the aides strict instructions not to allow Mama even to try to get out of bed.

Mama begged me, repeatedly, to help her get up and go outside. The discovery documents make clear that she had begged the aides to help her, too. They wrote about it in their notes.[316] The guardian insisted that the broken hip they had refused to splint could not bear Mama's weight. I could not take the chance that they might be telling me the truth and that Mama would fall if she tried to get up. They probably could have brought in a Hoyer lift and trained Mama's attendants to use it, just as they could have done that before the hip fracture, but once again, they did not choose to do this. If I tried to help Mama get up, and she fell again, it would be my fault. She only stopped asking me to help her up after I told her that, if I helped her and she fell, the commercial guardian would probably never let me see her again.

After noticing that the guardian would not let Mama get out of bed, after the hip fracture, I brought a measuring tape with me one day, to compare the width of the doors to Mama's room and the width of her bed. As I had suspected, Mama's hospital bed, which was on wheels, would not fit through the doorway to the hall. To wheel it thorough, that area would need to be widened by several inches.

Unfortunately, Mama's bed was also too wide for either individual door of the pair of French doors leading to the garden. In order for Mama's bed to be wheeled outside, both of the French

---

316 Caregiver Activity Log, December 14, 2008; Rosenstiel(2)017529; Caregiver Activity Log, May 23 , 2009.

doors would have to be opened. However, the door to the yard still had no ramp. The only door with a ramp was now the one by the kitchen, an area of her home that Mama had not been able to access since August 2008. She still could not, because she could not get into the hall leading to it. That made Mama, to my way of thinking, a prisoner in her bedroom. A proper ramp outside the French doors would at least allow the bed to roll down, safely, to the outside.

Attempting to discuss these issues with the guardian got me nowhere for a long, long time. This was no big deal, they said, because, in an emergency they would simply throw Mama down on the ground, on a blanket, and pull her outside.[317] Were they calculating that they would upset me by saying this? They were right. Throwing Mama anywhere would likely break other bones in her body. I begged them that, if an emergency ever did arise, at least one of the aides should carry Mama out in her arms. By then, Mama weighed about 90 pounds, so I did not think this was a totally unreasonable demand.

The guardian had given Hospice strict instructions not to tell me anything (they rarely did). When I asked the guardianship firm what was happening with Mama, they referred me to Hospice. When I contacted Hospice, Hospice referred me right back to the guardian. Or, if I asked an aide or one of the nurses from the home nursing service, they referred me to Hospice, who then referred me to the guardian, who then referred me to Hospice again. It only took me a couple of go-arounds to figure out the patterns, here. I kept asking, anyway.

Nevertheless, my gratitude for having Hospice on the job that one year is boundless. The best thing about Hospice was that it left a paper trail. That paper trail proved that the guardian had not prepared the aides for power outages, nor indeed for any other unexpected eventualities. They did not know where the flashlights were, or even whether any existed. They did not know what to do for Mama's oxygen when the lights went out. They had no idea how to raise or lower the head of Mama's bed when the electric

---

317 Deposition of Léonie Rosenstiel. Vol. II. March 22, 2017, Exhibit 130.

failed. They did not even know whether they had any supplemental oxygen. I discovered these things when Hospice produced their documents after I demanded some explanation of Mama's mushrooming expenses.

Mama's reported home health care costs rose from $258,313.91[318] in the guardian's annual report for 2007-08 to $565,689.55[319] in the guardian's annual report for 2008-09. (Those amounts would be $322,545.04 and $706,351.28, respectively, in 2021.) Furthermore, these were just the expenses for Mama's health care attendants; they did not include any of Mama's other expenses. At that point, it seemed to me that an explanation, at least for the attendants, might be in order.

---

[318] 03-Item65 in TOC Report 11.14.07-11.14.08
[319] 03-Item66 in TOC Report 11.14.08-11.14.09

CHAPTER IV

As One Nightmare Ends, Another Begins

I have often thought back to a question Dr. Ewing asked me when I met with him and Elizabeth Church in Mama's kitchen in 2007:

"Do you understand why the [commercial] guardian acts the way it does?"

"I can't imagine why they do what they do. What they do doesn't make any sense to me. Never has. They never explain why they do anything."

In a world where I normally presumed people to have relatively benign motives, I would never expect anyone to act as they had acted. Part of the problem, I now realize, comes from training everyone in the eldercare industry to assume only competition and conflict (and, of course, cupidity) as dictating the behavior of relatives who spend time near the prospective ward. Sometimes—as with my younger cousin—this acquisitive motive is obvious, but only after previously secret material surfaces. And she was an ideal person to support the guardian's actions. Betty, in my opinion, did not know Mama very well. Over the years when she was growing up, she had only seen Mama, perhaps two or three times a year. Then, too, for the almost four years during which Mama was losing her ability to think clearly, my cousin saw her only once, back in the summer of 1999. She did not see Mama again before the court decided that Mama needed a guardian.

Relatives often have goals in common, however. They might even care about each other, and this adversary legal model does not seem to consider that fact. Even worse, all court cases seem to consist of adversaries, at least according to all the dockets I have ever seen.

The fall-out from Mama's birthday in 2009 finally convinced me to sue the guardianship firm after Mama passed, although the commercial guardian had acted as if that was destined to happen even before the 2008 hearings, and I had also begun to prepare, just in case.

I was standing in Mama's room one day in 2009, next to one aide, when another walked in, carrying several small packets.

As the second aide entered, she handed two of them to the aide standing next to me and kept the third one for herself. The aide standing next to me thrust the second object she had received into my hand.

"You're the daughter. You should have one of these."

"What's that?"

"Pictures they took on your mother's birthday."

"Thanks."

Mama had made me promise to "remain standing." My on-going terror of being the only one on "my side" had kept me from accepting the commercial guardian's invitation to Mama's ninety-eighth birthday party. They did not offer to allow me to invite any of my friends to the party. I could not pay for Debbie to be there because that would mean that Ruth Pregenzer would also have to be there (at Mama's expense, of course). I am not even sure that, as my attorney, Debbie would have been allowed to speak to Mama; there is some legal protocol surrounding an attorney talking to a non-client who is supposedly on the "other side" of a legal case.

If I attended, without at least one witness whom I could bring, perhaps a dozen guardian firm loyalists would be the only other attendees. The odds were not good that I would come through that event unscathed, so I skipped the party. Why did even an apparently straightforward social event require prior extensive tactical analysis?

They did, however, stipulate that they would pay a commercial company to take a series of photos of Mama and me. They had final approval of the photographer and used Mama's funds to pay for the bill. Above, one of those photos. Léonie Rosenstiel and Annette Rosenstiel in the living room of Annette Rosenstiel's Albuquerque home (2008).
Photo: C & H Productions (Albuquerque)

I started looking through the photos. They were not pictures of the party itself.[320] I do not recall seeing pictures of any groups. Instead, they were all pictures of Mama. Mama with a birthday cake on her dresser, the cake posed, carefully, under those infernal photos. Mama, dressed in a nice robe, but still in bed, where she was going to remain for the duration of the party. Mama answering the phone. ("That's Betty on the phone," the aide told me.) Mama nude, looking rudely surprised and trying to pull the covers up around her. What?

The aide must have noticed my face change. "We call that one 'bath time,'" she explained, smiling, as if that made it all better.

"Who took these?"

"Someone at the birthday party. They gave copies to all the aides, as keepsakes."

"Not you?"

---

[320] According to the aide's notes that day, there was no birthday party, although the aide wrote "Happy Birthday, Doctor!" On the page and mentioned that Mama "Had [a] piece of cake Mary brought." Caregiver Activity Log for June 29, 2009

"No."

That much seemed clear because it was another aide who had entered with the copies. I thought I had better not say anything more. The second aide was on the other side of the room, looking over her own copies, so she was not likely to be the person who took them, either. With my peripheral vision, I tried to see Mama's expression. Her face looked both impassive, and determinedly set that way. Who were "they," the people who had taken these photos? Were other people there, also taking pictures? Were other pictures, even more revealing than the picture that had set me off, taken that day? I was afraid to ask. Even if I asked, they had now intuited that I was displeased with that photo, so they might not tell me anyway.

Their primary trial attorney, Greg MacKenzie, asked me at my deposition, somewhat apologetically, whether I knew who had taken the offensive photo. I answered that I did not know the names of most of the aides, that the aides almost never wore any nametags, and that they had not told me who had taken the photos.[321]

Oddly, for all the press the estate's case against the guardian received,[322] even after the gag order was lifted, the *Albuquerque Journal* never mentioned the part of my complaint involving this nude photo. The money seems to have interested them more.

Over the summer of 2009, someone rear-ended my car again. Of course, I missed my usual visit to Mama, that day. I was in the ER, for the first hour or so, believing that Bill Clinton was still President. I never told the guardian about my accident. This time, it had caused another concussion (fortunately I only had the new concussion symptoms for a few months) and a knee injury. Over the course of the next few months, I started needing a walker

---

321 For some reason, I was unable to find this exchange, even by repeatedly reviewing the transcripts of my two depositions; how it was omitted from the transcript is a mystery to me, because I clearly recall this exchange.
322 Colleen Heild, "Journal seeks to open guardian mismanagement suit," *Albuquerque Journal*, March 31, 2017, p. A1, A6; Colleen Heild, "Plaintiff in guardianship case wants judge to step aside," *Albuquerque Journal*, May 22, 2017, pp. A1, `A3; Colleen Heild, "Judge in guardianship case denies bias claims," *Albuquerque Journal*, June 29, 2017. pp. A1, C2; Colleen Heild, "Who Guards the Guardians: High-dollar 'malpractice' case unsealed by court order," *Albuquerque Journal*, July 23, 2017, pp. A1, A8.

because of the injury. The day I started using it, the aide (or was she a nurse?) standing by the kitchen door saw me opening the sliding door by the kitchen.

"Hi! When's your surgery scheduled for?"

"I don't plan to have surgery."

She looked shocked.

I did not know her, other than perhaps having seen her around Mama's home before. I complained to the guardian about inappropriate questions being asked of me by Mama's staff and was rewarded by one of the partners writing that she would instruct the aides not to mention my "cane." One invoice entry reads for December 4, 2009, "Please do not acknowledge Leonie's [sic] cane or ask any questions."[323]

Although I wanted to do something about the photo, I had to recover first, after the accident. I had already discovered that, if I complained about anything within the guardianship, the District Attorney and the police, equally, would simply refer me back to the civil (in this case probate) court system for redress of grievances. After some months of reflection on what I could do about the photos, and after I started feeling better, Debbie wrote a letter of introduction for me.[324] Then she and I made a stop at Attorney General Gary King's office. For one thing, I complained about that photo. For another, I described the massive hemorrhage of money out of Mama's accounts. King ignored the money questions. Totally. First attorney I ever met who did so. The millions that appeared, then disappeared, did not seem to interest him at all. He did at least look at the photo. We were only there a few minutes.

King patted me on the head, as Debbie and I were leaving his office. (I do keep wondering whether my need for a walker induced everyone to condescend to me.) Drawing himself up to his full six feet, so he would tower over me, at my own not quite five feet, he said, "I know exactly how you feel. My mother has dementia too." Then, he shepherded us out of his office. I did not hear from him

---

[323] Rosenstiel-22275 (As before, footnotes with names and numbers only refer to specific documents in files offered as part of discovery in Leonie Rosenstiel (PR) v Decades, LLC (et al) D-202-CV-201304646
[324] Rosenstiel(2)021016

again about this matter. Neither, to the best of my knowledge, did Debbie.

No, Gary King, you did not know how I felt, back then, and you do not know now, either. Unless you would have felt just fine, knowing that unnamed individuals might have been taking nude photos of your mother when she had dementia, and that they were taking those pictures apparently without her permission. Because she was no longer capable of giving it. And, oh, yes, those photos were being distributed in multiple copies (I think this is one definition of the word "publication"), to an indeterminate number of strangers who were then free to recopy and redistribute them, at will.

If you believe that taking nude pictures of elders with dementia is absolutely acceptable, Gary King, and you think that commercial guardians, appointed by the court, and paid handsomely for their efforts by their wards, should treat their wards this way (or allow others to do so), then that is how *you* feel. But it is not how I feel.

Did they take—or allow others to take—nude photos of Mama every year, and did I simply accidentally find out about it this one time? How many other people might have been there, taking pictures that day? Who were they? If the photographer made multiple copies of the photos, then the commercial guardian was presumably not objecting to this practice either. If this is standard practice in the commercial guardianship industry, how many nude photos of elders are floating around? How else might they be used? Do people "in the business" trade them, like baseball cards?

I started to wonder whether, perhaps, commercial guardians might routinely take—or allow others to take—nude photos of wards at other times, as well. Might that have been what Rev. Smith's hospice supervisor meant, when she said that a particular aide, who seems to have worked once per week, was "intrusive"? Mama did react to her ministrations exactly like the children I knew in nursery school, after our own experiences of abuse. We withdrew and refused to communicate with the outside world, for a while. If Mama's dementia had progressed far enough, she might well have reacted on that same level. Regardless of her degree of dementia at that point, since she was immobilized in bed and unable to escape, what other option than withdrawing into herself did she have? Why, since it seemed that everyone, including supervisors, knew how Mama reacted to this particular aide, did the commercial guardian not replace her?

There is an extremely odd notation in the commercial guardian's invoices. Dated January 19, 2010, it reads "Update Values History."[325] How could it possibly have changed?

After Mama died, I discovered, in the guardian's invoices for March 1, 2010, that Gary King had picked up the phone,[326] and called Ruth Pregenzer to tell her about the visit Debbie and I had paid to his office. Debbie's name was not mentioned, however, only mine. (During the time I was meeting with other families who had been seeing former attorney Stuart Stein—about whom more, later—the families of three other wards all said they had had appointments with King, to complain about the treatment of their loved ones, then under the court-appointed guardianship of the same commercial firm; he had done nothing about their complaints either. They all also told me that the firm had made their lives more difficult thereafter.)

King had called Pregenzer. She, in turn, called the commercial guardian's office. The guardian's billing record, for that date states, "PC from attny Pregenzer, re; Leonie/AG's [sic] office."[327] The guardian then billed at the rate of $110 per hour, in ten-minute increments, for this sort of work. (They billed very low-level office work at $70 per hour.) Getting information about my visit to Gary King to someone at a supervisory level in the guardian's office cost Mama $22. Of course, Pregenzer billed, too.

The commercial guardian said Pregenzer took 20 minutes, speaking to their office, longer than I had spent talking with AG King in the first place. The commercial guardian redacted Pregenzer's billing records, submitted as part of discovery, so I was not allowed to see the subjects of her calls that day, only the durations and fees charged. Pregenzer billed Mama for three separate jobs

---

325 Rosenstiel-22040
326 I would have expected King to have done something more about these complaints.
327 Rosenstiel-22046

that day, for a total of $280—three different calls, one of them lasting 48 minutes ($160), the others 18 minutes ($60) each. So, Mama paid more than $300 for my temerity in visiting the AG in the first place. But I did not know anything about all the billing my visit caused until after Mama died.

By then, I had become convinced that others in New Mexico had to have similar issues. I started looking, actively, for them, and particularly for a family whose members might allow me to make a documentary about them that I could present on my Channel 27 show. Originally, I did not want to take on events in New Mexico, but I had started to change my mind. Reading an internet post, I found someone from another state who claimed to be related to a New Mexico ward. The family, she said in that post, was very unhappy with the progress of events in her relative's guardianship case. I found her address and contacted her.[328]

Afraid to speak to me unless someone she trusted vetted me first, she referred me to Stuart Stein, a New Mexico transplant from Florida, who described himself as a retired attorney at that time. I learned that this avuncular ex-criminal attorney with the elegant clothes (rather like Mickey Barnett) had been serving, for some time, as the volunteer nexus of a group of victims who had clustered around him.

Everyone felt safe in his presence; we had all learned, early on, about his absolute antipathy to the abuses of the commercial guardianship industry in New Mexico and elsewhere. He used to tell us stories about his prior work in Florida, getting elders released from their "mandatory three-day commitments" under Florida's "Baker Law,"[329] arranged by hostile parties trying to separate them from their freedom and their assets. He said the game was to drug them, prior to any competency evaluation, so that they

---

[328] This family is still afraid to come forward and I am respecting their privacy by not naming them here.

[329] Clearly, there are arguments on both sides of this issue. Existing laws can sometimes be applied in an abusive fashion. For a positive view of this law, and an argument that it doesn't go far enough see Sullivan, Dan, "Five things to know about the Baker Act and why prevent attack on New Tampa bike family," *Tampa Bay Times*, June 26, 2018, accessed July 2, 2020, from: https://www.tampabay.com/news/courts/Five-things-to-know-about-the-Baker-Act-and-why-it-didn-t-prevent-car-attack-on-New-Tampa-bike-family_169491866/#:~:text=The%20Baker%20Act%20is%20a,doctors%20or%20mental%20health%20professionals.

were unable to respond, then to declare them "mentally incompetent." We all shuddered at his tales of the Florida abuses. If it could happen in one state, why not in another?[330]

It looked as if Stuart's zeal on behalf of one of his clients might have resulted in his disbarment, because his frankly skeptical and sometimes outright critical attitude certainly did not endear him to the professional guardians and their lawyers, and they seemed to wield considerable influence over the Bar Association. He had tangled with them before, when he tried to provide low-cost trust-creation services to the public. He had advertised, which was not then allowed. Now, attorney advertising is commonplace, expected. In the midst of the COVID-19 pandemic, I was not surprised to hear Ruth Pregenzer's law firm advertising frequently on the radio. Back in the early 2000s, however, Stuart found himself in front of the Bar Association, accused of an ethics breach for advertising his services.

A later complaint of making a new will for one of his clients was the immediate cause of his disbarment, as far as I could tell. Unfortunately, the fact of his then-recent disbarment (executed in New Mexico, and then occurring automatically, out of "legal reciprocity" in Florida as well) seemed to make currently-licensed attorneys shun him like the latest potentially fatal virus. There is rampant fear in the legal profession, too. Is disbarment a communicable disease? After Mama died, Stuart seemed genuinely touched when my then-new attorney, David Garcia, actually shook hands with him when I introduced them at a legislative committee hearing at the Roundhouse in Santa Fe.

I am not sure how many family member-victims of commercial guardianship Stuart ultimately sheltered under his wings. During the years when I knew him, at least a dozen people, from different families, were telling him about complaints against the commercial guardianship system in the State of New Mexico. I certainly was not alone anymore. However, as someone who currently

---

330 There was no similar law in New Mexico, back then. However, there is now a law in New Mexico that can be misused similarly, and can be set in motion by almost anyone. It is intended for people who might harm themselves or others but can easily be perverted by unscrupulous individuals, of whom there seem to be far too many.

had an attorney, I spoke a lot less and listened a lot more than the others.

We had different attitudes toward publicity, Stuart and I. He thought the more publicity, the better. In fact, I later recalled that I had heard him, several years before I met him, speaking with Art Bell on *Coast to Coast*, a radio show on which he had appeared in his capacity as the attorney for Melvin Dumar, who for years had been claiming an interest in the Howard Hughes estate.[331] (Stuart had gone into probate, guardianship and estate planning after he left criminal defense work.)

Several times, over the course of the years when I saw him relatively frequently and we corresponded, more than once he asked for permission to write about me (or about Mama and me). Having seen friends of mine destroyed by publicity, I always asked him to refrain from doing so. I still greatly appreciate his respect for my wishes in this matter. He has been similarly discreet with the others with whom he commiserated over the years.

Fear dominated the lives of family members whose loved ones were under commercial guardianship. However, only those who had actually been emotionally close to the ward truly suffered. Those who had been estranged before or were not close to the ward did not seem unduly upset by what had happened. Stuart vetted me, for his "friend" family. I do not say "client," because he had long ceased acting as their attorney and become a friend to all the family members. To say "ex-client" or "former client" sounds too much like "ex-spouse," and he had remained on very good terms with all of them, it seemed. He could have just forgotten them and gone on living, but instead he chose to stay and try to fight. From the complaints I heard, many other attorneys had fled, instead.

Multiple members of the ward's family said they were convinced that making a documentary about them would put them in danger. Several elderly members had concluded that the guardian firm would quickly be after them, to take them over as wards, if they poked their heads up and spoke, in public, about

---

331   Accessed January 28, 2020 from: *https://www.morelaw.com/verdicts/case.asp?d=37224&s=NM*

their concerns. (By now, most of them either have passed away or moved out of state, to places where they believed that they would be safe; I hope they are right, but with the current digitized medical record-keeping, GPS and facial recognition technology, I seriously doubt that anywhere on earth is truly "safe.")

Separately, and at different times, a number of individuals in that family told me about threats against them by the commercial guardian, including one time when they ran to get out of the way, because it looked as if one of the partners in the guardianship firm was trying to run them down with her car. They all said they were afraid to go to the police, lest they be called crazy and guardianized themselves.

I was not a journalist on a deadline and I could not see myself potentially putting people who did not need commercial guardianship into a potentially dangerous situation, so I dropped the idea of making a documentary about the New Mexico abuses and concentrated instead on seeing what I could do to be useful to this new community I had discovered. Like all support groups, we needed a safe place to discuss our trials with other people who had experienced similar things; I could use my pastoral counseling training to some good effect there. We ended up meeting, usually monthly, to commiserate and support each other. Sometimes, Stuart joined us. We all came to regard him as one of the victims of the system too. He was one of us.

By early 2010, Debbie and I had already been in the process of obtaining invoices from the health-care companies involved in Mama's case. Debbie engaged the late Tom Burrage, a grandfatherly type and perhaps the most distinguished forensic accountant in the state at that time, to analyze the invoices that Debbie had managed to extract, on my behalf, from the home care agencies. They covered the period from August 2008 to December 2009. Being Mama's only heir helped, here. If there had been multiple heirs, and they had disagreed about whether the expenses were reasonable, probably no entity would have complied with Debbie's requests. Or, if there had been a trust and the trustee thought the expense of auditing would not be worth the trouble, there would not have been any oversight at all. This did not occur to me until much later, but if I had ever agreed to be co-trustee with the guardian, back in 2008, they would have had a way to block any sort of audit, no matter when conducted. Simply object, take the matter to court, the judge sides with you, and the heir is in the doghouse for wanting to waste money.

Expense factors in here. Experts and attorneys must be paid. Over the years Mama was under commercial guardianship, particularly after Arthur died and the situation became even more intense, I spent on my personal expenses only what was required to survive. Everything else, I devoted to the legal battle. My perception is that the legal system bleeds people dry. It is not really designed for individuals; it is designed for corporations. I was not a corporation, but I had to act like one.

Burrage filed an affidavit on May 3, 2010, in district court.[332] This supplemented his first affidavit, filed on March 25. Among other new information, for an invoice paid on October 14, 2009, he had found an overpayment of $900. This was news to the guardianship firm. Their copy of that affidavit, produced as part of discovery in the case against the commercial guardian contains the handwritten notation "He's right. Requested refund." (They had had no idea about the overpayment, apparently, until an outsider pointed it out on May 3, 2010.)[333] Tom had found so many irregularities that I (through Debbie, of course) requested a forensic accounting, from Judge Baca.

At the same time, the guardian was asking me to sign off on "decreasing" the number of Mama's attendants. The fallout from my visit to AG King probably led the commercial guardian to feel even more threatened than that firm had, back in 2007 and early 2008.

Mama's commercial guardian now claimed that an appliance had recently been invented that would permit a single attendant to turn Mama, in her adjustable hospital bed, in a manner satisfactory to the firm. After doing some research and asking around, I could not find any such newly-invented medical device. At no time before they delivered the documents in response to subpoenas during discovery did the guardian firm admit that, in October

---

[332] Rosenstiel(2)020020-020024
[333] Decades 03442

2008, they had already received a formal report stating that Mama needed only one non-medical aide after the end of that month, and so none of these "additional" home health care expenses was medically necessary. Of course, I did not find out about this report until discovery in the estate's suit against the guardian.

According to all the records, Mama had to be turned every two hours, to prevent bedsores. Over a period of almost two years, between May 2010 and June 2012, I visited Mama almost daily. I never saw any freestanding "patient-turning device" in Mama's home, at any time. After Mama passed away, I had to return Mama's oxygen equipment to the firm that had leased it to her. The guardianship firm had bought Mama's hospital bed, so I donated it to a charity. However, after a thorough search of Mama's premises, I still was not able to find any evidence of the existence of a freestanding device of the sort they seemed to be describing to the judge. Nor did any firm contact me, asking for the return of their patient-turning device. The guardian's financial records show that they never seem to have purchased or rented any appliance that would serve the purpose they described to Judge Baca, either.

During discovery, my expert on home care testified that, to the best of her knowledge, no such "device" was invented or for sale in 2010, and that any properly trained single aide should have been capable of turning any patient comfortably, without the intervention of any appliance. And particularly someone like Mama, a frail, elderly woman weighing 100 pounds or less. In my experience, nurses, even LPNs, did not seem to help in turning Mama. That task, they relegated to the aides.

Not until 2019 did I discover that a product called TOMI Turn likely was what they had been using. It consisted of a pad, with attached handles that would enable someone who is not trained as a health aide to move a heavy patient in bed. I did see pads on Mama's bed at various times, but I did not see any handles. A wife had invented this pad-with-handles to turn her quadriplegic, 270-pound husband after he had had a stroke in 2006.[334]

The T. Rost Corporation had been marketing this product since 2008; the commercial guardian could have used it from at least the

---

334 "Our Story" accessed February 7, 2020 from: *https://www.tomiturn.com/our-story/*

end of October 2008, or at the latest anytime during 2009. However, Mama was under five feet in height and weighed only 90 pounds, according to the records of the Albuquerque Ambulance Service, dating from when they moved her for one of the 2010 renovation projects on her home; TOMI Turn was intended to help a slender, petite caregiver turn a patient who was much larger and heavier. I had always seen something called a "draw sheet" on Mama's bed, anyway; it served a similar purpose. Interesting that they did not even think of using this relatively new invention until I started demanding an accounting.

Our counter-argument at the 2010 hearing hinged on the fact that I had little to no medical information about Mama's condition. For that reason, I had no way to judge the merits of their request. Besides, Judge Baca had given the guardian plenary medical power over Mama only two years earlier. They had never asked for our permission before, for anything. Quite the contrary, in 2008 they had explicitly petitioned the judge to stop me from "meddling" in Mama's medical care. In reaffirming their plenary power over Mama[335], the judge had granted their request. From then on, I was under instructions to know my place, under threat of the guardian returning to court to strip me of visitation rights. Welcoming input? The 2008 court order explicitly forbade me to "meddle" in Mama's medical care, under threat of the guardian returning to court to strip me of visitation rights. Both sides were then requesting a hearing, but for different reasons.[336]

Judge Baca scheduled a hearing on both sets of requests for May 5, 2010. However, after we got started, she absolutely refused to allow Tom Burrage to testify. Nevertheless, she did agree to appoint a different forensic accountant, Judith A. Wagner, to look over the home-health-related invoices.

---

335 The commercial guardian, Judge Baca wrote, "has full power to make all end of life and emergency decisions for Dr. Annette Rosenstiel...[and the commercial guardian] shall continue serving as Dr. Annette Rosenstiel's court-appointed conservator." Decades 02987

336 Debbie elaborated on these facts during her arguments in 2010, explaining in detail to Judge Baca why I had not accommodated the guardian and told them what to do. Doing so, she argued, would have violated the order Judge Baca had signed in 2008 giving the guardian plenary power.

Back on March 10, 2010, Wagner had been appointed by the court as the trustee overseeing the bankruptcy of local real estate magnate Bruce Vaughan's recently failed property scam. The real estate agent who sold houses to Arthur and me, and to Mama when we moved to Albuquerque, had been working for Vaughan's real estate firm, back in 1997. Well, all of New Mexico is really one large small town; in terms of the people you are dealing with, you are never more than a couple of degrees away from where you started.

Debbie's final argument to Judge Baca had been that we wondered about the guardian's priorities. I had been asking, for almost two years, for them to install a ramp so that Mama's bed could be taken out of the house safely; the regular ramp, by the kitchen and the only door that could accommodate a wheelchair, could not accommodate Mama's hospital bed. Besides, there was no way she could be wheeled out into that hall by the kitchen in the first place. The guardian, it seemed to us, had been delaying on installing a ramp for Mama's hospital bed. However, here that firm was, asking for my agreement to save Mama money by giving her fewer aides. These contradictory positions seemed illogical to us, since the guardian's primary job was to protect the ward. The lack of a ramp got Judge Baca's attention, inducing her to demand an answer from the guardian about whether this was true.

After a bit of fumbling around at the guardian's table, the partner seated there admitted that it was.

Judge Baca then demanded that they install a ramp. (Judge Baca herself had been wheeled into this hearing, in a wheelchair. Might the change in her personal situation have made her more sympathetic to Mama's? I wondered.)

When Judge Baca commanded the commercial guardian to install the ramp, I started to hope, again, for a good outcome for the whole hearing. What a mistake!

Wagner, a high-powered, rising forensic accountant had serendipitously identified the involvement of Manny Aragon, a powerful New Mexico politician, in a million-dollar construction scandal that had led to his imprisonment in 2009[337]. The judge's

---

[337] Gallagher, Mike "How an Accountant Helped Unravel a Crime," *Albuquerque Journal*, March 25, 2009, p. 1

charge to Judith Wagner I found very disappointing. Judge Baca saw her role as simply to make recommendations, providing that she found anything that might be "corrected." She should let the guardian know, Judge Baca instructed, and then it would be the guardian's choice whether or not to implement her "suggestions." Furthermore, she told Wagner not to look for wrongdoing. Judge Baca forbade Wagner to say that she had found any, if she happened to identify some. She was not to present her findings in a court hearing, either, just in a report.

What is a "forensic accounting," if not an examination designed to determine whether there is any existing impropriety? It seemed to me that Judge Baca had commanded Wagner not to do her job, but to do something else, instead. Forensic accountants, says *Investopedia*, "...are trained to look beyond the numbers and deal with the business reality of a situation. Forensic accounting is frequently used in fraud and embezzlement cases to explain the nature of a financial crime in court."[338]

In addition to naming Judith Wagner as the person to do the "audit," at that same hearing Judge Baca appointed Barbara Buck as "special master." Buck, a Canadian-born attorney, seemed to specialize in "high end" cases, as I later discovered. In another case where she was the guardian ad litem, she had been seen traveling around in the same car as one of the partners in the same commercial guardianship firm caring for Mama. She was supposedly overseeing the guardianship firm in that case, on behalf of the ward, and of course with the blessing of the court. Because New Mexico guardians ad litem had recently gotten judicial immunity when this incident happened, it would have been unlikely that anyone could ever call her actions into question in any meaningful way. The special master is like an extension of the judge, and in New Mexico, judges have "judicial immunity," too. If everyone acting in a questionable manner has judicial immunity, what legal recourse is there?

One person who worked for the guardianship firm at that time, however, was incensed at this close social relationship. If acting ethically, the GAL is not supposed to be unduly close to the

---

338 Chen, James "Forensic Accounting," Investopedia. Accessed 1/21/20 from: *https://www.investopedia.com/terms/f/forensicaccounting.asp*

commercial guardian. Nor is the special master, for that matter, ethically supposed to be closer to one side of a case than another. It is likely that this social relationship tainted Buck's position as special master in Mama's case as well, although Judge Baca seemed to tolerate the situation. That employee signed an affidavit, complaining about it.[339]

The guardian, from what I heard later, successfully prevented that affidavit from being introduced into the record of that case. Soon after the commercial guardian discovered the existence of that affidavit, the person who had attested to the close relationship of the guardian ad litem and the commercial guardian left New Mexico.

What was the background of this event? According to the verifiable information I received at the time, the commercial guardian had promised not to block a family member's bid to take over as guardian. The person who thought she was about to assume the guardianship if she dropped her charges of impropriety against the current guardian, and had initially planned to use that affidavit as evidence, found her way blocked anyway. Instead of the current guardian objecting, as expected, the guardian ad litem objected instead. Instead of obtaining the guardianship through dropping her charges against the then-current guardian, the family member ended up only with the "non-disparagement" agreement she had signed with the guardian, as evidence of good faith, and that, henceforth, could not be broken without legal penalty. Commercial guardians play hardball.[340]

By the time all this had played out in the other ward's case, the then-current commercial guardian had proposed to the court a different commercial guardian, if anyone involved wanted to make a change. At that point, another interested party objected that one commercial guardian was pretty much like another, so there would be no reason to subject the ward to the stress of changing guardians. The original commercial guardian ended up keeping the ward, and the "malcontent" not only got nowhere in taking

---

339 I was given a copy of this affidavit, but do not choose to release the names involved, out of concern for their safety.
340 Because of the non-disparagement agreement, she cannot come forward and I am respecting her privacy by not naming her.

over the guardianship, but she was also now subject to strict limits on her freedom of speech. Guardians have a lot of experience with complex legal maneuvers. In my opinion, family members believe such offers and promises at their peril.

Buck's appointment in Mama's case ensured another on-going set of invoices for Mama to pay, because Buck "oversaw," at $200 per hour, various "projects" relating to Mama. I noticed, from the discovery documents, that Buck always asked the judge to approve her invoices before she submitted them to the commercial guardian, thereby making her suit-proof because, once the judge approves an expense, it is almost impossible to countermand that.[341]

The commercial guardianship firm told a second forensic accountant, appointed after Mama died, and who had questioned certain high expenses involving birdseed, the following "Barbara Buck was special master (appointed by court) for a while and was a bird enthusiast. She took Margot [Keener, recently appointed Mama's case manager] to Wild Birds Unlimited to find the best stuff. Once Barbara was out of the picture, they started going to Walmart to get these materials."[342] What is the going rate for a special master, appointed by the court, traveling to Wild Birds Unlimited to buy birdseed? In this case, $200 per hour for Buck. Plus $110 per hour for Keener's services. So, birdseed is billed, at a perhaps inflated cost, plus $310 per hour for the services of these two experts. Not that Buck's own invoices ever suggested that any of her time had been spent buying birdseed. Quite the contrary, they spoke of having meetings with Margot.

On one occasion, I saw Margot arrive, alone, bringing 20-pound sacks of birdseed. Which means that Mama was paying at least $110 per hour to her, plus of course the cost of the birdseed.

Why could home health aides, at a cost of, then, under $20 per hour, not be trusted to go and buy birdseed, while they were doing their regular marketing, even if the store in question was a couple of miles away? In Albuquerque, two or three miles each way

---

341 Decades 33647-33680
342 Rosenstiel(2)019859; Rosenstiel-22079 shows the guardian charging for Buck being at the birdseed store with Margot.

is practically next door. And particularly if the ward is not being left alone because there is a second aide present with the ward in the home? Is a special master or a case manager really needed to accomplish this task?

Buck's more substantial jobs included supervision of interior work on the house, particularly the first $20,000 of alterations that allowed for the installation of a ramp, so Mama's hospital bed could be wheeled out of the bedroom, into the backyard. Buck had decided that more concrete needed to be put down, so that bed could be wheeled to a gate leading to the front of the house. The only problem with that plan was that the bed would have ended up in a group of plants, rather than able to continue on, to the street. The other side of the house, already well paved, could have accommodated Mama's bed; all they had to do was widen the gate leading to the driveway, which they never did.

Buck and Keener had decided to widen both of the French doors, leading out to the backyard from Mama's bedroom, instead of just opening both sides whenever Mama's bed needed to be wheeled outside. They also decided to alter the paving in the backyard substantially, to add a stationary sun sail over the back door, and to do considerable additional landscaping that Mama, with her severely compromised eyesight at that point, was likely unable to see.

I objected, in emails exchanged right after the hearing, that the stationary sun sail was going to be installed on the west side of the house. In the morning, the house shaded that area. However, in the afternoon, the time of day when Mama was generally awake, now, the sun would keep changing position, in relation to objects in the backyard, which lay on the west side of the house. If you could not move the sunshade, it would be useless. Buck called me cheap. The sun sail was estimated to cost over $1,000. An adjustable sunshade only cost about $300.

Buck did not attend the May 5 hearing. I met her for the first time when I was summoned to a May 14, 2010, meeting with her and Margot Keener.[343] (Keener, whom I think I had already met,

---

343 Rosenstiel-22065

earlier that spring, I later discovered was a disbarred lawyer from another state. She had lost her license for stealing and cashing for herself a settlement check intended to be paid to one of the firm's clients.)[344]

My attorney did not attend that meeting because the guardian's attorney was not going to attend. The special master was there, in theory representing the judge. As I understood the purpose of the meeting, we would be making final decisions on the changes needed to allow Mama's bed to be taken outside. But it was still two trained attorneys and me having a conversation in Mama's bedroom.

I was standing by Mama's bed, visiting with her, when Buck arrived. Slender and expensively dressed, Buck looked to be all business. Instead of any pleasantries, she started right in on me:

"Do you know who I am?"

"Barbara Buck?"

"Surely you know (the name of the lobbyist)?"

"I know who he is." (He was someone I had locked horns with a couple of years earlier in Santa Fe. He represented, among other people and organizations, someone who had been trying to do me professional harm, for years.)

"He's my husband."

"Good to know. You know, I'd like to ask a couple of questions about that proposal for the sun sail. It's on the west side and you won't be able to adjust it, so it will be useless in the afternoon. That's when Mama seems to be awake, now. Can we discuss this?"

"It's not a proposal. I met with Margot yesterday. We've made all the decisions. We're only here, today, to tell you what they are."

---

[344] According to the *Albuquerque Journal*, Margot Keener set up, her own guardianship firm, "Transitions: Fiduciaries and Care Consultants, LLC" (November 28, 2016, Business Outlook, p. 16. She also has used the name "A & M Fiduciaries," but that name does not show in the court dockets. Since 2016, Keener's business has had six wards under its official name, "Transitions: Fiduciaries and Care Consultants." The "A & M" in her LinkedIn profile refer to "Anne C Keener" and "Margot Keener." According to various internet listings, Anne C. Keener, a criminal defense attorney, works in the Public Defender's Office. Information accessed January 26, 2020 from: *https://portal.sos.state.nm.us/BFS/online/CorporationBusinessSearch/ CorporationBusinessInformation and https://www.lawyerdirectory.legal/usa/lawyer/ New-Mexico/Albuquerque/criminal-defence-lawyers/38949-Anne-C-Keener.html*

At that point, Margot arrived.

"Hi. See you've met Barbara."

"Hi. Yes. I'd really like you to reconsider using an adjustable sun shade."

"You're just saying that because you're stupid."

"I'm saying that because it's on the west side of the house."

"Is it really?" Margot smiled sweetly.

"Yes, the mountains are in the east. The backyard is on the opposite side."

"Are the mountains on the east?"

At that point, I gave up. This was not going to get me anywhere. Keener had been living in Albuquerque for years. So had Buck. Everyone who lives in Albuquerque for any length of time quickly learns where the Sandia Mountains are. The view of those mountains absolutely dominates the eastern side of the city.

We were standing around Mama's bed, talking, so Mama had to listen to all of this. Fortunately, Mama was able to remain impassive. I guess she had gotten used to hearing outrageous discussions, held in her presence, with the participants all treating her as if she were invisible.

We went outside. They pointed out to me the extensive changes they had agreed on, the day before. Margot pointed to the sun and the mountains, "Well, the mountains really are in the east!" she exclaimed, as if this had been a new discovery for her. Not that this "discovery" was going to induce her to change the plan.

Margot had decided that the backyard needed extensive, additional landscaping, if Mama was going to go outside. Otherwise, it would not look nice enough for her. The backyard was then more or less the way Mama had wanted it, simple, with tasteful plantings. They totally ignored the fact that Mama could not see more than a few feet from her own face now.

Again, I objected that Mama was not even going to be able to see these landscaping alterations; they were too far away and too small. Apparently, expense (having as much as possible of it) was a deciding factor; if it was going to be expensive, then it must be the right thing to do. I kept trying to remember that I was only there to listen, not to have any input.

They told me that big plans were being made. During the bedroom renovation that would accommodate resizing the backyard doors, they were going to put Mama in an open area of the den of her home, surrounded by piles of stuff that had been removed from the master bedroom.

I objected to this, too, once more forgetting my place. It meant workmen would be walking past Mama at irregular intervals, and that she would have little to no privacy for a period of a couple of weeks. I suggested that they place Mama in a facility for the week or two involved, so she could have some peace and privacy, only to hear the values document quoted on the subject that Mama wanted, at all costs, to remain in her own home. Honestly, I do not think that anyone could have foreseen this. And, if I had been authorized to use "substituted judgement," I would have made a different decision. There was no further point to disputing anything; I was not going to get anywhere. I thanked both of them for their time, made my excuses and left.

That entire meeting lasted, perhaps, fifteen minutes. I did not have an unlimited appetite for abuse—either my own or Mama's—and wanted to get away as rapidly as possible. Buck billed for "1.8 hours" for that meeting. I do not know whether she got caught in traffic jams going both to and from her downtown office to Mama's home, but I know that I did not spend anywhere near that amount of time with her.[345] Margot, whose office was at least ten minutes closer to Mama's home than Buck's, billed for 1.3 hours for writing up the meeting and two hours for the meeting itself.[346] Perhaps, after I left, they met each other somewhere, and spent an hour or so, buying birdseed, because it looked to me as if, after the meeting, they left in their separate cars, just as they had arrived, at different times, in separate cars.

A word about the twenty-gallon, clear plastic, horizontal tubs of birdseed that ultimately piled up on the patio outside Mama's kitchen, and the resulting bird droppings that piled up around the door to the patio outside her bedroom. The guardian had never bought bird food in that quantity before. The seed, they stored, as far as I can recall, in six of those huge tubs.

---

345 Rosenstiel(2)33649
346 Rosenstiel-22064-22065

A couple of years earlier, when Mama was still able to use the table in her dining nook, she had spent time sitting, facing the sliding door to the side patio, watching the birds. Her feathered companions were then hopping around, merrily pecking at what looked to me to be normal, everyday crumbs, not more than eight feet away from Mama, just on the other side of the door. The commercial guardian told me that Mama loved birds. I knew that Mama had never had any special affinity with them before.

One day, I decided to ask Mama why she was so fascinated with birds now.

"Mama, why do you like to watch the birds, now?"

"They can fly away. I want to fly away, too."

Most likely by the time she was confined to her room, Mama could not see the wrens and sparrows anymore. When Mama was in bed, in her room, those wrens and sparrows must have been a good 15 feet away, at least. Maybe she could hear them, when the window or door was open. Even so, they would likely always remind her that she wanted to "fly away."

And the poor fish. Back in 2007, when they were planning to demolish Mama's reflecting pool, I think they took the carp out of it and put them into a 20-gallon tank in the den. The commercial guardian did not tell me this, but the carp I saw, when I started visiting Mama again, were huge, as if they had been alive for at least several years. Too big for a tank that size. No one seemed to want to clean it, either. Mama certainly could not, and the aides would not, as the discovery documents proved. This item was heavier than what they had agreed to handle. More likely it was not in their contract, because Mama was far heavier than the tank.

The aquarium developed a brackish, green film. The fish started dying. I complained. Mama had had lung issues, including more than one bout of pneumonia. Introducing unknown pathogens into her environment, in the den, a room where she then spent quite a bit of time, I did not think would be a good thing. Anyway, finally the commercial guardian got a professional fish-wrangler to come and take care of them because the aides had refused. Complaining about the fish had landed me in trouble with Elizabeth Church, too, who had insisted it showed my extreme pettiness, meanness, and lack of perspective.

When they confined Mama to her bedroom, they moved the aquarium to a nice, bright spot, on a table a foot or so inside of the west-facing windows, and restocked it with tiny goldfish and a catfish or two, because, predictably, its original occupants—8 to10 inch carp—had died, by then. They kept the blinds open all day, allowing the brilliant New Mexico sun to stream in. Fair enough, for Mama. But not for the fish. In the direct sunlight, they soon died and had to be replaced, repeatedly.

I complained, early on, that a bright window was a very bad location for an aquarium. Any aquarium. Having owned goldfish as a child, I already knew this. "Rule No. 1" in *Pets Keepers Guide* on the subject of fish, even today, states: "Do not set up an aquarium near a window where there is direct sunlight or very strong daylight."[347] The guardian told me they were being kind to Mama by placing the fish where she could see them. Again, I beg to differ. Mama had a bedroom, perhaps 25 feet wide. She might have been able to see the aquarium, although it was more than 12 feet away, but the fish were far too small. The commercial guardian still frequently replaced the unfortunate, tiny goldfish and catfish it bought and added to the tank. I was told that each one was granted a "funeral," before being flushed down the toilet.

Apparently, the expensive "fish wranglers" the commercial guardian hired never told the firm about Rule No. 1, and since I had told them that there are more healthful (for the fish) ways to take care of fish, they automatically discounted what I said.

The guardian insisted that keeping an aquarium in the room was always a "calming" influence. Agreed, but only if the fish stay well and are not being boiled alive, and if you are not frequently holding "funerals" for the dead fish. Mama likely grieved every time one of those tiny fish died. Why not put the aquarium in a darker corner, where the fish could have survived longer? The dresser only a few feet from Mama's bed was the right height and the furthest wall from the windows. On the wall by Mama's bed, the darkest one in the place, under those noxious photos, perhaps?

---

347 Accessed January 26, 2020 from: *http://petskeepersguide.com/the-location-to-set-up-a-home-aquarium/*

After Mama died, I found a little girl who really wanted the latest school of newly added goldfish and their accompanying catfish; presumably she knew better than to put them in a sunny window.

During the renovation period, Mama hated being in that open area, in the den. She had even less privacy, there, than she had had in her bedroom with two attendants staring at her, when they were paying any attention to her at all.

Margot said the "move" was traumatic for Mama and left her disoriented. Well, of course it was! They had an ambulance come, with ambulance attendants in uniform, to move her. She must have thought they were taking her to the hospital. If I had thought I was being taken to the hospital, but instead I ended up in my den for a couple of weeks, and I was lying in bed as workmen walked back and forth in the area where I was trying to sleep, I would have been confused, too. Mama had absolutely no choice; it was not as if she could get up and walk into another room, far from the frenetic activity.

They blamed Mama's state of agitation during this period on me because I was the malcontent who had forced them to make the renovations. I have always suspected that the outsized charges Mama paid for that renovation and landscaping work included some sort of retaliation for my futile visit to Gary King.

They finished widening the doors the week before Mama turned 99. In 2010, for the first time in years, Mama was able to go outside on her birthday. Typically, the commercial guardian's minions immediately realized that the sun sail did not work and wheeled her bed over to the area in back of the kitchen, where there was a covered patio that had come with the house.

While I rejoiced that Mama was finally going to spend some time outside, I remained afraid that it was too dangerous for me to attend the party they planned to give for Mama. Multiple people would be present at the formal party (they had told me that the food was either going to be Chinese take-out or pizza) from the commercial guardian's firm and those they employed. Anything I said or did could, and I was afraid, would be misconstrued. So, I got the guardian's permission to bring ice cream cake and celebrated with Mama, privately, on another day. Just knowing that she had been outside on her birthday was enough to make me feel that, maybe now, she would be allowed to get out a bit again.

They rarely took Mama outside, despite the fact that they now could, using portable oxygen tanks. It seemed to me that about 10 percent of the people I saw walking around on the streets of Albuquerque were using them. Why not Mama? Having apparently gotten Mama out the door and outside on her birthday, the aides soon started complaining that Mama's bed was "too heavy" for them to push. Or so the guardian told me. Nothing in the record substantiates this claim.

Would they have taken the trouble to push hard enough to wheel Mama's bed out of the house, if an emergency forced them to get her away from there, or would they still have thrown her on the floor, on a blanket, and dragged her out that way, as the guardian had threatened me that they would, back in 2007?

Over the course of 2010, Mama began to speak less. It seemed to me and any visitors I brought with me, that she understood what was being said. But more and more often, she would respond with signs or nods or smiles rather than words.

"You don't want to speak much now?"

Mama nodded.

"Does it hurt to talk?"

She shook her head.

"Is it too much effort?"

"Too much effort!" By late 2011, Mama rarely spoke at all. A friend who accompanied me to see Mama, early in 2012, noticed that there was a considerable time lag between when something was said and when Mama was able to process it and react to the speaker. Mama seemed to be processing information, but more slowly than before.

During the spring of 2011, Mama kept having problems with her lungs. I did not realize how serious the problems with her oxygen equipment had become until I read the clinical case notes during discovery. Over the first months, it repeatedly failed. I only saw Mama coughing and the guardian denying that anything was wrong, so I ended up blaming Mama's condition rather than the fact that she was oxygen-deprived, which ultimately seemed to have contributed to her almost constant coughing. The information I got at the time seemed confusing and contradictory. Problems with Mama's oxygen delivery system continued. That concentrator did not work satisfactorily between February 22 and March 15.[348]

Rather than fix Mama's furnace, so that her bedroom could have heat, the guardian elected to place space heaters on the rug in her room.

Discovery proved that I was not the only person who thought Mama's condition had changed for the worse during that period. Her guardian had hospice evaluations performed because of their belief that her condition had materially declined.[349]

I had been corresponding with the out-of-state relative of another of this commercial guardian's wards. She was coming into town. After we had lunch, I took her to see Mama. Mama had her eyes closed at the time. The visitor, who had been born again, prayed over Mama, in the name of Jesus. Mama was smiling all the while, although she still did not open her eyes. The visitor had brought Mama an almost-life-sized baby lamb, a stuffed animal, as a gift. I think Mama simply had not had enough energy, that day, to open her eyes, because she remained very fond of that particular stuffed animal, to the end of her life. (Her guardian used to give her expensive floral arrangements and expensive stuffed animals—almost certainly at Mama's expense—but none of those specific expenses seemed to show in their invoices, when I finally got to see them later.)

My friend and I referred to her gift as "the Lamb of God." Fortunately, I did not have to introduce my fellow-victim to the staff, because, as usual, they were not speaking to me. The visitor was terrified the whole time that the guardian might identify her, even though she had an entirely different last name from the commercial guardian's ward who had, entirely accidentally, brought my out-of-state friend and me together.

In August 2010, the electricity in the wall behind Mama's bed failed.[350] Meaning that her oxygen concentrator could not be

---

348 Decades 24665-24667
349 Decades 24668
350 Rosenstiel-22087

plugged in there and the aides could not use electrical current to adjust the head of her bed, so the commercial guardian had to get an ambulance, again, to move Mama out of the room, so they could repair it. I had learned, by then, not to suggest that Mama spend a day or two in some other, more tranquil, facility while repairs were made. They were not going to do it anyway.

This time, however, apparently at Buck's request, they decided to do a "lead paint remediation" job, despite the fact that Mama's home had been built after lead paint was no longer used in homes, and that nothing about lead paint had been mentioned during the previous job, only a few months earlier. It did not seem that they ran any tests to confirm the presence of lead-based paint prior to starting the work, either. Remediation increased the time needed and automatically increased the cost of the repair by thousands of dollars.

The prospect of fixing the electrical system (which meant opening up the drywall) and installing new heating ducts led to worrying about the air quality in Mama's home altogether. This entire set of questions (also raised by Buck, it seemed) they discussed, through the fall of 2010. They continued with air quality testing, at intervals, for the rest of Mama's life

Suddenly, they decided that expensive heating and cooling equipment needed replacement. They made what looked to me like ridiculously expensive, but simultaneously aesthetically repulsive, "repairs." Under Buck's supervision, Mama's home rapidly approached what I would call "decaying housing stock" status. After the 2010 renovations, an ugly, industrial-sized swamp cooler now sat on the patio, outside Mama's kitchen, leaking. It did not cool Mama's bedroom at all, but only the rooms in the other wing where the aides spent most of their time during that summer.

All of this newly installed equipment needed replacement again, in 2012, after Mama passed away. By then, it cost me $50,000 ($60,344.73 in 2021), just for actual work to be done, including a long-needed painting, to bring the house into decent condition so it could be sold. That did not include the $10,000 for an on-site supervisor while the work was in progress, nor did it include the cost of some of the remodeling materials, which ran a few thousand more.

Despite what I was told would be the goal of fixing the heating and cooling system, this second 2010 renovation ended up with the wing of the house that included Mama's bedroom lacking systemic heating and cooling, increasing the likelihood that a pipe on an outside wall in the guest bathroom might break during the winter.

That winter, after the renovations, they had initially brought into Mama's room several portable heaters (dangerous, I was afraid, since they had been placed on a carpeted floor). Eventually they installed a safer, but again repulsive, large stationary heater with a pipe that went out the window and they put a big, ugly, stand-alone cooling unit on the wall, above the upper corner of the door to the garden. I hoped that Mama could not see these things. These devices still did not take care of the heating and cooling issues in the other rooms in that wing, however.

As all this was happening, the guardian was losing even more of Mama's money by taking what I believed were dangerous chances betting on the market; I found out during discovery that they were buying what are called "European Options." These relatively rarely-used "investment vehicles" assumed that you could predict whether the actual price of a stock at a date certain in the future would be above or below a specific level. To me, that sort of foreknowledge requires a crystal ball. "European Options," says *Investopedia*, "are less common"[351] than regular options. Anyone can guess why.

The commercial guardian did luck out a couple of times. Once or twice, it was a wash. The rest of the time, they lost. Big. Regular options, I had always believed, were risky enough. With them, if the price rose above or fell below a certain level during a period that might vary from a day to a year or more, it triggered either selling or buying.

Mama would have to forego any regular dividend income from the stock being hedged using European Options. Standard practice in the investment world, although judging from the emails back

---

351 "Understanding Options," Investopedia. Accessed January 28, 2020 from: *https://www.investopedia.com/terms/s/stockoption.asp*

and forth to Winslow's office, the commercial guardian seemed not to understand this. Standard practice dictated that any regular dividends paid during the option period belonged to the person buying an option and not to the person selling that option (in this case, Mama).

The second tranche of the original shares, Winslow liquidated over a period of months. One of Winslow's arguments to Judge Baca had been that she wanted to save Mama capital gains taxes. However, Mama ended up having to declare an investment loss of more than $4.5 million for 2008, by far the majority of that negative income generated after Winslow took over.[352]

Winslow invested the remaining cash from that sale in mutual funds, the vast majority of which paid smaller dividends than the CME stock per year, or none at all. The third tranche of shares just sat in a separate account, for years, generating about 3 percent in income, annually. Even if it paid Mama $90,000 per year, that would only cover another month or two of expenses, the way the guardian was spending. Mama still had her pensions, but they barely covered another month or two of her currently high expenses. Add all Mama's pension money and all her dividends, and she would have less than six months of the money "needed" to pay her expenses.

At the same time, as I had predicted, the income from leasing the seat was drying up. It had fallen from $216,000 per year in 2006[353] to $28,200 per year, in March 2008.[354] The conservator had finally set up an ironclad plan that would eventually force Mama to use up her nest egg. The lack of income necessitated the periodic selling off the holdings from that mutual fund account for the rest of Mama's life, to pay for what I always considered her grossly over-inflated expenses.

Certainly, the way the guardian was spending her money, Mama needed the income from those CME dividends from the collared stock, if the guardian was going to continue holding that stock. At least in my opinion, she did. However, no one told me what was actually happening. The commercial conservator's

---
352 Annual Report 2008, p. 9
353 Lets of Guardian & Conserv 8-18-04 (Fax)
354 Ibid

annual reports did not have enough detail for me to realize the sorts of transactions in which they were engaging. I only learned about them during discovery.

On November 11, 2010, Ruth Pregenzer sent Debbie another letter about what the commercial guardian was still pleased to call "estate and tax planning." She reported, on behalf of her client, that the commercial guardian "wishes to revisit the need to make changes to Annette's current estate plan..." They proposed hiring Ken Leach, their preferred estate expert from the 2008 hearing, to do the work. The commercial guardian invoked "substituted judgement," once again. Pregenzer said that the firm believed "such planning would be consistent with Annette's wishes."[355] Really? Who told them that?

"If Leonie remains uninterested in participating," they threatened through the carefully crafted prose of Ruth Pregenzer, they would "discuss the matter with Barbara Buck."[356] Again, we told them to take a hike.

Had there been more than one heir, they might have been able to play one heir against another. "We're trying to help by saving you taxes" was the argument they were giving me. Maybe someone else might believe that they wanted to help, but given the firm's performance up to that point, I could not accept their argument. It did not look as if they had saved Mama all that much money. And Mama was their court-appointed primary responsibility.

If anyone had asked me to nominate the one entity in my life that had deliberately and consistently, over a period of years, predictably not acted in my best interests, I would instantly have named Mama's commercial guardian. As Mama's only heir, I objected, in the strongest possible terms, to changing Mama's will, just as I had before. The commercial guardian could not pretend that someone else also had equal or greater legal standing. Nobody had more standing than I did, at that moment. Not even Barbara Buck. Again, they had to drop the matter, but not for long, as I would soon discover. They even charged Mama $11 for reading Debbie's report of my refusal.[357]

---

355 Page 1
356 Ibid
357 Rosenstiel-22118

On November 15, 2010, just after the cutoff date for the annual report, Mama's commercial guardian removed $10,000 from Mama's checking account, made out to the firm. This, they put into a trust account, they said.[358] They had also removed the same amount prior to the hearing in 2008. I am assuming both amounts were intended to pay their legal bills related to my suits (although I had not filed any sort of suit in 2010); all I had done was to reject further "estate planning." They apparently used the second retainer for that purpose after Mama died, because they did not return any of it to the estate.

The commercial guardian's minions and whatever they might have told the aides made the end of 2010 more than usually painful for me. The aides kept intruding on the privacy during my visits with Mama that the 2008 court order supposedly provided. One aide (at least) would stand in Mama's room, or outside the window and stare at me, malevolently, during those times. It seemed as if we were going back to pre-2008 status. As the end of December approached, the aides were becoming almost intolerably intrusive before I managed to come up with a possible explanation. I could not figure out what happened until it occurred to me that 2010 was "The Year." By that, I mean, for any person dying during that year, all estate tax would be forgiven. "Dear Lord," I thought, "They can't possibly be expecting me to hurt Mama!" But, apparently, they were. Might that have been some sort of weird mechanism of projection?

Early in 2011, the aides started leaving the "turning log" out in the open. They left it where I could not avoid seeing that they often filled it out, hours in advance, the "future entries" already initialed by the aide. Theoretically, they were only supposed to initial it after the job had been done. The times that they initialed, however, ran to the end of the aide's shift. I began to wonder whether aides filled them out as soon as they signed in for the day. Maybe those aides did turn Mama on time, as the log says they did. Then again, maybe they did not.

Mama had been coughing for days. She also seemed to be having trouble breathing. The guardian's first reaction to my concern

---

358 Rosenstiel(2)014625

was to tell me that I was imagining this. Then, they tried to tell me this was Mama's new normal. Nevertheless, on April 5, 2011, the invoices show that the commercial guardian started trying to interest a hospice in taking Mama as a client. Not that they informed me about this. Whenever I asked, they told me Mama's condition was "stable" and that any concerns I expressed, from time to time, through Debbie, were unwarranted. However, an invoice entry for that date reads "T/C with Hospice."[359] Almost certainly this meant Hospice of New Mexico, where Dr. Morgan was one of the partners, because later on another entry for the same day reads, "Multiple calls, re; [sic] Doctors Request for Protocol/ Prepare Protocol."[360] With this commercial guardian, "Protocol," unless modified by another word, always seemed to mean "procedure to be followed after the ward's death."

A few days later, the aides left papers in various areas where they knew that I would spend time. Even before that, I had noticed that, if I arrived somewhat earlier than usual, there would be a second person present, often someone I had never seen before. And of course, all this was happening after the commercial guardian had assured the court that Mama needed only one attendant. I started noticing medical documents left around, showing that as many as three or four people a day were still attending to Mama, despite what the commercial guardian told the judge at the 2010 hearing. According to the guardian's clinical case notes, only on April 25, 2011, did two home health aides attend Mama during the day. Again, there was not a single aide during the day, as they had told the court there would be, but only at night, which had been true for years already. Even though Mama had two caregivers and Mama had been in essentially the same condition since August 2008, the guardian's representative said that neither aide admitted to knowing "how to plug [did she mean "move the head of"?] the bed if the power goes out or they need to take Dr. [that was what the guardian had told them to call Mama] outside."[361]

Not until April 14, 2011, did the guardian consider purchasing Mama's air mattress. If purchased, the note said, it would cost

---

359 Rosenstiel-22299
360 Ibid
361 Rosenstiel-22301

about $2000. The guardian had been renting it since August 2008, at a rate of $140 per month. That would be thirty-three months, which means they had already paid $4,620 for a $2,000 mattress and now apparently wanted to pay another $2,000.

The original set of "end of life" instructions still hung on the wall behind Mama's bed in mid-April. However, despite the stipulated order we had had with the guardian since 2008, a new set of "end of life" instructions now sat open, on Mama's dresser. The handwriting (the instructions were clearly so new that they had not even been typed up yet) was huge, none of it under 30-point size, so you could see it from a distance. The instruction sheet lay right where I had to walk past it to go up to the head of Mama's bed to talk with her. A Do Not Resuscitate order led the list. "Call Guardian First" the instruction sheet said, in case anything happened. I worried, seeing it, because Mama was so weak that day, simply lifting her eyebrows cost her great effort. She had managed to make a sound, when I approached and started speaking to her, but then sank deep into her bed, totally drained.

The guardian told me nothing about this problem at the time. However, according to those same April invoices, an electrical problem had prevented the oxygen equipment from functioning properly. Therefore, even after a new supplier provided the required oxygen devices, the electrical system still needed repair. This was not finished until April 25. [362] I had no idea why Mama's condition seemed to have declined so precipitously; I thought it was some physical problem she was having, without realizing that it was readily remediable with proper oxygen delivery, because Mama was always wearing her oxygen cannula when I visited.

Although I had first complained to the guardian about Mama's seemingly bad condition on April 4, not until I examined the guardian's invoices during discovery, did I realize that Mama's symptoms had resulted from problems with her oxygen equipment. Again, instead of putting Mama in a safe place while they obtained working equipment and fixed her home's electrical system, they kept her in her home, coughing and unable to get adequate oxygen

---

362 Decades 24661

into her lungs. Mama's breathing problems lasted from April 4 to April 12.[363] The commercial guardian remained in talks with Hospice through the end of the month. Ultimately, they elected to tell us that in the future they would give Mama only what they referred to as "palliative" treatment, but Mama would not be officially placed on hospice care. This turned out not to be what they did.

Electrical problems called, of course, for repeated consultations, bids from suppliers, and meetings. These undoubtedly added to the cost of the project. Mama had been having trouble breathing for a week. Not until April 11 was there the invoice notation, "Multiple pc's with caregivers, electricians, 911, care management [sic] team, troubleshooting loss of electricity to [oxygen] concentrator..."[364]

Meanwhile, the guardian agreed to respond to questions I had asked about their most recent annual report. It showed Mama with about 50 percent of the assets she had had in 2007-08. I did not have much confidence that their answers told the complete story. They never had before.

Although the commercial guardian had gone to court, in the spring of 2010, to get permission to use what they then referred to as a "new" assistive device to turn Mama, they do not seem to have brought one into her home until the end of March the following year. On March 28, 2011, according to the guardian's clinical notes, they first heard from the home aide service a proposal to have only one attendant for Mama and use the assistive device. Reading this during discovery was like being in a time machine. Had this not been one of the major reasons for the 2010 hearing? The purpose of a visit by a functionary from the guardian's office on March 30, 2011, the clinical case notes describe as "to demonstrate new assistive turning device. She [Mama] did appear to be somewhat anxious however...It was believed that the amount of people in her room was causing the anxiety...(there were 9 during demonstration)."[365]

On April 15, 2011, the commercial guardian at last created a

---

363 Rosenstiel-22303-223052
364 Rosenstiel-22304
365 Decades 24664

procedure for moving Mama's bed outdoors.[366] They had installed the court-ordered ramp, back in June 2010, but they rarely allowed Mama out of the room, regardless of the instructions currently in force.

While it is dangerous to assume that all these unpleasant events directly caused Mama's next medical emergency, I am sure they did not help, either. On Sunday, May 8, 2011, I was preparing to spend time with Mama, as I normally did on Mother's Day. However, before I left for Mama's house that morning, I got a phone call that she was already in the Emergency Room at Lovelace Women's Hospital in Albuquerque. I spent about an hour and a half, there, before anyone arrived from the commercial guardian's office to sign Mama in, officially, for treatment. Having arrived by ambulance, Mama had been taken directly into the ER itself, not into the waiting area.

I had been told that Mama was unresponsive. Well, she was not speaking with anyone, and the head of her bed looked a lot lower than I was used to seeing it. She seemed semi-conscious, perhaps due to dehydration.

Mama must have been dehydrated by the time I arrived, because she had been vomiting and had diarrhea. She only woke up a few times during her stay in the ER, but the doctor was not with her on any of those occasions. She did not seem to respond to the ER doc at all. Something about his attitude, perhaps?

The aide either knew nothing or had been instructed to tell me nothing, so she and Mama stayed in a private area. The aide did not allow me into the area, so I had to stand in the hall, waiting for the guardian's emissary.

The doctor supervising the ER, looking cranky and grossly overworked that day, walked up. His ID said his name was "Claman."

"Who're you with?" he barked.

I gestured toward the area where Mama was in bed, her aide sitting next to her.

"What's going on?"

"She's been vomiting green liquid. She has a history of gall

---

366 Decades 24661

bladder problems, but that was back in 2003. She spent time here, for that. I gather she has diarrhea, too, today."

"Is she on Actigal?"

"She was until about eight months ago. Then they took her off."

"Who're you?"

"I'm her daughter, but she has a legal guardian who signs the papers."

"What would make anyone *not* be their mother's guardian? My own mother's getting up there, so I want to know."

"My husband was dying when my mother got sick. I had to make a choice."

"You mean you didn't feel able to take care of them both?"

"I didn't think I could."

"Who else is interested?"

"I have a cousin, back East."

"Anybody closer?"

"No. They said someone from the guardian's office was on the way."

"Well, she's taking up a bed!" he complained, gesturing in Mama's direction. "Let me know when somebody gets here to sign."

Now he looked even angrier.

At that point, I was the only person standing in the hall. I watched, from a discreet distance as he examined Mama, never looking at the area around her gallbladder, only the central area of her stomach. A privacy screen stood at an angle to Mama's bed. No one bothered moving it into position.

The commercial guardian's emissary arrived about 30 minutes after that conversation. She was covering for everyone that day. Said she was unhappy about having to leave the festivities in the East Mountains to come into the city. I motioned to the ER doc across the room that the person who could sign for treatment had arrived. He strode over and took her to a more private position, just outside Mama's room. His voice was so loud that I could hear part of the conversation. At the beginning, hers was, too. I wondered whether Mama, also, could hear them. She was closer. Perhaps she heard more than I did.

"Why don't you just have her doctor come and give her fluids? That's all she needs. She doesn't belong here."

"Dr. Morgan's off today. She didn't have anyone to cover."

I did not hear the rest of the conversation, except for his parting shot:

"I wouldn't give her longer than another twenty-four hours!"

Again, I wondered whether Mama could hear him.

(I had certainly heard negative prognoses for Mama before. However, later I watched Mama's color improve after the administration of IV fluids, so I started believing that yet another doctor was wrong.)

The guardian's emissary stayed, altogether, about twenty minutes—long enough to sign the consent for treatment, which I think started just about as soon as the doctor knew she was willing to sign paperwork—before she returned to the East Mountains. Before she left, she made sure to tell me that she was not going to stick around, waiting for Mama to leave. She wanted to get back to the party at home.

Dr. Claman did not tell me that Mama had a day to live, maximum. He told me that she was living on "borrowed time." Anything, he said, could happen anytime. However, that is what most people would say, even about a perfectly healthy 99-year-old.

I wonder how they legally discharged Mama because I did not see anyone give the guardian's representative those papers; they were not near ready to discharge Mama when the guardian's representative left and I was not legally able to sign them. Who signed Mama out? I stayed another hour or so, until they discharged Mama to go back home. She had to travel by ambulance, both ways. Emotionally exhausted, I drove myself back home, to rest.

Someone prevailed on the doctor to prescribe antibiotics for Mama, despite the fact that the commercial guardian had told me, months before, that they would not do this anymore. I saw the bottle of them out when I visited, and I witnessed their side effects. Until Mama finished them, she had the dry heaves, off and on. Moreover, her aides who had not been trained (or licensed) to administer drugs, were doing so. By then Mama only had a nurse for a couple of hours per day, but the medicine had to be administered at 8 AM, noon and 8 PM. Or so the instructions said.

On May 23, 2011, the guardian's office received a call from the home-health aide service. The partner who took it said it came in at 6:35 P.M. "Dr. Rosenstiel had 'stopped breathing' when turned on her side ...this had first occurred earlier in the day when the Nursefinder [sic] nurse was there. When Dr. Rosenstiel was placed on her back she was fine...the DNR did not seem to be in the house..."[367] Another notation on May 25 stated that a nurse from Nursefinders had evaluated Mama "She advised that she had gone to assess Dr. Annette and believed that her difficulty [breathing] was positional."[368]

On June 7, a set of handwritten notes on the home visit of a functionary from the guardian's office included the following, "This writer removed old protocols from Bedroom [sic]."[369] These would be the protocols established by stipulated court order back in 2008. When those notes were written into the guardian's word-processing program, later, the writer added some flourishes, "This writer removed the protocols that were posted in bedroom, kitchen and CK staff [manual] and replaced with approved protocol. Discussed protocol with CK staff."[370] These would no longer be the protocols established by stipulated court order back in 2008. The guardian had just changed them unilaterally, touching off another round of legal negotiations.

A very odd notation in the guardian's notes for June 13, 2011, claimed that the guardian's functionary had phoned me to talk about Mama's birthday. The only times, after 2007, that I received calls from the guardian were when Mama was either in the hospital or dying. There was still a court order preventing me from contacting them, except through my attorney; they did not deliberately contact me directly, either, other than in an emergency, and even then, they generally did so through Debbie. Debbie had arranged for me to take an ice cream cake to Mama's for her birthday in 2010. When I was visiting Mama and someone from

---
367 Decades 24655
368 Decades 24656
369 Decades 24652
370 Decades 24647

the guardian's office arrived, whatever conversation we had was minimal. I do not believe that this reported conversation ever happened; I am convinced that the author imagined this fiction. She claimed I told her that the guardian did not need to do anything for Mama's birthday, other than "to know what her [Mama's] diet limitations are."[371] Nonsense! How would I have any standing to tell the guardian what to do about anything at all, anyway? Had the judge not given the firm plenary power, back in 2008?

Mama would be reaching her hundredth birthday on June 29, 2011. Again, they were planning to bring in Chinese food and chocolate cake and have a dozen or more of her caregivers and staff from the guardian's office present. Or so they told me. They told me it would be a big party, so again, I did not feel safe attending. After getting the guardian's prior express permission, I celebrated two days earlier with a couple of friends. We brought Mama some ice cream cake and party favors.

Unlike what I was told about Mama's later official party by the aides, the case notes for that date say, "This writer took Chinese food, chocolate cake, and flowers to ct. Ct was not awake during visit...The ct's room was decorated for her birthday."[372] That does not sound like a big blowout to me.

In 2011, the commercial guardian sent Debbie another letter, destined for me. The firm was, Ruth Pregenzer said, no longer able to guarantee the safety of Mama's possessions because no one from the guardianship firm was on the premises around the clock. True. However, theoretically, the conservator's court-given job was supposed to be to "conserve" Mama's assets, including her personal property. Dating from when Judge Baca had appointed them in November 2003, no one from the guardian's office had ever been on the premises twenty-four-seven. To me, this seemed like a formal denial of the legal responsibility they had assumed, back in 2003, and during all those hearings when they had asked the judge to confirm their plenary power to protect Mama and conserve her assets.

If I wanted any of Mama's possessions, they told me, I should

---

371 Ibid
372 Decades 24646

examine all of them, decide what I wanted now, and then take what I wanted. Anything not currently in Mama's bedroom that I wanted preserved, I should feel free to take. For months, I resisted doing this. I resisted saying goodbye to Mama while she was (to me, at least) still very much alive.

Finally, after some prodding from the commercial guardian, I started doing an inventory inside Mama's house. They told me to show them what I wanted, but I could not do that without taking photos. Ultimately, they allowed me to take pictures of the contents of the house. How they squared this permission with the prohibitions of the court order denying me the right to bring photographic equipment into Mama's home, I cannot imagine. The same with the shed. Old boxes in the garage or the shed would likely not attract the attention of anyone the guardians were suggesting might take things. At least they would not be the first things taken.

I inventoried everything, then attached little gummed, numbered labels to everything I could in Mama's home. Thousands of items. At first, I was only allowed to look inside the house and shed. Eventually, the commercial guardian allowed me to look in the garage, too. By 2011, multiple piles of boxes, sitting in rows since 1997, had collapsed on top of Mama's Acura. Some months later, as I was running on empty myself, I got a couple of friends to help with the list-making one day.

For the first time since 2004, I had been free to enter rooms other than the kitchen, breakfast nook, living room, den and Mama's room. What an unholy mess. Filthy floors. Commodes on top of papers. Broken glass in the garage. Broken controls on the washer and dryer. It was not only the rug in Mama's room that was stained, either. I would no longer trust the upholstery on some of the furniture; it would have to be discarded. I found an empty leather case for a small pistol. What had been going on in this house? Other than aides drinking on the job back in 2006, I mean. Apparently, inebriated caregivers had been a problem right along,[373] up there with the appearance of untrained caregivers, and caregivers inappropriately dressed. The clinical case notes from March 23, 2011, stated, "they have sent caregivers who have not

---

373 Rosenstiel(2)01575; Decades 24664

been trained about Dr. and were inappropriately dressed, which I myself witnessed..."[374]

I registered a protest with the guardian about the condition of many items and the general condition of Mama's home and garage. By late October, I had sent the guardian pictures of things I would want to take.

Fortunately, there is written evidence, from someone who would never deliberately have helped me, if she had been able to avoid it, that I was not the only one appalled by the condition of Mama's home. In her invoice for March 30, 2011, Barbara Buck wrote that she had discussed with Margot the following items: "House is filthy, need to come in and clean ceiling fans, window sills, upper reaches of bookcases. Need deep cleaning."[375]

On March 31, 2011, the guardian's clinical case notes state they, "received letter of Passover instructions from Betty Singer. Margot will deliver necessary supplies on Friday."[376] I guess that means Mama was about to get more mashed-up, microwave-heated gefilte fish that she did not like anyway. Unless Betty also sent them instructions that it was to be served cold. I doubt that, because anyone who ever attended a Passover Seder would have known how this dish was supposed to be served. And once again, the commercial guardian had decided to spend $110 per hour for an upper-level person to go and get these items, despite the fact that they were routinely available in local supermarkets, generally on clearly marked shelves at that time of year. An aide with a shopping list could have picked them up during any weekly shopping trip. I guess this means Betty was no longer sending Mama these supplies.

Meanwhile, Judith Wagner, deeply mired in the Vaughan bankruptcy by the time Judge Baca appointed her, delayed and delayed, and then delayed some more in finishing her examination. Months continued to drag on, with Mama sometimes well, sometimes ill. Wagner did not even have an initial conference with the guardianship firm and Debbie until October 12, 2010.[377] By April 2011,

---

374 Decades 24665
375 Decades 33674
376 Decades 24664
377 Rosenstiel-22337

Wagner appears to have issued some sort of preliminary report, but only to the commercial guardian. On April 19, 2011, this notation appears on the commercial guardian's invoice: "Mult emails re; [sic.] Judy Wagner's report."[378] However, almost a year after her appointment Wagner still had not issued any report so both sides could see it. The multiple emails mentioned in the invoice were not produced as part of the commercial guardian's discovery production, so I am assuming they were exchanged via the firm's internal, private server. Finally, on October 4, 2011, the case docket shows that Judge Baca sent Judith Wagner a letter. "Letter from Judge Baca to Ms. Wagner RE: Please submit your completed report as soon as possible," the entry states.[379] By November 4, the commercial guardian had started having intensive meetings on how to respond to Wagner's report. These consultations, along with the names of the participants, show in their invoices. Some included the special master. It seems that Debbie had no part in these discussions.

Not until seeing the invoices did I realize that some sort of report seems to have existed, back in April 2011. Why so long before we saw it? Perhaps a clue to this is the following, from Buck's "Interim Report," "The Special Master was mindful that the Court did not want a full analysis of the accounting..."[380] And then, there are two more clues, from her invoice items on July 18 and 19, respectively. "Discussion with Judge Baca re problems with Judy Wagner,"[381] and "Discussion with conservator re issues with final report from Judy Wagner,"[382] they read.

I was still working in Mama's garage, taking some things home with me in early November 2011. During the first days of that month, when the weather in Albuquerque cooled down abruptly, from highs in the 70s to highs in the 50s, and lows in the high 40s to lows in the 20s and 30s, there was no heat anywhere in the wing of Mama's home that housed her bedroom. Margot came, bringing a technician who struggled with that hideous, four-foot-tall heating unit they had installed in Mama's bedroom. The one referred to in

---

378 Rosenstiel-22305
379 Case Docket for Re: Annette Rosenstiel, Case #D-202-PQ-20030170. Accessed and downloaded 2/6/2020
380 Interim Report of Special Master, pp. 1-2
381 Decades 33679
382 Ibid

the guardian's records as a "heat pump." He wrestled with it repeatedly, but got nowhere. I told the aides where the floor heaters the guardian had removed from Mama's bedroom when they installed that now-useless unit had been stored. "The heating/cooling unit has not been fixed yet," complained Mama's clinical supervisor when she visited on October 4, 2011.[383]

I ran into Margot at Mama's home. She did not seem to remember that someone had stowed the space heaters in the back bedroom only a few months before. She looked angry, after I told her where they were, although she did not say why. After Mama died, I discovered that she had charged to go and buy a new one on November 4.[384] This additional, redundant unit, had I ever seen it in Mama's home, would have made a good companion for the three expensive, HEPA-compliant canister vacuums I also found in the same back room.

Mama had never enjoyed being kept forcibly in any room that served as her bedroom (even when the guardian put her bed in her den) with strange men moving around the place, seemingly at random, and out of her control. Even the commercial guardian admitted that Mama had not been comfortable during the two prior home improvement projects conducted by Margot. This was the third time. By then, Mama was not talking much, but her expression more than suggested to me that she did not enjoy the company of Margot, either.

The technician spent a couple of days in Mama's bedroom, troubleshooting the heating system, to no good purpose. The unit stayed broken, as Mama remained in her cold bedroom. The staff of aides did not turn over the way the nursing personnel did. Why would the aides not have spontaneously remembered to use the space heaters they had turned on, back in March, the same ones they had stored in the back bedroom? I am not sure whether the aides used the space heaters when I was not there; at least, when I was, Mama got some heat. The guardian continued to charge for troubleshooting problems relating to that apparently inoperable heating unit as late as December 29, 2011.[385]

---
383 Decades 24642
384 Rosenstiel-22320
385 Rosenstiel-22340-22341

The day after the tech seemed to have given up on the heater, I arrived to find one of Mama's aides waiting for me with a camera.

"I brought my camera today and I'm going to take a picture of you and your mother."

"Do you have permission from the office to take this picture?"

"I take these pictures of all my clients."

"I think you should ask first."

Seeing that the door to Mama's room was closed, I told the aide in the kitchen that I would work before seeing Mama. I went out to the garage to get together items I wanted to take back to my house. When I came back into Mama's house, the door to her room was still closed and the aide with the camera stood in the kitchen, baking cookies made, she said, with some sort of sugar substitute. I took things out to my car, came back, and the door to Mama's room was still closed. I asked about the closed door.

"She's probably still changing your mother."

I took more items out to the car. When I got back, the door to Mama's room was finally open. The aide with the camera ushered me in there. She was waving that camera, offering, again, to take a photo of the two of us.

"I don't have a photo!"

"Don't you have the photos from Mama's one-hundredth birthday party?"

"But you're not in them."

"I'm sorry, but I'm not permitted to allow you to do this."

"But there won't be a photo of the two of you together."

"I'm sorry. It's not allowed."

The other aide stood there, listening to us.

As I walked toward Mama's bed, I saw a note to Mama, in the handwriting of the aide who was brandishing the camera. It sat atop Mama's dresser. "Do you want me to take a photo of you with your daughter?" it said. Under any normal circumstances, that would be a fine request, but without permission from the commercial guardian that photo could be used to deny me visitation with Mama later, particularly since there was a witness, there to see whether I allowed the aide with the camera to take photos I knew had not been specifically authorized by the guardian.

The first aide made it seem that Mama had wanted this picture taken. The aides had dressed Mama up, make-up and everything. Did they really not know that I had no right even to call the commercial guardian's office on my own, to ask for permission? (I was almost certain they knew this.) Debbie could contact them, but then only through their attorney, meaning that it would be a matter of several days until a message got through. The aides could not call the guardian's office, either, barring an extreme emergency. If they had been authorized to call, they could have simply picked up the phone the moment I told them they needed permission. Almost certainly, they had to go through their employer, who then would have to contact the guardian. Another time-consuming process.

However well-meaning Mama's aides might have been (and I am not entirely sure their intentions were benign), they had spent a long time and a lot of effort getting Mama (and me) ready for disappointment. On February 29, 2012, Jennifer entered clinical notes, stating that, on February 12, "[client] had a red swollen eye,"[386] so likely the photo incident happened about the same time.

Perhaps they had made Mama up especially for picture taking on that occasion. But perhaps not. Sometime earlier, I had been working on the floor of a closet, in the room furthest away from Mama's, when I thought I heard her cry out. Needing the walker, back then, and having trouble getting up off the floor because of my knee problem, it took me a while to get to within view of the door of Mama's room. It was open and I was thinking of going in, when I noticed Mama's obvious black eye. The aides were some distance away, in the hall. If I reacted in any way, and particularly if I went in, when the aides were not in there, I would risk being accused of causing that black eye, so I continued down the hall, to my car, so I could come back with boxes to provide an excuse for me walking down that hall. Whatever damage had been done to Mama, it had already happened and I could not trust what anyone might tell me about the circumstances.

When I got back inside, I noticed that the door to Mama's room was closed. When I came back from the car, after doing more

---
386 Decades 24639

work, the door was open again, and Mama was all dressed up and wearing makeup. The black eye had been entirely camouflaged. At that point, it was safe for me to go in. The aides put makeup on Mama for several days thereafter. (They did the same thing, the second time, too.)

During discovery, I found documents confirming the existence of that first black eye; the doctor had been called. This accords with an entry in the case notes, on April 5, 2011. "Received email from Nursefinders from overnight report. It was noted that Dr. Annette's left eye was 'purple'...She also noted a bruise on her left hand, a cut-sore on her lip and she stated that she was having inspiratory/expiratory wheezing..."[387] In Mama's records, no determination was made about how it happened or who or what caused it. The second time, they did not bother to call the doctor. During discovery we did not receive copies of all those daily emails that the writer of these case notes says the guardian received.

Another set of items we did not receive were the notebooks Nursefinders kept. By 2012, the firm had been bought by Bayada. On April 1, 2011, the guardian's clinical case notes say "They [Nursefinders] also advised that they are on the last page in the notebook at the home. Notebook to be taken to the house on Monday. After discussing with Margot she was unaware of the notebook at the house..."[388] The notebooks belonged to Nursefinders, as it turned out, and we never got to see one.

Had they truly made Mama up for my benefit, on this particular day in 2011, because Mama wanted the aide to take a photo? Maybe. Then again, maybe this was just an elaborate way to hide another black eye while, at the same time, making me feel terrible in the process, for disappointing Mama. Certainly, Mama could not read, from bed, the handwritten message that lay on her dresser. Maybe the aide never showed that note to Mama. Maybe she just wrote it and left it on the bureau, so I would be sure to see it.

I was starting to think that all Mama's aides had cameras they could use, at will. Well, they all had cell phones, so it is a good bet that they could have used those anytime they pleased, if they had wanted videos or stills. How many photos of Mama were floating

---
387 Decades 24661
388 Decades 24662

around? A detail of the guardian's invoice for May 9, 2011, says, "Review of files/pictures."[389] During discovery, they did not produce any photos of Mama. It seemed to me, even at the time, that I was the only person on the premises not allowed to record or photograph anything without special permission from the commercial guardian.

The aides only left me alone with Mama for a minute or so that day. But I did have enough time to ask Mama whether she was feeling well. She looked unhappy, shook her head, and would not answer. By then, I was not even sure what I was seeing, or who was doing what to whom. After I said goodbye to Mama, I went home and cried. Briefly, I flirted with the idea of staying away from Mama's home for a while, but as far as I could see, that would likely make both of us feel even worse.

On April 15, 2011, a functionary from the guardian's firm was there when I arrived to visit Mama. She asked me whether there were any family customs that should be observed over Passover, which would begin on April 18. I said there were not. Her notes claim she had asked about Easter also, but I do not recall her asking about Easter at all. Unfortunately, the answer would have been, "For Easter, we would buy new clothes, exchange gifts and go out to dinner," all actions which would have been hard to duplicate under then-current conditions.[390]

Copious clinical case notes tracked Mama's progress from January through May 2011. Then, according to the invoices, there were no clinical case notes written between June and December.

The commercial guardian firm reminded me (through the relevant attorneys, of course) that they refused to be responsible for anything left outside of Mama's bedroom. I had best get on with removing anything I wanted from elsewhere in the house, they warned. Reluctantly, I started taking increasing numbers of things from the other rooms, eventually on January 2, 2012, paying several acquaintances to move into storage items that were too heavy for me. Then, the aides complained that I had taken too many things. By January 5, 2012, the commercial guardian complained

---

389 Decades 35011
390 Decades 24661

that I had already taken "too much,"[391] even though I thought that I had only followed their instructions by taking things I wanted to preserve from rooms other than Mama's bedroom.

The commercial guardian complained that I had demoralized the aides by removing these items. No point in retailing the entire, dispiriting exchange. "Some furniture was brought back to the house to make it look more liveable," read the clinical case notes for February 12, written up, it seems, on February 29.[392] Actually, this is not true. I moved a table and some chairs from another room into the kitchen area and convertible couches from the back rooms into the living room when I removed the living room furniture.

On Friday, October 28, 2011, Buck's invoice detail says, "Discussion with Judge Baca and drafting request for hearing."[393] According to the case docket, no request for a hearing was filed by any party to Mama's case until February 2012, and that one came—at least nominally—from the guardian's attorney, Ruth Pregenzer.

There is no entry on Buck's invoices stating that Buck consulted with Debbie about a motion. Was the special master, at the behest of Judge Baca (and in consultation with her) producing legal work specifically designed to benefit the guardian? Was Judge Baca telling the commercial guardian, through Barbara Buck, exactly how to file specific papers in order to get what that firm wanted? Buck charged Mama for almost an hour working on this project. And, of course, when Buck submitted her invoices to the court, Judge Baca approved this charge, just as she had approved all Buck's other charges.

After receiving Judge Baca's letter in October 2011, Judith Wagner quickly produced a draft report. In order to provide the judge with her tailor-made "accounting report," Wagner had to "compromise" with normal forensic accounting procedure. I refuse to call her report a forensic accounting, because I do not believe that it was. Judge Baca had made absolutely certain that it would not be one. Wagner's accounting-related novella was written and tailored to the judge's express order.

---

391 Rosenstiel-22347
392 Decades 24639
393 Decades 33678

Wagner examined only a two-week period during the year in question (mid-August 2008 to mid-November 2009).[394] She made a desultory attempt to see whether the prices being charged were in line with other prices charged for similar services in the area, during that period. Even so, she found over a dozen "non-standard" practices that she gently suggested the commercial guardian change.

Here are some items she did not consider: Was it standard practice, in the industry, to feed home health aides and their families, as well as the ward? She examined only invoices for health care and not all Mama's expenses to see whether the guardian's general practices were industry standard. Many shifts overlapped. She simply accepted the guardian's explanation that this was a fine procedure, and that it took 15 minutes, or more, for information to be exchanged at the change of shift, and the ward moved. She never tried to check on how many people needed to be involved in moving Mama or whether it took as long to convey information on one patient as on all the patients in a hospital ward. Even so, during that period, two people always attended Mama. She did not check to see whether the amounts being charged and the number of aides turned out to be fair, in relation to the amounts being charged to other clients in similar circumstances and the number of attendants hired for them. There is no evidence that she ever saw the Broadspire report, dating from October 2008.

Wagner deliberately ignored some other possible sources of impropriety. She insisted that the personnel, who were checking in by phone on their arrival, remained on Mama's premises and worked during the entire period of their shift, and that they then checked out, also by phone. How she could believe this, having never observed the situation in person, I cannot imagine. I knew this was not true, but Wagner never interviewed me; in fact, as of March 2021 I have still never met this petite blond, blue-eyed woman with her severe suits, although by now I have seen her picture, more than once, in the news.

By the time Wagner issued her report, I had had months during which I spent concentrated periods of four to six hours,

---

394 Despite this, Buck's "Interim Report of the Special Master" claims it covers the period November 28, 2008-January 5, 2009.

or more, at Mama's home, in order to complete the inventory, and then similar amounts of time as I was removing items from Mama's home, as the guardian had required me to do during 2011. While working at Mama's myself, I regularly saw aides check in for their shift. Some then returned to their cars to eat, drink or make phone calls, coming back in, seemingly at will. Others, after they checked in, disappeared for hours. Sometimes they returned with a bag or two of groceries from a supermarket a few blocks away. Sometimes, they just walked back in, without any pretense of shopping serving as a plausible excuse. Working at Mama's was easy duty, just as those two aides had told me, long before. Aides often absented themselves during weekdays, when most people were at work and the market was not crowded. Even if they had gone to one of the nearby markets, they ought to have been able to return, at the latest, within 45 minutes. It made me wonder whether they might be doing two different jobs, signing in for both of them, and being paid twice for the same time period. No way for me to prove that, of course.

Mama often was not getting all the services she was paying for. And particularly the intensive, hands-on services the commercial guardianship firm insisted that she needed so urgently at that time. On one occasion, they paid a bill for more than $6,000 to the same home health vendor more than once, on the same day. The commercial guardian seemed not to notice that it had the same invoice number for both checks until an outsider (Tom Burrage) told them before the 2010 hearing. Surely that invoice should have looked familiar, the second time around. The guardian said it was an accident and they would be more careful in future.

At another point, the home health service billed them for over $18,000, saying that they had raised the rates almost a year earlier, but had "forgotten" to bill for the additional charges. When Wagner asked them to produce the original contract, they could not. Both the guardianship company and the home health service denied there was any such contract; if any had ever existed, neither business could find a copy.[395] If there is one thing that, in my

---

395 Report of Rule 11-706 Expert, November 2, 2011, p. 5

experience, all health services (from doctors' offices to hospitals to home care services) require, it is copious documentation. Contracts, consent forms and payment agreements are required to be meticulously conserved and in order. However, apparently both the guardianship firm and the home health service insisted that they simply did not have one. Sometimes, the same aide was billed for at different rates. It looked to me as if Wagner picked a time when there was a bit less of this going on, but still she found quite a few things that she questioned. Wagner did not address the questions I submitted, claiming they were "not within the scope of my expertise and not within the scope of my assignment."[396]

Before Wagner issued her report, and while going through the contents of Mama's home, I had found a folder of health-related items. Mama was still alive, so I did not remove the papers. In addition, because of the court order, I could not copy the item, either. A contract with one of the home health care services, dating from right after Mama's hip fracture, was one of those documents. It called for providing aides at about $4 per hour ($8 on holidays) less than the invoices from that service showed (this was the contract the commercial guardian had told Wagner did not exist). After Mama's death, when I looked for it, it had disappeared.

Wagner had to keep her report within strict boundaries. Still, she found a dozen irregularities that she thought could be "corrected." The commercial guardian then started defending the firm against her "suggestions." A couple of minor ones, they said that they had already started using. To make systemic changes that instituted proper oversight, however, would place a great burden on the firm, they said. They appealed to Buck to decide, with them, that it would be more costly to be accurate, and they would have to charge Mama if the court demanded accuracy in the billing records. Buck concurred, so no, the changes suggested would not be made.

Judge Baca had denied my request for a real forensic accounting, even though Mama was paying quite a bit to get this report from Wagner. However, I had been clearly on the record, since the beginning, as repeatedly disapproving of the guardian's spending

---

396   Ibid, p. 3

habits. Had I not gone to court, multiple times, to register those protests, the judge would have automatically approved the guardian's annual reports, in a routine fashion, and I would have had no later recourse. As I got to know the family members of other wards, I discovered that this had happened in other cases. For various reasons, they seemed to have believed that they could raise these issues later, even after a judge had approved those expenses, and were devastated to discover that they could not.

Acting, she said, on behalf of Mama and to conserve Mama's estate, Barbara Buck told Wagner not to do any more work. Since she was acting in place of the judge herself, no one could argue. Her statements had the same authority as an order from Judge Baca. The $10,000 Wagner had billed, up to that point, were all she was going to get. After I looked at Buck's invoices, and at the commercial guardian's invoices, I was astonished not to be able to find any entry I could tie to a meeting in January 2012 that I had attended by phone. I heard her speak, but of course I was not allowed to do so; I knew Buck was there. So were the others—the guardian and Debbie and Wagner herself. Is it even possible that Buck forgot to bill for it? The only in-person meetings Buck mentions between October and March are with the guardianship firm's personnel.[397]

Listening to this meeting by phone from home, I heard Buck insist that she was concerned with saving Mama money. Of course, if Wagner had continued to dig, under the terms Judge Baca had set, Buck would have been quite right—further work would have been a total waste of money. The commercial guardian would simply have continued to reject her substantive "suggestions" as too burdensome. There should be a law against anyone calling what Wagner did "a forensic accounting."

All along, I had had to pay (and get a terrible reputation as intransigent) to register protests. Even worse, the guardianship system had saddled Mama with huge expenses so that the guardianship firm could defend itself against all of these complaints. The legal system works that way.

During January 2012, the commercial guardian cleaned Mama's home thoroughly. All the rugs looked (temporarily) clean.

---

[397] Rosenstiel-22343-22345

Then they took pictures of the "clean house" that would prove useful to them, later. They also took Buck there, to look around, right after that.[398] If she had asked me, I could have told her that, within weeks, the stains were going to reappear on the rugs, because the cleaning would only remove what was on the surface, not on the underside or in the pad underneath the wall-to-wall carpeting, but she never asked me.

Ruth Pregenzer had tried, again, to interest Debbie Gonçalves and me in more "estate planning" during November 2010.[399] They never told us that they were going to consult Ken Leach anyway, to the tune of $321 (including tax), on November 19, the same day that we rejected their idea.[400] I did not find that out until after we got the legal invoices during discovery. The commercial guardian's invoices show that they charged Mama $11 for reading Debbie's rejection, on my behalf, of their unsolicited offer on this subject.

Somehow, discontinuing Wagner's "forensic accounting" seemed to trigger yet one more attempt at "estate planning." By January 2012, we had heard from them again, asking to change Mama's estate plan (which, as it soon turned out, they had already started to do, without asking us).

On January 17, 2012, Dr. Morgan visited Mama. This seems to have been part of another one of the guardian's attempts to get Mama accepted by the hospice of which Dr. Morgan was a co-owner. Mama, however, was still too stable. Dr. Morgan did not refer her.

The commercial guardian started small, this time, with the estate planning, by removing Mama's TV and portable microwave from her home. Of course, visiting daily and coming in through the kitchen area, I had instantly noticed that the microwave that habitually sat on the south counter in the kitchen itself was not there anymore. Also, because Mama was confined to her bedroom now, and I visited her there daily, I discovered a large empty space on her bureau, where the big-screen TV had been. I could not have agreed more with the tone of Debbie's January 31 email to Barbara

---

398 Rosenstiel-22344
399 Letter from Deborah Rupp Gonçalves. November 19, 2010.
400 Decades 33621

Buck, Ruth Pregenzer, and other parties apparently countenancing these changes:

> I admit to being stunned that the conservator deems it appropriate to give away Annette's property, for whatever reason, without first asking Leonie if she has a preference or at least advising her. None of [the commercial conservator's] annual reports has indicated any charitable contributions made on Annette's part since 2003. I am unaware of any statutory provision that allows a conservator to simply give away or donate a ward's property in the manner you describe...[401]

No mention of this "donation" appeared in the conservator's 2012 annual report to the court. Just as in the previous eight years of annual reports, they listed no charitable contributions. Might this mean that the commercial guardian, using similar "substituted judgement," had decided to give away other property belonging to Mama? Might this account for the items that Mama had in 2003 and no longer owned in 2007? Had they been given to someone or some charity, and had the conservator similarly omitted this information from the corresponding annual report to the court? Well, at least they did not try to argue that Mama had outright told them to give away these items, and admitted that the firm had decided to do so. (Am I being too negative to think that, had I not complained immediately about these disappearances, other, larger items might have vanished?)[402]

Over the years of their tenure, the commercial conservator charged Mama what seemed to me to be tens of thousands of dollars for multiple unwanted and, at least to my way of thinking, unneeded attempts to change Mama's will. I had long ago started to wonder how many times they would try to push me in a direction I knew that Mama did not want to go. Each time they did, they claimed, through the magic of "substituted judgement," that they were the people who knew what Mama really wanted (as opposed to what Mama herself had always said that she wanted during the

---
401   Decades 03474
402   They also suggested that the appliances were defective or broken. Goodwill does not accept defective appliances as donations. Or at least they did not in 2012; I called them to ask.

many years when she was mentally competent). Each time, their efforts infuriated me more than the last time.

After Mama passed away, and I obtained Kathleen Winslow's back-office documents by subpoena through the probate suit David started, I discovered one possible reason why the guardianship firm had seemed so desperate, during the fall and winter of 2011-12, to gain control over me, and more particularly over the cash they knew would be available for me to use to sue them, should Mama pass away with at least some of her estate intact. Ruth Pregenzer, in checking over the firm's annual report before submitting it to the court, had discovered a $500,000 discrepancy between the assets the firm had reported on one day and the assets they had reported on the next. This loss, she warned them, had to be rectified, and the money "restored," unless someone could tell her (and, therefore, also the court) where that money went. Because she sent her letter to the investment house at the same time that she sent it to the guardianship firm, it ceased to be a privileged legal communication.

As the most ethical person in this situation, Pregenzer simply put everyone on notice that they could not do this to the court. They were going to have to find a way to fix things. There followed a mad rush to try to fix the numbers, although the commercial guardian did file the original figures anyway, on December 13, 2011.[403] The judge did not seem to notice.

On July 31, 2012, almost two months after Mama died, the guardian issued an "amended" report for this reporting period (November 2010 to November 2011). The firm's original report had claimed Mama had ended that reporting period with an estate worth $6,635,193.57. The amended report, however, listed her net worth as $6,071,293.68.[404] The inaccurate figures came, the commercial guardian told the court, from improperly reporting the actual numbers on three account statements—one by $77,839.08, the second by $170,201.34, and the third by $274,110.24. However, if you look at the actual statements for those three accounts, as of November 1, the date on the statement, which was the date nearest to the date of the original report, the original figures in

---
403 Annual Report, 2011-June 1, 2012, p. 4
404 Rosenstiel-24235-24237

that first report are correct.[405] In other years, the guardian simply reported the amounts on those statements, as I found out during discovery. Why the question here? Either way, Mama's net worth, now said to be in the neighborhood of $6,000,000, had shown quite a precipitous drop from the $20,499,511.29 the commercial guardian declared as the value of her assets in the report they filed on February 13, 2007, covering November 2005 to November 2006.

Ruth Pregenzer might be the only person who knows all the details of what happened. After Mama died, she resigned from the case, telling David that she thought she could not continue as the guardian's attorney in this matter because she might be called as a witness during the trial proceedings. Two other attorneys, from different legal firms, took over as the guardian firm's representatives—Dan Lewis, an attorney and a bishop in the Mormon Church who specialized in estate planning (now retired, he was then a partner in the firm of Allen, Shepard, Lewis & Syrah), and Greg MacKenzie, then a partner in Hurley Toevs Styles Hamblin & Painter.

On my side, I originally had "only" David Garcia, whom I quickly came to regard as a combination of Perry Mason and Matlock (at the time a partner in Mickey Barnett's firm), and his incredible paralegal, Jane, an extraordinarily efficient, slender middle-aged lady with a British accent. Both David and Jane seemed to have had photographic memories for the 40,000 documents produced during discovery. Somehow, it did not matter that there were two larger firms deployed against us. Eventually, there would be five.

Theoretically, the guardian was supposed to supply us, during discovery, with the same documents we got from Winslow, minus any internal documents from the investment house that they would not have had access to, but we did, via subpoena. They did not provide us with those documents. If there had not been a separate probate action, I would never have seen that email from Pregenzer, complaining about the numerical discrepancy, and many other pivotal documents, as well.

If Mama had had a trustee when she was guardianized, even if that trustee had been her daughter, once a commercial guardian entered the picture, I have little doubt that the judge would have

---

405 Decades 17112,

forced any family member-trustee to sign the trusteeship over to some "professional trust officer" of the guardian's choosing.

From what I have now seen of court dockets, the court tends to favor the trustee. To be fair, a couple of attorneys whom I have interviewed on this subject do insist that courts favor those who challenge trustees. However, my own normal probate experience (my grandfather's estate, my grand-aunt's estate, my father's estate, my husband's estate, and then my mother's), when contrasted with the painful experiences of friends of mine whose trusts were handed off to a commercial trustee or a commercial guardian's nominee, were quite different.

If the plaintiff loses, the plaintiff is often taxed with paying the court costs of the trustee, as well. Some judges also assess fines and other penalties. A corporate trustee with deep pockets might suit-proof a dishonest trust, preventing heirs of modest means from gaining any sort of redress. A friend of mine sometimes says that we have the best court system money can buy. Even exclusive of outright bribery within the court itself, I am afraid that I have to agree.

In my experience, and from what I have read in the news of lawsuits involving trustees, they rarely succeed. In fact, in one recent Albuquerque case, the person challenging a trustee of the trust for a local prominent New Mexico family ended up bankrupt. The judge complained that he did not approve of that heir's prior choices of investments and did not think he deserved any more money.[406]

(This was not a comment on the provisions of the trust; it appeared from this article, and from a couple of court documents I have seen, as if one or more judges might be barring the man from access to a hefty pile of money owed to him by the trust because of the first judge's low opinion of the man's prior investing history.)

---

406 Heild, Colleen, "Abruzzo trustee ordered to pay $250,000," *Albuquerque Journal*, July 10, 2017, p. A5. Accessed June 5, 2020 from: *https://www.abqjournal.com/1031145/abruzzo-trustee-ordered-to-pay-250000-2.html* and Heild, Colleen, "Abruzzo nemesis who 'squandered' his fortune faces tax evasion charges," *Albuquerque Journal*, September 9, 2019. Pp. A1, A2. Accessed June 5, 2020 from: *https://www.abqjournal.com/1364060/abruzzo-nemesis-who-squandered-his-fortune-faces-tax-evasion-charges-ex-husband-of-deceased-abruzzo-sister-spent-years-suing-his-inlaws.html*

If the beneficiary was entitled to the money, why is it anyone's right to judge what uses s/he chooses for that money, so long as those uses are legal? No one challenged the beneficiary's mental competency in that case, so far as I could see. Even though court dockets are supposed to be posted, and that one used to be, the docket for this case has mysteriously disappeared from among those posted on the internet. This is odd, because the gag order that originally applied to that case was lifted years ago. The docket had been posted before it was lifted; after that, however, the docket was suppressed.

Having, I hoped, fought this Judith Wagner round to a draw, I thought I would get some relief from the commercial guardian's machinations, at least for a while. Every so often, I would send them a question about Mama's condition. They would always answer that she was "stable." Not until discovery in a separate suit by her estate against Mama's then former guardians, did I realize the extent to which they had been trying to get various hospices in the area to sign Mama onto their services. Not only that, but they had been (so they said themselves) actively planning for Mama to die almost immediately. An invoice entry on January 18, 2012 describes various subjects discussed during a phone call with Ruth Pregenzer. "Potential estate gift- [sic] and related planning" caught my eye. Another catchy little item said, "final plan for disposing of personal property."[407] Whose "final plan" was that? Mama had clearly stated hers, in her will, back in 1997. Were these more projected instances of "substituted judgement?"

Some understanding of what was going on seems to have filtered down to the home health aides. One day, during early 2012, one of the aides looked up from her book as I walked into the den. (Interesting, I thought, that she is out here and not in the bedroom, with Mama.)

"I'm going to buy these bookcases at the estate sale," she informed me, gesturing at the bookcases lining the east wall of the room.

"What estate sale? Nobody said anything to me about any estate sale."

---

407 Rosenstiel-22343

Within a week or so, another aide tried to buy the car in the garage from me, asking how much I wanted for it.

"I don't have any right to sell this car," I answered. "I don't own it."

Later the guardian accused me of offering to sell that aide the car. Too bad I could not have recorded that conversation and played it back for them, later.

Another aide shocked me even more, "You know, it's traditional to offer the aides anything they want from a client's possessions, after she passes."

"Oh, really?"

Originally, I was going to grant another aide's request for all the cartons of photocopies, particularly those relating to Native Americans, that Mama had collected. No money was going to change hands; they would have been a gift. I took the boxes and put them on a then-empty shelf in the garage, for safekeeping. However, after Mama died, a friend of mine who volunteered to help me clean out the house, seeing that those cartons contained only photocopies, put them on the truck to the dump. They were already long gone when I noticed that they were missing from the shelf in the garage, where I thought that I had put them to keep them safe.

During discovery, I noticed a couple of very nasty things that particular aide had placed in the record about me, I am assuming after being asked, by her employer, to look for negative things to say. After that, I no longer felt as unhappy as I had before about having disappointed her.

Right after the notations about "final" disposal of property appeared in the invoices was when the large-screen TV in Mama's bedroom, and the microwave in the kitchen suddenly disappeared. When I asked about them, the commercial guardian claimed the picture on that TV was defective, that they needed to get a TV with a bigger, better screen. They suggested that the microwave was not working and needed to be replaced. (However, I had seen it in action just the day before it disappeared.)

The firm said it had donated both items to Goodwill, but the "receipt" they later produced for the TV did not follow the form of the receipt I had gotten when I had donated things to Goodwill myself a few months earlier. They said they could not find the receipt for the other appliance. After I complained, however, appliances stopped disappearing from Mama's home. They bought Mama another large screen TV to replace the one that had disappeared, installing it on January 20.[408]

During January, the commercial guardian spent a lot of time planning. The "final estate gift," when they ultimately decided to tell me about it, turned out to be for $5 million. They wanted to give me a gift of that amount of "appreciated" CME stock that belonged to Mama, in exchange demanding that I sign the same non-disparagement agreement that I later discovered that they had extracted or at least tried to extract from relatives of other wards. I had to promise never to say anything negative about them, on pain of legal sanctions.

Having spent almost nine years without freedom of speech, and having promised Mama I would write about what had happened to her, I knew immediately that I could not sign any such agreement. Regardless of what I said, the firm would be likely to find at least some of the things I said about them uncomplimentary.

Another consideration: How much had they spent since their last annual report in December? They were not saying. Theoretically, they would not owe the court another accounting until December 2012, almost a year from then. Would there be any money left for Mama's care if anyone took $5 million out of her account now? Did she even have that much left? They might be pauperizing Mama by giving me any substantial gift. I was afraid that I could not trust them to tell me the truth. Precedent was a good guide here, I thought.

The media had been running articles about the tax-planning strategy called "gifts of appreciated stock" for years. I already knew that it would be a very bad idea for me to accept one. People often give appreciated stock when they want to make a large donation to a nonprofit institution or organization. The donor gets

---

408 Rosenstiel-22344

the tax credit for the current value, and when the nonprofit later sells the stock at a higher value than the original purchaser paid, no capital gains tax is due because the organization or institution selling that asset is a nonprofit.

Heirs, however, are not nonprofit institutions. They owe any capital gains tax on the difference between the initial acquisition price of the gift stock and its now higher (appreciated) value, when it is sold. Which would mean that I could not sell anything for at least a year, in order to lower the capital gains taxes to 15 percent, which was what the federal government lowered these taxes to after a holding period of one year (plus whatever state taxes I would owe). Otherwise, any gain would count as ordinary income, and I would pay a high percentage—perhaps over 50 percent, including state taxes—in taxes.

After 2007, the guardian had not had any access to High Desert financial statements, only to my annual report on Mama's portion. Thankfully, Debbie had convinced the court to sever that entity, formally and completely, from the rest of Mama's estate. It looked, to me, as if they thought I had spent everything I had been saving, and that I had been counting on selling Mama's stock instantly to generate cash to pay attorneys. I came to the conclusion that they wanted to make it impossible for me to sue them without suffering a serious financial penalty.

Knowing that they would call me stupid or crazy, or both, unless I had a CPA to back me up, I called Dick Satter, who was still my accountant.

"Hi, Dick. It's Léonie. I've got this crazy offer, here, from Mama's guardian. They're saying they'll give me $5 million in Mama's appreciated CME stock, in exchange for signing a non-disparagement agreement."

"What? If you sold, you'd have to pay capital gains tax on her gain, too. That's a terrible idea!"

"Can I quote you on that?"

"Sure!"

"Thanks."

The third part of their "offer" made me white-hot-furious. They offered to *give* me Mama's guardianship, something they had no right even to offer. If you looked at it, what they were really saying is that they would have no objection if I wanted to take over Mama's guardianship from them, effective immediately.

By then, I had learned, by simple observation of all the court hearings in Mama's case, that guardians receive their power from the court. It requires a court order to become a guardian. The guardianship firm repeatedly asked the judge to reaffirm the company's status. Only the court, I had learned from that experience, can appoint a guardian. Therefore, by simple logic, only the court can remove one guardian and substitute another guardian.

Watching the events in Mama's case, over the years, and particularly during 2007-08, I noticed that regardless of what anyone else said, the judge would listen to the court-appointed arbiter. In 2007-08, it was Elizabeth Church. It seemed that, if you got into her good graces, you would be home free.

Judge Baca had officially passed all Church's power, and more, to Barbara Buck in 2010. To me, Buck's actions showed that the special master was firmly allied with the commercial guardian. She was not friendly to me. I concluded that Buck would likely suggest some friend of hers and the judge would agree. Maybe, the judge already had someone in mind and that person would simply walk in and take over the title. Or maybe the judge would even request Buck to step in and be Mama's guardian, because this was such a "difficult case" and needed special attention, and I would have no recourse.

I could not forget that the guardian had gone on the court record, saying that the firm had to "protect" Mama against me. And that it had to keep me from being anywhere near Mama when my younger cousin and my aunt were visiting. It did not matter that only Betty now survived, and that she had not come to Albuquerque to see Mama since the spring of 2008. They could still argue that, if given the power, I would try to stop Mama from getting Betty's phone calls. Whatever they might say, the judge would accept it; there would be nothing I could do to refute it because there was never a proper hearing and I had no access to the documents showing that what I was saying was true and what they were saying was false.

If the court awarded Mama's guardianship to a non-professional now, after more than eight years had passed, it would look as if the court might have done something wrong originally. The court would not want to make that suggestion of error—even a long-ago error—would it?

I have now heard several people say that the problem with the "courts of equity" (and guardianship cases fall within this category) is that they are not equitable. I would have to agree.

All they were really offering was the promise that the firm would not object to my appointment, at the same time knowing in advance that the judge would never appoint me. It was a sucker's ploy; I did not fall for it.

The commercial guardian had been actively planning end-of-life actions. On February 2, 2011, Ruth Pregenzer had sent Debbie an email:

"...all hospice evaluations for Annette Rosenstiel have been done either by Hospice de la Luz or Hospice of the Sandias. The latest evaluation was again done by Hospice de la Luz. The conclusion was that Annette is not yet eligible for hospice...On many days Annette is awake and alert, eating well and enjoying her life...[the company] is developing a protocol for end of life decisions... [the guardianship firm] will develop the protocol [for end of life care] based on the information it has in its file."[409]

Although the letter also asked for any new "input" I might give, I had already told them everything I knew, back in 2003. I told them similar things in 2008. Then I watched as they ignored whatever I told them. In the intervening years, I had given information to Mama's various doctors, both in the presence of the guardian and privately, at times when they were visiting Mama in her home and I also happened to be there. The commercial guardian also had the stipulated order that we had agreed to in 2008. It conformed to what I knew Mama wanted. By 2012, I had no hope of the commercial guardian listening to anything I said, regardless of the subject.

Once again, it only took a couple of days from my receipt of their tri-partite offer to Debbie's letter, telling the guardian of my definitive refusal.

---

409 Decades 24702

February 15, 2012, brought more than one event. According to the case docket, Judith Wagner at last filed her report with the court. On the same day, the commercial guardian filed a motion (was this the one Barbara Buck had been preparing a few months earlier?), asking Judge Baca to approve all of the commercial guardian's annual reports since 2008. If I allowed this action to remain uncontested, I would have no way to argue, later, that all they had done during the past four years was not correct and absolutely in order. To make clear to the court that I protested, I had to pay one or more attorneys to file an objection. By then Mickey Barnett's firm was actively involved. They knew about the guardian's recent "offer" and my refusal, as well as this latest filing by the commercial guardian.

Only the fact that the guardian had never before asked for judicial approval, during all the years they had been Mama's guardian, allowed me to file suit later. This motion by the commercial guardian started a legal clock that allowed me a specified time to contest the guardian's motion.

The commercial guardian wanted to make its position even clearer. On February 23, 2012, the firm amended the motion. No longer limited to the approval of the annual reports, its new title read: "Petition for approval of annual reports *and discharge of Guardian and Conservator from liability.*" [emphasis mine] David and I came to refer to this as their "motion for absolution."

Now, I really needed a litigator, to oppose this action. On March 15, 2012, the court posted Mickey's firm's official "order of appearance," listing David A. Garcia as one of my attorneys of record, along with Debbie Gonçalves. The guardian's invoices show that Ruth Pregenzer had emailed the guardian about this development on March 14. [410] At that time, papers were still being filed via snail mail. Most likely Mickey's firm mailed them out Monday, Ruth received her copy on Tuesday, and the court clerk had the document, then, but did not post the information until Wednesday.

By the end of March, the commercial guardian had billed over $1,000 during 2012, simply for trying to change Mama's treatment after she passed away and getting a hospice to take her as a client.

---

410 Rosenstiel-22358

It took me years to think up any reasons why they might have done this. Regardless of what I told them about Mama's religious beliefs, they always chose not to believe, me, but instead to believe the bogus "Values" document.

They could completely control the actions of hospice, whereas they could not control mine. I had a stipulated order that they were not to touch Mama's body, and that I was to be the first person called. If hospice was involved and hospice was responsible to the guardian, hospice would be called first, and treat the body however the guardian said that firm preferred. If the commercial guardian told hospice that the aides were to do something to Mama's body, that would happen, perhaps before I was even notified. Were they planning to do something to Mama's body, either before or after death, that they did not want anyone to know about? Or simply something they did not want me to discover? Even if they were, there was nothing I could do to prevent it.

On March 15, the commercial guardian requested yet another evaluation of Mama from Dr. Morgan's hospice. By the 19th, Hospice had already examined Mama.[411] Again, they refused to accept her. Mama was still too stable for hospice care. From the frequency with which the word "protocol" appears in the commercial guardian's invoices during that period, it seems they were simply itching to find some way to change what happened during Mama's final illness (assuming that she had one) and after Mama passed away.

Complications from outside of the case had affected my legal representation, early in 2012. New Mexico holds annual legislative sessions, starting in mid-January. Mickey had decided that he wanted to lobby in Santa Fe instead of working on this case, and had passed the matter on entirely to David A. Garcia. At the time, I felt shunted aside. I was so wrong! It turned out that Mickey was the wise one; David proved to be the ideal attorney for this case. Or rather, these cases, because Mama's guardianship eventually spawned two additional cases. Without both of those other cases, and the almost unbelievable sequence of events that gave rise to them and unfolded parallel to them, I would never have been free to write this book. Years later, I learned that Mickey tended to pass

---
411 Rosenstiel-22359

David the most complex of his cases. Watching David's actions, after that, I quickly came to understand why.

The commercial guardian's invoices, which I did not see until after Mama died, prove that they frequently saw and contacted Buck. On Friday, January 20, 2012, they "reviewed" my written rejection of their recent "offer." That would be the offer involving the non-disparagement agreement. They held a meeting on January 23 about what to say to Buck. Despite the exhaustive detail in those invoices, there is not the slightest suggestion that Debbie was ever included in any discussions with Buck. They might, perhaps, be what is called "ex parte" discussions. Only one side—the commercial guardian—habitually communicated with the special master who was standing in for the judge herself. Buck then discussed matters with the judge and got back to the guardian.[412]

On April 2, 2012, Judge Baca presided over the hearing at which Barbara Buck resigned as special master.

David and Debbie were sitting with me at "our" table. The commercial guardian and Ruth Pregenzer were sitting at "their" table. Barbara Buck flounced into the room. The only reasonable description of her demeanor would be "flirtatious."[413] She sat at the commercial guardian's table, next to the guardian, smiling broadly, and said, in a stage whisper in the direction of the guardian's ear, "Just came from the judge's chambers. It's all arranged. She's gonna do what we want." I am sure that she intended me to hear her, because I certainly did.

It looked as if the commercial guardian and her friends felt totally in control of the situation. This seemed of a piece with how Buck had behaved the first time I met her. And it was exactly the same behavior with respect to the partner in the guardianship firm described by the affidavit I saw, relating her actions in a totally different guardianship case.

Special Master Buck truly belonged on the other side of the room, on the side of the commercial guardian. However, my

---

412 Decades 33677-33678
413 An affidavit exists, describing Buck traveling around with the commercial guardian. The witness who wrote that affidavit and I both were seeing the same sort of inappropriate behavior between a court-appointed GAL or special master and one of the parties she was supposed to be supervising.

theoretical understanding is that a special master, acting as the judge's representative, is supposed to be just as impartial as the judge. It certainly did not happen that way in Mama's case. Nor, I understand, did the judge, special master or guardian ad litem seem impartial in other guardianship cases. At least, not in the ones I had heard about.

Barbara Buck stood up to speak at the hearing, explaining to Judge Baca that she had not been able to finish writing her final report as special master. A few days earlier, she said, a dead body had been found in front of her office, so the place was still a crime scene. The corpse, Buck said, had proven very distracting.

The *Albuquerque Journal* at first reported that the corpse of the initially unidentified Kennard Chee, a homeless man who died from drinking mouthwash and hand sanitizer and then being beaten to death by two companions, had been found on the 600 block of Roma, South West. By April 7, they had corrected this to "the 500 block of Roma SW."[414] The *Albuquerque Journal* ran a photo on Saturday, March 31, 2012, showing the body outline outside of Buck's place of a business. Judge Baca, of course, forgave Buck for her tardy report. Instead of a final report, Buck filed only an interim report. Or I thought that she had, from sitting in the hearing room, although I have still never seen it. As far as I can tell from the case docket, Buck never did issue her final report.

At that hearing, Judge Baca also appointed Geraldine Rivera, a retired judge herself, as the new special master.

Despite the time they had already spent on this matter, as soon as Buck withdrew, the commercial guardian started having conferences and discussions, again, to plan the protocol surrounding Mama's death. They do not seem to have included Judge Rivera in these activities. In returning to this subject, once again, they totally ignored the fact that, back in 2008, this entire protocol had been spelled out, in detail, in a stipulated order, an order that was still posted on the wall behind and just above the headboard of Mama's hospital bed. Mama could not see it, but all visitors to her room could.

---

414 "Body Found," Albuquerque *Journal*, March 31, 2012, p. D2; "Hand Sanitizer a New Danger for Homeless," Albuquerque *Journal*, April 7, 2012, p. D2

The commercial guardian and conservator would have had no reason to revisit this protocol unless they intended to change it, unilaterally. Otherwise, they would not need to discuss the matter again (and, of course, to charge Mama, once more, for this redundant service). Despite the number of times they discussed this subject, they never informed me they were thinking about treating Mama in ways that violated the 2008 order. Of course not. They knew, in advance, that I would have objected strenuously, and in court, if necessary.

They marked these new discussions with such titles as "end of life protocol concerns," "plan and status," and "end of life." Five such discussions, internally at the commercial guardian's office, with Ruth Pregenzer, and with the home-health aide service showed in their invoices during April 2012. They even queried the Albuquerque Ambulance Service on "questions regarding [death] protocol."[415]

Interesting, I thought, going over these invoices, that they never included Bayada, the nursing service, in these discussions. Not even once. In fact, they never had, even in earlier years, when the nursing service had a different name. One invoice item on April 9, says "Multiple calls with R. Pregenzer & care conferences, re; [sic] end of life." [416] How many times did they plan every aspect of Mama's demise? Many, apparently. There might even have been other occasions during that month when this topic arose, but I simply could not identify them from the names given to them on the invoices.

What possible motives could the commercial guardian have had in wanting to maintain control over Mama's body, particularly when both parties had signed a stipulated court order that stated exactly the opposite? All I can go on here is conjecture. As of April, all the hospices they had consulted—including the one in which Mama's then-current doctor was a partner—said Mama was stable. A rejection from hospice meant that Mama had a prognosis of more than six months of life.

The most benign explanation for the commercial guardian's actions is that they believed their own records. Despite the fact that

---
415 Rosenstiel-22363
416 Rosenstiel-22364

this had always only been a myth from the beginning, their paperwork stated that Mama was an Orthodox Jew. And as I discovered after Mama died, they told people that I was also an Orthodox Jew.

Orthodox Jewish customs used to dictate bringing in a special group of dedicated people (members of a religious society) to wash a person's body in a ritual manner, to dry the body, and to clothe the body in a ritual shroud, in preparation for burial. Another custom was for the body to have a "watcher" from among the faithful, from the moment of death until the time of interment. The Hasidim and the very Orthodox still tend to follow these customs.

In fact, back in 2006, my younger cousin had officially advised the commercial guardian of the existence, in Albuquerque, of just such a group.[417] The sex of the group performing the ritual washing had to match the sex of the deceased. Rarely, a family member of the same sex might take care of this religious obligation. The customs were usually referred to, collectively, as "Taharah."[418] It is possible that the commercial guardian intended to frustrate anyone's ability to perform this religious ceremony, including the "ritual watching" of Mama's corpse.[419]

A witness to the same firm's conduct with another of their wards told me that a Christian representative from the guardian's office insisted that a daughter, who was similarly non-Jewish, was made to wash her father's body. In life, her father had been the most non-observant of secular Jews. The daughter, according to my witness, knew nothing about this ceremony.

The commercial guardianship firm, imposing its own understanding of the ritual on this particular man, seems more than passing odd. Was this a case of substituted judgement gone stark

---

[417] Rosenstiel(2)017041
[418] "Taharah," The Jewish Encyclopedia, New York, 1906. Accessed February 10, 2020 from: *http://www.jewishencyclopedia.com/articles/14199-taharah*
[419] The religious problem, the guardian never resolved, primarily because Betty kept insisting that Mama was an Orthodox Jew. The case notes for March 14, 2011, (Decades 24665) state that Betty had just emailed the firm to object, strenuously, to what Mama had eaten for dinner the night before. Mama's caregivers had told Betty that Mama ate shrimp for dinner. Betty cautioned the guardian that eating shrimp was forbidden on a kosher diet. Kosher diet, my eye! Mama had never been on a kosher diet all the time I had known her, and she certainly was not then either. Although I cannot say that I ever saw Mama eat shrimp or seafood as a separate main course, she certainly did eat pork in Chinese dumplings and pork slivers in wonton soup.

staring mad? Had the guardian firm simply decided that the man would have decided to become Orthodox, after death? In any case, the witness told me that the representative of the guardianship firm stood by the man's bed, insisting on giving directions to the daughter, demanding that she perform this ceremony on the bed. As I have researched this ceremony, the washing ritual is not supposed to be performed on the deceased's bed anyway.

In the case of the male ward, the commercial guardian seems to have imposed a total travesty of an Orthodox Jewish rite on a man who was not Orthodox. If the firm had intended to follow Orthodox tradition, then a woman washing a deceased man's corpse, whether naked or almost-naked, was expressly forbidden in Orthodox Judaism. The ritual washing of a corpse is not performed on non-Orthodox Jews.

In practice, what actually happens in New Mexico is explained by Natural Burial New Mexico.[420] Here, a local rabbi arranges for the ritual washing to be done at the funeral home, if it has to be done at all.

Is how the commercial guardian acted, with this male ward, a case of having a smattering of knowledge and applying it across the board, even in situations where it is arguably inappropriate? Or is it a willful and deliberate attempt to terrorize and outrage grieving family members? The male ward was cremated. There is no good argument that he really was an Orthodox Jew, or even that he intended to become one, on death, since Orthodox Jews do not accept cremation.

In Mama's case, I am not sure things worked out exactly as the commercial guardian wanted. We had already filed our response to their "request for absolution" on March 26, 2012. We demanded a jury trial to determine, in front of members of the public, whether what the commercial guardian had done during Mama's guardianship was good practice. I wonder whether this was the first time, in the history of guardianships being under sequestration in New Mexico, that any party to a sequestered guardianship case had requested a jury trial.

---

420 "La Puerta del Cielo" by Marc Yellin. Retrieved February 16, 2020 from: *https://www.naturalburialnewmexico.com/blog/archives/03-2017*

By then the new special master had taken a look at the financials. She noticed the money hemorrhaging out of Mama's accounts during the entire period the guardianship had been in place and decided to appoint Sam Baca, a tall, florid, overweight partner in the firm of Baca & Redwine[421] as the forensic accountant. Both sides, the commercial guardian acting, at least theoretically, on Mama's behalf, and David and Debbie, acting for me, agreed. Neither Sam Baca nor I attended the hearing, in a conference room at Mickey Barnett's offices, at which this appointment was made.

On May 17, before Baca started to work, I had to sign a contract agreeing to pay his firm, no matter what happened. The commercial guardian signed this same agreement, on Mama's behalf. Therefore, Baca's firm would be paid by Mama's guardian if she survived, and by me, as the personal representative of her estate, if she did not survive until Sam finished his work. (Neither Tom Burrage nor Judith Wagner, having served before in this same case, was eligible to serve again.) On May 23, 2012, the commercial guardian paid Baca's firm an initial retainer of $5,000, equal to half the entire fee Wagner had charged.[422] Mama's estate would eventually pay him an additional $141,000 for his work. As the order itself said, "the Court finds that such an appointment would be beneficial for the resolution of the matters at issue in [the commercial guardian's] Petition for Approval of Annual Reports and Release of Liability."[423] With typical legal restraint, both parties described the primary reason for drafting this order as, "to resolve controversies that have arisen over expenditures, investments and accounting practices... from the time of its [i.e., the guardian's] appointment..."[424] [sic] In this, the order seemed to differ greatly from either of my two other attempts to get a forensic accounting.

I will always be grateful to David for negotiating the final order. One of the last stipulations, particularly, "this Order shall not in any way be construed to extend" the guardian's term.[425] In other words, should anything happen to Mama, the estate would

---

421 Now Baca & Howard, PC.
422 CV-PQ-200300170 Order for Forensic Accounting, May 17, 2012, p. 3
423 Ibid
424 Ibid, p. 1
425 Ibid, p. 5

take over, not me, personally (even though I would be in charge of the estate, as its personal representative), and the guardianship would immediately end at the normal time prescribed by law.

An estate would be a new legal entity, with powers that I never possessed, as simply an interested party in the guardianship case, even though I always had an attorney representing me. As I had discovered by then from other relatives of wards, one of the biggest problems was the guardian or conservator or trustee of a person's trust hanging onto power. This would sometimes go on for years, the estate bled dry after the demise of a ward and the heirs forced to sign an agreement not to sue before distributing any remaining money or property in the estate or trust.

Finally, in 2018, three New Mexico state senators co-sponsored SB 19, to prevent this abuse. "No person," it states, "shall request, procure or receive a release or waiver of liability, however denominated, of a conservator, an affiliate or a designee of a conservator or any other third party acting on behalf of a conservator." [426]

As shown in the annual report, Mama's guardian had taken a $10,000 "retainer" out of Mama's funds the previous fall.[427] That would be all the money they could continue to hold, as conservator, which meant that, after Mama died, they would have no additional money of hers that they could use, at will. Given the magnitude of Mama's losses before that, it would not pay an estate to go after this amount of money. They also kept a retainer for Ruth Pregenzer, out of Mama's estate, this time, for $5,000. Between November 13, 2011 and June 1, 2012, Mama had paid out over $23,000 in retainers to various entities (including Ruth Pregenzer, the guardianship firm itself, and Judith Wagner.)[428]

As personal representative of Mama's estate, I had to sign all the checks for Sam's firm, except for the initial retainer. This particular exercise in accounting work (I still absolutely refuse

---

426   It seems to have taken all the adverse publicity from media articles pointing out this abuse to induce the legislature to act, but act it eventually did. This bill passed 40-0 in the New Mexico Senate and 63-0 in the New Mexico State House, and was signed by the Governor within two weeks of passage. See: *https://www.nmlegis.gov/Legislation/Legislation?Chamber=S&LegType=B&LegNo=19&year=18*
427   Amended Annual Report 20011-2012
428   Rosenstiel-24235-24236

to call it "forensic accounting") cost Mama herself and her estate $146,000 ($167,993.34 in 2021), enough to buy a decent townhouse in Albuquerque.

An accountant who worked in the same office building as Sam told me that, at the conclusion of Baca's work on this case, both Sam and his son (also an accountant at the firm, although not working directly on this project) bought matching, new red Range Rovers. I did see two cars, matching that description, in the parking lot when I later visited that building, to see the other accountant. Even if this is true, it is no proof of any necessary direct connection between the size of the fees paid and the cars bought, though it is suggestive that the firm had recently been enjoying a nice, healthy income stream.

By April 17, 2012, Ruth Pregenzer had been in contact with the commercial guardian about Sam Baca's pending appointment.[429] Not until May 17, 2012, when the final order was signed, was there a mutual agreement by the principals that one side could not have ex parte contact with him, except through their attorneys. It looks as if the commercial guardian took full advantage of these intervening weeks to talk to Sam's firm and communicate whatever it wished about the case. Sam did not bill me for actions that happened prior to everyone signing the contract, so I do not know how much contact they had with him.

What I do know is that Sam and his assistant seemed to accept, uncritically, any explanation the commercial guardian gave them. At one point, his assistant noticed that during the guardianship Mama seemed to have paid utility bills for a building with a different address from hers. The guardianship firm told her that this was a building owned by High Desert.[430] Looking at the address, in the discovery documents, I immediately knew that it was not, but the accountant, apparently never checking the county real estate records, had accepted their explanation of an impropriety as being my fault, somehow, when actually that building housed another of the firm's wards.[431]

---

429 Rosenstiel-22363
430 Decades 24137
431 Decades 07382-07385. Through the years of the guardianship, the commercial firm caused Mama to pay a number of bills for other wards. Sometimes, the guardian caught this and reimbursed her.

Later, Sam would tell David and me that he had seen Mama's home and it was in great shape. The guardian's invoices mention taking photos at Mama's home just after cleaning it. None of the guardianship firm's invoices, before Mama's death, mentions Baca actually being at Mama's home before she died. Nor do any of the aides' log entries mention his visit. Baca's firm charged and mentioned out-of-office work on its invoices; it did not mention any home visit on these invoices.

Mama's home returned to its previously filthy conditions after the intensive cleaning required by the special master in January 2012, and the taking of pictures immediately after that. I did not take Sam there, myself, until the summer of 2012; both David and I accompanied him and his assistant on that occasion. Mama's home was in terrible shape that day, as it had been for months before that. Had Baca's firm examined Barbara Buck's invoices, they would have seen, there, her complaints about Mama's home being "filthy."

Perhaps what the commercial guardian told Sam about me before he met me made him adopt a permanently contemptuous attitude toward me. Or, maybe it was the fact that, in 2012, I needed a walker most of the time. He might simply have thought that all people who need a walker are also mentally challenged. Perhaps his actions resulted from some combination of both attitudes.

Whatever his reasons, Sam never treated me with less than total disdain. At the beginning, I still had hopes that he could be impartial. Over the time Baca & Redwine worked on the case, he grudgingly consented to have several conferences with David and me, at his office. While we were there, Baca steepled his fingertips together and rolled his eyes whenever I started to speak. If I entered the conference room ahead of David and Sam, I could see, in my peripheral field of vision, Sam standing to one side, making faces and hand signs to David.

Once, as I recall, Sam sat as far away from me as he could, at the long wooden conference table in his office, right by the window, reading what looked like a newspaper. His assistant did the talking, that time. Of course, he billed for that session, just as if he had truly been mentally present. During conferences, he made dismissive gestures to David that I thought translated into, "We all know she's nuts. How do you tolerate her?"

I tried, hard, to ignore his attitude and get on with the meeting, hoping that he did not realize that I saw what he was doing. Having already agreed to underwrite this accounting, I was stuck having to pay his firm anyway. Refusal would mean that I had violated a court order; Judge Baca could call that "contempt of court." Regretfully, I concluded that I was going to have to pay, regardless of Sam's attitude. No sense in having an argument into the bargain.

Laura Beltran-Schmitz, Baca's assistant (who also charged for being at these meetings), also a CPA, was then a petite, slender, youngish woman. When not in Sam's office, I heard that she wore a huge diamond ring. People who saw her in other contexts told me so. However, in these meetings at the home office, she did not seem to wear it. After I heard about the ring, I looked for it at our next meeting in Baca's office, but I did not see it. At our initial meeting, she told us that, although she had been an accountant for a while, this would be her first "forensic" accounting case.

The Baca & Redwine invoices showed a number of times when both CPAs were charging for meeting with each other. For some odd reason, Laura always said she was meeting with Sam for longer—usually about half-an-hour longer—than he said he was meeting with her. The younger accountant seems to have spent about a year at Baca & Redwine. She left the firm a couple of weeks after she finished her work on this project, to go back to her prior firm. Her current biography, on LinkedIn refers to her stint at Baca & Redwine, dismissively, simply as time spent at a-"local CPA firm."[432]

One of the major questions I had had for forensic analysis was to explain why thousands more shares—amounting to millions of dollars in value—of CME stock had cleared through one of Mama's securities accounts than she actually was known to own. I asked Sam and Laura this question, for months. Even told Sam where he could find that information, using a subpoena. However, he always refused to use the power to issue subpoenas that the court

---

[432] "Laura Beltran-Schmitz," LinkedIn bio. Accessed 2/14/2020 from: *https://www.linkedin.com/in/laura-beltran-schmitz-cpa-cfe-cgfm-cica-12621411*

had given him to get me an answer. How much of the estate's money did he waste stone-walling?

After I became personal representative, it took me only a few days after I got the thousands of pages of Winslow's back-office records, through a subpoena issued by Judge Campbell as part of a new suit in probate court, to find this information for myself. Winslow, it turned out, had at first tried to transfer more stock, worth more money, than her superiors had authorized her to transfer at any one time. She had to get special permission to give orders for moving that much money, because it seemed that she had never handled that much before with this regulatory entity.

Did Sam have some foreknowledge that the answer would look bad for Winslow's organization, and did he not want me to find out? Or did he automatically assume there was no reason to be concerned about why the statements made it seem that millions of dollars' worth more of negotiable stock was bouncing back and forth, through Mama's accounts, than there should have been?

When Baca eventually issued his report, this was not the only question he did not answer. He deliberately made no attempt to decide whether day-to-day expenses were reasonable. This included the $15,000 worth of grocery bills per year, at a time when Mama was going out to eat for many or even most of her meals. He did not consider whether Mama ought to be feeding her aides and her aides' families. He did not consider whether the costs of home health aides were in line with local charges. He did not do a lot of things.

Perhaps the most egregious of these: Baca's firm absolutely refused to consider or evaluate whether the commercial guardian, when acting as Mama's conservator, had saved and invested money wisely and prudently. In other words, whether this firm had truly acted to "conserve" her assets, in accord with its charge from the court. The commercial conservator's more than two-year failure to diversify Mama's assets had been a part of my initial complaint with them, repeated many times in the guardianship case's court record and in the guardian's own files.

Baca and his firm behaved, without a specific charge from the judge not to find any wrongdoing on the part of the commercial guardian, exactly as if the forensic accounting firm had received a signed order from Judge Baca not to find any. After my experience with Sam, it seemed to me that, within the context of a *sequestered* guardianship case, it is almost impossible to take a guardian to task for wrongdoing. Even when there is no court order, there seems to be a "gentlemen's agreement" that the court will protect its own appointed guardian. The existence of some sort of understanding (if not a written agreement) not to hold commercial guardians accountable would have become clear, if a jury had heard the matter, and if the hearing were made public rather than sequestered. It is as if the maxim I quoted before, from a former judge, directed at an attorney, is always in play, "Clients come and go, but colleagues are forever."

If the guardian had been a family member, would the court's and Baca's attitudes have been very different? Would they have been actively looking for fraud?

One of the most unfortunate provisions of the agreement I signed with Baca was that I would not publish any part of his report without the firm's prior permission. I am positive that neither they nor their successor firm will never grant permission. However, I would far have preferred to let everyone see these statements of what that firm refused to do, in Sam's own words.

Early in May, the guardian's records suggest that someone had stolen Mama's identity. The firm sent out fraud alerts to Social Security and credit reporting agencies. One of these even seemed to require them to contact the Federal Trade Commission.[433] Oddly, I could not find any supporting mentions of this episode in the 40,000 pages of discovery documents, including the guardian's own "Case Notes."

Meanwhile, since its deep cleaning in January, Mama's home had returned to its prior condition of filth and disarray. Part of that problem comes from Albuquerque being in the desert. Fine sand manages to enter homes, sometimes even overnight. But some of it comes from underlying problems that can only be abated by changing out seriously stained and damaged carpet; all the latent stains on the wall-to-wall carpets in various rooms had reappeared.

---

433 Rosenstiel-22372

By May 8, the guardian was invoicing for scheduling "yearly deep cleaning."[434] Funny about that, because no such notation appears in the May 2011 invoices. Nor, indeed, on any other invoices. I am assuming that this resulted from Buck's efforts. Had it been completed, this would have been the very first scheduled annual "deep cleaning" during the almost nine years of the guardianship.

On April 5, we had filed a request for a six-person jury. The guardianship firm objected strenuously to the whole idea of a jury trial. This was a sequestered proceeding, they argued; everything should happen in secret. Even I could not figure out how to keep six people quiet forever. However, jury trials are supposed to be guaranteed by the U.S. Constitution, which is what David argued in his brief.

During May, I had started wanting to revive my old idea about making a documentary film. This time, however, my public health training kicked in; I wanted the canvas to be larger. The problems I had experienced were not unique to me, and I was sure they were not unique to New Mexico, either. In fact, I did not really want the New Mexico situation as my primary focus. This needed to be a documentary about the whole problem of guardianship in the United States. I went back to the video producer who had worked on my Channel 27 program. We drew up a contract that we both signed in May 2012. I would put up $25,000 and she had agreed to put in sweat equity while she was on location for other jobs, outside New Mexico. It would take longer to get things done, that way, but we thought we could manage.

In May, the commercial guardian started writing up "case notes" like crazy. During the 102 months of the guardianship, the invoices show that the guardian wrote no case notes for 43 of those months.[435] Not all of the firm's claimed notes were provided during discovery, and for many of those from the years prior to 2011 what we got were simply unsigned, word-processed pages. They could have been written at any time, by anyone, and stuck into the guardian's Case Binders, since these were loose-leaf notebooks. Proof of this is that, during discovery, I found scrawled, handwritten notes

---

434 Ibid
435 Rosenstiel-21890-22387

describing discussions that were supposed to have taken place on "2/14" (but no year indicated). From the invoices, I know that they actually happened in 2004. These were salted in with computer-generated ones from 2011.[436] Fees charged for writing up case notes went from $11 per month, in March and April, to $100 for the month of May 2012. For the entire period from June 2011 to February 2012, the invoices mentioned no case notes being written at all. There were no notes listed as having been written between June and September 2009, either. Almost nothing between May 2007 and March 2008 concerned anything other than financial matters. For nine of those months, the invoices do not show any notes being written to the file at all.

On May 23, 2012, Sam Baca's retainer of $5,000 cleared through the checking account Mama's guardian maintained for her at Bank of the West.[437]

One of the subjects the notes from May 2012 did not seem to mention was the atmosphere around Mama. Late spring is wildfire season in the West; 2012 was no exception. By mid-May, fires in Colorado, northern Arizona, and in both northern and southern New Mexico were sending out smoke that the *Santa Fe New Mexican* warned, was "expected to be noticeable across both states [New Mexico and Arizona] for the next couple of days...The wildfires are burning along the Mogollon Rim in Arizona and within the Gila region of New Mexico."[438]

Having been diagnosed with asthma back in the 1980s, I was particularly sensitive to the way the air quality seemed to be deteriorating, even before May 25. I could already smell the smoke before Saturday, May 26, when the *Albuquerque Journal* ran an article enttled, "Haze Warning For Metro Area."[439] The author cautioned, "Poor air quality is expected into Sunday morning. The smoke could impact visibility and health."

By then, the Whitewater-Baldy complex fire had been burning, out of control, in rural Catron County, since May 9. It was to

---
436 Decades 24661-24671
437 Rosenstiel-06738
438 "Smoke to push across New Mexico," *Santa Fe New Mexican*, May 18, 2012, p. C-4.
439 Ashley Trevizo, May 25, 2012, p. C1-2

destroy 298,845 acres of Gila Wilderness land between then and July 23.

Advising the public to take the well-known, standard precautions, the authorities warned all residents to keep their windows closed and shut off their swamp coolers, and to use only air conditioners or heating systems (well, we could not really use heating systems in Albuquerque at that time because it was too hot). This warning applied to all times of visible smoke or fire odor, and both were in evidence twenty-four-seven, for days. I knew perfectly well there was a problem, because, not only could I smell the smoke, but I was also having trouble breathing when I was not in an air-conditioned place. Mama's room, at that point, was not an air-conditioned place.

The following day, the *Albuquerque Journal* featured a striking front-page photo of the previous day's air pollution, under the headline "Another Hazy Day in ABQ." Albuquerque's normally brilliant sun and clear blue sky were both obscured by clouds of orange and purplish-grey ash that made the city's skyline resemble a post-Apocalyptic sci-fi movie. High winds in the fire areas, the media reported, made containment unlikely in the near term. The worst of the pollution was then heading directly for Albuquerque, making life miserable for all who had to be outside and, of course, for anyone whose respiratory system was in any way compromised.

By May 30, the Gila wildfire had become the largest in the history of New Mexico. On that date, Albuquerque sent a five-man crew to help battle the blaze. At that point 170,000 acres were burning, almost 20,000 acres more than in the wildfire that had threatened Los Alamos in 2011. "The fire has not been contained," warned Russell Contreras, writing in the *Santa Fe New Mexican*, "and officials worry that shifting winds and dryness related to the state's record drought may cause the blaze to grow even more."[440]

Again, we are reaching the territory of "substituted judgement." Were I Mama's guardian, hearing this prediction for a week or more of air quality that was potentially dangerous to my ward,

---

[440] "Gila wildfire becomes largest in state history," Santa Fe New Mexican, May 31, 2012, p.A-6.

I would have tried immediately to find a place where I could have placed my ward so that she had reliable air conditioning and did not have to open a window for a week or two. I would have considered it a matter of safety. Because, at that point, the air conditioner in Mama's room did not seem to be working (or, at least, the aides were not turning it on) and temperatures were in the 80s, sometimes the high 80s. It did not cool down all that much during the night, either. There is no indication that Mama's commercial guardian tried to take any such evasive action.

The commercial guardian had instructed the aides to monitor Mama's fluid intake—a wise precaution in a desert climate. They had been doing this for years. They always left these sheets around, in the open; I found them reassuring. During May 2012, they discontinued logging Mama's fluid intake. (I did not find any recent ones after Mama passed away.) Meaning that Mama, who was now unable to speak, would not have been able to ask for water and no one would know whether she had had any recently. When I visited, I often asked the aides to give Mama some water. Whether they gave it to her when I was not there, I do not know.

During this particular week, when everyone had been warned to keep doors and windows closed, I realized that the aides had suddenly started opening Mama's door to the backyard, letting in a lot of burnt-smelling air, polluted with the residue of the wildfires. They had not done this before. I asked them whether they had heard the public announcements about the pollution, and keeping doors closed, particularly in situations where people had breathing problems, but they laughed at me and said it did not matter. They said they had been told that Mama needed some good, fresh air. The new, open-door policy, allowing the acrid pollution into Mama's room, continued until June 1.

One of Mama's aides asked me, around this time, what Mama liked to eat. I had seen that aide around Mama's place for years. A few years earlier, she had told me that Mama loved the seafood paella she had made. Did she not know what Mama liked to eat by now? Then I realized that, sometime before, the aides had forbidden me to sit with Mama anymore, while she ate. Was she even eating? Looking at the grocery receipts during discovery, I realized that my reply that Mama liked steak had induced someone to make a trip to the supermarket to buy hamburger. Of course, it might just as easily have been that it was very hot in Mama's room, that Mama was not getting enough fluid, that she was dehydrated, and that this made her unable to eat. I know that, during this period, her forehead was warm to the touch and I used to go and get her washcloths, dipped in cold water from the sink in her bathroom, to cool her down a bit.

I walked into Mama's room one day toward the end of May, to find her color a bit bluish. She did not move when I greeted her, and her breathing was shallow. I turned on the ceiling fan, because, as usual, the room was uncomfortably hot. Then, I realized that Mama's oxygen cannula was draped over the railing of her bed. Mama, unable to move, could not reinsert it herself. Rather than taking the chance of maybe causing Mama a bloody nose if I inserted it at the wrong angle, I called the aides, who came back into the room. I asked if one of them would please reinsert it. One did. Mama's color came back in a couple of minutes and she became responsive again. I do not know whether they kept the ceiling fan on, after I left. I doubt it, because the next day, when I arrived, it was off again.

This ritual continued for several days. The cannula either would be on the nightstand or draped over the bed rail. On arrival, I would find the ceiling fan off, the room beastly hot, the air conditioner off. Mama's color would be a bit blue and she would be unresponsive, at first, until I put the ceiling fan on and got an aide to reattach the cannula. Then, after a few moments, Mama's color returned and she became responsive, again.

On the afternoon of May 31, the same drill played out, but with a difference. The high temperature at the airport that day was 88 degrees; I am sure the temperature in Mama's room at that point was well over 95 degrees, with the afternoon sun pouring in, along with the acrid air entering through the door to the garden. I turned on the ceiling fan. This time, the cannula was not only out of Mama's nose, it was in a far corner of the room, on the floor by the window, at least 10 feet away from Mama's bed. Mama could not possibly have thrown it that far, even if she had accidentally knocked it off her bed railing. They either would have to clean this cannula or get Mama a new one, I thought; the floor was too dirty for them to reinsert it without at least cleaning it. Only one of the aides was willing to come back to Mama's room, with me, this time, when I requested that someone come and reinsert the cannula.

"The cannula's over there, on the floor. Ya gonna need a new one?"

"No. Not gonna put it back."

With that, she turned on her heel, flashed me what appeared to me to be an evil look, and strode toward the door.

"Are you serious?"

"Isn't it great that she's improved so much she doesn't need oxygen anymore?" the aide said as she passed me, on her way out the door.

Stunned and shocked, I just stood there for a moment, gaping at the aide's retreating form, as she turned right, on her way down the hall, from Mama's room toward the kitchen, where there was some nice, cool air from that ugly, industrial-sized swamp cooler. Then I went over to Mama's bed.

"Mama, something terrible's happening. I don't know what. Not sure I can find out in time to do anything."

I turned away and grabbed a couple of Kleenexes out of the box on the nightstand, to wipe away my tears. I could not let the aides see me upset. I was afraid they would put me on report and prevent me from seeing Mama again.

Overnight, I ran through my options. There were very few. I could complain to the police. Considering what happened in 2007, they would probably just refer me back to court. That would take too long. The same thing for the DA. Would either entity care at all about a 100-year-old woman who had a court-appointed legal guardian? Probably not. No one had cared before.

All it would take to remedy Mama's problems, judging from what I had observed the past week or so, was some oxygen, a cool room, and some hydration, and Mama would come back to herself. However, the guardian would not allow anyone to give Mama those things, or the aides would have replaced her cannula and they would still be keeping a hydration log. I thought about this all night.

On the morning of June 1, 2012, I was about to call Debbie when I received a phone call from her. She had just had a phone call from the guardian, saying that Mama was unconscious. She was told that had happened before (this was then news to me), but this time, they had been unable to wake her up. "Unresponsive" was the word they used. Very clinical.

During discovery, as I have said, I learned that one of the aides had realized that, if Mama herself were placed in a particular position, she would lose consciousness. When the aide discovered this, about a year before Mama died, she called the guardian; they simply told her to reposition Mama, and all was well. Positioning Mama's head too low also contributed to other problems. I do know that, when I arrived on the morning of June 1, 2012, Mama was a lot more horizontal than I had seen her, except the time when she was vomiting. That time, they said it happened because the aides had put the head of the bed too low, just after lunch. I did not know this that morning, but the same aide who had discovered the difficulty Mama had breathing when she was lying on her side-was also with her when Mama was discovered to be unconscious on June 1, while also lying on her side. She was the only aide on duty, the commercial guardian never really having had two aides on the overnight shift for years, despite what it told the court. Since she was the overnight person, she was gone from the scene for hours before anyone bothered to call Debbie.

Driving from different directions and in our separate cars, Debbie and I went to Mama's home immediately. Debbie arrived slightly before me. We went into Mama's room. A smallish man with a serious expression, someone I had never seen before, was standing there.

"You the daughter?"

I nodded.

"I'm from hospice. I was called this morning. You have to sign these."

He thrust some papers in my direction.

"I'm sorry. I can't sign anything. There's a legal guardian. Any legal papers, the guardian has to sign. I doubt you can be of much help to Mama now."

"I can help you."

"I doubt it. The guardian didn't permit hospice to help me last time."

"It's our job."

"You were hired by the guardian?"

"Yes."

"I'm unlikely to accept any gift they give me."

He looked shocked.

I could not deny my intuition not to accept any presents from the commercial guardian. Later, I discovered that Dr. Morgan, who had been attending the guardian's homebound patients for years, at that point, was listed as a founding partner in that particular hospice, so there would have been no privacy for me in anything I might have said to them, in the process called "grief counseling." The guardian would have been their "employer" and, as with Hospice de la Luz, anything I might have said would have been reported right back to the commercial guardian. Some "gift."

At that point, the commercial guardian tore into the room, face contorted with fury. She had apparently been listening from around the corner, in a side hall. She screamed at me.

"I'll bet you told *her* everything!"

"She's my mother. I talk to her."

Mama's face remained impassive; she did not open her eyes.

Leaving Mama flat on her back in bed,[441] all of us went outside for a while into the breakfast nook and the adjoining, open den area, in the other wing of the house, to talk. Or rather, Debbie and I sat there while the commercial guardian spoke with the hospice representative. In the course of the conversation between the guardian and the man from hospice, I heard Mama's commercial guardian say that the aides had the authority to increase Mama's oxygen dosage at will to 5LPM, the highest setting on her oxygen concentrator.

---

441 This was a position in which I had not seen Mama for the almost four years since she had been confined to bed. Normally, they kept the head of the bed raised, to one degree or another, to help her breathe. But then, they had always kept Mama connected to an oxygen tank or to an oxygen concentrator for the same reason. Now, neither oxygen device was in use.

"Are you sure about that?" the hospice man asked.

"We have authority to change the dose at will."

By then, Mama had only home health aides, except for about two hours, in the morning. These would be untrained people who apparently would be making potentially major health decisions. Not LPNs. Not RNs. Simply home health aides, trained to cook and clean and give Mama a bath and talk to Mama and periodically move Mama around in bed. Mama did not seem to have been hooked up to the concentrator for days before this, either. Might that possibly have been the aides' call?

(Hospice, although hired by the guardian, was, if somewhat tentatively, questioning the firm's medical judgement, just as I had. Increasing oxygen to too high a concentration for a particular individual eventually prevents the lungs from getting enough carbon dioxide to induce them to contract. In other words, the ward might stop breathing. From what I had observed over the last week or two, they had first placed Mama on the highest level of oxygen, and then reduced it drastically or removed it from her altogether. I had complained, both about the high level and about the aides removing Mama from the concentrator totally. Later still, some of the medical records disclosed that the oxygen levels were changed, sometimes greatly, over short spans of time. What this sort of procedure might have done to Mama's already-fragile lungs, I cannot begin to guess. During discovery, I found a couple of complaints written into her notes by Dr. Morgan that, when she had arrived to examine Mama, the attendants had been using too high a concentration of oxygen.)

Mama's skin color had turned a reddish purple. She did not seem to be struggling or panting for breath, but her breathing was very shallow and she did not open her eyes when I went back in, either. I felt she could still hear me.

"I don't know what else I can do, Mama. Would you like me to recite the Twenty-Third Psalm?"

I thought I saw a flicker of understanding, perhaps even acceptance on Mama's face, as I started to recite the words from memory. From the King James Version Mama liked. A small smile played on her lips when I got to "Thou preparest a table before me in the presence of mine enemies." I was standing on the east side of Mama's bed. The bed table on the west side of the bed that usually held supplies was bare of contents. Sun streamed in through the windows on the west side of the room, facing me. About halfway through, I became conscious that the two aides on duty that day were standing in the flowerbed, just outside the window to Mama's room, staring hard at us. What, in the name of all that is holy, did they expect to see? What sort of spectator sport is that? I finished the psalm, said goodbye to Mama and left the room. Debbie was sitting in the den, waiting for me, as was the commercial guardian. The hospice man had left.

"The aides were standing outside the window, staring at us," I said.

"They shouldn't be doing that," Debbie ventured.

"I'll tell them not to do it again," the commercial guardian said, already knowing, I think, that there was not going to be a "next time."

"Thanks."

"Nothing is going to happen for at least 24 hours. Maybe longer," the guardian assured us both, then ushered us to the door. Debbie returned to her office. I went back home, to gather up some things and return in the afternoon. I was planning to spend the night on the filthy floor in Mama's room, since the chairs belonged to the aides and I did not want to leave Mama alone.

At that point, if Mama's commercial guardian had insisted that the sun was shining, I would have made sure to pack a good umbrella. I had finished packing a kit to return to Mama's and was just about ready to leave when the phone rang.

"I'm the hospice nurse. Your mother just died."

"I'll be right over."

"I got to the kitchen door just as she was drawing her last breath."

I rushed to Mama's, only a few minutes away. As I recall, Debbie was there waiting for me when I arrived.

"Didn't they clean her up nicely?" the hospice nurse began.

Already, I was getting suspicious. If they needed to clean Mama up, and had already had the time to clean Mama up, then she must have passed away some time ago; I had arrived less than five minutes from the time I got the call.

Considering that up until that morning, we had had a court order that said they were not supposed to do that, I guess they did do a good job. But there was something they had left undone.

The original notice, posted above Mama's bed to reflect the stipulated court order, said that in the event of Mama's death, I was to be notified first and that I was to be the first person notified. The guardian had unilaterally broken that agreement once hospice was on the scene, posting a new notice above the headboard. Apparently, they had done this after I had left that morning. Now, the instructions stated that everyone else was to be notified before me. Now I understood why Debbie had gotten there first, despite the fact that her office was further from Mama's home than mine. The agreement about not doing anything to Mama's body was not in the new posting.

Whatever they meant by cleaning Mama up had not applied to her face. Mama had the oddest, distorted look on her face. As if she were saying, "Oh!" Her mouth was wide open, and awry. Why, I wondered, did they have to "clean her up"? She had been clean earlier in the day, when I had last seen her. And in the morning, her face had been in a normal state of repose.

Debbie and I sat down, next to each other, on chairs in Mama's room, facing the bed, and started to swelter until we were both feeling faint. It was painfully hot in there, even with the ceiling fan at its highest setting. The air conditioner on the wall by the door had not been in use for weeks; it seemed to be broken. If I had not put on the ceiling fan during my visits, Mama would not have had any relief from that heat wave; every time I arrived, the fan was off. Now, the hospice nurse sat in another chair, on the other side of the room, watching us.

Debbie tried to call the medical investigator's office, as we had previously agreed. She could not get through to anyone.

"What're you trying to do?" the hospice nurse asked.

"Calling the medical investigator's office, but I can't seem to get through."

"Oh, that's fine. I'll do it for you. I work there part-time. I have the private number."

And, indeed, she did. Got right through.

I am not sure to whom she spoke, but apparently someone with decision-making authority.

"I have a crazy relative here who wants an autopsy on a 100-year-old woman," she informed the person at the other end of the call. "She's pristine."

If I had not witnessed the events of the past few months, I would never have wanted to ask for an autopsy in the first place. At that point, I decided this upcoming medical procedure was already tainted with prejudice injected into the situation by the hospice nurse; instantly, I decided that I would not be able to trust the Bernalillo County Medical Investigator's autopsy. Poor Mama would need a second one.

How had Mama spent her last night on earth? Mama's aide said that her dinner consisted of fruit salad and "a few sip [sic] of juice," of which she ate about 15 percent.[442] The aide who spent the night with Mama stated that she ate 20 percent of her "dinner," really a bedtime snack, which consisted of some raspberry sorbet and a bit of banana. At 4 AM, she noted, that, after positioning Mama on her right side, "Dr. spit up...the sorbet."[443] (This was the same position in which Mama had stopped breathing in 2011.) Mama's breathing then changed. By 4:30 AM, Mama was no longer responding or taking in any fluids. No mention of repositioning Mama.

Her commercial guardian did not appear on the scene until 10 AM, hours after the change of shift. Then hospice appeared, and finally Debbie and I were called.[444] The same relief aide (or one of them, since the commercial guardian was still employing two, during the day), reported that Mama was pronounced dead at 3:45 PM. Again, I heard about it later.[445]

What did Mama's guardian tell the court about Mama's last meal? "Until the morning when she slipped into a coma, Dr. Rosenstiel enjoyed relative [sic] good health. The evening before she

---

442 Decades 28472
443 Decades 28476
444 Decades 28478
445 Ibid

passed, she had a full dinner and was drinking fluids through a straw." Either the guardian had not read the aides' notes before writing her report, or she wanted to misinform the judge.

Any aides I had seen taking food into Mama's room over the past few months, placed her nourishment in small ramekins that looked as if they held about four ounces. That is not much to survive on, in the first place. What is 15 percent of four ounces? A little over half of one ounce. Twenty percent of four ounces is still shy of a single ounce. Perhaps Mama had eaten a total of 1.4 ounces of food that night.

The commercial guardian had already completed a questionnaire for hospice before I had ever arrived on the morning of June 1, 2012. In answer to the Hospice of the Sandias question on the section intended for the Office of the Medical Investigator asking "Length of caregivers' preparation for patient's death," the professional guardian answered, "6 months." In the comment section, Mama's commercial guardian added, "Daughter Leonie [sic] was estranged from her mother.[446] Hospice then transmitted this information to the medical investigator's office.

Now I needed to fulfill my promise to Mama. First, I had to get the information necessary to organize the estate. Too many stories about New Mexico wards are hidden behind an iron veil of secrecy. I needed to make sure that New Mexico's restraints would not prevent me from telling Mama's story.

---

446 Rosenstiel(2)017011

CHAPTER V

Waking Up

No notice of Mama's passing appeared in the press; I was afraid of attracting any unwanted attention, whether from Mama's long-ago-fired caregiver and her family, or anyone else. Because no messages from Betty appeared on Mama's voicemail in the two weeks after her death and before it was disconnected, I assumed that Betty already knew. She did not contact me to offer condolences, so I did not contact her, either.

After we received the invoices from Mama's former guardian, I could not find any evidence, there, that the guardian had called Betty to tell her. The last mention of anything that would have involved Betty came on May 7, 2012, "Phone call and fax to Comfort Keepers re [sic] letter for Jewish Holiday,"[447] it read.

The eve of Passover had already come, on April 6. The first day of Passover would have been April 7, that year. It had ended on April 14. Betty's letter then would have to have been about a holiday Mama had never even considered celebrating for all the time that I had known her, *Pesach Sheni*, a ritual that the Chasidic community celebrated, exactly a month after the first day of Passover. Why Betty would have tried to induce Mama's guardian to enforce Mama's celebration of this specific holiday, I cannot imagine. The

---

[447] Rosenstiel-22368. Again, footnotes with names and numbers only refer to specific documents in files offered as part of discovery in Leonie Rosenstiel (PR) v Decades, LLC (et al) D-202-CV-201304646

guardian did not include this letter in their discovery documents, so I have no way to know for certain.

David and Jane started looking for an independent pathologist immediately. Contrary to all those TV shows featuring kindly state and county coroners, when someone from the Bernalillo County Medical Investigator's office called me, it was to bark, "Why did you order an autopsy on a 100-year-old woman?" I tried to explain, but he hung up the phone, saying I could "call anytime." He sounded annoyed that I had bothered them. When I tried to call back, I never could get through. Perhaps because I was using the public number, rather than the private number the hospice nurse had called, back at Mama's home. It was 2019 before anyone representing that office called me back. Someone who said that she was doing a survey wanted to know how I found the "service" in the medical investigator's office.

David had located Dr. Amy Gruszecki, a Texas pathologist who frequently consulted with both families and law enforcement on criminal cases.[448] She was willing not only to look at Mama but also to review any associated information. (Many other similar practitioners are only willing to look over the written report of the first pathologist.) The Albuquerque autopsy had detected no skin lesions or irritation, whereas the Texas autopsy identified a number of areas in which Mama's body was less than "pristine," as the hospice nurse had told the medical investigator's office:

> EVIDENCE OF INJURY: A superficial excoriation measuring approximately 2-inches is on the posterior aspect of the sacrum. An area of ecchymosis measuring 1/2-inch is on the dorsal aspect of the left hand. Small superficial excoriations are in the right groin area. Slight excoriation is present beneath the left breast.[449]

Mama had four areas of skin irritations, the largest on her sacrum (a common place for what nonprofessionals call a "bedsore"), a smaller one under one breast, and a number of small

---

448 She ran—and still runs—a firm called American Forensics, which was then located in Dallas.
449 Rosenstiel(2)018679

areas of irritation in the groin area. She also had a nasty bruise on her left hand that might well be due to rough handling, either in transit or at the medical investigator's office. However, it might also have been due to some physical reaction where Mama was trying to wave off someone trying to do something she did not want done. Perhaps an automatic reaction, even if she was otherwise unresponsive. On the other hand, it might have happened a day or so earlier and I had not seen it because that hand had been under the covers when I visited. It was on the arm furthest from me while I was in Mama's room after she died. I did not go over to that side of the bed before the drivers from the funeral home came to get Mama. At the funeral home later, I did not see that bruise because they had hidden Mama's hands. They might also have used make-up to cover it.

Dr. Amy wrote me an email on November 20, 2012 that said, in part, "As for the bed sore, 'bed sore' is a layman's term. Your Mom did have an ulceration..."[450]

The temperature range the week after Mama died was about the same as it had been the prior week. For almost a week after Mama died, I put a thermometer on Mama's pillow and took photos of it, at different times during the day. Rarely did the temperature on that pillow dip below 85°F. Often, it was close to, or even over, 100°F.

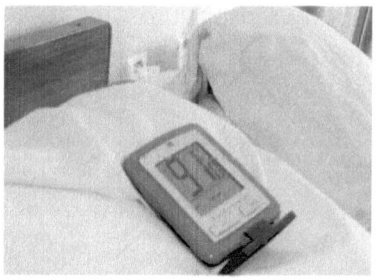

The temperature at noon on Mama's pillow. June 2012.
Photo: Léonie Rosenstiel

That fall while just finishing the clean-up and renovation of Mama's home for its sale, I was standing in the kitchen with the person supervising the work when a woman arrived at the door. She lived in the area, she said, was also a real estate agent, and had noticed that the house seemed to be getting fixed up for sale. In fact, we were just about to put a "for sale" sign out when she arrived.

I told her I was the daughter of the owner, Mama had passed away, and I would be selling Mama's home.

---

450 Amy Gruszecki, email to Leonie Rosenstiel, November 20, 2012

She said, "Oh, I know. You were estranged from your mother. Everyone knows that."

Until discovery, I did not realize that the guardianship firm had told everyone they came into contact with that I was "estranged" from Mama. Most likely, that was the primary reason I was getting nasty treatment from everyone, except Dr. Amy (she wanted me to call her that), who had never spoken with the commercial guardian, as far as I know. Everyone else, including hospice and the medical investigator, apparently believed I knew nothing about the situation and was simply intruding on the beneficent commercial guardian's territory, after the fact. As before, the commercial guardian had created a situation in which everyone in any way connected with Mama's care treated me as if I had some sort of dread, communicable disease.

On January 29, 2019, at 11:25 AM, I received a call from UNM. I had received two prior recent messages from the university. Both times, the caller, identifying herself as what sounded to me like "Emily Mose," had said she was a student at UNM and was conducting a survey, but I had no reason to call back, because I had had no contacts with UNM in years. I did not recognize the number, other than it had "UNM" above it. I generally do not participate in phone surveys. I had simply assumed that whoever called had spoofed that number. However, this time, I answered.

The person on the other end of the phone had the same voice as the person who had left those earlier messages. She asked for me, by name. I said, yes, I was on the phone. She then identified herself as Emily Mose (but she did not spell her name). Emily said she was conducting a survey about people's satisfaction with the medical investigator's office and wanted to ask me questions about "Annette Rosenstiel's autopsy."

I said, "I'm sorry, I don't answer any questions on that subject," and hung up the phone.

Considering that it took anyone at UNM six-and-a-half years to show any curiosity about whether I was satisfied with their "service," I did not think they cared enough to make it worth my time to bother to answer. Any office that can ignore a commercial guardian saying, in writing, that they have been "preparing for" Mama's death for six months, while at the same time assuring me that there had been no change in her condition, I should think would raise questions. In fact, that part of the form the guardian had filled out for the medical investigator did have someone's handwritten question mark in the margin of that statement, but perhaps it was not enough to raise serious questions in the mind of whoever made decisions in that office.

Had I been the doctor in that office, I would have been curious. Why had this relative been worried? What is the back-story here, particularly given that Mama had not been on hospice until the last few hours of her life and that the guardian had been, for the past six months, trying to enlist hospice organizations to take Mama under their care? They had been refused, meaning, as the commercial guardian later told the court, that they believed Mama was in stable condition and had a prognosis of more than six months of life. Is the negative reaction of the medical investigator's office simply age discrimination, or is it an attempt to punish a "meddling daughter" for wasting their valuable time examining someone whose length of life, in their opinion, had already been too long? How strange. I had always thought that my tax money (and Mama's) helped to pay the salaries of the people in that office.

The omniscient internet says that there is an Emily Mose Romero, but she lives in California. There is also an "Emily Romero;" in January 2020, she was a first-year law student at UNM, but there is no guarantee that she is the same "Emily Mose Romero" I found in California or the person who called me. There is no "Emily Mose" that I could find. UNM has several people with last names of "Morse," one of whom is a chaplain, but none of them is named "Emily." The only "Emily Morse" I could find on the internet bills herself as a "Doctor of Sexology." Thinking maybe I had not heard the last name right, I tried "Moses" too, but no luck there, either. The medical investigator's office website showed no staff with either a first or last name similar to the one my caller gave me.

As with many major developments in Mama's case that seemed to happen over weekends and on holidays, Mama's death took place on a Friday afternoon. The medical investigator's office said they could not accept the body at that time on a Friday and I would have to have Mama stored at a funeral parlor over the weekend. Once that was done, something called the "chain of custody" had been violated, making any normal sort of prosecution (should any sort of wrongdoing surface) almost impossible.

The guardian had immediately given me a key to Mama's home, but I could not change the locks. Because the courts had not yet appointed me as personal representative, I did not have title to the premises, so they still technically owned the place and I could not ask them to give me their key. On Saturday morning, I started cleaning up Mama's house and sorting out what should be kept. Albuquerque was still in the midst of a heat wave. Temperatures in the afternoon were in the mid-90s at the airport. In the far northeast heights, the temperature was more like the mid-to-upper 90s, and sometimes reached 100ºF or higher, as the thermometer I placed on Mama's pillow proved.

Because there was no air conditioning in that entire wing of the house, I had to get to Mama's home early, around 6 AM, while the temperature was still in the 70s and 80s, if I was to get any work done at all before the oppressive heat that arrived at noon. The commercial guardianship firm was still using its own key.

Walking around Mama's room made me cry, so I only stood on one side of the bed and then went out the door. However, it seemed to me things in the house had been moved around a bit by Saturday morning. I checked on some antique textiles that I knew had been stored in the closet of the guest bathroom. Some were still there.

On Sunday morning, I went back there just after 6 AM. I still needed a walker most of the time, because of my 2009 car accident. I had not needed to use it the day before, because I was not doing much standing or walking, but I knew that I would have to carry some supplies into Mama's home on Sunday and would need to wheel them in, on my walker. As I was taking supplies out of the back of my car, I was surprised to see in my peripheral vision a car approaching the house. It was a residential area, and the speed limit was 25 miles per hour. I turned to face the car in time to see it speed up as it entered Mama's driveway, threatening to run me over. If I tried to run away, I would fall, either on the concrete or on the xeriscaping stones. My walker would at least provide some sort of barrier.

I recalled the other family who had run when threatened, and determined that I would not. If she were going to hit me, she would have to do it with me staring at her. The person in the car looked exactly like the head of the guardianship firm, and for that instant, I was not all that sure she was not going to run me over. She had written an email stopping the aides from discussing my "cane," but I am not sure she realized that I needed a walker because, as usual, she had not paid attention to me or what I had said. In order to do me any damage, she would have to do damage to her car by hitting the walker first. I could see her jump in her seat. I am pretty sure she did not expect to see me there at that hour, on a Sunday. It is an understatement to say that I did not expect to see her there, either.

She had entered the area from a street that ran east-to-west. Another road ran from north to south, parallel to the east side of the house. She shifted into reverse, then tore down the road on the eastern border of the property, going south. Only a few weeks earlier, speed bumps had been placed there. I heard a terrific crash a few seconds later. She had already received punishment for threatening me. I blessed the other family whose information permitted me to have some confidence that she only wanted to terrorize me and not actually kill me. I concluded that she was unlikely to return to bother me. At least not that day.

I entered Mama's home and started to work, soon realizing that objects, placed in position Saturday so I could accomplish various projects on Sunday, had been moved. Antique textiles, some of which had belonged to my French great-grandmother, had vanished from that bathroom closet overnight. This relatively minor gaslighting continued for as long as I had to refrain from changing the locks. At the time I first discovered this was happening, I took a deep breath, reminding myself that the car incident I had just experienced had come out of some sort of existing playbook. This "trick" would likely continue to be played on me until I could assert some real authority over the situation, and that would not happen until after I was named Mama's personal representative.

However, I had to keep working because otherwise I was concerned that more things would disappear.

Stuart and the relatives of wards I had met had told me that commercial guardians routinely tried to disorient their wards by doing the same thing to them. Thank Heaven for Stuart Stein and the other victims! Without their insight, I might have tried to complain, perhaps triggering a guardianship proceeding against me by Mama's former guardian. Even earlier on, I had had some experiences that might have fallen into this category. Around the time of the 2008 hearing, someone broke into my garage (well, it was not alarmed or locked up tight, like the rest of the house, so they did not have to disarm an alarm system to enter it). Oddly, all that intruder did was to move things around in the garage and did not even take anything. I did not bother calling the police. What would I tell them? "Someone I don't know has been moving things around in my garage?" Another time, there was a large SUV parked across the street from my home. I would see it there, just at an angle where I could not see the license plate from my window. It came back daily for about a week, and it was not a car that belonged in the area. I still have no clue whether all these events are related.

I worked on my own, daily, mainly outside of Mama's room, because it was too painful for me to stay in there for any length of time. I would leave the thermometer on Mama's pillow, then do other work around the house and come back to photograph it, before leaving.

One day the following week, I brought a friend who noticed the slightly-soiled white vibrator on the nightstand by Mama's bed. "Look!" she said, pointing. "Well, good for her!"

I followed her pointing finger with my eyes. My friend had not seen Mama in about ten months, at that point. I did not have the strength to tell her that, to the best of my knowledge, Mama had been unconscious all day, the day she died, and that she had been entirely unable to move on her own for quite some time before that. She could not have asked anyone to give her any sort of massage, sexual or otherwise, if she were unconscious.

One or two of Mama's aides had spoken to me about being expected to provide mechanical sexual satisfaction to paralyzed clients. At that point, Dr. Amy's autopsy did not exist yet, so I had no way to connect the torn skin in Mama's groin with the possible use of that vibrator on her nightstand. Was that another evidence of "substituted judgement"? Or was this another evidence of gaslighting, where Mama's commercial guardian placed something potentially upsetting on the nightstand, intending to make me hysterical? If she wanted to give me an experience I could not forget, and raise questions I could never successfully answer, she certainly succeeded. The device could only have been left there deliberately, since the aides had had the time to "clean up" Mama and the room before I arrived on the afternoon of June 1. It would have cost no real effort to have it removed. That is, if it were not simply planted there later by the commercial guardian.

There is no direct proof of any connection, but the proximity of that object to Mama's bed is certainly suggestive. I was not able to speak or write about this to anyone between June 2012 and January 2020; simply thinking about someone possibly having treated any dying woman, much less my mother, that way was far too painful. However, in an extremely perverted way, it certainly did bring Mama's life full circle; a life begun in abuse might have literally ended that way.

By June 7, 2012, I was eligible to file for the probate of Mama's will. I did. Every day after that, I arrived at Mama's home, early in the morning, to continue cleaning up.

On June 10, after that filing appeared on the case docket, but I had not yet become Mama's personal representative, I arrived at Mama's home, as usual, to work. Not until after I took title to Mama's home, something I could not accomplish until after the judge appointed me Mama's personal representative, would I be able to change the locks on the doors to Mama's home. As far as I knew, only Mama's ex-guardian and I had keys.

I walked into Mama's bedroom to do some additional tidying up, only to be met by a strong odor of feces. The source? A small trash container in Mama's bathroom that had been entirely empty ever since I saw Mama's aides leaving on June 1, placing all the plastic bags of trash from her bedroom in one of the trash carts in the side yard.

Temperatures in Albuquerque had reached at least 88º F every day since Mama died, so I concluded that someone must have left that little package for me, quite deliberately, after I had finished my work at Mama's the previous day, knowing the odor would be become noxious in the heat within a few hours.[451] I disposed of it and got on with my work. Interesting that any visits the guardian might have paid to Mama's home during this period were now "free" and not listed on their invoices (which continued to be charged against their trust account).

Mama's ex-guardian and I continued to share access to Mama's home, with "incidents" of one sort or another happening almost daily. Finally, I had the legal right to get those locks changed. Other than the incident in Mama's driveway, I never saw anyone else when I was there. Complaining to the police would only have encouraged the guardian to use more of whatever might be left of Mama's money on additional expensive attorneys, and perhaps gotten the police to label me as a hysterical female into the bargain. I took a deep breath and decided to wait out this nasty period that was, fortunately, limited by law.

By June 19, the estate was an official, legal entity and I could request transfer of title of Mama's home, car, and any other remaining assets, directly to the estate. I also had the requirement, set up in Mama's will, to fund a trust. Originally, the purpose of that trust had been to benefit Arthur and me. However, by 2012, I was the only beneficiary left. There was no good legal purpose served by continuing to pay the legal and accounting fees for maintaining a trust. Another—to my mind—essentially useless expense required by law.

Although I had to set up that trust, other matters took priority before I attempted to take any action to get rid of it. In July 2013, we petitioned for and received permission to dissolve that trust.

---

[451] Temperatures retrieved on May 8, 2020 from: *https://api.wunderground.com/ history/airport/KABQ/2012/6/1/DailyHistory.html?req_city=&req_state=&req_statename=&reqdb.zip=&reqdb.magic=&reqdb.wmo=*

Again, as with Mama's will, since there were no other interested parties, there was no possibility for contention. Of course, these actions took place in a public proceeding in district court.

Winslow, apparently concerned that I would sue her firm for the money that Mama lost under her management, refused to release any remaining money directly to the estate, or to allow her firm to let me draw money out, through what is called an ACATS (Automated Customer Account Transfer Service) form. Instead, her company demanded that I sign to create a new estate account, inside of her firm. I understood what she was doing, and paradoxically it later saved me a lot of money in legal fees. Under the circumstances, I am pretty sure this was not her intention.

By signing to create an account at a brokerage house, you are also agreeing not to sue in court, should a dispute of any sort arise. Instead, the new client promises, in advance, to go to arbitration instead, if there is ever a disagreement. However, I had already determined that the major issues, including Mama's largest losses, were overseen (or actually, in my opinion, created) by the commercial guardian and conservator. Winslow had been following the orders of a court-appointed entity, and she had done so only after the guardian's choices had led to earlier, larger losses.

Opening this new account, however briefly, simply ensured that we would concentrate anything we complained about to the court on what the guardian/conservator had done. The lawyers for Mama's former guardian and her firm, apparently not realizing that I already knew there was no possibility of a suit against Winslow Wood, later kept suggesting that there were further legal actions David ought to have been taking to protect my interests. No, there were not.

On August 3, 2012, David became my primary attorney. Debbie withdrew from the case, officially, as of August 6, 2012, because it then became strictly a litigation exercise. David also was the attorney who had filed for the probate of Mama's will. Even before that, David had taken over as my primary emotional support. We spoke at least daily, and sometimes more often. Over the years, he was my lead attorney; our emails numbered in the thousands, perhaps even the tens of thousands.

I insisted that David accompany me when I signed to open that Winslow Wood account in the name of Mama's estate; my prior experience at the firm had been so unpleasant that I did not want to go back there alone. As before, it was a hot day. On this visit, two women cared for us, both suggesting there was something mentally wrong with me because I had told them that I wanted to transfer Mama's remaining assets elsewhere. The younger one had long, green-enameled fingernails. As in 2008, both wore long black dresses with long black sleeves. This was Albuquerque in the month of August. To me, their garments simply seemed strange.

As we turned down a long corridor, to leave, I thought I saw the outline of Winslow herself, a large cane next to her, seated in a corner office. She, too, was wearing a long, black dress. She did not acknowledge me, so I did not say anything to her, either. Once again, there was a thunderstorm as we left. As soon as the new account had been established at Winslow Wood, I immediately transferred everything it held into a new account, with my long-term broker, Erik Gallegos, using a standard ACATS form.

Although I was now Mama's court-appointed personal representative, I found that the former conservator waited until the very last moment, just before we were about to go to court to compel action, to give the estate any of Mama's remaining assets. In my opinion, just as when Mama was alive, they never made a transaction or event either easy or pleasant.

The best feature of the probate case was my ability to subpoena material, for good reason, from financial and medical entities. No one else had any legal standing there, and therefore no one had the ability to object to what I, as Mama's personal representative, did in that case. In my opinion, had Mama's assets been overseen by a commercial trustee, that person would have said, "I won't fund this nonsense. Take the money and run!" If I had done that, I would never have gotten any meaningful answers to my questions.

Probate court proceedings are not secret, the way that guardianship cases still seem to be in New Mexico. If there is a problem, it cannot be disguised in probate court.[452] I do not hear much about gag orders in probate cases, either, although they sometimes crop

---

[452] Perhaps part of the reason I had a relatively pleasant time in probate court is that this was an uncontested action. The more different attorneys and conflicting interests, the more complications.

up there and in family trust cases. How odd that theoretically guardianship law is a division of probate law, but the assumptions are very different; the statutes governing guardianships are found among the probate statutes, I guess because they relate to people's assets. Why do people want their assets transferred in secret, through trusts that are not transparent, when it is possible to do everything out in the light? In all fairness, just about every attorney I have ever spoken to about the subject disagrees with me on this point. From what I have seen, it is the secrecy in guardianship proceedings (and sometimes in trust proceedings, as well) that encourages all sorts of abuse.

As we waited and waited for Sam to make some progress, odd things were happening in the guardianship case, which was still hanging on. Judge Baca retired in August 2012. On August 31, Judge Denise Barela-Shepard was assigned to the case. The problem with having her as the judge was that Dan Lewis, one of the ex-guardian's attorneys, was the "Lewis" in the law firm of Allen, Shepard, Lewis & Syrah. The "Shepard" in the firm was Denise Barela-Shepard's husband, Ned. Therefore, Denise Barela-Shepard had to recuse herself from the case.

Over the summer of 2012, I was among a group of relatives and friends of people under guardianship who attended an Albuquerque meeting of the New Mexico Health and Human Services Committee where attorneys Greg MacKenzie (then the lobbyist for the New Mexico Guardianship Association) and Darryl Millett (later skewered for his treatment of the Darnell family by Diane Dimond in her series of award-winning *Albuquerque Journal* articles[453]) were speaking on behalf of the guardianship profession. The lawyers described how they wanted attorneys to control any substantial gifts anyone over 65 might want to give to anyone else. It sounded as if they wanted attorneys to have running lists of all

---

453 Diane Dimond, "Who Guards the Guardians? Third in a Series," *Albuquerque Journal*, November 29, 2016, pp. 1, 4 and Diane Dimond, "Investigative Report—Part 4. Who Guards the Guardians?" *Albuquerque Journal*, November 30, 2016, pp.1, 4 and Diane Dimond, "Investigative Report—Part 5. Who Guards the Guardians?" *Albuquerque Journal*, December 1, 2016, pp. 1, 4. Followed by Millet's attempted rebuttal, arguing that the state's strict privacy laws required him to treat family members as he did—Darryl Millet, "Attorney reacts to series on guardianship process," *Albuquerque Journal*, December 7, 2016, p. 7. Greg MacKenzie had also been involved in the Darnell case early on.

the specific assets of everyone over 65, so they could make sure an older person did not give "too much" away. My issues with this are first, the person's privacy, and second the fluctuations in the value of assets. Stocks, bonds, and real estate all fluctuate in value; asset value does not always go up.

The two attorneys, along with a functionary from the Senior Citizens' Law office, wanted to introduce legislation to that effect at the next New Mexico legislative session in January 2013. (Despite its name somewhat misleading name, the Senior Citizens' Law office is a private, not a public, organization.) Those of us present were aghast. Even the committee itself did not vote the proposed bill onto the legislative agenda.

Millet, MacKenzie and the Ellen Leitzer of the Senior Citizens' Law Office, all seemed to think that anyone over 65 was both daft and easily manipulated, and that attorneys should keep track of things so that Medicaid was not scammed. It did not seem to me that this was an ultimate issue, since any improper gifts that some people might want to give to defraud Medicaid would be clawed back into the Medicaid system if any irregularities were discovered later. To me, it seemed like just another way for attorneys to collect fees and exercise control. All those present who were involved with wards of commercial guardians were horrified by this proposal. Part of the meeting had been filmed, but that part (unfortunately, in my opinion) was not.

When Sam had not delivered his report by December 2012, both sides agreed to vacate the guardianship hearing that had been scheduled for that month. Originally, it had been calendared primarily to listen to what he had to say.

When David and I met with Sam Baca in January 2013, he said he was about to issue his report. He did not.

Legislation about guardianship was pending during the 2013 legislative session, which in New Mexico that year ran from mid-January to mid-March. Emily Darnell told the rest of the group of family members of wards that she had known the bespectacled, avuncular, seemingly ever-smiling Sen. Jerry Ortiz y Pino for years. She got a couple of lobbyists she also knew to make an appointment so that we could go and talk to him, in his office at the Roundhouse, about possible legislation. I went up there, to see him along with a group of family members of other wards. I was not going to be able, however, to give any details of Mama's case, just as I could not do that at the legislative hearing a few weeks earlier. We had made clear to the senator, in advance, that we only felt safe speaking if the senator and a staff member were the only people in that gathering with us. No one from the guardianship industry, Sen. Ortiz y Pino assured us, would be present. Just us.

As that meeting started, it seemed to me that there were some eight family members of wards, seated around the senator's conference tables. (They seem, in memory, to have been a number of individual tables, pushed together.) He and an aide were at the other end. We were just about to begin introducing ourselves.

"We all have to communicate," the Senator said. "Everyone has to participate."

Then he sent his aide out, into the anteroom. We waited, silently, for a few seconds, as the aide came back with a man and a woman.

The senator introduced the two new people as members of the guardianship community, whose names and affiliations I no longer recall. "Please introduce yourselves," Sen. Ortiz y Pino said, motioning to the rest of us.

"I'm sorry," I said, without introducing myself first. "I'm afraid that I have to leave, Senator. You said we'd be speaking with you and your aide only." I got up and left the meeting.

Having had some experience with legislative negotiation on other matters, frankly I had been surprised that we had been told we could meet with the senator, but no one else, other than perhaps his aide. We were all representing one constituency and asking him to take some action on our behalf, without the opposition present. Our legislature runs on balancing the interests of competing groups. They primarily want to deal with representatives of structured, large groups. The larger, the better. Numbers elect legislators. And all stakeholders have to sit together, to hammer out compromises.

At that point, guardianship was kept so secret in New Mexico that nothing about it was automatically made public. The case dockets were not published and families of wards only met families of other wards with difficulty, or through nexus people like Stuart Stein. We had trouble canvassing to see how large our group was, due to the judicial secrecy of the cases and the gag orders already in force in some of our cases. As a group, we had never had any representation in the legislature, as opposed to the legal, judicial, guardianship and social work professions. Those people's interests would be directly affected by whatever a legislator might do to solve our problems. Those other groups all had a long history of successfully lobbying legislators. I had been afraid, in advance, that we would be out-flanked by the other groups, but decided to try. We were.

From my point of view, Senate Memorial 94, introduced by Sen. Ortiz y Pino as a result of that meeting, was bruised and bleeding when it passed. The final version ended up creating yet another task force, the "Guardian & Conservator Working Group," scheduled to start work by August 1, 2013, to examine practices within the guardianship and conservatorship industry. Once more, that new group included only certified "professionals" in the field, representing various professional interest groups (but not the families of wards, since being the adult child of a ward is not a "profession"). The Developmental Disabilities Planning Council had the responsibility of setting up the group. Their recommendations, that would normally have been enacted during the 2014 legislative session, did not pass.

During the legislative session, I participated on March 18, 2013, in a podcast on guardianship in New Mexico with Marti Oakley. Guests on Oakley's broadcasts frequently discuss guardianship matters. I gave out no information at all about Mama or her guardianship, only about pending and recently passed legislation in New Mexico. I was trying to be very careful that any possible publicity would not be about me, personally, or about Mama or her case.[454]

Another member on Oakley's panel that night strongly suggested that I must have done something very, very wrong for a judge

---

454 *https://www.blogtalkradio.com/marti-oakley/2013/03/18/elder-abuse-new-mexico-passes-baker-act*

not to want me to be my mother's guardian. I answered that the case in which I was involved was not the subject of this broadcast. Besides, the show was announced as a discussion of the potential abuses of a new law the New Mexico Legislature had just passed that was the equivalent of Florida's Baker Act, the sort of law that confined people for several days after a relative or friend says they are not behaving normally.[455] This was the law Stuart had told us all about several years earlier. During such a confinement, they could be drugged and then fail competency exams as a result. Stuart Stein used to tell us that his efforts had managed to release quite a few people from this potential "reason" for placing them under guardianship. These people were not incompetent; they were simply drugged.

Meanwhile, the legal clock continued to tick. Sam, despite his promises, had produced nothing. But he did continue to bill. As we entered the second quarter of 2013, it began to become likely that he would not issue anything until after the one-year statute of limitations for filing a separate, non-sequestered civil suit against the guardian. We got our material together and David (primarily) along with his co-counsel, Dan Pick, prepared papers to be filed in a civil suit in district court, totally outside of the guardianship case itself.

Mama had died on June 1, 2012. We had a deadline of May 31, 2013, to file any new civil action. I did not have the time, energy or money to file a wrongful death suit, although I badly wanted to. With that avenue closed, all I could complain about was money. Fortunately, knowing that I could not sue Winslow Wood in a court of law, and also realizing that what that firm had done might not have been as terrible as what the former commercial conservator had done (or, in some cases, not done), narrowed down the people we could sue to the guardian and conservator.

When we still did not have Sam's report by two days before the statute of limitations would have expired, we filed our fifty-page complaint in district Court on May 30, 2013, charging Mama's former guardian and conservator with malfeasance. Because of the intense secrecy that guardianship material then commanded in

---

455 "Baker Act," University of Florida Health, Retrieved February 22, 2020 from: *https://ufhealth.org/baker-act*

New Mexico, we felt obliged to file the initial complaint under seal, so that my attorneys would not be subject to sanctions for violating the sequestration of material in the guardianship case, with the understanding that we would get that secrecy lifted later.

I was confident we could do this because I was Mama's sole heir. All the rights that had been legally vested in her, and then in the commercial guardian and conservator, were now vested in me, including the right to publish material Mama had created or paid for, or to write about her, as she had wanted me to do. All those documents had belonged to her. Mama had paid for every record produced during the guardianship, whether by the guardian, the conservator, or anyone working for them. We also filed for a jury trial.

Mama's former commercial guardian spent months, attempting to consolidate the new district court suit into the old guardianship suit. Fortunately for me, the estate was a new and separate legal entity, even though I was its personal representative and I had personally been an interested party in the guardianship case.

We were forced to make the arguments, repeatedly, that the estate did not exist, as a legal entity, during the guardianship; it was only established after Mama died. Mama might have named someone else as personal representative in her will, someone who had not been an interested party in her guardianship case. On the other hand, I, personally, had existed all along and, theoretically, I, as an individual, had had the ability to defend my rights and get redress of grievances along the way. Even though I would argue that was not really so, it was a potential legal argument that the ex-guardian's attorneys could and did make.

The estate, however, had had no rights during Mama's lifetime. Had there been a trust that had existed throughout Mama's lifetime, and had I simply taken over the trust, I am not at all sure that I would have had any cause of action, either. I suppose that an incoming trustee can challenge an outgoing trustee, but that situation certainly would not have been any more pleasant than mine was.

As the various attorneys were sinking their teeth into the legal meat, in the estate's suit against Mama's former guardian, according to the docket, Shannon Bacon was appointed the new judge in the guardianship case on August 27, 2013, the same day Judge Barela-Shepard was recused.

True to the by-then-established pattern, the latest judge had a conflict, as well. Judge Bacon turned out to be Dan Pick's cousin. She was recused within weeks. After Judge Campbell, the same judge from the probate case, replaced her on September 4, 2013, the ex-guardian's attorneys used a peremptory challenge to get him excused. Within a day, Judge Valerie Huling was the next one appointed to preside over the guardianship case. I started to get dizzy, watching all the judges come and go.

Meanwhile, the former guardian's attorneys filed another motion, trying to roll the new, malfeasance suit into the guardianship case, a move we fought because we wanted the information out in the open, not hidden.

Right after we filed, Sam finally produced what I regard as his perfunctory report, barely the length of an undergraduate college term paper, and to my mind, not as rigorous. The estate had paid, effectively $7,300 per page for this document. Had there not been a court order, specifically directing me to pay him, I would not have.

The ex-guardian's lawyers quickly challenged Carl Butkus, the first judge assigned to the new case. On July 17, 2013, the court substituted Alan Malott, an acerbic jurist who had previously been a personal injury lawyer. Starting on July 13, 2009, about seven months after his initial appointment to the bench by Gov. Bill Richardson, he had started writing a column, "Judge for Yourself," that appeared every other week in the *Albuquerque Journal*. He seemed to like to appear on the radio, too, which he still does even though he is now theoretically retired. (I am not sure whether he frequently appears on television; I have not watched television since 2001.) It later turned out that he most emphatically wanted to keep me from writing, publishing or making any media appearances.

Malott remained the judge on this case until it settled. Once Judge Malott arrived on the scene, Mama's ex-guardian's attorneys decided to drop their motion in the guardianship case to consolidate the new case in district court into the old guardianship case. They had previously tried to argue that there would have been no new case without the guardianship case, and so the "new" case was really an extension of the "old" case, suggesting that it was really all the same old case anyway.

We argued (once more) that Mama's will could have appointed anyone as personal representative. She could have appointed a bank or a trust officer or her third cousin twice removed. She simply happened to have appointed me. My capacity and responsibility as personal representative differed from my personal interests.

As far as I was concerned, it would have been in my personal best interest, and definitely the easiest thing to do, to take whatever might have been left in Mama's accounts and abandon any attempt to grant Mama's request that I write about the past and try to correct any problems that Mama had experienced. However, the personal representative, regardless of who that person or business entity is in relation to the deceased person, has a responsibility to redress any possible existing grievances of the decedent at the time of the person's death. I was not suing to fix my own issues, caused by the commercial guardian (of which there were quite a few); I was only suing to get redress for Mama, and hence for her estate. In fact, my name appeared only as personal representative in the caption of the case. I—as an individual—was not even a party to the suit.

In December, I attended and spoke at another legislative hearing of the Health and Human Services Committee in Santa Fe, at the Roundhouse, in my capacity simply as a New Mexico resident with a master's degree in public health who had a strong interest in the subject of guardianship. I discussed general problems in the field, and quite deliberately did not mention anything about Mama's case. My documentary partner sent along a cameraman who took a video of the proceedings, but I never got to see it. I saw at least a half-dozen guardianship victims in the audience, all family members of wards of commercial guardians. Not all were the same ones who had attended the meeting in June.

Mama's ex-guardian also attended, sitting all the way up front, in the audience. She and Greg MacKenzie were sitting next to each other. When the camera panned to the audience, she hid the face of Greg MacKenzie, who had been the president of the New Mexico Guardianship Association a few years earlier and continued to lobby for the industry. I have no idea what happened to that video. I kept asking my then-partner for a copy, but never got one.

One of the biggest problems I had seen (and, of course, all family members and friends of wards had also seen) in other guardianship cases was that they seemed to drag on and on, always sequestered and also often with gag orders on the participants. When Mama's former guardian dropped the petition for absolution, Special Master Geraldine Rivera resigned. Both entries were posted on the docket the same day—October 30, 2013. This fact strongly suggested that there would be no further motions or legal arguments made in that case. There had been no legal events in the probate case since the order terminating Mama's trust in July 2013.

All the action then moved to the district court estate suit against the guardian. David and I had made sure that Mama had all the terms of her will carried out in accordance with her wishes in the probate case, however, before proceeding to other matters.

Theoretically, that effectively left two cases pending, the probate action and the suit of Mama's estate against the former guardian. The probate case was uncomplicated and public. I was the only person with any legal interest in the matter, so no matter how long it lasted, there would be no opposing parties. The complaint against the guardian, however, can only be described as byzantine and, originally at least, filed under seal. We had asked for a jury of six. The former guardian, after filing an answer to our complaint, also under seal, then "raised us" by requesting a jury of twelve, rather than six.

There could be no legal case without evidence, so David then filed to unseal the court record in the guardianship case so the documents could be used in this case. The former guardian objected. They claimed that Mama—regardless of the fact that she had passed away more than a year earlier—would be "embarrassed" by having any of the information made public. They claimed that they were still protecting Mama, despite a court document that stated that even the existence of a pending forensic audit did not mean that the guardian could remain Mama's guardian after she died. We answered that, as personal representative, I was the only person with the legal power to judge what was or was not in Mama's best interests. Furthermore, we believed that the only person secrecy served, at this point, was the defendant. That defendant no longer had any legal claim to be representing Mama's interests at all.

Judge Malott denied our motion to unseal on October 15, 2013. There followed months—no, years—of wrangling over this issue, which my attorneys and I considered affected our First Amendment rights (or, in this case, the lack thereof). We needed to move forward into the process of discovery, but we could not show experts anything if all documents were considered sequestered.[456]

Arguments and counter-arguments continued until August 2014, when the defendants filed a new motion, demanding that Judge Malott grant them a global gag order. Part of their argument was that I had spoken to a legislative hearing in 2012. They said they wanted to make sure that I spoke neither to legislators, nor to the media, and that I definitely should not be allowed to issue the documentary I had said, during the 2012 hearing, that I had been preparing[457].

As of Labor Day weekend in 2014, acting on accusations from Mama's ex-guardian that I was essentially simply seeking publicity and was about to put out a documentary video critical of the guardianship firm Mama's estate was then suing, Judge Malott imposed a total gag order on me and on my legal team as well, forbidding any of us to say anything about Mama, the guardianship, or the subject of guardianship, that Mama's ex-guardian found offensive.

Theoretically, this order also affected the guardianship firm, but they stood to benefit greatly if the case took place in total secrecy. Should anyone on my side violate that order, we would all be subject to imprisonment and fines. All of us, not just me. There

---

456 This was one of the problems Stuart Stein ran into, he used to say, when trying to defend his license. Because the client involved was a ward in a sequestered case, and the court denied him the right to use documents from that case to support his position, he had been unable to offer any evidence in support of his legal position. I was afraid they were trying to do the same to the estate, here.

457 Defendants' Motion for Protective Order (D-202-CV-2013-04646) , p. 8. They also seemed to be claiming that the documentary was about them. It was not. It was about the abuses of guardians and conservators, in general.

was no hearing in advance of the imposition of that order, and no opportunity to argue about what was in the rough video footage itself, as of that point. The judge never saw or asked to see it. Neither did Mama's ex-guardian.

Believing that prior censorship was unconstitutional, we immediately appealed to the New Mexico Supreme Court, which meant that I, as Mama's personal representative, had to sue Judge Malott himself. When the New Mexico Supreme Court refused to hear our petition, and gave us no explanation of why, we started to think about going directly to the federal district court, but various pre-emption doctrines (areas in which the federal courts say they will not intervene in State-court decisions) prevented us from taking this sort of action at that point.

It is one thing for legal experts, whose only contacts with Mama and me related to this case, not to speak about it. It was quite something else, for me. My only clues to how Mama's ex-guardian might react to something I said was how they had reacted, in the past, not only to things I had actually said that I came to believe they had misunderstood, but also to things third parties might have told them I had said, even if I had not said them. Those reactions, it seemed to me, had been uniformly negative and punitive. Now, the defendant had told the judge that I was creating a documentary about them, when I was not. And it seemed that he had automatically believed them without ever asking me a single question about the situation. All I knew was that, over the years I had known these people, they had often accused me of things that I had not done. It then became impossible for me to discuss anything about my life or my family with anyone without worrying about their reactions.

To be relatively safe, I then concluded that I could not say anything about my life. Or Mama's, for that matter. At one point, I was having an old robe of Mama's framed. The pale blue, satin-textured cloth was embroidered with a large gold dragon, a striking item. The gag order produced this rather surreal exchange between the elderly man who owned the framing shop and me:

"What an interesting textile! Who did that belong to?"

"I really can't say."

I could not attend reunions for my high school and college classes; people who had known Mama and had not seen either of us for a long time were likely to ask after her. I also had to discontinue work on the documentary, because I could not authorize the release of a documentary about the subject of guardianship, a subject that the judge had just forbidden me to discuss in public. This also meant writing off the $25,000 I had already spent. I could not attend any meetings of a politically active group for which I had been the secretary since 2005, because, even though it was a non-profit, under the terms of the gag order, I was not allowed to speak to legislators or lobbyists. I was afraid that simply being in the room with politicians (some members of the group ended up in the legislature or as mayors or city councilmembers all around New Mexico; there was even a future lieutenant governor in the group) would be all I would have to do to get an express ticket to jail. I could no longer go to the legislature in Santa Fe to lobby, which I had done as a citizen (i.e., unpaid) lobbyist for years.

The gag order also directly prevented me from doing as Mama asked and "telling the story," which she had made me promise to do, back in 2008. Living in the United States, I would never have imagined that a judge would one day bar me from speaking about any period of Mama's life, and certainly her years under commercial guardianship during which I had seen her just about every day. I would never have been able to conceive of the possibility that someone would take away my freedom of speech when talking about my own life. And all this on the basis that someone the judge knew well had said he believed that I would commit a future infraction. Somehow, someday, I would have to see that the gag order was lifted or I would never be able to keep my promise to Mama.

Had I gone to jail for contempt of court, the imprisonment term would have been entirely at the judge's discretion. I wonder whether I would still be in jail. At the time, I even wondered whether, in a secretly conducted case, anyone would ever find out that I was there. A fine would also have been at the judge's discretion. I considered the $25,000 write-off of my contribution to the abandoned documentary as the first installment of a much larger fine the judge would very likely levy, if I was not extremely quiet.

Perhaps my isolation and lack of social activities during that period helped, because the defendants asked a series of Interrogatories that required 48 single-spaced pages to answer. Ultimately, there would be two such long documents. The first, we delivered to them on December 17, 2014. After scrutinizing that one, they produced another set of questions that took another 48 pages to answer. The second set of answers, we delivered on February 2, 2017.

While all this was happening, I had been looking for a new single-level house. I was still having trouble with stairs and needed to move from the three-level home in which I had lived since 1997. My former business partner kept saying she wanted to buy the home I was leaving. She said that she wanted to pay whatever an appraiser reported its worth to be, and asked me to get an appraisal. I went to a bank I had been dealing with since 1997 and asked for the name of an appraiser.

Of course, my documentary partner had known Mama too, so she was on a now-secret witness list. I could not violate the gag order to tell her that, of course. I could not even give her a Christmas gift anymore, in order to avoid worrying that someone might call it "bribing a witness." So, I did not. Once my former business partner saw the appraisal, she asked for a huge discount from the appraised valuation. In order for this to be an arm's-length transaction, I could not give her a discount off the valuation. She started insisting, "You can afford just to give it to me!"

"No, actually I can't."

"Haven't I been nice to you? Haven't I treated you well?"

I had begun to feel that somehow the other side had gotten to her just before we quit work on the documentary. We had agreed not to interview people in the guardianship industry in New Mexico, but in the end, she refused to conform to our agreement. She insisted on interviewing an attorney in the circle of friends of Mama's former guardian, and then started admiringly telling me how much money the guardianship firm was making.

A few months later, I sold the house to someone else. Later, I discovered that my former associate had bought a different house, from an attorney in the former guardian's circle of friends, right after the owner had reduced the asking price by $180,000.

Of course, as soon as I could not speak about Mama or the case, on pain of serious legal reprisals, everyone wanted me to do just that.

"You're no fun anymore!" one of my friends complained. "I can't even ask you a question about your mother, or even whether there's a case."

"Well, you can ask, but I can't answer."

Even during the guardianship, I could not speak about on-going legal maneuvers, because that might compromise my right to attorney-client privilege. I would become primarily a listener when people were discussing their personal lives. Now, I was even more socially passive than before. After the gag order, I withdrew, in fear, from most social activities, particularly those in which there was even the remotest possibility that anyone present might think I had said something that could be reported back to the defendant's side of the case as a negative comment about them or about their profession.

Several months after I moved into my new home, I looked out my window one night. It was already dark outside. I saw the outline of someone sitting in a white SUV that looked exactly like the one I had seen Margot Keener driving, back in 2012. (There are a great many white SUVs in Albuquerque, however.) The car was parked facing my home. I could not see the license plate, which would have been on the back of the car anyway, but I turned on all the lights in the front hall and the front rooms, where they could easily be seen from the street. Whoever was in the car drove away.

I was already bound by the gag order, so I did not dare complain to the police, and there was no evidence that whoever was in the SUV had trespassed or done anything to my property. A police complaint would have involved, perhaps, speaking ill of the defendant in the case, and I wanted, above all, to stay out of jail. Shortly thereafter, the city installed an extremely bright streetlight, directly across from my driveway. I did not see uninvited nighttime guests watching my house anymore.

The case docket published on the internet makes it seem as if there was next to no legal activity in the estate's case against Mama's former guardian, between December 17, 2014, and October 30, 2015. However, I know that intensive gathering and analysis of documents was closely followed, on both sides of the case, by the crucial search for expert witnesses. Watching the mad scramble to get everything done by court deadlines, I came to realize how misleading the naked online docket could be.

On October 30, 2015, the defendants filed a brief, arguing (at great length) that they had done nothing wrong in their handling of Mama's assets. They asked the judge to agree, by issuing a "summary judgement" saying that they had acted in a blameless manner. We, of course, argued exactly the opposite, that not only was preserving Mama's assets their responsibility, it was actually a major, court-imposed responsibility of any conservatorship. The legal struggle continued for months. These positions, the attorneys argued in briefs sometimes exceeding 50 pages in length. Because court filings usually do not exceed ten pages, they needed special permission from the judge to submit longer "briefs."

Beginning in February 2016, the *Albuquerque Journal* started publishing articles about problems in the commercial guardianship industry. Syndicated columnist Diane Dimond was writing about guardianship problems from around the country. The *Albuquerque Journal* published the first of them on February 20, 2016.[458]

A family member of another ward told me that she had initially contacted Diane, after the first of those articles appeared, and asked her to investigate some of the most egregious guardianship cases in New Mexico. While Diane's investigations were in progress, I was still under a blanket gag order, and therefore not allowed to talk to the press. I nearly fainted when I got the following interrogatory from the defendants, "Please explain whether or not you contributed, financially or otherwise to Ms. Dimond's book or newspaper stories."[459] To the best of my recollection, neither my name nor Mama's name had ever appeared in her articles.

---

[458] "Guardianships can easily turn to abuse," *Albuquerque Journal*, February 20, 2016, p. A9.
[459] Estate Response to Oriola Discovery, February 13, 2017, p. 48.

On April 5, 2016, the docket listed the appearance of yet another attorney in my camp. It did not mention his name. Now that the gag order has been lifted, I can say that it was Hank Bohnhoff, the earnest and formidable former chief assistant attorney general and deputy attorney general of New Mexico, who was then a partner in one of the largest law firms in the state—Rodey Dickason Sloan Akin & Robb, P.A. (colloquially known as "The Rodey Law Firm"). Rodey itself had been around since 1883; more than 60 attorneys worked there. David had worked with Hank before, years earlier.[460]

The docket did not recognize the fact that David filed both the notice of Hank's appearance and his last argument on the summary judgement matter on the same day. The docket says David filed his brief later, on April 8, 2016. Perhaps the clerk of the court submitted one document to the judge before the other.

Hank's new presence, I think, might have conveyed a dual message. First, it signaled that David, who had become a solo practitioner in 2014, knew how to get help, when he wanted it. (By then, there were some 40,000 documents included in the discovery portion of the case.) Second, it meant that one of the largest firms in the state, and one of their most distinguished practitioners, knew about my case and believed in my side of it enough to be willing to enlist in trying to help me.

Whatever his reasons, Judge Malott denied the defendants' petition for summary judgement, and in a very timely manner. His order made its way onto the case docket on May 5, 2016.

Judge Malott issued both a scheduling order for the case, and his order, denying the summary judgement motion, on the same day. Shortly after that, odd things started to happen.

I lived in a very quiet area. My house had had an antiquated alarm system installed before I moved in. That system had recently malfunctioned but I had not yet replaced it. Suddenly, it began to appear that things had been moved in my home, when I was not there. A roll of stamps that had calmly resided in the cubbyhole of a closed, drop-leaf wall desk the previous day ended up on the floor

---

[460] After a stint on the Court of Appeals, Hank returned to Rodey in April 2019. He was sitting on the Court of Appeals when this case "went critical" in the spring of 2017.

the next day, where I was not expecting it to be. I tripped over it. Checking around to see whether any doors or windows had been tampered with, I discovered that a door I had not used in months, and had kept locked, was now no longer locked. I quickly installed a new burglar alarm. After that, I was careful to keep all the doors and windows locked and alarmed. The gag order was still in force; I did not even think of calling the police. There were no further problems, at least for a while.

After buying a new car that spring, to replace the one I had owned for the past seven years, I started to find that when I parked in an open lot, and particularly when I had my cell phone with me at my attorney's office, things had been moved around in my car when I got back. Once, whoever had entered the car in my absence simply opened the overhead area where most people keep their car registration. It was as if someone was saying, "We know where you are at all times." Someone certainly seemed to. Not until 2020, on a day when I accidentally locked my car keys inside my car while shopping, did I discover that my then-new car had a special feature, specifically designed to facilitate entering the vehicle if you had locked the keys inside. It seems that whoever was opening it, years earlier, had read the owner's manual a bit more carefully than I had. I started leaving my cell phone at home. These episodes greatly decreased.

After I had alarmed the house again, a still-shrink-wrapped VHS version of the film *Gaslight* appeared, standing up in an open box, in my garage, where I could not miss seeing it. I alarmed the garage as well.

Finally, at about 12:30 PM on Sunday, May 29, 2016, I went out to my street mailbox—a group mailbox. It had separate, locked compartments for each house on my street. For years, I had received most of my mail at a post office box. Everyone from whom I habitually received mail knew to send it to my post office box, so I only checked my street box a couple of times each week.

The weekly circulars for supermarkets and the postcard decks advertising local services arrived on Wednesdays, so I always picked up the mail on Wednesday or Thursday. Monthly postcard decks, advertising local services, always came on the first of the month. However, on this day, what appeared to be a heat-sealed glassine envelope full of advertising postcards was all that my street box contained. I recall thinking, "That's strange! I shouldn't be getting these until Tuesday." All other such envelopes I had gotten had either my name, or a prior occupant's name, or simply the word "Occupant" in the address section of the postcard or pasted on the outside. This one left the address area blank. These were glossy, expensive-looking postcards.

I decided to look them over after a late breakfast. Having felt a bit tired, I decided to take a high-dose Vitamin B-12 lozenge. After breakfast, as I opened the envelope, I was suddenly overwhelmed by the smell of bitter almonds. At first it was just a subliminal recognition of an odd odor. I started going through the postcards. One had the headline, "The Boys of Summer." The title made me think about a book by that title reviewed in *The New York Times Book Review* years earlier. That volume was a history of baseball, but this card seemed to be an ad for a performance by the Santa Fe Gay Men's Chorus.

Now, the bitter-almond stench hit me full blast. I started choking. It was hard to breathe. My eyes watered. I felt suddenly nauseous. My nose burned, and I simultaneously got a blinding headache. Two of my fingers were numb. My literary imagination kicked in immediately, with thoughts of Agatha Christie and William Styron. I ran out of the room. After I stopped retching, I put on some vinyl gloves and one of the heavy masks I generally used for cleaning the garage. (We are all advised, here, to use them while cleaning enclosed spaces, because plague infects some of the local rodents.)

I opened every door and window in the area, to clear out any residue. Finally, I came back into the breakfast nook. While holding my breath and trying to keep my eyes as far away from the noxious stuff on the table as possible, I transferred the postcards and the envelope to a Baggie that locked tightly shut. That Baggie is still in a safe place.[461] Since I had survived that long, I assumed that there was not enough poison in the envelope to do me serious injury and, although my head still felt as if someone had just hit it with

---

461   Fear of violating the gag order prevented me from contacting the authorities.

a boulder, I concluded that I had already been through the worst of it. Thinking that I had just had a brush with hydrogen cyanide (because I saw no residue of any sort in the area where the packet of postcards had been), I took more of the high-dose B-12 lozenges. A handful of them. If I went to an urgent care office, or the police, or even to the postal authorities I risked running afoul of the gag order. I looked it up on the internet. The only known antidote for cyanide is a hefty dose of injected B-12. Because I believed that I could not tell any medical personnel how I came in contact with the poison, I decided those lozenges would have to do. Until then, I had never consciously realized that my freedom was more important to me than my life.

Unfortunately, I was wrong about not having lasting effects from that encounter. After about ten hours, I realized that I was not urinating. I took some dandelion tea and that problem resolved, at least temporarily. I started having painful spasms in my hands and legs and feet, at odd intervals. Sometimes they woke me during the night. Sometimes, I would wake up with one or more fingers curled into an odd position.

Within a few days, my legs were swelling up and I was getting short of breath. I had gained rather a lot of weight, perhaps ten pounds, although I was not eating more than normal. The weight gain and bloating continued and the shortness of breath worsened.

By then, I was avoiding seeing people. Anyone who had seen me a few months before would have been bound to ask why I looked so different. I had gained about 40 pounds of water weight. Desperate, I looked on the internet for a doctor I could be sure was not allied with the other side in my case. (Sometime earlier, I had discovered that at least one medical doctor had brochures from Mama's guardian's firm in her office. The relative of another ward had seen them there, several years earlier, and reported the incident to the group. Perhaps others did, as well.)

The person I found was William Sommer, an Albuquerque specialist in internal medicine as well as a psychiatrist, who had had massive run-ins with the New Mexico medical establishment, perhaps in part as some sort of retribution for his attempts to help Stuart Stein with a guardianized person. He saw me, told me I had heart failure, and prescribed massive doses of potassium. Perhaps ten times the normal amount. He said I could expect to lose about 30 pounds of that water weight in about three days on the high dose he was prescribing.

I was afraid to follow his orders. Dr. Sommer insisted that I had to have someone with me when I took each dose, because my heart might stop and I would need emergency medical treatment immediately. I thanked him, took his prescription with me, but did not fill it. I lived alone. I had told him that. No one would be able to come, several times per day, to stay with me for half an hour or more while I took the medicine and we found out whether my heart was going to stop, that particular time. Besides, no one would be willing to do that without asking a lot of questions about what had happened to me, and why this sort of extreme prescription was now necessary. I could not risk blurting something out that I would regret later.

After thinking about the problem, I hypothesized that perhaps three times the normal dose of potassium, also taken orally, might get the job done, along with a topical herbal application I had patented years earlier. This combination would likely work slower than the medically prescribed dose, but it would not be strong enough to kill me either, so I would be able to get the job done alone. I had seen the topical oil help a patient lose a pound or so of water weight in a day. The extra potassium, I reasoned, should improve those results.

This regime seemed to work, but the process did take a lot longer than three days. Years before, an accident attorney showed me an instructional video, before a scheduled deposition that never did take place. The video made clear that you had to disclose any prescription drugs you were taking when you gave a deposition. Fortunately, the medication regimen I was following did not entail taking any prescription drugs, so I would not have to say I was taking any when I gave my deposition. All I was taking, at that point, was a hefty amount of a non-prescription potassium supplement and that same B-12 I had been taking back in May, but a lot less of it. However, I still had severe leg and foot cramps that forced me to take breaks, periodically, during my testimony.

Fortunately, I did not finish losing all the weight during the period between my two depositions. Afterward, I discovered that I had developed a periumbilical hernia. It did not show while the excess water weight was in that area. Sometimes these things develop spontaneously, but I have always thought this one came originally from the uncontrollable retching I had, after I opened that noxious package I had received in the mail. Of course, I could not, and did not, tell this to the doctors who examined the hernia.

In late February 2017, two more attorneys entered the case, representing two insurance companies involved with the defendants. For the most part, they simply observed, but they would certainly have an interest in the outcome. I started looking at the army of attorneys on the other side—sometimes as many as four or five at a single deposition—and felt thankful for the efficient way the commando-attorneys on my side operated. There was never a deposition that required more than two of them. So many defense attorneys also posed the more-than-implied threat that, if I lost in court, the judge would force me to pay all those attorney fees and court costs for the defendant.

Greg MacKenzie chose to take my depositions in a rickety old clapboard building in downtown Albuquerque. The gravel parking lot made it hard to use a walker. Approaching the building for the first time, I realized that I would not be able to take my walker up the few steps to the front door. I would have to leave it in the car, and crawl up and down, with help from David and James, to get into and out of the building. I would have to hold onto the building on one side, and one of my attorneys on the other.

The structure had a side door, but the steps there did not even have a railing I could hold. I sat at one corner of the table in a long, narrow room. The dark wood conference table that dominated the space looked as if it seated a dozen people. There was almost no space between the table and the outside walls. Before the deposition started, my public health training kicked in. I amused myself by speculating on what would happen if a fire broke out. The "food-heating" and "coffee-making" equipment occupied a very narrow hall, just outside the door on the west side of the room. A small window was on our side of the south wall. The north side, where the other side sat, featured a solid wall, all the way around the north wall, to the door to the hall and "our" window, behind us, on the south side. The only other exit was right behind David, James and me. In the event we would need to evacuate the building, those on the plaintiff's side could somehow get out the exit behind us. The people sitting on the defendant's side would likely burn to a crisp before they could escape.

My side was seated, but Mama's former guardian had not gotten all the way to her seat yet. As she passed the area where the court reporter sat, the woman jumped up and embraced her, gushing about how delighted she was to see Mama's former guardian again.

During my first deposition, the only remaining partner in the guardianship firm sat diagonally, at the furthest seat away from me, wearing one of her seemingly-endless array of expensive-looking kimono jackets, munching Cheetos out of a large bag and, as I recall, drinking a monster-sized drink of some sort, out of a cardboard cup. I could not tell, from that distance, what it was. She read the paper, worked on her cell phone, and did assorted other fidgety tasks. Not very often, she just sat there and stared, hard, at me. Was she trying to distract me?

Fumbling with some busywork while trying to hold onto her Cheetos, she lost control of the bag. Out of the corner of my eye, I could see it seem to leap out of her hands and fly down the length of the table, finally tipping over and spilling dozens of Cheetos diagonally in David's and my direction. Finally, she had succeeded in disrupting the proceedings, but only for a couple of minutes, as various attorneys helped her gather up her Cheetos. I think David said something like, "Thanks anyway." We all chuckled a bit uncomfortably.

At the other end of the defendants' side of the table, near the court reporter, sat Greg's associate, eating nuts and consulting with Greg about the exhibits in the boxes she and Greg had brought. Next to her, stood the videographer the defendants had insisted on hiring to tape my deposition. I still have not seen a copy of that video. Just never ordered one.

Greg asked me questions, as Dan Lewis and one of the upcoming defense expert witnesses, seated between Greg's associate and

Mama's former guardian, looked on. By the time of my second deposition, I was no longer Dorothy thinking of Greg MacKenzie as the Wizard of Oz behind the curtain anymore. The former guardian chose to eat something else the second time, but it did not jump across the table. Greg's associate ate nuts again. I no longer cared that they were treating my deposition like a circus sideshow.

As soon as Hank Bohnhoff entered an appearance in the Estate's case, the defendants started complaining that one of the older attorneys at Rodey had once served as the defendant's attorney on this case. No attorney from Rodey had ever put in an order of appearance on the defendant's side of the case. Not in the guardianship case and not in this case.

All law firms conduct a "conflicts check" prior to accepting any client. I had been run through that test by Rodey's own ethics department and passed, prior to them taking on my case. The partner the defendants claimed had discussed my case with the head of the guardianship firm said that he did not recall having any conversation about my case with anyone. Just to be on the safe side, however, Rodey withdrew from representing me on September 9, 2016. That was months after Judge Malott denied the defendants' motion for summary judgement, meaning that we would still be proceeding to trial, albeit with a slight delay, made necessary by Hank's withdrawal and the substitution of attorneys James E. Dory and Patti Williams to help David, instead of Hank, which did not happen until January 2017. Patti entered on January 17, James on January 25.

The defendants started demanding to see my personal financial records and copies of my personal emails. They tried to subpoena Erik Gallegos, who had been my personal investment advisor since 1999. We fought against these actions. My personal financial history had nothing to do with Mama's estate. Nor could how I had handled my personal investments while Mama was alive have had any influence over the decisions Mama's conservator had made while Mama was alive. My financial decisions after Mama's passing similarly could not have had the slightest influence over what had happened years earlier. David addressed the question of how I had handled Mama's finances with Mama's ex-guardian at her second deposition on May 9, 2017:

Q: Okay. Was there any concern that Annette's daughter Leonie had exploited Annette Rosenstiel?
A: There was not a concern.
Q: No evidence of that either?
A: No evidence of that that I'm aware of.
Q: Either before or after the guardianship commenced?
A: You know, that's never been something that I considered a problem.[462]

We kept repeating that Mama's estate was a separate legal entity. Only Mama's estate was involved in the lawsuit. I, personally, was not. My name could as easily have been "John Smith," and I would still be suing, as the personal representative of the estate. We reiterated that the estate was suing the guardianship firm, and not me, personally.

By consensus, we kept the suit to what we identified as the most important and most egregious actions of the defendants. In other words, I could still be personally hurt and offended by the defendants' actions in essentially preventing me from seeing Mama for years, but legally, I (as an individual) had no recourse. If I allowed my personal feelings to intrude, it would be far easier for the defendants to continue to manipulate me, emotionally, as I firmly believed they had been doing during all those years of the guardianship.

I had seen what happened to other family members of people under guardianship who had tried to come to court with a laundry list of grievances, throw them all up against a wall, and try to get a few to stick. All foundered as the guardian (or even ex-guardian) twisted them up into emotional pretzels. The commercial guardian tended, from what I had heard, to pick a small item and suggest that the complainant was a chronic complainer, picking all the time on small things. That was the way Elizabeth Church had handled her report as GAL, back in 2008. I did not want this case to go that way.

The legal machinations made me feel like a young child in a strange world. I started asking questions, early on. In return, I got fascinating lectures, explaining that the current problems with

---

462 Nancy Oriola Deposition, Albuquerque, New Mexico, May 9, 2017, p.21.

guardians and trustees denuding the trust of assets and doing things that scandalized people were as old as the Crusades, when the predecessors of our current guardianships were first established. Crusaders originally had to transfer their lands into the name of a friend or relative. They would return from the Holy Land to find that their trusted relative or friend had bankrupted them and married their daughter, in their absence, and petitioned the Court of Chancery (the model for our courts of equity) for justice.

Later, an institution called a "trusteeship" fulfilled the same function, but sometimes trustees also either made off with trust funds or refused to return the property to its rightful owner, when requested to do so. The remedy—petitioning a court of equity—remained the same. Simply knowing that I stood in a long line of petitioners with similar issues improved my mood. My general complaint was nothing new, but everything rested, just as it did during the Middle Ages, on having an honest judge who could—and would—grant redress.

Fortunately, I had patient attorneys who were willing to take the extra time to explain why they were doing what they were doing. During 2017, I started to see angry web postings about how terrible certain attorneys in the trust and estate fields were in New Mexico. One of the common woes of my fellow victims: the uncommunicativeness of their attorneys. They got no progress reports, no information until everything was resolved. Sometimes the legal experts made agreements in their clients' names that the clients later regretted.

In my life, I have had, if I am counting correctly, a total of 11 attorneys who have worked on various projects for me. I had had this experience of non-communication with three other attorneys, working on other issues for me, one of them in New York, before I even moved to New Mexico, but definitely not in this case. Sometimes, I might not hear from an attorney for several years, and then all of a sudden, I would get a settlement offer. Of all of them, only one attorney who said she represented me—Cristy Carbon-Gaul—had ever made any agreements by which I was bound but with the details of which I totally disagreed.

At that point, speaking about my conversations with my attorneys would have lost me the coveted attorney-client privilege. By the time 2017 arrived, I would probably have gone to jail, into the bargain. Fortunately, I had only praise for my attorneys working on the case against Mama's former guardian. I felt frustrated by the fact that I could not write in, at the time those internet posts appeared, disputing them. Fortunately, they now seem to have been deleted, with more reasoned and helpful articles substituted.[463]

Watching so many complain about the excessive expenses incurred by hiring an attorney, I also wanted to write in, to react against them. In fact, I had a running joke with David that he was not charging me enough. That is only because I was allowed to see how much work the lawyers on my side were doing for me. If all I had done was to drop the problem on their desk, instruct them to "fix things," and then come back only when there was a deposition or court hearing to attend, I, too, might have believed that nothing had happened for a year and objected to the billing during that period.

My attorneys also made me aware that "legal ethics" and what non-attorneys consider "ethics" differ materially. Many things that a defendant might have done that are, strictly speaking, within the law are also detestable, from a moral point of view. To my mind, it is detestable to make someone observe an Orthodox Jewish ritual on Tuesday, particularly when they themselves have not voluntarily observed it for more than half a century, and then on Thursday, feed them shrimp. Or to continue to try to force a ward to see a rabbi, when that ward has said clearly to the guardian, on more than one occasion, "I don't want to see one!" Another ward I met during my time seeing her relatives, saw her beloved pet (a teacup-sized dog) taken away because her home health aides did not want to bother walking it or cleaning up after it. These traumas cannot readily be quantified. The court prefers numbers and statistics. They are easier to analyze.

During the fall of 2016, first, syndicated columnist Diane Dimond, and then *Albuquerque Journal* investigative reporter Colleen Heild took on the subject of the harms guardianship and

---

463 *https://aaapg.net/page/1/?s=%22new+mexico%22* Various pages on this site detail abuses in New Mexico, over the years since 2016.

conservatorship were wreaking on New Mexico families. Suddenly, the plight of such families started to make the national news. One day, I came home from some errand or other and checked my voicemail, to find a message there from veteran newsman Sam Donaldson, asking whether I would be willing to speak with him. I did not return his call. Diane Dimond got my email address from someone and emailed me. I did not answer her email. I have probably been rude to just about every legitimate reporter who was researching guardianship during that period.

I had no desire to be rude to anyone. I was simply afraid of going to jail and being fined if I violated the gag order. Somehow, this makes me think of Mama saying she had grown up in a Hasidic area, just to please her questioner. I was trying to ensure that I kept my promise to Mama to "remain standing," so that I could tell the story she wanted me to write. Which in this case required me to make sure that absolutely no one could say I had violated the gag order so that I eventually could get it lifted. Seeing what had happened to others, I realized this was my only way out, to eventual freedom.

Obviously, I would have had no idea who could do a good job, replacing Hank. Again, David found exactly the right people. James, a protégé of David's who had also worked with The Barnett Law Firm for a while during David's tenure there, was an up-and-coming sole practitioner. David had worked with Patti Williams, a partner in the firm of Williams, Wiggins & Williams too, years earlier. Blonde, brilliant, and a bulldog when pulling the truth out of someone at deposition (while not seeming to expend any special effort doing so), Patti also made a fine substitute.

Patti totally nonplussed one of the defendants' expert witnesses at a video deposition by simply positioning her chair so that he could not see her. The attorney-witness was, perhaps, a thousand miles away. Where Patti sat made her questions appear to come from everywhere and nowhere. I gathered that this witness was used to garnering visual cues from the people questioning him. When he could not, he fell apart under her questioning. What a relief! The other side was experiencing some manipulation, for a change. I pray that my attorneys only use their skills on the side of the good and the holy, because they are formidable, the lot of them!

But that was later. As the complainant, my deposition came first. The hype surrounding Greg MacKenzie had me terrified to start with, but he turned out to be the Wizard of Oz, so his exalted reputation ended up being fake news. He was only as good as his research; it turned out that mine was at least as good as his. By then, having been, for a couple of years, in something approaching solitary confinement, I had had time to read and digest the 40,000 pages of documents. At times, I was able to tell him that there was a document in the pile that specifically spoke to a particular issue he raised, because I knew I had seen it there.

The gag order had prevented me from socializing for about two years, at that point, except for my daily conversations with David. Unwittingly, I think, the defendants had given me nothing much more to do than to read those discovery documents, repeatedly, and get to know them fairly well. After I had finished the first morning's deposition, I had also realized that I probably knew those documents better than Greg did. He was carrying a caseload, perhaps, of a couple of dozen cases at any one time. I had certainly had more opportunity to spend time directly studying those estate-related documents than he had. I speculated that he relied on the documents his associate had picked out for his attention. Even feeling secure in that belief did not induce me to forget about having the gag order lifted. If it remained in place after the case was over, I could never write about Mama, as I had promised her I would.

Over the years after the gag order was in place, I started taking writing courses, online, from New York University. Among other things, completing innumerable writing exercises, a number of short stories, and the beginning of a science fiction novel. I always felt that my freedom of speech had been taken from me because I could not write what I had promised to write. However, I wanted to believe being prodded to practice writing, even on other subjects, would eventually help.

Oddly, these academic exercises made me feel young again, even though nothing I wrote for those courses has ever been published. Back in 1977, I had taken a single, omnibus course in publishing from NYU that later developed into their now-famous master's degree in publishing program. As general as it had been, this introductory class taught me enough to run the little publishing house that Arthur and I had owned in New York and to help him in his literary agency. I hoped these courses would ultimately be equally valuable. At least they kept me thinking. And writing. Having seen what happened to Mama when she stopped writing regularly, I would have done just about anything to avoid the same fate.

I continued to try to keep my mouth and my computer from getting me into trouble with the judge by isolating myself from social activities and concentrating on the wildlife in my backyard. I watched the animals learn new things. At the beginning, I put out organic apples. For some reason, the rabbits were designated by their backyard brethren to examine new things. The first day, a rabbit crossed the patio, looked carefully at the red apple from a safe distance, then hopped off. The second day, he came much closer. The third day, he tried to have sex with it. When it did not respond, he started nibbling at it. Only then did any of the other animals seem interested.

At the beginning, they came, in size order, to eat the fruit I put out for them. First the house wrens, then the larger birds. Mourning doves, generally, arrived as the last of the birds. Then squirrels, and finally rabbits. The order was invariable, until one day a dove and a squirrel sat on the back patio, at the same time, eating peaceably, side-by-side, different grapes in the same bunch. After that, pairs of animals sometimes arrived together, sharing a meal. Or was it a date? My roadrunner couple generally surveilled the others eating, from a safe distance, not bothering them at all. Geckos sunned themselves nearby, waiting for a stray ant or other insect to approach the banquet table. They kept the patio clear of insects.

All the critters loved grapes, above all, followed by soft-peel fruit. To keep them wild, I never wanted to provide their entire diet, so I never fed them seeds or salad, only treats. Strangely, I never saw any of the animals fighting over the food. And they generally removed rinds and bits of grapevine from the patio, cleaning it up nicely for me. Even after years of this, I have never had to hose animal waste off the patio; there simply has not been any there. Not even from the birds.

My furry and feathered acquaintances have always brought me tangible tokens of their thanks. Tiny matchbox cars, taken from heaven-knows-where, now dot my backyard. I have lost count of the whiffle-balls they have dumped by my back door, inside my fence, and in my driveway. Where did they get these? No young children lived in the near vicinity at the time.

Then, there were the peaches. I do not know which animal it is, but one of them drags peaches from under the big peach tree in the backyard, all the way to the other side of the house, just outside the door to my bedroom that opens to the backyard. Once, at the end of the season, I found a perfect, ripe peach that had clearly been moved carefully (so it did not get bruised). Whichever animal moved that one put it directly in the middle of the front of the door to the patio, where I had always put the grapes.

On March 1, 2017, we held the first deposition of Mama's former guardian at the office of the court reporter David liked to use, in a downtown office building, around a large conference table. Although she admitted to having held more than one securities and insurance license, which she had used as a financial planner at Winslow's original investment firm for almost nine years, she said she had let them lapse because investments did not interest her.

Some friends of mine told me that the *Albuquerque Journal* was going to run a town hall on the subject of guardianship on March 22, 2017. They said that they wanted to save me a seat. I said I could not be seen anywhere people were even discussing this issue, and all the more if politicians and journalists were going to be present. A family member/victim in another case called me the next day.

"A group of us went out afterwards, with some people from the *Journal*, and we were all discussing you!"

"How's that possible? I haven't spoken to a single reporter, the whole time."

"Well, they all know about you, particularly that man from the *Journal*. What's his name? Walz?"

"You're kidding! I've never met him. Never even spoken to him. How does he know so much about me?"

During the many months of journalists being interested in my story, and me trying hard to avoid them all, I was relaxing at home one Sunday. Someone rang my bell. I answered to see a slender, petite woman standing there. She looked a lot like pictures of Diane Dimond I had seen, but my visitor gave a different name.

In opening the door, I had forgotten to put on sunglasses, and had been temporarily almost blinded by the brilliant Albuquerque afternoon sun. My visitor kept wanting to show me something on a laptop computer screen on which, at that moment, I could only see glare. Flashing a nametag at me, she wanted me to believe that she was from the Census Bureau. However, it was not a census year. Then she flashed a "Homeland Security" badge, instantly putting me on notice that she was some sort of pretender. The census is run out of the Commerce Department, not Homeland Security.

"Do you have a problem with your eyes?"

"No. I got a lot of sun in them when I opened the door. Should have put on sunglasses first. I'll be fine in a while."

"Can I come in?"

"I'm sorry! I'm under a strict gag order. I can't let anyone in. If you come in and see anything at all and talk about it, I might go to jail. I just can't risk that."

She tried a couple of times more, unsuccessfully, to convince me to let her in, so she could look around, "for the government." When nothing she said worked, she eventually left, looking very dissatisfied.

For many months, I did my best to avoid publicity, as Judge Malott had commanded me to do. The more I hid, the more the press seemed to follow me around, like a Chihuahua, nipping at my heels.

We were at Dan Lewis' law firm, listening to the deposition of Doug Schulz, my expert witness on investments, on March 29, 2017, when a junior member of Lewis' firm came in, looking agitated, and whispered to one of the people on the defendants' side of the table. Present, that day, in addition to David, Doug, the court reporter and me, were a future expert witness for the defendants, three attorneys and the defendant; this additional junior practitioner was a new addition. He pointed, and the next person on the defendant's side of the table looked at his computer screen. This set of actions went down the line of people on the other side of the table—and very quickly, too. From my side of the table, it looked like a weird exercise in synchronized swimming, but on land instead of in water.

Suddenly, instead of continuing with the deposition, which had sometimes been a bit heated, not only Greg MacKenzie (who had been questioning our expert), but also everyone else on the other side of the conference table from us was staring, silently, at the screens of the laptops, perched in front each of them on the table. All except Mama's former guardian; she was staring at her cell phone. Without saying anything to us, they all turned pale, got up, and rushed out of the room, leaving Doug and me looking at each other, totally bewildered.

David took us outside, to a separate private room, to show us the new message that had just arrived on his cell phone: The *Journal* had notified all the attorneys involved in the case that it had filed a brief, requesting that Judge Malott lift the gag order in this case, in the interests of informing the public about what was going on in the guardianship industry in New Mexico. The defendant's side clearly was not as delighted as I was.

On March 31, 2017, the *Albuquerque Journal* ran a feature article about the estate's case against Mama's former guardian. As much, that is, as could be found in currently available public sources. Of course, Colleen Heild, the author of the piece, could not interview me because I was still gagged by Judge Malott. Somehow, she managed to get a photo of Mama and me together that I did not even have anymore.[464] Mama had gotten a copy of the DVD containing those formal photos of us that had been taken by my photographer friend, back in 2008, but they were missing after she died. After I moved, I could no longer find my copy.

The gist of the article was that the *Journal*, like me, wanted the case to be opened rather than gagged and sequestered. Again, I could not write in to the *Journal* to support their position. My own

---

464 https://www.abqjournal.com/979809/journal-seeks-to-open-guardian-mismanagement-lawsuit.html

earlier efforts (David's, really), in filing petitions to open the case up had already done that, however. As Colleen wrote, "What happened to her [Mama] and her assets during the nine years before her death in 2012 is mired in court-ordered secrecy that is opposed by her only child." So true.

By April 1, 2017, the New Mexico Supreme Court had announced that, in reaction to all the recent bad news about guardianship and conservatorship in New Mexico, it had set up a special commission to study the subject. That was a technical working group, primarily, concerned with rules, that issued its report on December 28, 2017.[465] Its conclusions, as might be expected, were those that most people expect from a government committee—it recommended the establishment of more new committees.

This followed the demise of the prior group that had recommended legislative reforms, some of which were enacted by the legislature in its January to March 2018 session; that first group disbanded on January 1, 2018. Twenty-two people applied for positions on this new "rules committee," but there were only eight slots. Gaelle McConnell, the guardianship attorney my ex-documentary partner had interviewed just prior to asking me to give her my house, was named to chair it. McConnell had also served on the prior commission.

Emily Darnell Nunez, whom by then I had known for about seven years, was the only family member of a ward appointed to that new rules committee. She, her sister Mary and her mother, Blair Darnell, had figured prominently in the prizewinning exposé articles on guardianship that the *Albuquerque Journal* had run the previous fall. Except for Emily and a court visitor, Mary Galvez, the other members were all attorneys. This situation seemed perfectly natural to most attorneys; regulatory language is notoriously prolix. To the families of victims, however, it seemed as if the foxes once again were being appointed to guard the henhouse.

For some reason, the Journal did not mention that Galvez also served as a guardian. Another known guardianship reform activist had applied but had not been named to serve in this group. Judge

---

465 See: *https://supremecourt.nmcourts.gov/uploads/files/AGSC%20Final%20Report.pdf* accessed June 25, 2020.

Shannon Bacon, also a critic of the status quo, was appointed. So was Ruth Pregenzer, who told the *Journal* that she was "no longer accepting new guardianship cases."[466] But of course she was not saying that she had reassigned all of her current ones.

By April, the Abruzzo Trust case had hit the headlines. The widower of the daughter of one of the wealthiest families in Albuquerque, the Abruzzo family who had developed the skiing on Sandia Peak and near Santa Fe, and after whose patriarch the Albuquerque Balloon Museum is named, wanted more money from the trust his wife had set up for him. According to legal papers posted on the internet, Kearney, the widower of Abruzzo's daughter, claimed that, under the terms of his wife's trust, he was owed 30 percent more money than he had been paid, over a considerable number of years.[467] He and his wife's brothers were joint trustees, but he was automatically outvoted as a trustee because his wife had had two brothers, both of whom she also had named as trustees. Had she wanted her brothers to control her husband? Or had she (mistakenly, as it turned out) thought the three of them would always agree on everything?

One of the major charges against Mr. Kearney, and the reason why hefty fines were levied on him, was that he had violated the gag order Judge Malott placed on him. Just as in the estate's case against Mama's former guardian, the side opposed to Kearney had requested one.

The *Journal* badly wanted to cover the details of this major local story about the Abruzzo family. However, Judge Malott, who had been sitting on that case as well, had declared everything about the case gagged. He had threatened to jail any of the members of the audience or any journalists who spoke about or published anything about what they might have heard in his courtroom.

Not only the *Albuquerque Journal* but also the New Mexico Foundation for Open Government took a position that the proceedings should be opened.[468] Judge Malott refused to lift the gag order

---

466 "Critics say insiders dominate committee working on guardianship reforms," Colleen Heild, *Albuquerque Journal*, April 1, 2018. Retrieved February 20, 2020 from: https://www.abqjournal.com/1153215/critics-say-insiders-dominate-committee-working-on-guardianship-reforms.html

467 IN RE KEARNEY, Case No. 17-12274-1, September 14, 2018. Accessed February 23, 2020 from: https://www.leagle.com/decision/inbco20180917529

468 "Judge's orders on privacy in Abruzzo trust trial defended," Katy Barnitz,

in that case, leading the newspaper to appeal this matter to the New Mexico Supreme Court. That process, however, took so much time that the case was long over before the State Supreme Court lifted the gag order. By then, however, the verdict was no longer news. This case did not get coverage in the *Journal* again until 2019.

On April 5, 2017, the Albuquerque Lawyers Club had held a meeting at which it announced that both Judge Malott and Greg MacKenzie, along with Ellen Leitzer (representing the Senior Citizens' Law Office), would be speaking on a panel about guardianship. A timely subject, given all the recent press. However, the title of the panel discussion, "The Truth Underlying the Reporting on Guardianships/Conservatorships in New Mexico," suggested that some debunking might also be on the agenda.

It was. Someone recorded the proceedings. I heard that recording. Greg MacKenzie disclosed, during the discussion, that the panel had had an emotional teleconference, the night before this meeting, talking about the subject. From a legal point of view, this raised the potential issue of *ex parte* communications between the attorney for the defendants and Judge Malott. The entire thrust of the panel's comments went to how unfair the reporting had been to upstanding, concerned guardians and conservators. And to their honorable attorneys.

I had then heard Judge Malott on the radio, most recently on March 22, 2017, stating that he thought all medical and financial records of a ward should be kept secret. By then, I was also familiar with how Greg MacKenzie sounded when he spoke. The purpose of this panel was to criticize and decry the recent press attention to the abuses some commercial guardians (even non-profit guardians) had visited on their wards, particularly in New Mexico. The panelists, generally, ended up calling family members unjustified, and their criticism unwarranted, unfair and skewed.

Everyone on the panel seemed to agree that family members would not be sitting in a guardianship hearing if the family were not dysfunctional, and it was not the court's job to fix dysfunctional families.[469] Judge Malott, sitting there, although he said he was

---
Albuquerque Journal, April 28, 2017. Accessed February 20, 2020 from: https://www.abqjournal.com/994810/judges-privacy-orders-defended.html
469   This ignores the fact that even 100 percent-functional families (do any truly

not going to comment on any specific case, seemed to concur in the negative opinions of families expressed by the other panelists.

The ironic nature of the guardianship profession's sanctimonious stance shows in the fact that, only a few weeks before her first federal indictment on multiple criminal charges, Susan Harris, who headed the now-defunct Ayudando Guardians, appeared at a meeting of the state commission discussing guardianship reform. She accompanied her business partner, Sharon Moore, who on that day excoriated the family members of wards, accusing them of monstrous ingratitude for what the generous-spirited guardians and conservators were doing for their families. Harris and Moore were both indicted in July; a federal grand jury added new charges in December 2017. "She was the picture of Charity," charged yet another new complaint, filed by the U.S. Attorney in Albuquerque in January 2020.[470] She "deceived almost everyone around her," he continued.

During the panel discussion on April 5, 2017, each participant spoke. Then they all fielded questions from the audience. Greg MacKenzie, the chair, spoke first. The media had misunderstood the entire Darnell case, he asserted. Multiple *Albuquerque Journal* articles had needlessly raised strong public indignation against what had happened to that family. To him, it had seemed a routine case. He contended that the facts about the family reported in the press and the statements made about financial actions were wrong. No one on the panel represented the other side of the issue. Apparently, no one representing that side of that case was present. Perhaps no one on the other side of the argument even knew about this event.

Then Judge Malott spoke. He contended that the courts could not possibly be held responsible for monitoring a guardian's performance. Did the public want the court system to hire yet more experts to monitor the expert guardians? If so, the courts would need much more money. He riffed on one of his major March

---

exist in a world filled with fallible humans?) may see their members' relationships strained and distorted when one person in the group becomes irrational. I suspect that, if everyone were rational at all times, no one would need a court of any sort in the first place—not just a probate court, any court.

470 "Ayudando founder to face day of reckoning in court," Colleen Heild, Albuquerque Journal, January 12, 2020. Accessed February 19, 2020 from: *https://www.abqjournal.com/1409024/ayudando-founder-to-face-day-of-reckoning-in-court.html*

themes, also, while responding to a timidly-asked question from the audience about whether some complaints might, perhaps, be justified. He averred that anyone who complains about the court's actions (or the guardian's or conservator's actions) is wrong.

Family members who complain, he seemed to be telling the assembled attorneys, are more in the wrong than most other people who complain because they are almost certainly simply mercenary. Worse, they are sore losers. (What about the many court decisions that go up to appeals court[471] or state supreme court[472] ?)—or even federal district court or ultimately the United States Supreme Court—because one of the parties disagrees with a judge's decision? More than 48,000 arguments found their way into federal appeals court during 2020.[473] A district court judge's original decision might be overturned there, too.[474] Are all those litigants simply sore losers? In guardianship cases, he seemed to be saying, there should be no right to appeal. District civil court judges hear all sorts of civil cases. Are district court judges infallible only when they are hearing guardianship cases?)

To me, Judge Malott still did not sound particularly friendly to the families of wards. After discovering this, David felt obliged to ask Judge Malott to recuse himself from our case, since he mentioned no redeeming features of family members, only their most negative aspects, and the others on the panel argued strongly against the *Albuquerque Journal* articles on guardianship. Anyone unacquainted with the inner workings of the system might have listened to the panel discussion and concluded that the primary problem was that the courts needed more money to hire more people and that the families of wards should be grateful to the court for its efforts on their behalf.

---

471 The federal government, unlike Judge Malott, considers district court—where guardianship cases are heard in New Mexico—as the lowest rung of the state justice system and its rulings subject to appeal. See: https://www.uscourts.gov/about-federal-courts/court-role-and-structure/comparing-federal-state-courts Accessed October 12, 2021

472 Ibid.

473 2020 End of Year Report on the Federal Judiciary, p. 5. *https://www.supremecourt.gov/publicinfo/year-end/2020year-endreport.pdf,* Accessed October 12, 2021.

474 According to a recent article in *SearchLight New Mexico,* the entire purpose of New Mexico's Appeals Court is to catch "mistakes made by lower courts" See: *https://nmpoliticalreport.com/2020/02/24/full-court-pressed-new-mexico-court-of-appeals-is-swamped-with-backlogged-cases-leaving-hundreds-in-limbo/*

David's argument to the court featured calmer, more reasoned general statements about the appearance of impropriety presented by the judge's closeness to the attorney for Mama's former guardian. This included prior information that Greg MacKenzie seemed to have had private communications with the judge that were directly related to this case, and earlier ethics pronouncements within the legal profession about the appearance of rectitude being very important if a jurist wants to be perceived as impartial.

The *Albuquerque Journal* appeared to have been watching the case docket. On May 15, the court clerk posted notice that we had filed a motion to recuse the judge. On May 22, Colleen Heild published a front-page story on the subject.[475]

On June 11, Colleen Heild named Paul Donisthorpe's Desert States Life Management as having made hundreds of thousands of dollars in trust funds intended for a victim of a traumatic brain injury disappear. Generally, the courts appoint professional conservators in cases where someone receives a court settlement, particularly if the family is not accustomed to handling large sums of money. This ward had been a court-mandated client of the firm. Donisthorpe's company was a non-profit conservatorship organization. We were then halfway through 2017. Donisthorpe had been running Desert States since 2006, but had not been audited since 2008. This exposé started a new inquiry, into his firm and all the money it was supposed to have been managing. It later turned out that Donisthorpe was spending millions of dollars of his wards' money on ranches and other luxuries for himself.

I felt scorched by the emotional sparks in the air at Judge Malott's recusal hearing, on June 26, 2017:

> THE COURT: We are convened in this hearing today on plaintiff's motion for my recusal...I have read the material over three times, possibly four...I would appreciate if you don't read your briefs back to me...[476]

---

475 "Plaintiff in guardian case wants the judge to step aside," Colleen Heild, *Albuquerque Journal*, May 22, 2017, pp. A-1, A-3.
476 Hearing, June 26, 2017, T-3, ll.19-25

MR. GARCIA: The panel...discussion [held on April 5] appears...as an exercise in damage control for the commercial guardianship industry by members of the panel, except for Your Honor...although I would submit that you are a customer of the conservatorship/guardianship industry in this court, and the judges are the ones that have provided much of the business of the commercial guardian companies...[477]This is the first time I've filed a motion to recuse a judge in 30 years of practice...I read the Code of Judicial Conduct over many times...This is awkward for me to stand here.

THE COURT: And I understand.[478]

MR. GARCIA: The inherent problems with the panel are enhanced by prior ex parte communications in this case...The Court did grant my motion regarding prohibiting ex parte communications in this case; entered an order to that effect addressing that [issue]...the order granted the relief requested...[479]all of these communications [a prior incident in 2014, the panel, the subject-matter of the panel, and the fact that one major defendant in this case is the same as in the Darnell case] would reasonably create a perception that Mr. MacKenzie or the defendants are in a position to influence the court.[480]

THE COURT: So far you haven't come up with a single incident showing...that I made any comment whatsoever about this case or as to any subject related to this case.[481]...I have a constitutional obligation to stay on cases to which I'm assigned unless it is shown by

---

477 Hearing, June 26, 2017, TR-6, ll. 12-25
478 Ibid, TR-8, ll. 7-22
479 Ibid, TR-9, ll. 9-22
480 Ibid, TR-11, ll. 18-25.
481 Ibid, ll. 22-25.

reasonable evidence that I have some trouble being impartial...⁴⁸²

THE COURT: So if I, for example, appeared on a panel of civil procedure and I opined, for example, that I think the most recent revisions to Rule 93, the contempt [of court] rule, are counterproductive, would I then be prohibited from ever hearing a contempt case...?⁴⁸³

MR. GARCIA:...The panel discussion—the panelists were one-sided industry advocates, industry lobbyists. You're there on a panel with a bunch of industry lobbyists refuting articles that the industry hates. And the composition of the audience does not make a difference...It's a one-sided panel discussion or discussion that the judge is being subjected to.⁴⁸⁴

THE COURT: Anything else you want to tell me, Mr. Garcia?⁴⁸⁵

MR. GARCIA:...During that presentation [a panel discussion on March 22], Your Honor stated that you believe medical and financial records should be sequestered from the public...The defendants in the guardianship industry are committed to maintaining secrecy...in all these guardianship proceedings, including the one involved [here]...That isn't the way it is in any other case that I'm aware of, including contested probate cases...⁴⁸⁶ The law [on the subject of confidentiality of records] only pertains to the court's own records...And the court, in entering the confidentiality order [in this case] even went beyond the

---

482   Ibid, TR-13, ll. 22-25.
483   Ibid, TR-13, ll. 4-9.
484   Ibid, TR-15-16, ll. 18-24; 11. 2-3.
485   Ibid, TR-19, ll.21-22.
486   Ibid, TR-20, ll. 3-25.

relief requested and made everything in the case confidential...What the judge may or may not have said [on April 5] is not an issue. It's the fact that the judge was subjected to a one-sided panel. [487]...if the judge is going to decide to not recuse himself, I would ask for an evidentiary hearing...The basic issue is whether a reasonable person would think that the judge lacks impartiality when he sat with my opposing counsel and parties aligned with the industry represented by my opposing counsel, discussing articles that pertain to the defendant in this case, pertain to issues in this case...if it comes down to an evidentiary hearing, we'll find out what was discussed there...[488]

Greg MacKenzie, sitting at the defendants' table that morning, remained silent throughout. Another attorney, present on behalf of one of the defendants' insurance companies, said he had no comment. Dan Lewis, however, rose to his feet to object to our motion recusing the judge:

MR LEWIS: What do we have in this case? The plaintiff wants to suggest that by the mere title of the panel discussion that there must have been...something that went on there...that would put the court in a place that would create a perception of a lack of impartiality...There was not even a discussion [on that panel] of something indirectly that was about this case. There's no reason for the court to recuse, as suggested by the plaintiff, and we ask that the motion be denied. So, while they have no burden to bring forth witnesses to an evidentiary hearing, they have got to at least present to the court and say, "Your Honor, we understand, we have an affidavit. (T)here is no reasonable appearance of a lack of impartiality in this case..."

---

487 Ibid, TR-32, ll.12-24.
488 Ibid, TR-33, ll.6-20

To me, all of Judge Malott's statements about family members (both in March and in April) sounded extremely critical. I have since heard now-retired Judge Malott speak on the radio multiple times. Whenever the subject of guardianship arises, I always hear him criticizing the families of wards for thinking badly of the system. In the now three years since that hearing, I have never heard him say a single good word about any family member of any ward under commercial guardianship.

Charles R. Peifer, the *Albuquerque Journal's* attorney, represented the newspaper at the hearing to recuse Judge Malott. Peifer paled and looked as if he might be about to faint when Judge Malott alluded to the contempt of court rule, even though this remark was aimed at David, not at him. The *Journal* did not really attend in order to argue actively against Judge Malott continuing to try our case. This was our motion. They had filed as an "intervener" in our case, which automatically made them entitled both to notice of any hearings and the right to speak, should they choose to do so.

We were going to be minimally active, also, when their motion to ungag the case went before the judge. However, David had finally managed to argue a good part of his thinking on the subject of confidentiality of records during this hearing, the words he had never had the opportunity to say, back in 2014 to the judge because Judge Malott had issued the gag order without ever scheduling a hearing on the defendants' motion. Our request for the opening of the records was a lot more comprehensive than the Journal's, which I suspect made the *Journal's* job that much easier at the next hearing.

A motion like this one, to recuse a judge, and to ask for a hearing on the matter, is very rare. It is almost unheard of that a judge will refuse to resign if someone involved in a case perceives him to lack impartiality. It is even stranger, to me, that a jurist would sit as the judge on a hearing, in open court, regarding a motion to recuse himself. For the sake of impartiality in the decision-making process, would it not be natural to hand the final decision-making authority over to some neutral third party? The desire to be perceived as impartial, and thereby keep a judge's reputation pristine is, for most jurists, more important than maintaining control of a particular case. But, apparently, not this time.

A friend of mine had attended that recusal hearing. She later told me that she had been sitting in the audience (the place was jammed, that day, with spectators) among a dozen or more law students whose professor at UNM had sent them over to observe. Sitting here, now, I still wonder why the courtroom was open to spectators on this then-sequestered case, but it was. No direct information about Mama made its way into anyone's argument, however, which might have been a factor in Judge Malott not clearing the courtroom.

On the way out of the hearing room, most people were staring at their shoes, afraid to look anyone else in the eyes. I heard, from someone else who had attended, that this was what court observers did in banana republics. They found themselves ashamed, and unable to look each other in the eyes after such a hearing.

Ultimately, Judge Malott said he was staying on the case. He officially denied our motion for recusal as of July 10. "Malott ruled that attorneys for Leonie Rosenstiel presented no evidence to show that he couldn't act impartially in the case," Colleen Heild wrote on June 29.[489] Unfortunately, as I understood things, we were not supposed to be required to prove that this judge—or any judge, for that matter—could not be impartial, only that he appeared to have expressed opinions in public, while the case was in progress, that made him seem partial to one side rather than the other.

We supported the *Albuquerque Journal's* motion to unseal that was scheduled to be heard on July 7, 2017, but it represented only a small part of what we had requested, back in 2014, and what I needed from the court if I planned to keep my promise to Mama. In some limited ways, they were also supporting our own motions to unseal material from years past. I still believed that, as Mama's sole heir, I had the right to decide whether I supported making this information public; I did. Through David, I gave the *Albuquerque Journal* a statement to that effect, to be entered into the court record, so that Judge Malott would have proof that I did not object

---

489 "Judge in guardianship case denies bias claims," Colleen Heild, *Albuquerque Journal*, June 29, 2017, p. C-17.

to what the *Journal* was trying to do. That hearing was the *Journal's* show. James attended, to give further proof of our agreement, but not to argue the matter. David was busy elsewhere; I could not go either.

At the hearing, Judge Malott had made a positive comment about Ellen Leitzer, whom Lewis also referred to at the June hearing, as only being a sometime guardian ad litem. (However, there is plenty of evidence that she was also a guardian herself.) Leitzer, who had also been on the April panel with Malott, garnered the judge's praise because she worked for a non-profit organization. This suggestion that workers for non-profits are somehow special resounded in my memory when a federal grand jury indicted Susan Harris and her partner on July 17, 2017, on 28 criminal charges. Over the years, her non-profit organization had served as guardian for hundreds of court-mandated wards.[490] She and her partner had made off with millions of dollars of their money.

As I was seated in Judge Malott's courtroom that June day, it was the first time since the suit was filed, back in 2013, that he had actually held a hearing in this case. His contention about Ellen Leitzer immediately recalled to my mind that Al Capone had established a huge soup kitchen during the Great Depression. It has been said that during those years, Capone did more for starving Chicagoans than the state.[491] Did Capone's generosity in feeding his compatriots mean that he was not a major gangster?

Not at all. No more than the façade of kindness that Susan Harris projected and the "injured dignity" demeanor she and her partner Sharon Moore presented at the May meeting of the New Mexico Supreme Court's Guardianship Panel meant that they were not stealing money from their wards to pay their own personal bills. Sharon Moore had spoken in defense of the rectitude of the guardianship community at that hearing, while Harris approvingly looked on, a point Colleen Heild made handily in her front-page

---

490 "Fraud charges leveled on state guardianship firm," Susan Montoya Bryan, *Santa Fe New Mexican*, July 20, 2017, p. A-8.
491 "During the Great Depression, Al Capone created one of the first "Soup Kitchens" for the unemployed," by Ian Harvey, October 26, 2016. Accessed February 19, 2020 from: *https://www.thevintagenews.com/2016/10/26/during-the-great-depression-al-capone-created-one-of-the-first-soup-kitchens-for-the-unemployed/*

article, on July 26, less than a week after the pair had been arrested by federal authorities.[492]

By then, I had seen plenty of evidence that Mama's commercial guardian, too, often participated in charitable causes, particularly those related to dementia victims. But that did not necessarily mean that she treated her clients or their family members with equal charity.

What better cover is there, after all, for malfeasance, than to have a bright and shiny local reputation for kindness and charity? Perhaps at times these individuals do want to help others. If so, I am glad they have a charitable impulse to balance the other impulses that might not be so nice. How many people have lived this sort of double life?

After all, in his native Colombia, drug kingpin Pablo Escobar built an entire neighborhood to house the poor.[493]

David and Mama's former guardian had two go-arounds about her business interests, one at her March deposition, the other at her May deposition. The discussion in March seemed clearer to me:

Q: So, currently, the only business you have an ownership interest in is [the guardianship firm]?
A: No.
Q: Oh. What businesses now do you have an ownership interest in?
A: I have a second LLC called the Care Management Group of New Mexico.
Q: And what does that LLC do?
A: Provides fee-for-service case management for families and financial management.
Q: Does it do the same sort of work as [the guardianship firm]?
A: Similar.
Q: And how many employees does Case Management Group— or, excuse me, Care Management Group of New Mexico currently employ?

---
492 "Ayudando exec testified for industry before arrest," Colleen Heild, *Albuquerque Journal*, August 26, 2017, pp. A-1, A-3.
493 "Incredible Charity Work Done By...Wait, Organized Crime?" Modern Rogue, September 12, 2018. Accessed February 19, 2020 at: *https://www.themodernrogue.com/articles/2018/9/11/incredible-charity-work-done-by-wait-organized-crime*

A: None

Q: None? Are you the only principal of Care Management Group?

A: Actually, Care Management Group is an LLC, it's owned by a general partnership.

Q: General partnership. And who are the partners?

A: I am the general partner.

Q: Are there limited partners?

A: Yes.

Q: And who are they?

A: Myself and my daughter, through a grantor trust.[494]

By the time of her April deposition, her answers to some of David's questions seemed a lot cloudier:

Q: Are you a trustee or co-trustee on any trust?

A: No, not that I'm aware of.

Q: Okay. That's fair. The reason I'm asking is it was mentioned at the last deposition—you had mentioned a trust involved with your daughter, I think.

A: Oh. I think it's a—I didn't even know I had one until I did my taxes. So it's a grantor trust, and for some reason, it may not require a trust document. It's just part of an ownership structure. You have to talk to my lawyer. I—

Q: Okay. And did you say there were no trust documents, or you didn't know whether it had to have a trust document?

A: Right. I don't know whether it's required. I think it might have been due to her age at the time, and—

Q: Do you know if there are trust documents?

A: I've called and asked, and I've not gotten a return call.

Q: Who was the grantor?

A: Me.

Q: Okay. And what—what generally is in this trust?

A: I think it's a 10 percent limited partnership interest.

Q: Okay. In what partnership?

---

494 Nancy Oriola, Deposition, March 1, 2017, pp. 36, l.7-37, l.7

A: The Care Management Group of America.
Q: What's the Care Management Group of America?
A: It's a partnership.
Q: And who are the partners?
A: Myself and my daughter under a grant or a trust.[495]

All this "confusion" came into the discussion, I suspect for this reason:

Q: And let your attorney object, but what was the—for 2016, what was the gross revenue of Care Management Services [the company that was the partnership]?
MR. LEWIS: I will object to that...
Q: (BY MR. GARCIA) Do you have any business—yourself, have any business relationships outside of New Mexico, particularly in
Nevada?
A: I think the partnerships are registered in Nevada.[496]

By then, it was spring. The case was already set to go to trial on October 23, almost the next day, from a legal point of view. As I was sitting, listening to the commercial conservator's depositions, I first started to think that, if possible, I should try to settle the case. I thought about Dickens' *Bleak House*. A case could drag on almost forever and destroy everyone involved.

There are many horror stories, too, of people who get big money awards, afterwards spending the rest of their lives, first trying to find the money and then attempting to extract it from wherever the other person put it. Often you cannot even spend enough money to track down the money you are owed. The federal government has these sorts of search capabilities and personnel who know how to use them; most of the rest of us do not.

If I involved myself in the sort of exercise that following the money required, it might well take the rest of my time on earth. I did not want to be emotionally tied to the head of the guardianship firm. I had promised Mama some sort of redress, but being

---
[495] Nancy Oriola, Deposition, May 9, 2017, pp. 59, l. 1-60, l.7
[496] Nancy Oriola, Deposition, May 9, 2017, p. 63, l. 24-p. 64, l. 11.

"still standing," which was another of her major requirements, also made it necessary that my fortunes would not forever be connected to those of her former guardian. At some point—hopefully in the near future—I had to be free to write about Mama and what happened to her.

Perhaps Dan Lewis and Greg MacKenzie and Judge Malott did not think that the comments he had made about the family members of wards were negative. I did. Particularly so because they never seemed to be balanced by anything positive that the wards' families might have done in trying to help or protect their loved ones. This strongly suggested to me that he might not have wanted to believe that he had a negative bias against me, but that he did, in fact, have an unacknowledged prejudice against me simply because I was the daughter of a ward. I had never met Judge Malott, of course, and so he would primarily have relied on what people he trusted (in this case, Mama's commercial guardian and her attorneys) said about me.

Should this matter go to trial, it was beginning to seem increasingly likely that I would have to appeal the verdict. Just getting this far had taken more than four years after Mama died. Spending another four or five years in court, during an appeal, seemed more like a punishment, to me, than an opportunity to redress grievances.

Even if an appeal went in my favor, what if the insurance companies involved, who arguably had deeper pockets than I ever would, decided to appeal the case again? People who are old enough to have relatives under guardianship as a result of dementia are not all that young themselves. How old would I be by the time all appeals had actually been exhausted? I kept reminding myself that I had promised Mama that I would "remain standing" to tell the story. I had not written anything yet, fearing it would be subpoenaed during discovery. What if I did not even start to write for another five or ten years?

By the time I started seriously considering these questions, we were in the process of scheduling the required pre-trial mediation session with James A. Hall, a retired judge from Santa Fe. The proliferation of legal papers scared me. These, of course, were all in addition to the tens of thousands of pages of documents unearthed during discovery. At one point during the spring of 2017, David had seven different motions due on the same day. Rumor has it that he slept on the couch in his office for a week, making sure that he finished and filed them all on time. He would call me, periodically, when he wanted to take a breather from this work.

Originally, we were slated to have our mediation session in the case on July 5, but with the *Albuquerque Journal's* hearing scheduled for July 7, that date had to be postponed.

Because the primary thrust for making the material public came, this time, from the *Journal*, their appearance, that day, to speak in front of Judge Malott, was essentially their hearing. As I have said, James represented our side, to show our support for their action, and to reaffirm, to the judge, that we had no objection to what they were trying to do. As it turned out, Judge Malott asked James whether the current state of the gag order would affect our preparation for trial. James said it would, particularly for lay witnesses, who would not be allowed to see any exhibits, should it remain in force.

The *Journal* used several arguments David had previously made and some of its own that most people would be familiar with, involving the public's right to know and my own lack of objection to the release of this information, because I would be the only person holding whatever right to privacy remained. What surprised me was Greg MacKenzie's statement:

> MR. MACKENZIE: (I)f for some reason the *Journal* in their motion has caused the court to reflect on that [motion to seal the documents] and change its mind, our position is if the court is going to release anything, it should release all of it...[497]

Judge Malott went even further in his order in opening up the case than the *Journal* had requested. He did what Greg MacKenzie seems to have asked, which was exactly what David had originally requested. The judge went back and, finally, granted the motion we had initially made, back in 2014, to open up the case.

---

497 Hearing, July 5, 2017, TR-29, ll.11-15.

Perhaps I am the only family member of a ward who has ever been declared "competent" to make a decision by the judge in a case that had any relation to guardianship. Judge Malott declared that I was, indeed, competent to decide to release information relating to Mama and me. At that point, I had already attained the most important of my major goals, the right to speak my mind again, but a little financial redress would also be welcome. After all, As Mama's personal representative, I had spent $146,000 on Sam Baca's "work" alone.

The *Journal* seemed to have been waiting, eagerly, for Judge Malott to release the documents in this case. Judge Malott lifted the gag order on July 10, 2017. On July 23, 2017, Colleen Heild had already published a front-page feature article on the subject, in which she gave a quick summary of our initial complaint. At the end, she also interviewed Mama's former commercial guardian.

By the time we got to August, and of course the mediation, motions had been flying like arrows. The people on the other side started accusing each other of improprieties, too. At least, so it seemed to me. An attorney from another state, connected to one of the defendants' insurance companies asked for leave to enter the case on behalf of the defendant. One of the insurance companies had not been vigilant enough in its defense of her, the defendant claimed.

David, James and I arrived at the boxy, severe New Mexico Bar building, on the morning of Monday, August 7, 2017. Thinking things over, in preparation, I had decided that, no matter what else happened, I had had this particular legal scene for as long as I had been able to stand it. The case, I had already decided, would end on that day. Meanwhile, the defendants had been threatening to make another grab at my personal correspondence and personal financial records.

David, James and I had been preparing, intensively, for this day's mediation with Judge Hall and had not taken time off to read the Sunday papers. One of the few things about this case that everyone involved agreed to do was to keep secret the mediation proceedings themselves and the specifics of any settlement.

We had just arrived when the opposing attorneys and the

defendant entered the lobby, looking unnaturally glum. Something had changed. Normally, they were almost ebullient, as well as dismissive of everyone on our side. Before August 7, 2017, it had seemed as if great actors were arriving, onstage, and demanding an ovation. However, the defendant's side had an even more dour demeanor as we saw them return from lunch. How odd. We all noticed it.

The mediation that had lasted almost to the end of the day now successfully concluded, all of us left, exhausted. The case was over at last. (At least we had agreed and now the final papers had to be drawn up and signed.)

Only then did anyone on my side read a Sunday paper. As part of her series, "Who Guards the Guardians," Colleen Heild had written another front-page feature article, "Reforms starting for guardianship system," describing the early attempts of Shannon Bacon and then-Chief Judge Nan Nash to require conservators to post bond when managing assets over $30,000. Bacon also requested that then-State Auditor Tim Keller conduct audits of all commercial guardians who had received any state funds. Including fiscal year 2018, then still in progress, Mama's commercial guardian's firm had received $352,029.95 from the New Mexico Disabilities Planning Council since 2010. That amount of state money might well be large enough to interest the State Auditor in tracking where the state's money went.[498]

Another non-profit firm was currently under extreme scrutiny by both the FBI and the New Mexico Attorney General's Office, Heild reported. This time, Paul Donisthorpe's Desert States Life Management, a company entirely dedicated to conservatorship and trusteeship, was the target. Primarily it administered the trusts of poor clients who had received legal settlements. Between the $4 million Susan Harris and her firm had been accused with taking and the $4 million Donisthorpe's firm was now being accused of taking, the total that professionals in the guardianship industry had been accused of stealing had now climbed to $8 million taken from defenseless wards, and possibly that amount would climb higher. State and federal authorities had just informed the public

---

[498] Retrieved on February 22, 2020 from: *https://ssp2.sunshineportalnm.com/#*

that they believed that, in recent years, at least $8 million had been stolen from some of the state's most vulnerable citizens.[499] While we were making our point in the negotiating room, Colleen Heild and the *Journal* had been making it in the press.

One of the defendants' strongly argued positions had always been that court-appointed conservators are, by nature, virtuous. Public recognition of numerous criminal infractions by two of the most prominent guardianship and conservatorship firms in the state would have made it easier for our side to argue, in court, if the case ever got to court, that guardians and conservators should not always be presumed to be virtuous. Perhaps the defendants had been just as motivated to settle, that day, as I was. The *Journal's* timing could not have been better (from my point of view, at least).

I hid out until after the final agreement was signed. I did not speak to anyone. Because the *Journal* contacted David asking for comment, I gave a written statement. I wrote Colleen Heild that now that the case was over, I planned to go on with my life.

One thing I had long wanted to do was provide a road map for others to get to the stage I was at now—released from the onerous silence imposed by a gag order that lasts forever. Had Judge Malott not lifted it, mine would quickly have become a federal case. Even with the pre-emption doctrines in place, there are still some legal ways to accomplish this.

New Mexico, I believed, needed to rid itself of the court system's imposition of this infernal secrecy on the subject of guardianship. This put me at odds with Kelly Smoot Garrett, a Texas-based writer who had declared herself the leader of a group consisting of family members of wards. Lift the secrecy, I argued, and most of the other abuses will naturally vanish. Having been through Mama's guardianship case, and then the just-settled case, I had become convinced that light, and not increasing numbers of laws and regulations and committees, provided the best disinfectant. People would not dare act, in public, the way they acted when they knew no one was looking and, as a result, they believed that no one would ever find out what they were doing.

---

[499] "Reforms starting for guardianship system," Colleen Heild, *Albuquerque Journal*, August 6, 2017, pp. A-1-A-2.

Although I would not say that my case was the only catalyst for the changes that were about to take place in New Mexico, it was certainly a public demonstration of the evils of secrecy in the courts. Added to the exposé articles over the months since the fall of 2016, recognition of a terrible situation had finally inched New Mexico toward reform.

For loved ones of wards or former or deceased wards who want to get gag orders lifted, I hope that the legal papers in the estate's case against Mama's former guardian can now provide guidance or even blueprints.

Back in 2013, when New Mexico's version of the Florida Baker Act passed the legislature, it offered miscreants more chances to guardianize elders. I hope that, if competency hearings can be held in the open, tests can be performed on the spot to determine whether someone has been drugged, and so prevent any railroading of hapless seniors.

As a result of the 2017 New Mexico Supreme Court Commission's actions, guardians and conservators now must file detailed reports, on time. (They were always supposed to do so, but, as in Mama's case, often that did not often happen.) Commercial guardians handling over $30,000 for a ward theoretically now must post bond (although I see from the dockets that this requirement is still often waived, and the money for the bond probably comes from the ward's funds anyway).

By 2019, the New Mexico Legislature had enacted SB 395, sponsored by Sens. Damon Ely and James P. White. (Ely had, for a time, been involved in the Darnell case.) Professional guardians and conservators had to have certification. (My mother's guardian had been certified as a "National Master Guardian," and for years before that, as a "Master Guardian," so I am not sure this is the best answer, but they are trying.)

Almost as if my case had been a blueprint, a guardian is now forbidden to refuse visitation to a family member of a ward for more than a week without an evidentiary hearing. (Am I the only one to worry that the testimony of health aides, whose livelihoods depend on the good grace of the guardians, might be influenced by the guardian's interests?) Finally, there is a mechanism that allows family members to communicate directly with the judge, to lodge grievances, without being considered to be acting in an ex parte manner. Hearings may be held in open court (but they still are not required to be). The only possibility for trouble is that a judge can decide to exclude some people and include others within the group that receives information about a ward.

The only absolute requirements are the most important from my point of view. These cannot be legislated. What are they? The intelligence, compassion and good faith of the judge and the honesty of the attorneys, guardians, conservators, GALs, court visitors and medical professionals.

On the negative side of the ledger, during the 2020 session of the New Mexico legislature, I saw the beginning of an initiative to bring "supported decision making" into the guardianship discussion. Having had extensive experience with "experts" deciding what Mama would want after knowing her not at all, I would seriously question the wisdom of going further with this idea. Fortunately, HM 23 died without a vote in the House. But I am afraid that it will be back. It sounds lovely, but in practice, I have seen it work to harm or upset the ward. It might work, temporarily, for a dementia patient whose condition is worsening, but only if the ward undergoes frequent re-tests, to see whether the "support" has become "control" due to the ward's mental decline. Certainly, those whose condition is expected to remain stable for years or who might recover need to be treated differently.

I have now spent almost three years writing this manuscript so that I can keep my promise to Mama. With the help of a few good attorneys I believe are on the side of the angels, and with the assistance of some honorable and honest jurists, we can make more progress.

Knowing more of the truth has set me free. Free of the belief that all government functionaries and everyone they appoint are saintly. Free of the fear of not living up to the ghostly expectations of perfect forebears. Free of the responsibility to be perfect so that I can emulate Mama's perfection. Free of believing that most of my friends are really my friends. Because so few really are.

In February of 2020, news of the COVID-19 pandemic began to spread in the States. David began to call more frequently, sometimes several times a day. Within a few weeks, we were both under isolation conditions caused by the COVID-19 pandemic. As an attorney, his was considered an "essential" profession. Most of his face-to-face meetings were now teleconferences. Even the court had begun to hold telephonic hearings. Since I was in a high-risk group, we had not had lunch or dinner together for quite a few weeks.

Now I was providing more support to him, it seemed, than the other way around. By late March, I got the feeling that he had not been shopping for months. I had tried to warn him about the lines and separation demarcations if he wanted to go shopping.

"I went to two supermarkets, but both of them had lines around the block. And those yellow lines separating people! Couldn't stand it. Had to leave."

"I have some extra food."

"You know I don't believe in this COVID stuff, but I'd never forgive myself if it really existed, and I gave it to you."

I suspect that he ate after that only what he could pick up from the takeout window of a restaurant or have delivered. He hit the same wall, looking for an open barber.

"Do you know an open hair place?"

"Won't be any till the governor allows them to open."

"Damn! 'Scuse me."

"Don't worry. I want a haircut too. Don't wanna look at myself in the mirror in the morning anymore. Even worse if I tried it myself."

The first week in April, David asked, "How did you manage, during the gag order?"

"You mean, not seeing people, not speaking to them?"

"Yeah!"

"Well, I had you. I could talk to you. We could go have coffee. Or lunch. Or dinner. That fixed things for me."

By then it was clear that COVID-19 was no joke.

"Do you mind if I call you more?"

"Call anytime. Always great talking to you. You know, I'm pretty much staying in these days..."

We both chuckled.

"And you're always welcome to come over, too. Wouldn't be too many people."

"I want to, but I can't. Damn COVID! Can't have you sick."

On April 6, 2020, David called me. We spent quite a bit of time on the phone.

"What about pumping gas? You use wipes for afterward?"

"Nope. The old exam gloves I brought home when I closed my acupuncture office, back in 2012. Still have some boxes of 'em."

"Should have known."

"Thanks for asking."

David, it turned out, had a long list of things he wanted me to make sure I did to protect myself. Almost like a pilot's pre-flight checklist. He made a couple of jokes about his anxiety over these details. Probably the result of not sleeping recently. "No problem. Just get some rest."

"Call you tomorrow morning?"

"Looking forward to it!"

As the COVID-19 pandemic progressed, David had sounded more and more pressured. Some of his emails conveyed this same feeling. On the phone, there was just something different about his voice.

As often happens when multiple people experience a traumatic event, different people experience it differently, emphasize different aspects of it, then color it with details from their own mind that seem congruent with their real or imagined relationship to the deceased. Sometimes the story varies from one telling to the next, even with the same witness. This is why eyewitness testimony is often suspect in court and must be verified.

I did not hear from David in the morning, but I did get an email from him at 1:53 PM. By mid-afternoon on April 7, 2020, I already knew, instinctively, that something was very wrong. The first story I heard was not until Saturday morning. Walter, the attorney who owned the building where David had his office, returned my voicemail to tell me that David had had a massive coronary at about 2 PM Tuesday. (David had always told me that he expected to die at his desk, over a weekend, and they would find him on Monday. He came close, but the day he died was a Tuesday.)

No one who worked in the same building with David, and who had seen him that day, had noticed anything unusual about him, even a few minutes prior to his coronary. All the time I had known him, he had always been pale, just under six feet tall, and heavy. None of that had changed.

David A. Garcia

Walter told me that the attorney who had an office across the hall from David's had found David unconscious and then dragged David's body out of the men's room into the hall. All this time, David was bleeding profusely from what the people in the building all believed to be a superficial head wound. The same man knew CPR and used it, but it took 20 minutes for the EMTs to arrive, and by then they could not revive David. Their efforts took another 20 minutes.

After my conversation with Walter, I kept thinking that I might have been able to do for David what he had done for me, but the pandemic prevented me from getting him whatever help he needed, or even just some basic companionship. Although he worked in a building with peers, David needed some of the pressure of isolation relieved, before it killed him. Might spending some time together have helped? Over the years, we had spent birthdays and holidays together. David was also a big "luncher." Used the time to socialize and network, but with all the restaurants closed by the governor's health emergency orders, he could not do that anymore. Sometimes he had power breakfasts too.

Walter and David's other office-mates seemed to have no sense of how David was feeling during those months. James and I knew, I later discovered. I did not realize that while David was alive. James and I were not in touch directly, after the case was over; we only reconnected after David passed away.

As with so many events I have to relate, there is a second story circulating about David's death. Different but with some points of congruity. In that one, the person who ultimately performed CPR found David at a much earlier stage. David was conscious but unable to get up. He was cracking jokes about his situation. Although he was bleeding profusely from the head, he said not to call an ambulance. While this conversation was in progress, it apparently did not occur to David's conversation-mate that anyone with a profusely bleeding head wound might not be fully in intellectual control of what was happening. He might easily have suffered a concussion or be in the early stages of a "brain bleed." These injuries often impair judgement. Judgement such as the ability to make a well-considered decision about whether to call for medical assistance.

For whatever reason, the other man (so goes this version) seems to have done nothing (other than talking to David) until David fell unconscious. Then, instead of checking for a pulse and respiration, calling immediately for medical help, leaving David where he was and immediately starting CPR, he took the time to drag David out into the hall. Only then did he check for pulse and respiration (so the story I heard goes) and then the others present called for an ambulance while he was performing CPR. The story then continues that it took 20 minutes for the ambulance to arrive. This would have been in a city in the midst of a COVID-19 lockdown, a city with no traffic on the road, in an office about five minutes from two different hospitals. The ambulance, this version of the story insists, stayed there, with the EMTs performing CPR for another 20 minutes before they pronounced David dead and took him away.

The second story I find really hard to credit. There is a 40-minute time frame of essentially treading water that follows some amount of time spent in casual conversation with a profusely-bleeding man. Knowing very well how easy it is to get a concussion, and how that scrambles anyone's logical thinking, many people would have called for an ambulance immediately and let their colleague refuse the assistance. I have had situations in my life like that and I always chose to let the potential patient—if that person was still conscious when the EMTs arrived—accept or refuse their help.

What do both stories lack? Any discussion of chest pain or of David clutching his chest or saying he could not breathe. No mention of arm pain. Or any other specific pain. No sense that he was struggling to breathe. Most people with severe heart attacks have some discomfort of that nature, even if it is just a feeling of intense pressure on the chest.

What else do they have in common? An astounding delay in actually summoning medical help. This was a small, one-story office building. Open areas and offices totaled perhaps a dozen and you could easily hear a cry for help from one end to the other. In one story, a groan was heard. In the other, the sound of someone falling. And then there's that 20 minutes the EMTs are supposed to have spent doing CPR in the front hall of that office building after David's office-mate had already supposedly spent 20 minutes on CPR. I do not think I will ever really know what happened to David.

David and I had adopted each other, all the way back in 2012, spontaneously and mutually. I had gone to Mickey's office for one of the early status conferences about my case. We had finished the business of that meeting, and Jane had just left the room. I was about to get up to leave, when suddenly David started talking again. So did I. Finally, it occurred to me that time was passing. When I glanced at the clock on the wall, an awful lot of time had passed. I must have looked anxious.

"Don't worry!" David, the expensive litigator, said. "I've been off the clock for the past 45 minutes."

We had been "intentional family" for the eight years since then. He told me his family stories and I told him mine. We used to kid each other that eight years are longer than most people stay married. We both hoped that, someday, everyone would be blessed with family they actively chose.

Acknowledgments

Many individuals and organizations offered information and supported me emotionally during the years when the events described in this book were taking place, as well as during the writing and publication process. I am grateful to them all. So many have assisted me that I am probably going to leave someone out. Please be assured that any omission is inadvertent; I apologize for that possibility in advance.

Two of my most active supporters and advocates are no longer among the living. I need to thank, first of all, my late husband, Arthur Orrmont, who passed away in April of 2007, after a long illness, and second my longtime attorney and closest friend David A. Garcia, who died suddenly in April of 2020.

Another friend now among the departed is Tom Burrage, long the dean of forensic accountants in New Mexico. His own desire to know why so much money was seemingly flying out my mother's window during her guardianship spurred me to keep digging.

Another emotional supporter and adviser has been Brad A. Thompson, a London publisher and old friend of Arthur. He always encouraged me to see the absurd in my situation. Exercising my laugh muscle helped greatly.

Stuart Stein, no longer practicing law when I met him, remained a protector and supporter of many enmeshed in the guardianship swamp (including me) over a period of some twenty years. Other survivors of similar ordeals were mutually supportive—particularly Mary Darnell, Emily Darnell-Nunez, Elizabeth Thornton, Kaylynn Holloman, Elizabeth Brown, and Marcia Southwick (who shared Elizabeth Thornton's trials).

Authors do not normally thank stockbrokers and CPAs, unless they are writing financial textbooks, but I must. Erik Q. Gallegos, a friend and sounding board since 1999, was always generous in providing reality checks and otherwise confirming that I was right to question what was happening to my mother's investment accounts. Dick Satter, CPA, now retired, did the same to help me confirm suspected accounting anomalies.

In addition to giving me emotional support, Deborah Rupp Gonçalves and her always-calm paralegal Tina Kelbe provided the best possible legal holding action between 2005 and 2012. I would like to express my gratitude to her for her cooperation with Mickey Barnett, whose firm took over my case in 2012 and who was responsible for David (his then-partner) taking on this work.

My gratitude also to the excellent attorneys Dan Pick, James E. Dory and Patti Williams who collaborated on various legal duties with David along the way. James E. Dory also helped me in transferring documents from David's office after David's passing.

Libraries always deserve recognition. The reference librarians at the Cherry Hills branch in Albuquerque accommodated my requests for sometimes-obscure interlibrary loan books and the University of New Mexico welcomed community members wishing to use university facilities in their research.

Jenna Viscaya and Laurel Schillke, supported me emotionally even when the gag order prevented me from sharing much with my friends. They have always provided oases of calm and understanding, both during the main events and during the cataclysmic emotional shocks that followed.

Rev. Ife Majkia-Gaston and Rev. Herbert S. Gaston, Sr. were dear friends as well as sources of strength and emotional healing.

Without the intervention of the media, it would have taken months—perhaps even years—longer to lift the court-imposed gag order that prevented me from communicating openly with my friends as well as from writing, publishing, or speaking in public about guardianship. Many thanks to the *Albuquerque Journal*, and in particular to Kent Walz (then the editor of that newspaper, a benefactor whom I have never met), who took an active interest in seeing my gag order lifted; Diane Dimond, whose multi-part series on guardianship started the most recent impetus toward open up this pressing national issue for public discussion (and with whom I was able to speak only after I finished writing *Protecting Mama*); and my special appreciation goes to Colleen Heild, whose articles about Mama's estate's complaints against her former guardian made it clear to all the *Journal's* readers how illogical and legally untenable the gag order was in the first place. I apologize, once more, for having been unable to speak with her at the time, due to the restrictions imposed upon me by that same gag order.

Béatrice Hérold helped during my attempts to identify the photographer who took the 1933 picture of my mother, and shared information about her family's decades-long relationship with my mother.

Thanks to Jose Z. Garcia for supplying the photo of David A. Garcia.

Some of the entities that have recently taken on the herculean effort of helping those under state-imposed guardianships and their families deserve special accolades—the National Association to Stop Guardianship Abuse (NASGA—and particularly Elaine Renoire and Marcia Southwick), the Center for Estate Administration Reform (CEAR—and above all Rick Black), Stop Probate Fraud (especially Brett Darken), the Life Legal Foundation (most especially its Executive Director Alexandra Snyder) and Americans Against Abusive Probate Guardianship (thanks to its founder, Dr. Sam Sugar).

C & H Productions obtained the guardian's permission to take the photos dating from 2008.

Thanks to Steve Csipke, my able indexer.

Finally, my profound gratitude to those at Calumet Editions who had faith in this project and so expertly shepherded this book through the editorial-and-production process—Ian Graham Leask, Gary Lindberg, Susan Thurston-Hamerski and Sue Stein.

Index

AARP, xiii
Abruzzo Trust case, 362–63
abuses
    in guardianship. *See* guardianship abuse
    Mama's experience of. *See* CHILDHOOD ABUSE under Rosenstiel, Annette
ACATS (Automated Customer Account Transfer Service) form, 327, 328
accounting. *See* forensic accounting
Adair, John, 39
Administrative Office of the Courts, New Mexico, x–xi
advertising by attorneys, 233
aides. *See* home health aides
aide services. *See* home health services (home aide services)
air conditioner problems, in Albuquerque house, 252, 253, 306, 313, 322
air quality, wildfires affecting, 304–6
Albuquerque, New Mexico
    air quality issues from wildfires near, 304–6
    house-hunting in, 12–13, 20
    Jewish congregations in, 28–29
    Léonie and Arthur's wedding in, 11
    Mama's and Léonie's decision to move to, 10–11
    Mama's home in. *See* Albuquerque home *under* Rosenstiel, Annette
    Orthodox Jewish burial customs in, 294

Albuquerque Ambulance Service, 238, 293
Albuquerque Journal, 213, 292, 362
    Abruzzo Trust case gag order and, 362–63
    air quality in wildfires covered in, 304, 305
    article on guardianship case by, 360–61
    brief requesting lifting of gag order filed by, 360
    Diane Dimond's series on guardianship industry problems in, 329, 343–44, 355, 361, 365
    guardianship reform article in, 379
    Léonie's complaint about Mama's nude photo not covered in, 228
    Léonie's written statement to, about guardianship case, 380
    lifting of guardianship case gag order and, 377–78
    motion for Malott's recusal from guardianship case and, 365, 369–70
    motion to unseal guardianship records by, 370, 371–72, 376–77
    questions in the guardship case about – Léonie's involvement in the series, 343–33
    Malott's "Judge for Yourself" column in, 335
    town hall on guardianship held by, 358–59

"Toy Box Killer" reporting in, 35
Albuquerque Lawyers Club, 363–64
Alibi, The (newspaper), 29–30
Allen, Shepard, Lewis & Syrah, 281, 329, 359–60
Alzheimer's disease. *See also* dementia
   inability to handle financial and personal affairs in, 54
   Mama's diagnosis of, 39
annual reports by conservators
   charitable contributions on, 279
   court requirement for first-year report, 84
   financial transactions on, 254–55
annual reports by guardianship firm
   aides expenses detailed in, 93–94
   amended after Mama's death, to rectify inaccurate figures, 280–81
   court's requirement for, 83–84
   court's routine approval of, 276–77, 289
   expenses detailed in, 83–84, 90–94, 96–97
   financial manager Winslow's collaring of stock issues on, 190
   financial reporting in, 89–94, 98–99, 100–01
   guardian's motion for approval of, and "discharge of Guardian and Conservator from liability," 289–90
   home health care expenses in, 224
   inaccuracies in, 84, 85, 100–01, 280
   Léonie's objection to guardian's motion for approval of, 289, 296
   Léonie's questions about, 259
   Mama's awareness of, 136
   Mama's estate value on, 135–36, 280
   Mama's health noted in, 97
   Mama's hospitalizations reported in, 81–82
   Mama's net worth over time on, 73, 84, 89, 90, 101, 280–81
   Mama's social life reported in, 87–88
   reporting period discrepancies in, 98–99, 135
   retainers reported on, 297
   tracking lawyers' work using, 156
   wheelchair ramp installation on, 189
appreciated stock, gifts of, 285–86
Aragon, Manny, 239–40
aquarium, in Mama's house, 247–48
aromatherapy, 45–46, 51
assisted-living facility. *See also* nursing homes
   Mama's visit to, 52–53
assisted suicide, 208–9
attorney advertising, 233
audits. *See also* forensic accounting
   of guardians receiving state funds, 379
auditors, court-appointed, 41, 93–94
autopsy
   evidence from second autopsy (Texas autopsy) in, 318–19
   Léonie's decision to have a second autopsy, 314
   Léonie's request to the medical investigator's office for, 314, 318
   medical investigator's office's survey about their first autopsy, 320–21
   report from first, 318, 321
   search for independent pathologist for autopsy by, 318
   state of Mama's body described in, 318–19
Ayudando Guardians, xiv, 364

Baca, Sam, 296–302
   appointment as forensic accountant, 286, 298
   CME stock transfer issues and, 300–1
   contract signed for services of, 296, 300
   final report of, 301, 330, 333, 335
   finding on possible guardian wrongdoing by, 301–2
   guardian's work with, 298–99
   inaccurate information given to, 298–99

Léonie's treatment by, 299–300
payment for expenses of, 296, 297–98, 300, 333, 377
share accounting as task of, 300–1
Baca, Theresa
agreement about Léonie's visitation without taping and, 188
Buck's special master appointment by, 287
Buck's resignation and, 291–92
competency hearing and, 58, 59–61
conference on guardian's management and financial losses and, 97–99, 104–05
financial manager Winslow's collaring of stock issues and, 190–91, 192
forensic accounting hearing and, 236, 238–39, 240, 241
forensic accounting report from Wagner to, 266–67, 273–74, 276–77
guardian's annual report amendment and, 135
guardian's annual report approval by, 289
guardianship firm's petition for instructions from, 173
guardian's power to protect and conserve Mama's possessions and, 264
hearing on money manager selection and, 174, 176, 178, 179, 181, 184
hearing on redrawing Léonie's visitation agreement and, 187, 188, 189
High Desert agreement changes and, 83
Léonie's authority over Mama's medical care and, 82
Léonie's High Desert management and, 189
Léonie's withdrawal from end-of-life decision-making and, 107–8
Mama's "completion" of Value History Form and, 179
Merc asset management and, 204, 206, 254
patient-turning device purchase and, 237–38
permanent guardian ad litem appointed by, 187
possibility of naming Léonie as guardian and, 168, 169
retirement of, 329
Rivera's special master appointment by, 292
wheelchair ramp installation and, 239
Baca & Redwine, 93, 296, 299–300
back-office documents, 178, 190, 301
Bacon, Shannon, 335, 362, 379
Baker Law on mandatory commitment, Florida, 232–33, 380–81
Bank of the West, 304
Barela-Shepard, Denise, 329, 335
Barnett, Mickey, 195–96, 290
Barnett Law Firm, 281, 289, 296, 355, 387
Bayada, 271, 293
Bear Canyon Senior Center, Albuquerque, 48–49
Beaulieu, Serge (nephew-in-law), 3
Beaulieu, Sondra ("Sondie"; niece), 3, 31, 37–38, 151
Becker, Cathy, 153, 154–55, 183
Bell, Art, 234
Beltran-Schmitz, Laura, 300
Bengen Rule, 16–17
Bennett, Jane, 196, 281, 318
Bernalillo County Medical Investigator. *See* New Mexico Office of the Medical Investigator
Bitterman, Julius ("Grandpa Julius"; father), 49, 151
Black, Rick, xiii, xiv, 167, 391
Bohnhoff, Hank, 344, 351, 355
Brinks guard, 117
Broadspire, 221, 274
Brown, Martha ("Marty"), 171–72
Browne, Graham, 24, 25–26, 40, 50, 53, 55
Buck, Barbara
air quality issues in Mama's house and, 252

appointment as special master, 240, 287
appointment of new guardian and, 287
birdseed purchase by, 242–43, 246
close social relationship between Mama's guardian and, 240–41
dispersal of Mama's property and, 278–79
drafting a request for a hearing with Baca and, 273, 289
estate and tax planning with Mama and, 255
guardianship firm's rejection of suggested invoice changes and, 276
guardian's frequent meetings with, 291
intensive cleaning of Mama's house and, 266, 277–78, 299, 302–3
lead paint remediation and, 252
renovations of Mama's house and, 243–45, 246, 252
resignation as special master, 291–92
Wagner's forensic accounting report and, 267, 276–77
burial customs, in Jewish Orthodox religion, 294–95
Burrage, Tom, 235–36, 238, 275, 296
home-care agency invoice analysis by, 235–36
Butkus, Carl, 335

Campbell, Clay, 301, 335
capital gains taxes
financial manager Winslow possible talk with Léonie about, 175–76
gifts of appreciated stock and, 286
Winslow's use of European Options and, 254
Carbon-Gaul, Cristy
agreements made by, as Léonie's representative, 79, 354
attendance at hearing by, 59–60, 61
competency hearing paperwork and, 53
creation of trust and, 54, 82, 90, 146
disposition of Mama's car and, 74
guardian's battle with Léonie over ownership of items and, 66, 74
High Desert agreement changes and, 83, 108
lawyer's recommendation of, 50, 55
Léonie's objections to guardian's report and approval by, 88
Léonie's seeking permission to visit Mama and, 80
Mama's payment for services of, 79
remark about collecting Mama's money after the hearing, 61–62
resignation of, 88–89
revocation of Léonie's power of attorney and 58–59
Care Management Group of New Mexico, 373, 374
caregivers. *See* home health aides
care plans, in guardianship, 111–12
case manager. *See also* Keener, Margot
aide's firing and, 116
birdseed purchase by, 242–43
niece Betty's letter to, about her visit to Mama, 84
caseworker
meeting between Mama and Léonie after Arthur's death and, 120, 121–22
physical therapy for Mama's legs and, 129
Center for Estate Administration Reform (CEAR), xiii, 167, 391
certification of guardians, xii, 115, 381
Channel 27, Albuquerque, 142, 232, 303
Chicago Mercantile Exchange (CME) stock
investment loss in trading of, 254
Léonie's questions about amount of stock in trades, 300–1
Mama's need for income from, 254–55
planned merger between Merc and, 40, 146

Index

projected estate gift of appreciated stock, to Léonie, 285–86
Church, Elizabeth, 225
    court's reliance on opinion of, 287
    guardian ad litem appointment of, 168
    opinions about Léonie's complaints held by, 177, 186–87, 247–48, 353
    Léonie's petition to become Mama's guardian and, 168–71
    wheelchair ramp installation and, 189
Claman, David M., 260–62
cleaning of Mama's Albuquerque home, 266, 277–78, 299, 302, 302–3
CME stock. *See* Chicago Mercantile Exchange stock
commercial conservators. *See also* conservators
    use of term, xi
commercial guardians. *See also* guardians
    use of term, xi
commercial trustees. *See also* trustees
    use of term, xi
competency hearing, 53–62
    accuracy of court visitor's report in, 56–57, 61
    aide's offer to testify at, 53
    aide's hiding of Mama from experts for, 54–55
    court-appointed experts' interviews with Mama in, 55–56, 59
    discussion with Mama about her needs for "help" and, 63
    future role of conservator and guardian explained in, 61
    hearing with the judge presiding over, 57–61
    interested parties' attendance and secrecy of, 59
    Léonie's communication with Mama before the hearing, 54–55, 57, 58
    Léonie's end-of-life authority over Mama's medical care granted in, 61, 82
    Léonie's reactions to hearing, 58, 60, 64
    Mama's meeting with her lawyer in, 57–58
    Mama's presentation in, 60, 61
    Mama's reactions to hearing, 63, 64
    niece Betty's concerns about, 57, 70
    paperwork compiled and filed for, 53–54
    people attending and setting for, 59–60
    recommendation of Cristy as Léonie's lawyer for, 50, 55
    timing of Mama's revoking of power of attorney and, 57–58, 58–59
Compitello, Steven ("Steve"), 206
Computershare, 103, 191
confidentiality orders, 164, 368
Congregation Albert, Albuquerque, 28, 29
conservators (guardians)
    annual reports by. *See* annual reports by conservators
    attempts to change Mama's will by, 209-11, 279–80
    bond requirements for, 379
    certification of, 381
    commercial aspects of work of, xi
    competency hearing judge on role of, 61
    duty to ward by, 175
    fees charged by, 110
    guardianship case argument about virtuous nature of, 379–80
    handling of settlements to wards by, 366
    Léonie's filing of lawsuit against. *See* : guardianship case and probate case and estate's suit against the former guardian.
    Léonie's petition to become guardian and conservator, 166–68
    Mama's access to financial information and, 134–35
    Mama's estate value and, 135–36

New Mexico's prosecution of
abuse by, xiv–xv
NYMEX account management and,
191–92, 206
substituted judgement used by,
107
transfer of assets to Mama's estate
by, 328
use of term professional
conservators for, xi–xii
conservatorships
Albuquerque Lawyers Club panel
on guardianship in, 363–65
Brian Wilson example of
successful use of, 105–6, 109
as business opportunities, and
possible criminal infractions,
138, 366, 379–80
guardian access to privileged
information during, 183
hearing reconfirming the
authority of, 187
Léonie's documents on financial
losses of, 195–96
New Mexico Guardian &
Conservator Working Group
on practices of, 332
New Mexico Supreme Court
commission on rules of, 361–
62
newspaper articles on families
harmed by, 355, 379
preserving assets as court-
imposed responsibility of, 343
Contreras, Russell, 305
Corless & Winslow, 104, 159
court visitor (court observer)
accuracy of report of, 56–57
competency hearing and, 53, 59,
60, 61
discussion with Mama about her
needs for "help," 63
Mama's sending money to sister
Vicki and, 47
courts of equity, 167, 288, 353
COVID-19 pandemic, x, 382–84, 386

Darnell, Blair, 361
Darnell, Mary, 361

Darnell Nunez, Emily, 330–31, 361
dementia, in general. *See also*
Alzheimer's disease
commercial aspects of businesses'
interest in, 144–45
possibility of manipulation in, xvi
supported decision making
during, 382
treatment using early life
memories in, xix, 152
dementia, Mama's experience of
aide's photographs taken during,
230–31
competency hearing for. *See*
competency hearing
confusion and other possible early
signs of, 38–39
diagnosis of Alzheimer's and, 39
doctor's recommendation for
guardian in, 49–50
easy manipulation of individuals
in, xvi
factors in worsening condition in,
129
forgetfulness while teaching a
class during, 48–49
frequent visitors needed for
monitoring conditions in, 206
guardian's request to relatives
about limiting discussions
with Mama, 95
improbable stories confabulated
in, 55, 60
inability to make decisions in, 193
increasing inability to pay
concentrated attention to
matters, 42
intermediate solutions for
isolating Mama from
consequences of, 53
loss over control over impulses in,
45
need for aides due to, 39–40
reminders of childhood abusers
and, xix
reply to letter from Great Neck
widow as possible early sign
of, 32
Desert States Life Management (Desert
States Trust), xiv, 365–66, 379

Developmental Disabilities Planning
  Council, 332
Dimond, Diane, 329, 343–44, 355, 359
discovery (legal process)
  case notes provided during, 303–4
  documents found through, 133
  lack of photos in, 272
  Léonie's deposition in suite
    against former guardian case
    and knowledge of, 356
  niece Betty's letter to the guardian
    about Passover not found in,
    317–18
  possible identity theft involving
    Mama not found in, 302
DNR (Do Not Resuscitate) order
  aide's loss of, 263
  guardian's attorney seeking
    court's approval of, 179
  letter to the guardian about
    pressure for Mama's signing
    of, 119, 187–88
  posting in Mama's bedroom of,
    258
documentary on guardianship abuse
  decision to quit work on, 340–41
  fears of family members about
    publicity from, 234–35
  filming of committee meeting in,
    336–37
  gag order effect on, 338–39, 340–41
  Léonie's expansion of focus to
    entire United States in, 303
  Léonie's first proposal about New
    Mexico families, 232, 234–35
  write-off for, 340, 341
Donaldson, Sam, 355
Donisthorpe, Paul, 138, 365–66, 379
Dory, James, 161, 351, 355, 371
driver's license renewal, 41–42

eldercare industry. *See also*
    guardianship firms, in
    general; home health service
    (home aide service)
  guardianship in. *See* guardianship,
    in general
  relationship between relatives
    and, x, xvii, 225

screening of potential guardians
  in, xi
elders
  abuse of by guardians. *See*
    guardianship abuse
  family disagreement and possible
    manipulation of, xvi
  Florida's law (The Baker Act) on
    mandatory commitment of,
    232–33
  frequent visitors needed for
    monitoring care of, 206
  home care versus institutional
    care for, 203
  Mama's book about loss of
    autonomy by, 55, 63–64
  New Mexico (Las Cruces) radio
    show panel on care of, x–xi
  New Mexico's law on mandatory
    commitment of, 381
  number of under guardianship,
    xiii
  restrictions on substantial gifts by,
    330
  violent shaking by aides and, 116
electrical system failure
  guardian's lack of instructions to
    aides about, 223–24, 257
  oxygen supply issues and, 223, 258
  repairs after, 252, 258–59
  single incident of, 251–52
Ely, Damon, 381
end-of-life authority. *See also* protocol
    of guardians over wards, 209
  granting to Léonie for Mama, 61,
    78, 81, 82
  removal of Léonie's ability in, 83,
    107–8, 209
end-of-life care
  guardian's answer to question
    about length of preparation
    for, 315, 321
  guardian's instructions on, 258
estate (Mama's estate)
  conservator's transfer of assets to,
    328
  as legal entity, 326
  financial manager Winslow's
    refusal to release money to,
    327

Léonie's lawsuit against guardians
and conservators and. *See*
guardianship case
Léonie's transfer of titles and
assets to, 326
opening of estate account within
Winslow's film and, 327–28
estate planning
annual spending from Mama's
accounts in, 183–84, 204
expenses for, 278, 283
guardian's initial steps in, 278–79
guardian's substituted judgement
in, 255, 283
guardians' work in, 196
hiring of expert in, 255
Léonie's refusal to participate in,
255
letter to Léonie about creation of
trusts in, 209–11
stepped-up basis in, 146
estrangement story about Léonie
guardian firm's use of, 315, 320
niece Betty's creation of, 85, 86–87
European options, 253–54
Ewing, David N., 225
executor/executrix. *See* personal
representative
expenses. *See also* invoices
for birdseed, 242
for Brinks guard, 117
for Buck's work as special master,
242
for buying versus renting an air
mattress, 258
for case manager's meeting, 246
for case note writing, 304
for a chaise longue and a recliner,
97
for complaint in offensive nude
birthday photo, 231–32
for conservator's attempts to
change Mama's will, 279
for documentary on guardianship
abuse write-off, 340, 341
for estate planning, 278, 283
for forensic accountant Baca, 296,
297–98, 299, 300, 333, 377
for forensic accounting by
Wagner, 277, 297

for groceries, 93–94, 141, 166, 301,
307
for guardianship case attorneys,
354
for guardianship firm's defending
itself against complaints, 277
for guardianship firm's handling
of problems with the original
aide, 102
guardian's reports on, 83–84,
90–94, 96–97
for heating equipment, 268–69
for home health care, 224, 237, 275
for hospice care, 224
for landscaping project, 125, 189,
243, 245, 246, 249
for legal advice on NYMEX asset,
155–56, 189–90, 204
for legal representation for
guardians, 189–90
for Léonie's attorney's replies to
letters from the guardianship
firm, 155
for Léonie's complaints to a judge
about high amount of, 97–98
for Léonie's legal battle against
Mama's guardianship, 236
for Lifecare Plan on Mama's
health, 221
for Mama's care after hip fracture,
203
for Mama's funeral, 200
for oxygen equipment, 258
for Passover supplies, 266
for preparing to sell Mama's
house, 252–53
for relatives' visits in
Albuquerque, 95, 96, 147
for sending Léonie lawyer's
letters, 255, 278
for special master's drafting a
request for a hearing with
Baca, 273
for stipulated order for planning
funeral arrangements, 221
for utilities, address issues with,
298
for wheelchair ramps, 124, 189,
243

experts at competency hearing
  aide's hiding of Mama from experts for, 54–55
  discussion with Mama about her needs for "help," 63
  interviews with Mama by, 55–56, 59
eyesight changes, 212
  ability to recognize people and, 123–24
  driver's license renewal and, 41–42
  landscape changes and, 243
  Mama's denial about, 41

families
  Albuquerque Journal articles on guardianship's harms to, 329, 343, 355, 372–73
  communication of grievances to judges by, 381
  complaints about guardians ad litem made by, 170
  Desert States' handling of settlements of, 365–66, 379
  Guardian & Conservator Working Group on guardianship practices and, 332
  guardianship's threats against, 235, 323
  guardian's involvement with more than one member of, over time, 143
  legislation on visitation rights of members of, 381
  lengthy resolution of guardianship cases filed by, 297
  Léonie's documentary on guardianship abuse and. *See* documentary on guardianship abuse
  possible New Mexico legislative changes to guardianship and, 330–32
  relationship between guardianship firms and, 167, 171
  secrecy of medical and financial records of wards and, 363–65, 368–69

family guardians
  close relationship of guardian ad litem and the commercial guardian and appointment of, 241–42
  court's preference for commercial guardians over, 138
  instances of abuse by, xiv, xv
  number of, xiv
  preference for using over commercial guardians, xi
  prosecution of for abuse, xv
  request for replacement of a guardian with, 138
Federal District Court, New Mexico, xiv, 339
federal grand juries, 364, 372
Federated (Macy's) stock shares, 63
Financial Investment Network Corporation, 104
First State Bank, 90
financial affairs. *See also* Chicago Mercantile Exchange (CME) stock; estate planning; High Desert Holdings; New York Mercantile Exchange (NYMEX; "Merc")
  aide's knowledge about, 43, 73, 74, 101
  annual report coverage of, 89–94, 98–99, 100x1
  annual spending from Mama's accounts and, 183–84, 204
  closing of account with Macy's shares during guardianship, 63
  CME stock transfer issues and, 300–1
  collaring of stock issues and, 190–91, 192
  conservators' role in managing, 61
  contractors and Mama's access to, 134–35
  court visitor's report on Léonie's handling of, 56
  guardian's use of European options and, 253–54
  expenses for groceries and phone calls by Mama's aides allowed by guardianship firm, 93–94, 141

expenses for legal representation for guardians and, 189–90
guardian and lawyer's meeting with Mama over, 73
guardian's access and decision-making role in, 75–78
guardian's annual reports on, 89–94
guardian's meeting with lawyer over, 70–71
guardianship firm's understanding of, 104–5, 135–36
handling financial details after husband's death, 4–5
hearing on money manager selection and, 174–85
Léonie's compensation for managing investments in, 80
Léonie's criticism of guardian's spending habits and, 276–77
Léonie's financial background as help in interpreting, 144
Léonie's power of attorney over, 39, 40, 43
Léonie's push for diversification and, 159–60
Léonie's questions about changes in Mama's assets and, 259
Mama's competency hearing presentation on her role in, 60
Mama's difficulties paying bills and using checkbooks and, 38–39
Mama's estate value and, 135–36, 280
Mama's inability to understand details of, 54, 98, 103–4, 135
Mama's net worth over time, 73, 84, 89, 90, 101, 280–81
Mama's poor judgement in, 91
Merc cash flow and, 40
need to hire and pay aides and, 39–40
real estate investments with family of aide and, 44–45
retainers from Mama's accounts and, 297
sending money to Aunt Vicki, 47
stock gift to son-in-law Arthur and, 76–77, 82, 91, 108
trust needed for guardianship and, 54
use of aide's family for repairs and, 41, 45
Florida, Baker Law (Baker Act) on mandatory commitment in, 232–33, 380–81
food preparation
aide's query about Mama's food preferences and, 306–7
aides' grocery shopping for, 275
aides's work in, 36, 140–41, 218
cost of groceries for, 93–94, 141, 166, 301, 307
Léonie's complaint about food handling in, 186–87
Mama's last meal and, 314, 315
seafood meal and, 140–41, 306
serving sizes for meals in, 315
forensic accountant. *See* Baca, Sam and Burrager, Tom
forensic accounting. *See also* Wagner, Judith A.
guardian's choice about implementing "suggestions" by, 240
of home-health-related expenses, 238, 239–40, 266–67, 275–76, 278
Léonie's questions about amount of stock in trades and, 300–1
Foundation for Open Government, 363
fraud
big business aspects of conservatorships and guardianships and, 138
forensic accounting and, 240
identity theft and, 302
Medicaid and, 330
funeral arrangements
guardian's planning for, 196, 200, 221
for Mama's husband, 1–3
Mama's "instructions" to Léonie about, 31, 121
Mama's "instructions" to guardian firm about, 221

niece Betty's making in advance for Mama by, 95, 196, 200, 219, 221
stipulated order giving Léonie authority in, 221
funeral homes
guardian's contract with, 195, 201
Mama's body stored at, before autopsy, 322

gag orders (secrecy)
Albuquerque Journal brief filed requesting lifting of gag order by, 360
demand for and granting of new global order in estate case against Mama's guardian case, 338–39
difficulty determining number of people in guardianship cases due to secrecy, 332
estate case's imposition of, 338–39
estate case's lifting of, 377–78
Hammond's deposition on guardians given during estate case, 110–11
Kearney in Abruzzo Trust case fined for violations of, 362
in lawsuit against a trustee involving a prominent family, 283
lengthy resolution of guardianship cases and, 337
Léonie's personal life affected by, 339–40, 341–43, 356
Léonie's release from, at case's end, 380
Malott in Abruzzo Trust case with order for, 362–63
possible penalties for violating, 339, 340–41
in probate cases, 328–29
GAL. *See* guardian ad litem
Galindo, Patricia, x–xi, xii, xiii, xiv
Gallegos, Erik Q., 181–82, 328, 351–52
Galvez, Mary, 361–62
garage storage, Albuquerque homes
cleaning out after Mama's death, 284
intruder's moving things around in Léonie's, 324

Mama's storing of old Jewish family items in Mama's, 29, 52, 66
ownership questions in returning Léonie's items in, 66–68
Garcia, David A., 233, 376, 382–87
Albuquerque Journal's motion to unseal guardianship case records and, 371
appointment of Baca as forensic accountant and, 296
Baca's final report and, 330
Baca's treatment of Léonie and, 299–300
COVID-19 pandemic and, 382–84
death of, 384–87
deposing ex-guardian about her business interests, 373–75
deposing head of guardianship firm on her work history and financial management, 104, 161, 164, 173, 375
deposing Jacobson on her guardianship experience, 111
deposing Jacobson on the writing of Mama's Value History, 180
importance of work on Mama's guardianship case by, 281
judge's recusal hearing and, 366–69
Léonie's carrying out the terms of Mama's will with, 337
Léonie's complaint about food handling in Mama's kitchen and, 186
Léonie's filing for probate of Mama's will by, 325
Léonie's inspection of Mama's home with, 299
as Léonie's lead attorney and primary emotional support, 327
Léonie's management of Mama's estate and, 327
Léonie's objection to guardian's motion for approval of all annual reports and, 289, 290–91
Léonie's opening of Winslow Wood estate account and, 328

motion for Malott's recusal from guardianship case by, 365, 366–69

motion to unseal guardianship case records and, 337–38, 370, 371, 377

negotiation petition for absolution resolution by, 296–97, 301

preparing for Mama's guardianship lawsuit by, 195–96

Pregenzer's resignation as guardian's attorney and, 281

search for independent pathologist for autopsy by, 318

testimony of Winslow about conversations with Léonie, about capital gains tax 175–76

Garrett, Kelley Smoot, 380

gaslighting experiences, 323–24, 325, 345

Gaston, Herbert, 3, 11, 13, 23

Gelberman, Joseph, 1–3

gifts
of appreciated stock, 285–86
in guardianship, proposed changes to, 329–30
Mama's stock gift to son-in-law, 76–77, 82, 91, 108

Glad, Tad (brother-in-law), 47, 151

Glad, Victoria ("Vicki"; sister), 9, 47, 151

God's House Church, Albuquerque, 23–24

Gonçalves, Deborah Rupp Gonçalves ("Debbie"), 171
aide's ability to contact, 270
appointment of Baca as forensic accountant during her tenure as attorney, 296
appointment of new guardian and, 172
Buck drafting a request for a hearing with Baca and, 273
Buck's work as special master and, 291
call to medical investigator's office by, 313–14
concerns about NYMEX account management and, 105, 193

dispersal of Mama's property and, 278–79

estate and tax planning and, 255, 278

group meeting with doctors about Mama's hip fracture and, 200–1

guardian's access to High Desert information and, 286

guardian's concern about safety of Mama's possessions and, 264

guardianship firm's funeral arrangements for Mama and, 221

guardian's opinion of Léonie and, 140, 142

guardian's proposal to change Mama's will and, 209

hearing on money manager selection and, 174–85

hearing on redrawing Léonie's visitation agreement and, 185–89

home-care agency invoice analysis requested from Tom Burrage, 235–36-

Léonie's communication with guardianship firm through, 155, 263

Léonie's complaints about Mama's health transmitted to guardian by, 148, 150, 195

Léonie's decision to sue the guardian and, 194, 196, 229–30, 231, 289

Léonie's objections to level of guardian's expenses and, 98

Léonie's selection of, as her attorney, 89

Léonie's visitation rights and, 120, 161, 188

Mama's death and, 312–14

Mama's "fall" getting out of bed and, 195–96

Mama's hospice care and, 257, 288

Mama's lapse into unconsciousness and, 309–11, 312

Mama's ninety-eighth birthday party and, 226

Mama's request to replace her
    guardian with Léonie and,
    138
notification order after Mama's
    death and, 313, 314
photographing Mama's
    possessions and, 149
Wagner's forensic accounting
    work and, 267
wheelchair ramp installation
    issues and, 189, 239
withdrawal from Mama's
    guardianship case by, 327
groceries
  aides' shopping for during shifts,
    275
  cost of, 93–94, 141, 166, 301, 307
Gruszecki, Amy, 318–19, 320, 325
guardian ad litem (GAL)
  appointment of permanent GAL,
    187
  case involving close social
    relationship between a
    commercial guardian and,
    241–42
  Church's appointment as, 168. See
    also Church, Elizabeth
  competency hearing and, 53, 60
  complaints about the commercial
    guardian to, 139
  hearing reconfirming the
    commercial firm's
    guardianship and
    conservatorship authority
    and, 187
  impartiality of special master and,
    292
  judicial immunity of, 170, 240
  lack of wheelchair ramps and, 137,
    187, 189
  Lavelle appointment as
    permanent GAL, 187, 213
  Léonie's complaint about food
    handling in Mama's kitchen
    and, 186–87
  Léonie's concerns about Mama's
    accounts and, 193
  Mama's hip fracture and
    convalescence and, 200–1
  Mama's inability to complain
    about her guardian to, 139,
    140
  Mama's request to replace her
    guardian with Léonie and,
    139
  proposal for Léonie's care of
    Mama and, 168–70, 177, 183
  requirements for, 381
  visitation agreement with Léonie
    and, 185
Guardian & Conservatorship Working
    Group, 332
guardian firms. See guardianship firms
guardians (commercial guardians),
    for Mama, 53–315. See also
    guardian firms, for Mama;
    guardianship, for Mama
  aide's action in Mama's pulmonary
    embolism emergency and,
    95–96
  aide's advocacy for Mama, 157
  aide's asking Léonie personal
    questions and, 229
  aides' complaints about Léonie's
    visits and, 161
  aides' complaints about Léonie's
    removal of items from the
    house and, 272–73
  aides' firing and, 64, 65, 102, 116–
    17, 127, 135
  aide's help with Mama's fall
    getting out of bed and, 195
  aides' inconsistent oversight by,
    141
  aides' reports read by, 163
  aides' supervision by, 156, 157
  aides' watching Mama and Léonie
    through a window and, 312
  attempt to connect Mama with
    a rabbi. See religious belief
    during guardianship
  attempts to get Mama accepted by
    a hospice and, 257, 278, 283,
    288, 289–90, 293
  baby monitor use in Mama's room
    and, 158, 170, 197
  ban on Léonie's taking pictures
    during visits and, 185, 265,
    269–70, 272

Brinks guard hired for protection by, 117
changes in number of aides needed over time by, 236–37, 257, 259, 309
charge that Mama had never given Léonie gifts made by, 69–70
cleaning of Mama's home by, 277–78
cleaning up Mama's body after her death by, 313
communications to Léonie about Mama's hospitalizations, 82, 83
competency hearing judge on role of, 61
concerns about Mama's health and meetings with a hospice by, 257, 278, 283, 290
concerns over aide's undue influence over Mama noted by, 100, 180
court order preventing Léonie's "meddling" in medical care by, 238
demand that Léonie call ahead before visiting Mama and, 157–58, 173
desire of for Mama to meet with a rabbi, 29, 215
dispersal of Mama's property while alive by, 278–79
dispersal planning for Mama's property after her death by, 283, 284
"donation" of Mama's property to Goodwill before her death, 284–85
electrical system failure instructions from, 223–24
emotional distance between Mama and, 71–72
end-of-life instructions and, 258
estate gift for Léonie planning by, 283, 285–86
estate planning and, 196, 278–79
excessive familiarity of, 71–72
existence of Léonie's TV talk show hidden from, 142
expectation about being sued by Léonie, 194, 226
expenses for legal representation for, 189–90
falls during wheelchair transfers and, 41, 133–34, 196
family photos copied by niece Betty and hung above Mama's bed by, 151, 152
financial access and decision-making role of, 75–78
financial planning for Mama's death by, 281
forensic accountant Baca's contract and, 296
forensic accountant Baca's findings on account management by, 301–2
forensic accountant Wagner's "suggestions" and action by, 240
gaslighting experienced by Léonie after Mama's death and, 323–24, 325, 345
Hammond's deposition on judgments of, 107, 108, 111
harpist's visit to Mama during hospice care and, 211–13
hearing on redrawing Léonie's visitation agreement and, 185–89
heating unit installation and, 268–69
High Desert account and, 70, 75–76, 77, 78, 90, 91, 92, 108, 182–83, 298
hiring of aide's family for house repairs and, 41
hospice employment and signing power of, 310, 311
inaccuracies in information from, 84–85, 88
inhibiting presence of, xviii–xix
instructions keeping Mama's health information from Léonie, 223
instructions limiting Mama to bed from, 222
Jacobson's deposition on the writing of Mama's value statement with, 112–13

key to house given to Léonie by, after Mama's death, 322
lack of chiropractic treatments for Mama and, 118–19
lack of communication between Léonie and, 225, 238, 257, 263–64, 283
landscaping project disagreements and. *See* landscaping project
Léonie given confusing and contradictory information by, 154
Léonie's ability to prescribe herbs and treatments for Mama and, 64–65
Léonie's accounting information sent to, 78
Léonie's complaint about the condition of Mama's house to, 265–66
Léonie's complaints about guardian's approach to relatives' visit, 148–49
Léonie's concerns about wards manipulated by, 108, 171
Léonie's contact with Mama blocked by, 68, 80–81, 82–83, 118, 148–49
Léonie's decision to find a litigator to file suit against, 194, 195–96, 226, 229–30, 231, 289, 327
Léonie's end-of-life authority over Mama's medical care and, 61, 78, 81, 82, 83, 107–8, 209
Léonie's fear of losing visitation rights and downplaying her TV talk show, 142
Léonie's filing of lawsuit against. *See* guardianship case
Léonie's information ignored by, 72, 100, 131, 137, 215, 248, 256–57, 288
Léonie's inventory of Mama's possessions and, 265
Léonie's open visitation with friends and, 165–67
Léonie's petition to become guardian and conservator, 137–38, 139–40, 166–68, 169
Léonie's power of attorney and. *See* power of attorney
Léonie's questioning priorities of, 239
Léonie's research materials kept by, 66, 67–68, 78–79
Léonie's visit restrictions and, 173
Léonie's visits and calls with Mama monitored by, 125–27, 153–54, 173
Léonie's visits without advance calling and, 157–58
Lifecare Plan on Mama's health and, 221–22
Mama as supposed co-author of book about Nadia Boulanger, 217–18
Mama's awareness of son-in-law Arthur's death and funeral and, 119
Mama's being outside at her house and, 249–50
Mama's birthday parties and, 133, 226–28, 249, 263–64
Mama's breathing difficulties and, 263
Mama's budget and, 77
Mama's confusion in recognizing Léonie from the aides and, 123–24
Mama's desire for companionship and, 128, 157–58
Mama's ER visit for dehydration and, 260–62
Mama's fear of offending, 41
Mama's feelings about, 169
Mama's hearing aid use, 156–57, 220
Mama's hip fracture and convalescence and, 127–28, 196, 199–202, 222
Mama's hospitalizations and, 80–81, 82
Mama's inability to complain about, 139, 140
Mama's lapse into unconsciousness and, 309–11, 312
on Mama's last meal, 315
Mama's letter about lack of respect by, 71
Mama's medical appointments attended by, 88

Mama's mental state and doctor's recommendation for, 49–50
Mama's need for social interaction and, 156–57
Mama's request to replace her guardian with Léonie and, 137–38
Mama's social life and, 87–88
Mama's violent shaking by aide and, 116
medical investigator's office's questions answered by, 315
meeting between Mama and Léonie after Arthur's death and, 120–23
meeting with lawyer over financial affairs, 70–71
meeting with Mama over her financial affairs, 73
moving Mama's bed outdoors, procedure for, 260
niece Betty's "estrangement" tale about Léonie and Mama and, 85, 86–87, 315, 320
niece's letter on advance funeral arrangements for Mama sent to, 95
niece's letters about Mama's health sent to, 118–19, 141
non-disparagement agreement for Léonie and, 285, 286, 291
notification order after Mama's death and, 290, 313
NYMEX account management and, 191–92
offensive nude photo from Mama's birthday party and, 226–28, 229–32
one-size-fits-all attitude of, xviii
opinions about Léonie held by, 142–43, 195
ownership questions in returning Léonie's items and, 65–68, 74–75
oxygen delivery problems and, 258–59
oxygen levels set by aides and, 310–11
palliative treatment recommendation and, 259
patient-turning device used by, 236–38, 256, 259
photographing Mama's possessions by, 149–51
physical therapist's resignation and, 131
policy of always hiring an aide's family and, 41
possible identity theft involving Mama and, 302
power over Mama's affairs by, xi, xviii, 83, 287
pre-approval for medical treatments needed from, 95–96, 99
pressure for Mama's signing of DNR order and, 119, 187–88
primary care physicians used by, 133–34
privacy during Léonie's visits and, 158, 165
problems with original aide noted by, 69, 80, 94–95, 99, 100, 101–2
proposed business venture by aide's family noted by, 46
protocol about Mama's death and. *See* protocol
refusal of hospice social services by, 216
relatives' visits with Mama and, 72–73, 84, 85–86, 95, 129–30, 147, 148–49
relief aides and, 65, 69, 70, 73–74, 79–80, 85, 195, 196, 314
reports to Léonie about Mama's declining health, 80–81, 82, 87
requirement to not touch Mama's body after her death and, 290, 293, 313
restrictions on private time with relatives during visits and, 84
retainer taken by, from Mama's accounts, 297
scheduling of Léonie's meeting with Mama by, 73
story about Léonie threatening to kill Mama spread by, 127, 158, 164
telling Léonie of Mama's hate for her, 66, 69–70, 76

Index   409

unsafe at home status and double coverage by, 114
vibrator discovery in Mama's bedroom and, 324–25
wheelchair ramp installation and. See wheelchair ramps
Wright's deposition on Mama's condition and work of, 113–14
guardians (commercial guardians), in general. See also guardian firms, in general; guardianship, in general
abuse by. See guardianship abuse
audits of guardians receiving state funds, 379
certification of, xii, 115, 381
charitable causes involvement as cover for malfeasance by, 372–73
commercial aspects of work of, xi
court's changing of, 287–88
court's preference for, over family guardians, 138
criminal charges in cases of funds stolen by, 364, 372–73
disorienting tricks on wards by, 324
expense levels of, 110, 111
fees charged by, 110
guardianship case argument about virtuous nature of, 379–80
involvement with more than one member of a family over time, 143
lack of reliable statistics on, xiii–xiv
lack of statewide standards or board requirements for, xi
maligning of family members by, 153
New Mexico standards for, 381
non-disparagement agreement used by, 241
number of complaints about, xi, xii, xiii
number of family members as, xiv
number of websites discussing abuse by, xii, xiii
power of, xi

preference of using family members as, xi
psychological screening of candidates for, xi
request for replacement of, with a family guardian, 138
stories about families unhappy with treatment in, 232–35
threats against family members by, 235
use of term professional guardians for, xi–xii
violent shaking by aide and, 116
visitation rights of family members and, 381
guardianship, for Mama. See also guardian firms, for Mama; guardians, for Mama
attorneys' fees paid by Mama in, 79
cards and flowers sent during, as only contact with Mama by Léonie, 115–16
charges for handling of problems with the original aide by, 102
closing of account with Macy's shares during guardianship, 63
concerns about sufficient income from Mama's accounts expressed by, 92
conflict of interest with Léonie's first lawyer in, 88–89
courts' approval of actions of, 139–40, 173
disposition of Mama's car during, 74
ending of, upon Mama's death, 296–97
guardian access to privileged information during, 183
hearing reconfirming the authority of, 187
keeping Mama confused and feeling isolated as ploy in, 71, 88
lack of cataract treatment or prescription glasses for Mama during, 123–24

Mama's admission of her
loneliness in, 217, 219–20
Mama's call to Léonie during,
115–16
Mama's desire to see Léonie
during, 115
Mama's lack of understanding of
her role as ward in, 64
Mama's opinion about, in Values
Document, 169
Mama's possessions moved or
missing during, 153
Mama's request to Léonie "to
remain standing" and "to tell
the story" about, 214–15, 226,
340, 355, 375, 382
Mama's request to replace her
guardian with Léonie, 137–38,
139–40, 169–70
Mama's stock gift to son-in-law
Arthur during, 76–77, 82, 91,
108
Mama's supposed Orthodox
Jewish belief during. *See*
religious belief during
guardianship
Mama's writing of values
document and, 179–80
niece Betty's letter on advance
funeral arrangements for
Mama sent to, 95, 196
ramp installation during. *See*
wheelchair ramps
religious issues with Mama
during. *See* religious belief
during guardianship
secrecy of records of, xiii, 133, 141,
143, 189, 204, 315, 329, 332,
334, 338–39, 341, 361, 380–81
stipulated orders in. *See* stipulated
orders
trust for Mama's holdings needed
for, 54, 82
unlicensed status of head of firm
managing, 104–5, 160
guardianship, in general
abuses in. *See* guardianship abuse
age of individuals under, xiii
Albuquerque Lawyers Club panel
on, 363–65
Brian Wilson example of
successful use of, 105–6, 109
Conservator and Guardian
working group on practices
of, 332
court's changing of guardians in,
287–88
discussion about gifts in, 76–77
Hammond's deposition on
buzzwords in, 106–11
Jacobson's deposition on person-
centered care plans in, 111–
12
lack of reliable statistics on, xiii–
xiv
monetary gifts to family members
by, 76–77
need for specialist's
recommendation for court
process in, 50
New Mexico Health and Human
Services Committee hearings
on, 329–30, 336–37, 338
New Mexico (Las Cruces) radio
show panel on, x–xi
New Mexico Supreme Court
commission on rules of, 361–
62
newspaper reports on families
harmed by, 355, 379
number of complaints about, xi,
xii, xiii
number of individuals under, xiii
secrecy of hearings on, 338–39,
341, 368–69, 378
standards for, xi, xii, 112, 113, 115,
205
supported decision making in, 382
use of term professional guardians
for, xi–xii
Wright's deposition on supervision
in, 113–14
guardianship abuse
attorney Stein's work with
families in, 233–34
business opportunities and
possible criminal infractions
in, 138, 379–80
family members as guardians and,
xiv

family members' lawsuits in, 67
guardians' threats against family members and, 235
Léonie's documentary on. *See* documentary on guardianship abuse
New Mexico radio show panel on complaints about, xi
New Mexico Guardian & Conservator Working Group on, 332
New Mexico's prosecution of, xiv–xv
New Mexico Supreme Court commission on rules of, 361–62
newspaper reports on families harmed in, 355, 379
number of websites discussing, xii, xiii
radio show panel on care of, x–xi
guardianship and related cases
Guardianship Case (2003-2013)
Action starts in, 53-54
Action ends in, 337
Albuquerque Journal article on
Baca forensic accountant in, 296-302, 329
Baca judge in,
Buck named special master in, 240
Buck resigns as special master in, 291-92
Buck tells Wagner to stop forensic work on, 277
Burrage analyzes healthcare invoices in, 235-36, 238, 275
Competency hearing
ex-guardian attempts to consolidate new suit against ex-guardian into, 223, 335-36
Lavelle named "permanent" GAL in, 187
Léonie's role as personal representative in, 328
Major filings in see: annual reports, motions
new judges appointed in, 329, 334-335, 337
Rivera named special master in, 292, 337

Probate Case (2012-2013) *see also*: autopsy, medical records
closed, 337
Léonie files to open, 333-34
Léonie's role as personal representative in, 334, 336
Leonie's writing and focusing on wildlife as distraction, 356-58
Winlsow's back office records and, 167, 176, 178, 191, 280, 281, 301, 328,
Suit against the former guardian (2013-2017),
Albuquerque Journal articles on the case *see: Albuquerque Journal*
Albuquerque Journal's motion (brief) to unseal sequestered guardianship records as evidence in, 360, 370, 371-72
array of defense attorneys in, 349
attempt to subpoena Léonie's personal financial records, 351, 378
deadline for filing civil suits, 333
defendants' argument about the virtuous nature of guardians and conservators, 379-80
defendants' brief asking for a summary judgement in, 343-44
defendants demand total gag order on guardianship records and plaintiffs in, 338-39
defendants' interrogatories in, 341, 343-44
defendants' questions about Léonie's involvement in newspaper guardianship series, 343
depositions of ex-guardian taken in, 103-04, 160-61 163-64, 358, 373-75
deposition of retired CPA partner in guardianship firm, 160
deposition of Terry Hammond taken in, 105-07, 108-111
deposition of Shea Jacobson taken in, 111-113

deposition of Doug Schulz taken in, 259-60
deposition of Susan Wright taken in, 113-114
filing of complaint in, 333
focus on most important actions of defendants in, 352
Garcia's motion to unseal guardianship records as evidence in, 337-338, 370, 371
impact on legislation by, 380-82
importance of David Garcia's work on, 290-91
lengthy resolution of, 297, 337
Léonie's depositions taken in, 182, 199, 201, 228, 348-352, 356
Léonie's projected documentary and, 338, 339, 340
Malott appointed judge for, 335
Malott grants total gag order without a hearing, 338
Motion for Malott's recusal from, 365-71
new judges in suit against the former guardian, 335,
New Mexico's law banning release or waiver of liability in, 367
New Mexico Supreme Court denies gag order hearing, 339
possibility of appeal in, 367
pre-trial mediation session in, 376, 378-79
questions about Léonie's involvement in newspaper series and, 343
guardianship cases, in general
family members' communication of grievances to judges in, 381
lengthy resolution of, 297
New Mexico's prosecution of, xiv–xv
number of wards involved in one case, xv
open hearings in, 381
secrecy about, in New Mexico, 141, 143, 332
secrecy of medical and financial records of wards and, 363-65, 368-69
guardianship firm, for Mama. *See also* guardians, for Mama; guardianship, for Mama
annual reports by. *See* annual reports by guardianship firm
annual spending from Mama's accounts by, 183-84, 204
attempts to find reasons to prevent Léonie's visits orchestrated by, 161-64
audit possibility for, as recipient of state funds, 379
awareness of conflict of interest with Léonie's lawyers and, 89
concerns over aide's undue influence over Mama noted by, 100, 180
contract between home health service and, 275-76
courts' approval of actions of, 139-40
criticism of original aide in her annual review by, 99
expenses for groceries and phone calls by Mama's aides allowed by, 93-94, 141, 301
funeral arrangement planning by, 196, 200, 221
gag order in guardianship case and, 338-39
Garcia's questioning work history of head of, 104
hearing on redrawing Léonie's visitation agreement and, 185-89
internal private server used by, 140, 150, 185, 267
keeping Mama confused and feeling isolated as ploy used by, 71, 88
lack of authority of Mama's High Desert account by, 75
lack of communication between Léonie and, 225, 323
lack of understanding of Merc asset by, 104-5, 160
landscaping project arrangements and, 124-25
Léonie's activities monitored by, 143

Léonie's attempts to advocate for Mama and, 137
Léonie's communication with through her attorney, 143–44, 155, 158, 263, 270
Léonie's experience of totally arbitrary actions of, 114–15
Léonie's fear of, 139–40
Léonie's filing of lawsuit against. *See* guardianship case
Léonie's petition to become guardian and conservator and, 137–38, 139–40, 166–68, 169, 171, 195
Léonie's rebuttal to charge by that Mama had never given her gifts, 69–70
Léonie's request to resume visiting Mama, 120
Léonie's surprise at sudden car incident by head of, 322–23
Léonie's visit with Mama in presence of aide and, 73–74
Léonie's visits without advance calling allowed by, 157, 158
Mama's failed attempts to get away from, 155
Mama's High Desert account and spending rate of, 131–32
Mama's hip fracture surgery and, 197–200
Mama's husband's experience with, in another state, 54
Mama's "instructions" as justification for financial decisions made by, 135
Mama's letter to about lack of respect by her guardians, 71
Mama's refusal of flu vaccine and, 92–93
Mama's stock gift to son-in-law Arthur arranged by, 76–77, 108
meeting with Mama's relatives during their visit, 72
niece Betty's letters to about Mama's health, 118–19, 141
NYMEX (Merc) account managed by, 76, 77, 78, 79, 83, 89, 91, 92, 102, 103–5, 135, 145–46, 153, 154–55, 189–90, 204

Orthodox Jewish burial customs as background for actions of, 294–95
ownership questions in returning Léonie's items and, 67, 74
as part of an interest bloc preserving and expanding their sphere of influence, 145
Passover observance and, 272
petition to Judge Baca for instructions, 173
ploy offer of guardianship to Léonie by, 286–88
possible use of Léonie's treatments for Mama and, 65
rejection of suggested invoice changes by, 276
rent for Mama's Merc account and, 77–78
restrictions on Léonie's visits by, 161, 173
restrictions on private time with relatives during visits set by, 84
stipulated orders covering actions of. *See* stipulated orders
thinking of themselves as being an extension of Mama, 145
trying to get rid of aide's problematic family, 41
understanding of Mama's financial affairs by, 104–5, 135–36
guardianship firms, in general
Albuquerque Journal on problems in, 329, 343–44, 355, 361, 365, 372
Albuquerque Journal on reforms in, 379
benefits of secrecy for, 338–39
charitable causes involvement as cover for malfeasance by, 372–73
family members' relationships with, 167
Guardian and Conservator working group on practices of, 332
Léonie's education and research on, 144

manipulations of families by, 171–72
observance of Jewish Orthodox burial customs by, 294–95
picking courts favorable to them for hearings, 167
podcast panel on, 332–33
possible New Mexico legislative changes to, 330–32
prosecution of for abuse, xiv–xv
ward's family threated by partner in, 235, 323
Guardianship Panel, New Mexico Supreme Court, 372

H & R Block, 90
Hall, James A., 376, 378
Hammond, Terry, 105–11, 114
Harris, Susan, 138, 364, 372, 379
Hasidic Jewish religion
    burial customs in, 294
    Mama's story about growing up with, 355
"Healers, Health and Healing" TV talk show, 141–42
Health & Human Services Committee, New Mexico House of Representatives, 329, 336–37, 338
hearing aids, reason behind Mama's use of, 156–57, 220
hearings
    on forensic accounting, 236, 238–39, 240, 241
    on money manager selection, 174–85
    on redrawing Léonie's visitation agreement, 185–89
    secrecy of, 141, 143, 338–39, 341, 368–69, 378
Heild, Colleen, 355, 372
    Desert States' handling of settlements covered by, 365–66, 380
    guardianship case article by, 360–61
    guardianship reform article by, 379
    Léonie's note to, at end of suit against the former guardian, 380
    lifting of gag order on sequestered guardianship documents and, 378
    motion for Malott's recusal from the estate's case against the former guardian and, 365, 371
High Desert Holdings, LLC
    aide's interest in real estate held jointly with, 44, 56, 76
    building owned by, 46, 56, 286
    conservator's agreement on management of, 182
    creation of, for protecting Mama's interests, 42–43, 53
    criticism of Léonie's management of, 175, 181, 206
    financial manager Winslow's opinion of Léonie's management of, 175–76
    guardians and, 70, 75–76, 77, 78, 90, 91, 92, 108, 182–83, 298
    guardian's opinion of Léonie's management of, 188–89, 206, 286
    Léonie's annual report on Mama's portion of, 188, 286
    Léonie's compensation for managing, 80
    Léonie's refusal to sell Mama's share of, 126, 131
    Macy's shares in, 63
    Mama's income from, 83, 90
    operating agreement changes to, 83, 108
HIPAA, x, 85
hip fracture, 195–202
    aide's actions resulting in, 127, 197–98, 222
    aides' care during convalescence from, 204–5
    bedsores during convalescence from, 207
    group reading with doctor about, 200–1
    guardian's instructions limiting Mama to bed after, 222
    guardian's refusal of recovery in, 199–200
    harpist's visit during convalescence from, 211–13

Index 415

home health agency's version of, 127–28
Mama's desire to get out of bed after recovery for, 222
Mama's use of drugs during convalescence for, 206–7
possible blood clot treatment with morphine overdose prescribed during convalescence from, 208
social workers' recommendation on, 198–99
home care for elders, versus institutional care, 203
home care agencies. *See* home health services
home health aides
accuracy of information given to court visitor by, 56
activities with Mama, without the guardian's approval, 69
advocacy for Mama with guardians by, 157
air quality issues from fires and open door policy of, 306
antibiotic administration by, 262–63
aquarium care and, 247–48
aromatherapy therapy suggestions from family of, 45–46
asking Léonie personal questions by, 229
attempts to find reasons to prevent Léonie's visits and, 161–64
attempts to make Léonie angry by serving seafood to Mama, 140–41
belief in Mama's home as inheritance of, 53, 55
business venture requests from family of, 46–47, 61
chaise longue purchase and, 97
changes in number needed over time, 236–37, 257, 259, 309
cleaning up Mama's body after her death by, 313
colleague's report about Mama sleeping at home of, 79–80
companionship for Mama provided by, 128, 157
competency hearing and, 54–55, 59
complaints about Léonie's visits, 161
complaints about Léonie's removal of items from the house, 272–73
concerns about being seen talking with Léonie, 193
control over Mama's life by, 69
cost of, 224
Coumadin monitoring during treatments and, 96–97
dispersal planning for Mama's property after her death and, 283–84
drinking on duty by, 117–18, 265
electrical system failure instructions and, 223–24, 257
family of aides used for repairs, 41, 46, 130
food prepared by, 36, 140–41, 186–87, 218
forensic accounting report on work shifts of, 274
guardian's annual reports on expenses for, 93–94
guardian's concerns about original aide's undue influence over Mama by, 100, 180
guardian's frustration at policy of always hiring the family of, 41
guardianship firm's approval of expenses for groceries for and phone calls by, 93–94, 141, 301
guardian's hiring of second aide for relief, 70
guardian's inconsistent oversight of, 141
guardian's instructions limiting Mama to bed and, 222
guardian's lies about Léonie told to, 127, 158, 164, 315
guardian's notes on problems with original aide, 69, 80, 94–95, 99, 100, 101–2

guardian's pre-approval for medical treatments needed from, 95–96, 99
guardians' reading of reports by, 163
guardian's role in firing, 64, 65, 102, 116–17, 127, 135
guardianship firm's criticism of original aide in her annual review, 99
guardians' supervision of, 156, 157
information on Mama's health given to Léonie by, 194
knowledge of Mama's financial affairs by, 43, 73, 74, 101
Léonie given confusing and contradictory information by, 154
Léonie's complaints to a judge about high costs of, 97–98
Léonie's contact with Mama blocked by, 68–69
Léonie's experience of hostility and perceived threats from, 71
Léonie's feeling threatened by behavior of, 155
Léonie's hiring of, 40–41
Léonie's meeting with Mana and demands from, 74
Léonie's open visitation with friends and, 165–66
Léonie's taping of visits with Mama and, 185–86, 188
Léonie's visit restriction about meals and, 306
Léonie's visits blocked by, 157–58, 165
Léonie's visits and calls with Mama monitored by, 125–27, 158, 256
limits on sharing information with Léonie by, 137
notes about talk with niece Betty during a visit, 85
Mama and Léonie watched through a window by, 312
Mama's attempt to get out of bed and, 163
Mama's black eye incidents and, 270–71
Mama's call to Léonie and, 115–16
Mama's changing opinion about treatment and threats by, 50–51, 52
Mama's dependence on, 94–95
Mama's fall getting out of bed and, 194–95
Mama's feelings about, 165
Mama's fluid intake monitored by, 306
Mama's hip fracture story after fall "discovered" by, 196–97
Mama's hip fracture caused by, 127, 197–98, 222
Mama's hip fracture convalescence care by, 204–5, 206–8
Mama's kitchen knife accident with her thumb and need for, 38
Mama's lapse into unconsciousness and, 309–11, 312
Mama's last meal and, 314, 315
Mama's need for social interaction and, 156–57
Mama's pulmonary embolism emergency and, 95–96
Mama's talk attendance by, 49
Mama's visit to an assisted-living facility and, 53
Mama's work periods and, 94
Mama's writing produced with, 94
meeting between Mama and Léonie after Arthur's death and, 120–23
mental health of, 158–59
mistreatment of Mama by, 116
negative comments about Léonie placed into record by, 284
notification order after Mama's death and, 313, 314
notes about talk with niece Betty by, 85
not speaking to Léonie by, 251
nude photo of Mama taken on her birthday by, 226–28
oxygen cannula handling problems and, 307–9
oxygen levels determined by, 310–11

patient-turning device used by, 236–38, 256, 259
privacy during Léonie's visits and, 158, 165, 256
providing mechanical sexual satisfaction to paralyzed clients by, 325
query to Léonie about Mama's food, 306–7
real estate investments with family of, 44–45
request to be hired for private duty work, 36, 40–41
requests to Léonie for Mama's possessions by, before her death, 284
request to photograph Mama and Léonie, 269–70, 271
shifts and actual hours worked by, 274, 275
smoking by, and Mama's oxygen use, 157
story about Léonie threatening to kill Mama and, 127, 158, 164
"Toy Box Killer" case related to, 35–36
unrefrigerated leftover food issues and, 186–87
using someone else to stay with Mama while running errands, 51
visits from during Mama's hospitalizations, 49
warning to Léonie about "something about to happen" to Mama, 193–94
home health services (home aide services)
aide's contract with, 40
assistive device for turning Mama and, 259
baby monitor use in Mama's room and, 170, 197
billing irregularities and contract and, 275–76
complaints about Mama's dependence on an aide by, 94–95
contract between guardianship company and, 275–76
examination of invoices from, 238
lies about Léonie told to aides by, 158
limits on sharing information with Léonie required by, 137
Mama's hip fracture cause and, 127–28, 197
obtaining invoices from, 235
Wagner's forensic accounting of expenses by, 238, 239–40, 266–67, 275–76, 278
Mama's violent shaking by, 116
homes
Léonie's. See Manhattan home and Albuquerque home *under* Léonie Rosenstiel
Mama's. See Manhasset home; Manhattan home; and Albuquerque home *under* Rosenstiel, Annette
hospice. *See also specific hospices*
chaplain Smith's observations about Mama in, xix, 215–20
guardian's attempts to get Mama accepted by, 257, 278, 283, 288, 289–90, 293
Léonie's relationship with, 320
Hospice de la Luz, Albuquerque, 201–8
guardian's attempt to get Mama accepted by, 288
expenses for, 224
guardian's instructions keeping Mama's health information from Léonie and, 223
guardian's refusal of social services from, 216
Mama's discharge from, 220
Mama's hip fracture and care from, 201, 202, 203, 204–5
Mama's hospice evaluations done by, 288
Mama's meetings with chaplain Smith from, xix, 216–20
need for periodic certification for services from, 220
social worker reports from, 216
hospice nurses
call to, after Mama's death, 314
call to the medical investigator's office by, 314, 318

call to Léonie about Mama's death,
    312–13
on condition of Mama's body after
    her death, 313, 318
lawyer's attempted call to the
    medical investigator's office
    and, 313–14
presence in Mama's home after
    her death, 313
Hospice of New Mexico, Albuquerque,
    259
call to Léonie about Mama's death,
    312–13
guardian's attempt to get Mama
    accepted by, 257, 278, 283,
    290, 293
guardian's signing power and
    employment of, 310, 311
Léonie's lack of privacy in
    interactions with, 310
Mama's home lapse into
    unconsciousness and, 309–11
Morgan's ownership of, 257, 278,
    290, 293, 310
Hospice of the Sandias, Albuquerque
guardian's answer to
    questionnaire from, 315
guardian's attempt to get Mama
    accepted by, 288
Mama's hospice evaluations done
    by, 288
hospitals. *See* Lovelace Westside
    Hospital; Lovelace Women's
    Hospital
Hoyer lift, 133–34, 222
Huling, Valerie, 335

incapacitated/incapacity, xiii
    guardians' use of term, 106–7
    person-centered care plans for, 112
incompetent, use of term, 106
institutional care for elders, versus
    home care, 203
interested parties, in guardianship, 59,
    88, 141, 334
internal server, in guardianship firm,
    140, 150, 185, 267
Invest (investment clearing firm), 176
investments. *See* financial affairs; High
    Desert Holdings; New York
    Mercantile Exchange

invoices. *See also* expenses
    for attempts to get Mama accepted
        by a hospice, 289–90
    for case note writing, 303, 304
    for deep cleaning of Mama's
        house, 299, 303
    for dispersal planning meetings
        on Mama's property after her
        death, 283, 284
    double billing on, 275
    for electrical repairs, 259
    for forensic accountant's expenses
        and meetings, 299, 300, 331
    forensic accounting of. *See*
        forensic accounting
    guardian's communication with
        niece Betty noted in, 317
    from health-care companies, 235–
        36, 274, 275
    for home health aides' time,
        billing rate variations in, 275,
        276
    for oxygen delivery equipment,
        258
    for protocol reviews and revisions,
        257, 290, 291
    for special master Buck's work,
        242, 246, 266, 273, 277, 299

Jack White (brokerage firm), 15
Jacobson, Shay H., 111–13, 180
Jewish Chronicle, Newark, 29
Jewish Encyclopedia, 48–49
Jewish life
    Mama's experience as a Jewish
        woman in the army, 27–28
    Mama's knowledge of, 48–49
Jewish religion. *See also* Hasidic Jewish
    religion; Orthodox Jewish
    religion
    guardian's statement that Léonie
        was Orthodox Jewish, 72–73,
        140, 141, 216
    lawyer's assumption about
        Léonie's affiliation with, 62
    Mama's early refusal to have any
        contact with, 29
    Mama's family's observance of
        precepts in, 49
    Mama's husband's funeral and,
        1–3

Mama's storing of old family items
connected with, 29, 52, 66
Mama's later conflicts about.
See religious belief during
guardianship
Mama's story about growing up
with, 355
marriage age in, 48–49
niece Betty's insistence that Mama
was an Orthodox Jew, 72, 147,
180, 215, 216
perceived mercenary aspects of,
28, 29
Journal. See Albuquerque Journal
Judaism. *See* Jewish religion
judicial immunity, 170, 240

Kathleen Winslow & Associates, 174.
See also Winslow, Kathleen
Kearney, Victor, 362
Keener, Margot, 342
birdseed purchase by, 242–43
heating unit installation and,
268–69
landscaping project and, 243–45
Mama's discomfort during home
renovation and, 249, 268
need for deep cleaning and, 266
nurses' notebooks and, 271
Passover supplies and, 266
Keller, Tim, 379
King, Gary, 229–30, 231, 249
Krippendorf's Tribe (film), 30–31

landscaping projects
first project (2008)
assisted decision-making claims
and, 124-25
bulldozing of reflecting pool, 125,
245
cost of and, 124, 189
delay getting work done in, 130
neighbor's complaint about
condition of property during
delay, 130
second project (2010)
plans made between Buck and
guardian and, 243–46
Mama moved to den during, 249
Mama's deteriorated eyesight
prevents her from seeing,
243, 245
plans announced to Léonie about,
243-46
sun sail proposed for, 243–44, 249
Lavelle, Gerard, 187, 193, 198, 213
Leach, Kenneth C. ("Ken"), 163, 204,
210, 255, 278
Leech, David C., 198, 201, 204, 207–8,
220, 222
Leitzer, Ellen, 330, 363, 371–72
Lewis, Dan
deposition of ex-guardian about
her business interests and,
375
as guardian firm's representative
in the estate's case against the
former guardian, 281
Judge Barela-Shepard recusal and,
329
Léonie's deposition and, 351
motion for Malott's recusal in
the estate's case against the
former guardian and, 369,
375
liability, waiver of. *See* waiver of
liability
Lifecare Plan, 221–22
Lipsky, Mortimer ("Mort"), 4, 5
Loew, Alfred A., 4
Lovelace Westside Hospital,
Albuquerque, 128
Lovelace Women's Hospital,
Albuquerque, 95, 208, 269
LPNs (licensed practical nurses). *See
also* nurses
certification of Mama for hospice
services by, 220
music played for Mama by, 214

MacKenzie, Gregory A. ("Greg")
Albuquerque Journal's brief
requesting lifting of gag order
and, 360
Albuquerque Lawyers Club panel
on guardianship and, 363,
364, 369, 377
committee meeting on
guardianship profession
attendance by, 329–30, 336–37

as guardian firm's attorney in suit against the former guardian, 281
Léonie's deposition in suit against the former guardian taken by, 349, 350–51, 356
Léonie's deposition on High Desert account by, 182–83
on Léonie's preferences for Mama's care after her hip fracture, 199–200, 201–2
motion for Malott's recusal from suit against the former guardian, 369
motion to unseal guardianship case records and, 377
query about nude photo of Mama from, 228
Wright's deposition by, 113
Macy's (Federated) stock shares, 63
Majkia-Gaston, Ife, 3, 11, 13, 20, 23
Malott, Alan, 344, 351, 359
Abruzzo Trust case and, 362–63
Albuquerque Lawyers Club panel on guardianship and, 363, 364–65
appointment as judge in suit against the former guardian, 335–36
families of wards criticized by, 364–65, 369, 375–76
imposition of global gag order in suit against the former guardian by, 338–39
lifting of gag order by, 377–78
motion for his recusal from the suit against the former guardian, 365–71
motions to unseal guardianship case records and, 338, 371, 377
mandatory commitment laws, 232–33, 380–81
Manhasset, New York
Mama's home in. See Manhasset home *under* Rosenstiel, Annette
Raymond Rosenstiel Memorial chamber music concert in, 21, 30, 31
Manhattan, New York
Mama's later dislike for, 31
Mama's home in. See Manhattan home *under* Rosenstiel, Annette
McConnell, Gael, 361
mediation session, in suit against the former guardian, 376, 378
medical experts at competency hearing, 53–54, 59–60
Medical Investigator's Office. See New Mexico Office of the Medical Investigator
Merc. See New York Mercantile Exchange
Millett, Darryl, 329
Montebello assisted-living community, Albuquerque, 52–53, 117
Montoya Chavez, Maria, 79, 83, 88–89, 206
Moore, Sharon, 364, 372
Morgan, Elizabeth
complaint about aide's oxygen concentration for Mama in notes of, 311
hospice ownership by, 257, 278, 290, 293, 310
Mama's ER visit for dehydration and, 262
Mama's evaluation by, for hospice admission, 278, 290
Mama's refusal to communicate with, 220
Mose, Emily, 320–21
motion (petition, request) for absolution
commercial guardian's filing of, 289
guardian's dropping of, 337
Léonie's attorney's negotiation of resolution of, 296–97
Léonie's team's response to, with a request for a jury trial, 295, 303
Nash, Nan, 379
National Guardianship Association (NGA), xii, 111
disagreements over function of, 115

Hammond's deposition on, 109–10
Hammond's lectures for, 105–6, 108–9
Jacobson's deposition on, 112
Natural Burial New Mexico, 295
New Mexico
air quality issues from wildfires in, 304–6
audits of guardians receiving state funds in, 379
commission on rules of guardianship and conservatorship in, 364
guardianship abuse prosecution in, xiv–xv
guardianship standards in, 381
Hammond's deposition on guardians and familiarity with statutes of, 108, 110
judicial immunity of guardians ad litem in, 170, 240
lack of statewide guardian standards or board requirements in, xi
law banning release or waiver of liability in guardianship cases in, 297
legislative changes to guardianship in, 380–81
Léonie's proposed documentary on guardianship abuse in, 232, 234–35
Mama's and Léonie's decision to move to, 10–11
Mama's love of, 217
mandatory commitment law in, 233, 381
number of complaints about adult guardianship in, xi, xii
Orthodox Jewish burial customs in, 295
podcast panel on guardianship in, 332–33
secrecy of guardianship hearings, 141, 143, 338–39, 341, 368–69, 378
secrecy of guardianship records in, 133, 141, 143, 189, 204, 315, 328–29, 332, 334, 361, 363, 380

stories about families unhappy with their guardianship treatment in, 232–35
New Mexico Administrative Office of the Courts, x–xi
New Mexico Developmental Disabilities Planning Council, 332
New Mexico Federal District Court, xiv
New Mexico Foundation for Open Government, 363
New Mexico Guardianship Association, 329, 337
New Mexico Legislature
joint Health & Human Services Committee, 329, 336–37, 338
New Mexico Legislature
certification of professional guardians and conservators mandated by, 381
gag order barring Léonie's work or contact with, 340
guardianship reforms enacted by in 2018 session, 361
Health & Human Services Committee in, 329, 336–37, 338
mandatory commitment law and, 232, 381
Ortiz y Pino's pending guardianship legislation in, 330–32
podcast panel on pending guardianship legislation in, 332–33
proposed law on gifts and, 330
supported decision making legislation in, 382
New Mexico Office of the Medical Investigator
delay before accepting Mama's body for autopsy by, 321–22
guardian's completion of questionnaire from, 315, 321
hospice nurse's call to, on private number, 314, 318
lawyer's attempt to call, after Mama's death, 313–14
Léonie's relationship with, 320

Léonie's request for a second
autopsy and, 314, 318
survey about satisfaction with
autopsy done by, 320–21
New Mexico Senate
gag order preventing Léonie's
lobbying before, 340
Guardian & Conservatorship
Working Group, 332
changes to guardianship law in,
381
joint Health & Human Services
Committee, 329, 336–37, 338
legislation on guardianship in, 332
New Mexico State Auditor, 379
New Mexico Supreme Court
appeal of gag order in the estate's
case against the former
guardian before, 339
assisted suicide ruling of, 208–9
commission on rules of
guardianship and
conservatorship, 361–62
filing of guardian and conservator
reports on time mandated by,
381
gag order on newspaper coverage
in Abruzzo Trust case and,
363
Guardianship Panel, 372
New York City
Mama's later dislike for, 31
Mama's home in. See Manhattan
home *under* Rosenstiel,
Annette
New York Mercantile Exchange
(NYMEX; "Merc")
expenses for lawyers on, 155–56,
189–90, 204
guardian's annual reports on,
98–99
guardianship firm's management
of, 76, 77, 78, 79, 83, 89, 91, 92,
102, 103–5, 135, 145–47, 153,
154–55, 189–90, 204, 206
High Desert Holdings and, 43, 131
income from, 40, 54, 90, 91, 97,
101, 103, 153, 254
increasing value of seat on, 4, 98,
99, 104–5, 131–32

Initial Public Offering (IPO) of, 97,
136
lawyer's supervision of, 88–89
Léonie's push for diversification
and, 159–60
Léonie's refusal to sell Mama's
stake in, 126, 131
Mama's husband's original
purchase of seat on, 4
Mama's inheritance of seat on, 4,
13, 14–15, 17
refusal of long-term care
insurance through, 26–26
restrictions on communication
with Léonie about, 206
tax issues in selling shares of,
145–46
trust in Mama's name for, 54, 90,
146
New York Times, 105
NGA. *See* National Guardianship
Association
non-disparagement agreement
example of a commercial
guardian's use of, 241
demand that Léonie sign, 285, 286,
291
NurseFinders, 263, 271
nurses. *See also* hospice nurses; LPNs
(licensed practical nurses)
antibiotic administration and, 263
guardian's instructions keeping
Mama's health information
from Léonie and, 223
Mama's attempt to get out of bed
and, 163
Mama's breathing difficulties and,
263
Mama's hip fracture surgery care
and, 202, 203, 207
protocol update and, 293
nursing homes. *See also* assisted-living
facility
monthly fees for, 203
persons defined as being unsafe at
home and, 114
NYMEX. *See* New York Mercantile
Exchange

Oakley, Marti, 332–33

Office of the Medical Investigator. *See* New Mexico Office of the Medical Investigator
older people. *See* elders
order, stipulated. *See* stipulated order
Orrmont, Arthur (son-in-law), 4
    books by, 123, 166
    compensation for managing his mother-in-law's assets by, 80
    contact with his mother-in-law during her guardianship, 115
    death of, 119
    decision to move from Manhattan by Léonie and, 8
    decision to move to New Mexico by, 10–11
    donation to Aunt Vicki by Léonie and, 47
    family approach to stock investing used by, 15–16
    father-in-law's funeral and, 3
    guardian firm's gifts from his mother-in-law to, 76–77, 82, 91, 108
    guardian's changes to High Desert management and, 83, 91, 131
    guardian's knowledge of High Desert account of, 78, 182
    health of, 31, 50, 52–53, 203
    High Desert Holdings and, 42–43, 44, 75, 153
    house-hunting in Albuquerque and, 12–13, 20
    Léonie's hosting of TV talk show and, 141–42
    Léonie's relationship with her relatives and, 33, 34
    Léonie's proposed trip to Mexico and, 46–47
    life in Albuquerque with Léonie, 23, 24, 30
    Mama's desire to move in with Léonie and, 50, 52–53
    Mama's fall and, 24, 25
    Mama's growing agitation and, 45
    Mama's knowledge of death and funeral of, 119, 121, 122
    Mama's memory changes about, 85, 121
    Mama's move from Manhasset to Manhattan and, 14, 19
    Mama's visit to Manhattan and, 6
    Mama's will and, 25, 26, 37, 147, 210, 326
    new home in Albuquerque and, 20, 22, 239
    new will and power of attorney drafted and signed, 24, 25–26
    publishing house owned by Léonie and, 357
    Raymond Rosenstiel Memorial chamber music concert and, 21, 22, 31
    search for possible new home location by, 8–11
    stock investing with Léonie, 15
    trust bequest to Léonie by, 209
    wedding with Léonie, 11
    visits to possible new home cities by, 9–11
Orthodox Jewish religion
    guardian firm's understanding of burial customs in, 294–95
    guardian's statement about Léonie's belief in, 72–73, 140–41, 216, 294
    Mama's belief in. *See* religious belief during guardianship
    Mama's husband's funeral and, 2
    Mama's Values History document on identification as, 180
    Passover observance in, 266, 272, 317–18
Ortiz y Pino, Jerry, 330–31
O'Toole, Sean, 5
oxygen
    aides' authority in determining dosages for, 310–11
    aides' cannula handling problems and, 307–9
    aides' smoking and, 157
    cost of equipment with, 258
    deprivation effects with, 250–51, 258–59
    electrical system failure and, 223–24, 258, 259
    Léonie's complaints about levels of, 311
    Mama's lapse into unconsciousness and levels of, 309–11

Mama's use of, 129, 156, 237, 251, 307–8, 311

Passover observance, 266, 272, 317–18
patient-turning device, 236–38, 256, 259
Peifer, Charles R., 369–70
personal representative (PR)
 back-office records subpoenaed by, 190, 301
 collaring of stock issues examined by, 191
 conservator's transition of Mama's assets to, 328
 contract for Baca's accounting work and, 296–98, 377
 guardian's arrangements for funeral arrangements and, 221
 Léonie's personal interests different from responsibilities as, 336, 352
 Léonie's legal right to change locks as, 325, 326
 Mama's will naming Léonie as, 176, 336
 Mama's hidden family photos found by, 152
 ownership of Mama's house and, 322, 325
 possible contract with a funeral home and, 200
 probate court proceedings and, 328
 suits to get redress for Mama's grievances and, 336, 338, 339, 352
person-centered care plans, in guardianship, 111–12
petition for absolution. *See* motion for absolution
photos
 aide's request to photograph Mama and Léonie, 269–70, 271
 aide's taking of nude photo on Mama's birthday and, 226–28
 Attorney General King's lack of action in birthday photo complaint, 229–32
 family photos copied by niece Betty and hung above Mama's bed, 151–53
 guardian's ban on Léonie's taking pictures during visits, 185, 265, 269–70, 272
 guardian's photos of Mama's possessions and jewelry for Léonie, 149–51
 of Léonie and Mama, in article on guardianship case, 360–61
 Léonie's inventory of Mama's possessions in, 265, 274–75
 Mama's hiding of birth family photos, 151–52
 of Mama's home's conditions, 299
physical therapy
 for shoulder injury, 21, 26
 for legs, 129, 130–31
Pick, Dan, 333, 335
power of attorney held by Léonie, 54
 drafting and signing of new version of, in Albuquerque, 24, 25–26
 family stock trading and, 15
 High Desert Holdings and, 43
 Mama's difficulties in handling financial affairs and, 39, 40, 43
 Mama's revoking of, 57–58, 58–59
PR. *See* personal representative
Pregenzer, Ruth, 170, 273
 attempts to find reasons to prevent Léonie's visits and, 161, 163, 173, 185
 attitude toward Léonie by, 140
 attorney advertising by firm of, 233
 discrepancy in guardianship firm's annual report discovered by, 280
 dispersal of Mama's property and, 279
 end-of-life planning by, 288, 293
 estate planning and, 210, 255, 278, 283
 expenses for, 155
 financial manager Winslow's account management and, 190, 206
 forensic accountant appointment and, 298

group meeting with doctors about Mama's hip fracture and, 200–1
guardian's retainer for, from Mama's accounts, 297
hearing on money manager selection with, 174, 175–76, 178, 179, 181, 184–85
Léonie's objection to guardian's motion for approval of annual report and, 289, 291
Léonie's visit with Attorney General King and, 231–32
Mama's ninety-eighth birthday party and, 226
on Mama's writing of the Values Document, 179, 180
photographing Mama's possessions and, 149
preventing Léonie's visits by guardianship firm and, 185
reason for resignation as guardian's attorney by, 281
safety of Mama's possessions and, 264
working group on rules and, 362
Presbyterian minister, Mama's meetings with, xix, 216–20
probate of Mama's estate
advantage of open proceedings in, 328–29
Léonie's filing for, 325, 327
Léonie's transfer of titles and assets to the estate and, 326
professional conservators. *See also* conservators
use of term, xi–xii
professional guardians. *See also* guardians
use of term, xi–xii
progressive guardianship, 106
protected persons, 68, 106
protocol. *See also* end-of-life authority
guardian's work reviewing and revising, 263, 288, 292–93
invoices for preparing, 257, 290, 291
legal negotiations after guardian's unilateral change of, 263
posting in house of, 263
stipulated court order for, 263, 292
use of term, 257
psychological screening, of guardian candidates, xi
psychologists
easily manipulated individuals in dementia and, xvi
hearing on Léonie's becoming Mama's guardian and, 139
lack of wheelchair ramps and, 137
on Mama's inability to make decisions, 193
Mama's inability to complain about her guardian to, 139, 140
on Mama's lack of understanding of her assets, 104
on Mama's loss over control over impulses, 45
Mama's request to replace her guardian with Léonie and talk with, 139

rabbis
guardian's desire for Mama to meet with, 29, 215
Mama's husband's funeral and, 1–3
Mama's knowledge of Jewish life and, 48–49
Mama's refusal to have any contact with, 29
ramps. *See* wheelchair ramps
Ray, David Parker, 35–36
Raymond Rosenstiel Memorial chamber music concert, Manhasset, New York, 21, 22, 30, 31
Reardon, Walter, 384–85
REDW (accounting firm), 78, 153, 154, 182–83
Reform Jewish religion
husband's funeral in, 1–3
Mama's attending holiday services to revisit Jewish roots, 28–29
relatives. *See also* Singer, Betty (niece); Singer, Louise (sister)
adversarial position of, in court cases, 226
as guardians. *See* family guardians

Mama's desire not to see, 32
motives of, 225
relations with, in eldercare industry, 225
release of liability. *See* waiver of liability
relief aides, 65, 69, 70, 73–74, 79–80, 85, 195, 196, 314
religious belief during guardianship
   Betty's insistence on Mama being an Orthodox Jew, 72, 147, 180, 215, 216, 219
   guardian firm's lack of knowledge about Léonie beliefs and, 73
   guardian firm's observance of Jewish Orthodox burial customs in, 294–95
   guardian's belief in Mama being an Orthodox Jew, 140–41, 293–94
   guardian's desire for Mama to meet with a rabbi, 29, 215
   guardian's rejection of Léonie's thoughts on, 290
   Mama's meetings with chaplain Smith and, xix, 216–20
   Mama's rejection of Jewish religious belief for herself, 219
   Mama's statements about being an Orthodox Jew, 147, 216
   Mama's supposed Values document on, 290
   Mama's wrestling with issue of, 28
reports
   by aides, 163
   by conservators. *See* annual reports by conservators
   by court visitor for competency hearing, 56–57
   by guardianship firm. *See* annual reports by guardianship firm
   by Léonie on Mama's portion of High Desert Holdings, 188, 286
request for absolution. *See* motion for absolution
Reynolds, Charles A. ("Chuck"), 57–58, 59–60, 61, 66, 70, 73
Richardson, Bill, 335

Rivera, Geraldine, 292, 337
Rodey Dickason Sloan Akin & Robb, 344, 351
Rosenstiel, Annette ("Mama")
   book about older people losing their autonomy, 55, 63–64
   book on Native Americans being researched, 6, 60, 284
   photos of Mama, xviii, 2, 19, 22, 23, 150, 227
   FAMILY RELATIONSHIPS
   demand for perfection in family, xvi–xviii, 27, 382
   family's observance of Jewish religious precepts, 49
   family photos copied by niece Betty and hung above Mama's bed, 151–53
   husband's death, 1, 2, 86
   husband's funeral, 1–3
   husband's memorial chamber music concert and, 21, 22, 30, 31
   lies and cover-ups in previous generations, xvii
   Mama's changing feelings about relatives over time, 152–53
   Mama's hiding of birth family photos, 151–52
   Mama's desire for truth to be told, xvii
   Mama's gifts to Léonie, 69–70
   Mama's storing of old Jewish family items, 29, 52, 66
   relatives' pressure on Mama to move to New Jersey, 8, 37, 85
   sending money to sister Vicki, 47
   sister Louis's death, 215, 217
   sister Vicki's death, 47
   time gaps in relationship with Betty, 225
   CHILDHOOD ABUSE
   Mama's adult acknowledgement that she remembered the experience, 123
   Mama's possible later life abuse experience and, 325
   photo of childhood abuser copied and hung by Mama's bed by guardian, 151

CHILDHOOD AND EARLY LIFE
experience as a Jewish woman in the army, 27–28
Mama's story about growing up with Orthodox Jewish beliefs during, 355

HEALTH, MENTAL. *See also* dementia
depression, 147, 148, 151
diagnosis of Alzheimer's, 39
disorientation during home renovation, 249, 268
feelings of loneliness, 217, 219–20
impact of relatives' visits on Mama, 147–48
inability to make decisions, 193, 208–9
refusing to communicate with certain people as a means of control, 220
speaking less, 250, 260, 268
staying in bed for long periods, 140, 148, 152
treatment for increasing agitation and anger, 45–46

HEALTH, PHYSICAL
antibiotic side effects, 262–63
air quality changes from wildfires, impact of, 305–6
arthritis, 9, 23
bedsores, 207, 237, 318–19
beginning of wheelchair use, 129
black eye incidents, 270–71
breathing problems, 95, 198, 263, 255–56, 259, 263, 306, 307, 309, 311, 314
confusion and other possible early signs of dementia, 38–39
coughing and breathing problems, 256–57
Coumadin monitoring, 96–97
death of Mama, at home, 312–13
decline during house renovation, 251
dehydration, 260, 261, 307
eyesight changes. *See* eyesight changes
fall with broken ribs, 24–25
falls and knee problems during wheelchair transfers, 14, 127, 133–34, 196
fluid intake monitored, 306
gall bladder problems, 261
hearing aid use, 156–57, 220
hip fracture, 127–28, 195–202, 222
hospice rejection due to stable health, 257, 278, 283, 288, 289–90, 293
lack of cataract treatment, 41, 42, 123
lack of chiropractic treatments, 118–19
lapse into unconsciousness and oxygen levels, 309–11
Léonie's ability to prescribe treatments for Mama in guardianship, 64–65
Lifecare Plan on health status, 221–22
Mama's fluid intake monitoring, 306
Mama's concerns about using drugs for pain, 206–7
need for skilled nursing care, 221–22
oxygen cannula handling problems, impact of, 307–9
oxygen deprivation, effects of, 250–51, 258–59
oxygen use, 129, 156, 157, 223–24, 237, 251, 258, 311
physical symptoms after competency hearing, 64
physical therapy for shoulder injury, 21, 26
physical therapy for legs, 129, 130–31
pulmonary embolism, 95–96
refusal of flu vaccine, 92–93
refusal of long-term care insurance, 26–26
rotator cuff injury, 21–22, 26
stitches for kitchen knife accident with her thumb, 38

MANHASSET, NEW YORK, HOME, 1–11
classes taught by Mama, 6, 55
contractor's annoying behavior, 6–7
decision to move to New Mexico from, 10–11
desire to move from Manhasset home, 8

driving habits of, 5–6
family approach to stock investing used by, 15–16
financial planning by, 16–19
handling financial details after husband's death, 4–5
home repairs made by, 6
husband's funeral and, 1–3
husband's memorial chamber music concert, 21, 30, 31
inheritance from husband, 4, 13
Léonie and Arthur's wedding and, 11
Léonie's visits to Mama in, 3
Mama's lack of birth family photos displayed in her home, 151–52
new belief in supernatural forces, 7–8
preparations for moving from, 21
preparations for selling house before move to Albuquerque, 13–15
pressure on Mama from relatives to move to New Jersey, 8
search for possible new home location and, 8–11
selling of house, 21

MANHATTAN HOME
Léonie's visits to Mama in, 19, 21
Chinese language classes with Léonie, 19
renting of sublet apartment and, 19–20
rotator cuff injury, 21–22, 26

ALBUQUERQUE HOME
air conditioner problems in, 252, 253, 306, 313, 322
air quality issues from wildfires near, 252, 304–6
aquarium location issue in, 247–49
baby monitor use in Mama's room in, 158, 170, 197
decision to move to, 10–11
church attendance with Léonie, 23–24
costs of preparing to sell, 252–53
electrical problems and repairs in. *See* electrical system failure
fall with broken ribs, 24–25
family photos copied by niece Betty and hung by a guardian, 151
forensic accountant Baca's visit to, 299
garage storage issues. *See* garage storage, Albuquerque home
gaslighting experienced by Léonie in, after Mama's death, 323–24, 325, 345
guardian's photographing Mama's possessions in, 149–51
health problems with arthritis, 23
heating units in bedroom of, 251, 267–69
home health aides in. *See* home health aides
house-hunting for, 12–13, 20
intensive cleaning of, by order of special master, 266, 277–78, 299, 302, 303
interior painting by aide's family, 41, 130
interior renovation of, 243, 246, 249, 252–53
kitchen knife accident with her thumb, 38
landscaping at. *See* landscaping projects)
lead paint remediation in, 252
Léonie's cleaning of after Mama's death, 284, 319, 322, 323–24
Léonie's complaint to the guardian about the condition of, 265–66
Léonie's initial inability to change locks on, after Mama's death, 322, 323, 325
Léonie's inventory of Mama's possessions in, 265, 274–75
Léonie's legal right to change locks to, 326, 345
Léonie's receipt of key to, from guardian after Mama's death, 322
Léonie's removal of items from, 265, 266, 267, 269, 272–73, 275
Léonie's transfer of title to, 326
letter from Great Neck widow about proposed visit to, 32
Mama's fascination watching birds at, 246–47

Mama's hiding of jewelry in, 149
movement and disappearance of items from, after Mama's death, 322, 323–24
newspaper reading and letter to the editor, 30–31
niece Betty's call to Léonie about changing Mama's will, 33–34
niece Betty's visits and calls with Mama, in Albuquerque, 32–33, 34–35, 37–38, 57, 70, 72, 84, 85–86, 87, 91, 93, 95, 96, 99, 129–30, 147–48, 215, 225, 227, 287
new will and power of attorney drafted and signed, 24, 25–26
possessions moved or missing during guardianship, 153
posting of updated protocol in rooms of, 263
preparations for moving to, 21
preparations for selling after Mama's death, 252–53, 319–20
reaction to relatives' request to visit, 32–33
reflecting pool destruction during landscaping at, 125, 247
relatives' desire for Mama's property from, 33–34, 37
repairs to, using aide's family, 41, 46, 130
taking possession of, 22
temperature in Mama's bedroom in, during her last days, 307, 313, 318, 324
vibrator discovery in, 324–25
wheelchair ramp installation at. *See* wheelchair ramps
HOSPITALIZATIONS
aides' visits during, 49
doctor's recommendation for guardian due to Mama's mental state in, 49–50
guardian's annual report on, 81, 82
hip fracture and rehabilitation, 127–28, 198–202, 222
home health aide's family's visits, 49
Léonie's contact with Mama blocked during, 80–81
for pneumonia, 51–52
pressure for Mama's signing of DNR order during, 119, 187–88
for various ailments over five months, 49
GUARDIANSHIP. *See* guardians, for Mama; guardianship, for Mama
HOSPICE. *See* hospice *and specific hospices*
LAWSUIT. *See* guardianship and related case
Rosenstiel, Bessie (mother-in-law), 58
Rosenstiel, Léonie
FAMILY RELATIONSHIPS
decision to stop calling – and cousins in New Jersey, 34
finding a rabbi for father's funeral, 1–2
Mama's demand for perfection, 27, 382
Mama's gifts to Léonie, 69–70
niece Betty's call about changing Mama's will, 33–34
MANHATTAN HOME
Chinese language classes with Mama, 19
decision to move from Manhattan, 8
decision to move to Albuquerque, 10–11, 13
family approach to stock investing used by, 15–16
father's funeral and, 1–3
father's memorial chamber music concert and, 21, 22, 31
frequent visits to Mama and, 3, 19
Mama's financial planning with, 16–19
Mama's preparations for selling house with help from, 13–15
Mama's visits from Manhasset, 5–6
search for possible new home location by, 8–11
visits with Mama in Manhattan, 19, 21
wedding with Arthur, 11

ALBUQUERQUE HOME
church attendance with Mama, 23–24
cousin Betty's relationship with Léonie, 86–87
possible cyanide-tainted postcard episode and related health problems in, 345–49
decision to move to, 10–11, 13
description of new house, 22–23
fake census worker's appearance at, 359
"Healers, Health and Healing" TV talk show hosted by, 141–42
house-hunting in, 12–13, 20
movement of items in, and installation of alarm system, 344–45
need to change houses in, 341–43
new will and power of attorney drafted and signed, 24, 25–26
preparations for moving to, 21

CARING FOR MAMA
accuracy of court visitor's report on, 56–57
assistance during Mama's move to Albuquerque, 22
competency hearing and. *See* competency hearing
end-of-life authority over Mama's medical care, 61, 78, 81, 82, 83, 107–8, 209
ER visit with Mama for her dehydration, 260–62
first home health aide hiring, 40–41
guardians' blocking of Léonie's attempt to advocate for Mama, 137
involvement in relatives' visit to Mama, 34–35, 37
Léonie's authority over Mama's medical care, 82
Léonie's birthday celebrations with Mama, 52, 249–50, 263–64
Léonie's promise to Mama "to remain standing" and "to tell the story" about, 214–15, 226, 340, 355, 375, 382

Mama's desire for truth to be told, xvii
Mama's desire to move in with Léonie and Arthur, 50, 52–53
Mama's desire to never be on the public dole, 143
Mama's eyesight changes and driver's license renewal, 41–42
Mama's financial issues. *See* financial affairs
Mama's request to replace her guardian with Léonie, 137–38, 139–40
need to change first home health aide, 50–51, 52
power of attorney over Mama's affairs. *See* power of attorney held by Léonie
restrictions on Léonie's giving her treatments to Mama, 64–65
stipulated order banning participation in Mama's health care, 82–83
treatment of Mama for increasing agitation and anger, 45–46
Twenty-Third Psalm recitation, 311–12
visit with Mama to an assisted-living facility, 52–53
wheelchair ramp installation. *See* wheelchair ramps

LAWSUITS. *See* guardianship case and probate case and estate's suit against the former guardian

Rosenstiel, Raymond (husband)
death of, xix, 1, 2, 86
experience with guardianship in another state, 54
financial investments made by, 4–5, 12, 13, 14–15, 136, 182, 183
financial planning by, 4, 16, 144, 203, 211
funeral for, 1–3
Léonie's financial apprenticeship with, 144
Mama's move to Albuquerque and memories of, 23

memorial chamber music concert for, 21, 22, 31
safety issues
  air quality issues from fires and, 306
  individual defined as being unsafe at home as, 114
  guardianship firm on Léonie's threat to Mama as, 166–67
  stock certificate storage as, 15
St. Martin, Rhonda, 221
Sale, Nell Graham, 209, 210–11
Santa Fe New Mexican newspaper, 304, 305
Satter, Dick, 183, 286
Sauter, Ronald, 133–34
SBS Engineering, 12
Schrandt, Judith D., 79, 89, 95
Schulz, Douglas ("Doug"), 359–60
screening, of guardian candidates, xi
seafood meal, aide's serving to Mama, 140–41, 306
secrecy
  benefits for guardianship firm of, 338–39
  of competency hearings, 59
  of guardianship hearings, 338–39, 341, 368–69, 378
  of guardianship records, xiii, 133, 141, 143, 189, 204, 315, 329, 332, 334, 361, 380–81
  of mediation proceedings, 378
  of medical and financial records of wards, 363–65, 368–69
  New Mexico legislative changes to, 380–81
  of probate court proceedings, 328–29
  of sequestered proceedings, 189, 303
secret server, in guardianship firm, 140, 150, 185, 267
Senate Memorial 94, New Mexico, 332
Senior Citizens' Law Office, Albuquerque, 330, 363
sequestered cases
  court's protection of guardian in, 302
  depositions in, 164
  guardianship case as, 189, 361
  jury trial requested in, 295, 303
  lengthy resolution of, 337
  secrecy of records in, xiii
Shepard, Ned, 329
Shojai, Pedram, xix
Singer, Betty (niece)
  aides's notes about talk with, 85
  as possible interested party at Mama's competency hearing, 59
  assistance for Mama over car lock problem, 86
  calls to Léonie about visiting Mama, 32, 33, 34
  concerns about Mama's competency hearing, 57, 70
  desire for Mama's property and portrait, 33–34, 37
  end of visits to Mama by, 215
  estrangement story about Léonie created by, 85, 86–87
  family photos copied by Betty hung by guardian on wall near Mama's bed, 151–53
  attempt to make advance funeral arrangements for Mama by, 95, 196, 200, 219, 221
  guardians' allowing freedom of access to Mama by, 153
  guardian's caution to Mama about not speaking about her finances with, 73
  guardian's relationship with, 147, 153, 172
  guardianship firm's meeting with, 72
  hotel stays during visits with Mama, 95, 99–100
  insistence that Mama was an Orthodox Jew, 72, 147, 180, 215, 216, 219
  Léonie's decision to stop calling, 34
  letter to the case manager about her visit to Mama, 84
  letter to the guardian about Mama's DNR order, 119, 187–88
  letters to the guardian firm about Mama's health, 118–19, 141

Mama's death and, 317
Mama's husband's funeral and, 3
Mama's husband's memorial chamber music concert and, 31
Mama's meetings with a Presbyterian chaplain and, 218
Mama's will disinheriting, 37, 59, 210
Passover instructions for Mama from, 266, 317–18
possible visit with Mama, in Manhattan, 19
pressure on Mama to move to New Jersey, 8, 37, 85
relationship with Léonie, 86–87
relationship with Mama, 225
request to change Mama's will, 33–34, 37
sister Vicki's death and funeral and, 47
time gaps in relationship with Mama, 225
visits and calls with Mama, in Albuquerque, 32–33, 34–35, 37–38, 57, 70, 72, 84, 85–86, 87, 91, 93, 95, 96, 99, 129–30, 147–48, 215, 225, 227, 287
visits with Mama, in Manhasset, 86
Singer, Louise (sister)
as possible interested party at Mama's competency hearing, 59
death of, and Mama's reaction, 215, 217
guardianship firm's meeting with, 72
guardian's caution to Mama about not speaking about her finances with, 73
hotel stays during visits with Mama, 95, 99
letter to the guardian firm about Mama's health, 118
Mama's arguments with husband of, 212
Mama's husband's funeral and, 3
Mama's husband's memorial chamber music concert and, 31
Mama's will disinheriting, 37, 59, 210
photo of, copied by niece Betty and hung above Mama's bed, 151
possible visit with Mama, in Manhattan, 19
pressure on Mama from, to move to New Jersey, 8, 85
sister Vicki's death and funeral and, 47
visits with Mama, in Albuquerque, 32, 37–38, 70, 72, 84, 87, 91, 93, 95, 96, 99, 147–48
visits with Mama, in Manhasset, 86
Smith, Angus (chaplain), 216–20
guardian on Léonie's imagined reaction to, 72–73, 216
Mama's meetings with, xix, 216–20
observations about Mama during guardianship made by, 216, 217, 220
Smoot Garrett, Kelley, 380
social workers
guardianship firm employment of, 177
guardian's refusal of services from, 216
Mama's hip fracture and, 198–99
Sommer, William, 347–48
"Speak Up, Las Cruces" radio show, x–xi
special master
Buck's appointment as, 287. *See also* Buck, Barbara
Buck's resignation as, 291–92
drafting a request for a hearing with Baca and, 273
forensic accounting final report and, 267
guardian's being barred from touching Mama's body after her death specified in, 290, 293, 313
guardian's relationship with, 240–41, 287, 291
impartiality of 292

intensive cleaning of Mama's
home ordered by, 299
judicial immunity of, 240
meeting about taking Mama's bed
outside and, 244
Rivera's appointment as, 292
standards, guardianship, xi, xii, 112,
113, 115, 205
Stein, Stuart, 231–32, 324, 332, 333, 348
stepped-up basis, 146
stipulated orders
ban on Léonie's participation in
Mama's health care, 82–83
Léonie's open visitation with
friends permitted by, 165–68,
185
Mama's funeral arrangements to
be made by Léonie under, 221
notification order after Mama's
death specified by, 290, 313
protocol around Mama's death
and, 258, 263, 288, 290, 292,
293
trust for Mama's holdings
terminated in, 82
stock investments. *See* financial affairs;
High Desert Holdings; New
York Mercantile Exchange
substituted judgement
attempts to change Mama's will
and, 193, 279
guardians' charitable
contributions and, 279
guardians' use of term, 107, 111
guardians' actions and, 112, 115,
305, 325
justification for Jewish burial
customs using, 294–95
Léonie's objections to guardian's
use of, 279–80
Mama's estate planning and, 255,
283
Mama' use of the Hoyer lift and,
134
niece Betty's letter on, 118
supported decision making, 382
Sutin, Thayer & Browne, 24, 79, 88–89,
146
Swaim & Schrandt, 209

Tahara, 294
talk show, Channel 27, Albuquerque
Léonie's desire to make
a documentary for.
See documentary on
guardianship abuse
Léonie's hosting of, 141–42
taxes. *See also* capital gains taxes
gifts of appreciated stock and,
285–86
selling NYMEX shares and desire
to avoid, 145–46, 254
stepped-up basis in, 146
TIAA-CREF pension, 17
TOMI-Turn patient turning device,
237–38
trustees
commercial aspects of work of, xi
success of lawsuits against, 281–83
trusteeships, 353
trusts
Léonie's setting up after Mama's
death, as required in her will,
326–27
revocable trust for Mama's
holdings set up as advised
by attorney prior to
guardianship, 54, 82
trust set up as part of Mama's will,
25–26, 146
Twenty-Third Psalm, 23, 311–12
Twin Cities Board of Trade (TCBOT),
4–5

U.S. Army, Mama's experience as a
Jewish woman in, 27–28
United States District Court for the
District of New Mexico, xiv
Utah, guardianship of federal judge
case in, 110

Values Document (Values History,
Values Statement)
billing for update to, 231
court's approval of, 179
disagreements about Mama's
desired living arrangements
as stated in, 199, 246
guardian claims to have witnessed
Mama's writing of, 71

Jacobson's deposition on the writing of, 112–13, 180
lack of billing for guardianship assistance in writing of, 179–80
Léonie's doubts about Mama's authorship of, 179
Vaughan, Bruce, 239, 266
Vigil, Cynthia, 35–36
Voss, Dorothy Auringer ("Dottie"), 32, 37

Wagner, Judith A.
  Baca's appointment of, 238
  expenses of, 277, 297
  guardian's retainer for, from Mama's accounts, 297
  final report by, 267, 273–74, 276–77, 289
  forensic accounting of home-health-related expenses by, 238, 239–40, 266–67, 275–76, 278
  invoice changes suggested by, 276
  judge's charge about role of, 239–40
  Léonie's previous experience with, 239
  request for contract between guardianship company and home health service by, 275–76
waiver of liability in guardianship cases
  guardianship firm's request for, 289–90, 296
  New Mexico's law banning, 297
Walz, Kent, 359
wards
  court's preference for commercial over family guardians for, 138
  Desert States' handling of settlements of, 365–66, 379
  Florida's law on mandatory commitment of, 232–33
  guardians' disorienting tricks with, 324
  guardians' end-of-life power over, 209
  guardian firm's threats to, 235, 323
  guardian firm's understanding of Orthodox Jewish burial customs with, 294–95
  guardians' maligning of family members of, 153
  guardians' use of term, 106
  lack of reliable statistics on, xiii–xiv
  lengthy resolution of guardianship cases affecting, 297
  Léonie's documentary on guardianship abuse and. *See* documentary on guardianship abuse
  Malott's criticism of families of, 364–65, 369, 375–76
  Mama's lack of understanding of her role as, 64
  newspaper article on guardians stealing money from, 372–73
  person-centered care plans for, 111–12
  possible New Mexico legislative changes to guardianship and, 330–32
  secrecy of medical and financial records of, 363–65, 368–69
Wells Fargo, 90
wheelchair ramps
  charging for before installing, 189
  cost of, 124, 189, 243
  duty to protect the ward and need for, 187, 239
  guardian ad litem's lack of action about, 137, 174, 187, 189, 195, 223, 239
  moving Mama's hospital bed outdoors and need for, 222–23, 239, 243, 260
  kitchen-door ramp installed, 222–23, 239
  legal complaint filed about, 124, 189
  Mama's wheelchair use and lack of, 136–37, 158, 187, 195
White, James P., 381
will (Mama's will)
  conservator's attempts to change, 193, 209-211, 255, 278 , 279–80

drafting and signing of New Mexico will, 24, 25–26, 210
estate-planning letter to Léonie about creation of trusts in, 209–11
executor/executrix of. *See* personal representative
guardian's consulting experts about drafting, 193
Léonie's filing for probate of, 325
Léonie's setting up of trust as required in, 326–27
Mama's inability to make decisions and drafting of new will, 193
niece Betty's desire to change, 33–34, 37
relatives disinherited in, 37, 59, 210
substituted judgement and, 193, 279
trust as part of, 25–26, 146
Williams, Patricia ("Patti"), 351, 355–56
Wilson, Brian, 105–6, 108
Wilson, Harry, 30
Winslow, Kathleen
back-office documents of, obtained in the probate case, 68, 176–79, 190, 191, 206, 280, 281, 301
collaring of stock issues and, 190–91
complaints about financial decisions of, 178–79
estate planning and, 210
guardian's expenses on, for hearings, 190
hearing on money manager selection and, 168, 174–77, 178–79, 181, 182, 183, 184–85, 191
issues with losses during management of Mama's accounts by, 254, 327, 333
Léonie's access to Mama's estate funds and, 327, 328
Léonie's opening of estate account and, 327–28
Léonie's decision not to sue, 327, 333
Léonie's push for diversification and, 159–60
Léonie's questions about amount of CME stock in trades of, 301
Léonie's meeting about Mama's accounts with, after the hearing, 192–93
Merc asset disposition and, 204, 206
opinion of Léonie's management skills by, 175–76
refusal to release money to Mama's estate by, 327
Winslow Wood, 327–28, 333
Wooten, Patricia, x
Wright, Susan, 113–14

www.ingramcontent.com/pod-product-compliance
Lightning Source LLC
Chambersburg PA
CBHW022045160426
43198CB00008B/133